The Psychology of Sport

The Psychology of Sport

The Behavior, Motivation, Personality and Performance of Athletes

DORCAS SUSAN BUTT

University of British Columbia

VNR VAN NOSTRAND REINHOLD COMPANY
_____ NEW YORK

Library of Congress Catalog Card Number 86–9281

ISBN 0–442–21437–5

Printed in the United States of America

Van Nostrand Reinhold Company Inc.
115 Fifth Avenue
New York, New York 10003

Van Nostrand Reinhold Company Limited
Molly Millars Lane
Wokingham, Berkshire RG11 2PY, England

Van Nostrand Reinhold
480 La Trobe Street
Melbourne, Victoria 3000, Australia

Macmillan of Canada
Division of Canada Publishing Corporation
164 Commander Boulevard
Agincourt, Ontario M1S 3C7, Canada

16 15 14 13 12 11 10 9 8 7 6 5 4 3

Library of Congress Cataloging in Publication Data

Butt, Dorcas Susan.
    Psychology of sport.

    Bibliography: p.
    Includes indexes.
    1. Sports—Psychological aspects. 2. Motivation
(Psychology) I. Title.
GV706.4B87 1987   796'.01   86–9281
ISBN 0–442–21437–5

Preface

In the decade since my book, *The Psychology of Sport: The Behavior, Motivation, Personality and Performance of Athletes,* was first published, the field of sport psychology has expanded beyond my expectations. The expansion is due to several developments. There is immense interest in the field from students in colleges and universities, sports people, and the public at large. There are increasing numbers of researchers actively conducting studies in sport psychology from whom we have heard much, and will hear more, in the future. Practitioners of sport psychology are now more knowledgeable in appreciating and applying psychological perspectives than they have been in the past. For all of these reasons I feel I can be much more optimistic about the field of sport psychology than I was ten years ago.

Many of the old problems persist: the pushiness of some parents and coaches at the expense of young people; the drug, alcohol, and behavioral problems that plague people in sport; the overemphasis on competitive success in sport organizations without consideration of the developing individuals within them. Yet these essential issues and many more are being addressed by people with both the concern and understanding to correct them.

I hope readers enjoy this book and are stimulated to further work in sport psychology by the ideas within it. You will not agree with all my ideas, nor should you. A growing and healthy field is inevitably a controversial one. We do not know the answers to all questions, but we have the opportunity of proposing new ideas and new solutions until better ones replace them. We are not confined by method in the field of sport psychology. Experimental results, field research, clinical observation, and personal experience all have their place and contribution to make. I think that is why the field is alive and developing.

I have written the book as a source of ideas and research hypotheses, as a general reference text, and also in order to present my own theoretical and research approaches to sport psychology. I hope the book will be of interest to researchers and professionals as well as to advanced undergraduate and graduate students. I also hope that journalists, writers, and other social critics and/or enthusiasts of sport may find the book of use. The first edition was read by these groups and their reactions and comments provided a lively and challenging debate after the book's publication. In addition, many in the sports community — Pee-wee hockey coaches to national team coaches — contacted me with regard to their problems and concerns. These contacts generated new issues, new ideas, and new studies.

The health, vigor, and growth of sport psychology has brought the work of some well-established researchers to the forefront for study and application. I have attempted to cover the contributions of as many of these researchers as space would allow. At the same time, all fields of study need evaluation and criticism. I have not shied away from attempting to correct misinterpretations and misemphases within the field. Sometimes I have moved into the area of social criticism, as the study of sport is an ideal forum for the consideration of social issues. However, the ideas in the book have a solid theoretical and research basis. The theoretical basis is provided in Parts I and II of the book, on motivational theory. The research basis of the book is largely contained in Chapter 6 on competition and cooperation and in Chapter 9 on the personality of the athlete. It is essential that the reader consider the definitions and results contained in these first sections to follow the arguments put forward in the book.

The major basis a psychologist has in taking a position or in proposing an idea is that it be founded upon results which have been validated in several different ways — different lines of reasoning or methods of study. For example, one may replicate many minor points in the laboratory with regard to human behavior using only one method of study. Those results are so narrowly confined they cannot be generalized to real situations. In the psychology of sport we may combine many methods of measurement and study and need never stray far from real life situations. I have attempted to reflect this in the book by providing various examples and incidents from the world of sport to illustrate theoretical or research points.

Readers of the first edition will see that this is a much expanded coverage of the field of sport psychology. Several of the new chapters are devoted to a description of how sport psychology may help the athlete and to the description of clinical practices and issues (Parts IV and V, respectively). Students need to know the theory and research in a field of study. But they also need to know what sport psychologists do in practice. They need to know about the measures, tests, and techniques applied. And they also need to be disabused of any ideas with regard to quick and easy methods of improving performance.

Reading this book will not make you a trained clinician. The use of many of the techniques described requires specialized and professional training. Such training can be obtained from many graduate schools in psychology which are devoted to the training of researchers and practitioners. Some types of training can be obtained in graduate schools of health, recreation, and physical education. Issues involved in such professional distinctions are discussed in Chapter 20 on the ethics of clinical and consulting work. In summary, the clinical chapters in the book are included to impart information, to give a complete overview of the field, and to allow students to consider career goals and options.

I wish to thank several people who have read this manuscript for me. Professor Stephen Rubin, who teaches at Whitman College, gave up time from his busy teaching and clinical schedule (and his busy acting schedule while playing a lead role in *The Odd Couple)* to read the manuscript. Professor Gordon Russell, well-known researcher on aggression in sport from the University of Lethbridge, was tracked down during his sabbatical at his Piers Island retreat on the Gulf Islands — during a cold snap. He gave up time from his own writing schedule to read the manuscript. Professor James Nylander of Central Washington University made valuable suggestions which have been integrated into the manuscript. Jane O'Hara, Vancouver Bureau Chief and formerly National Editor of *Maclean's Magazine,* and Pat Hickey, while Sports Editor of the *Vancouver Sun,* gave generously of their editorial skills and comments. Needless to say, any errors remain my responsibility.

Several students have assisted me with the manuscript as assistants and I wish to thank Sandra Gamlin, Debbie Lee, Liz Tench, Margo Janz, Mark Ritchie, Brenda Bliss, Jay Lee and Pat Burdett. A leave fellowship in 1983-84 from the Social Sciences and Humanities Research Council, Ottawa and a sabbatical leave from the University of British Columbia helped me immensely in writing the book.

My purpose in writing this book is to provide a comprehensive review of sport psychology, including its theory, research, and practice. In order to do this I have maintained the theoretical framework of the first edition. The evolution of sport at all levels, the emerging psychologies of athletes, and new research emphases have clearly supported the framework that I proposed several years ago. I argued then that if competence motivation could be encouraged and if it replaced the competitive ethic in the minds of athletes, then the world of sport would offer a more constructive experience to many. In the last ten years, in both sport and psychology, we have moved toward theories of competence and cooperation, or prosocial behavior, toward studies of intrinsic motivation, and toward the critical evaluation of the external rewards to both athlete and society. The issues I raised ten years ago have clearly come to the forefront and have remained there. The continued examination of these issues promises to benefit us all.

DORCAS SUSAN BUTT

Acknowledgments

Grateful acknowledgment is made to quote from the following copyrighted material:

From "A Shropshire Lad" – Authorized Edition – from *The Collected Poems of A. E. Housman.* Copyright 1939, 1940, © 1965 by Holt, Rinehart and Winston. Copyright © 1967, 1978 by Robert E. Symons. Reprinted by permission of Holt, Rinehart and Winston, Publishers, New York, and by The Society of Authors as the literary representative of the Estate of A. E. Housman, and Jonathan Cape Ltd., publishers of A. E. Housman's *Collected Poems.*

From "Dulce et Decorum Est" by Wilfred Owen, *Collected Poems.* Copyright Chatto & Windus, Ltd., 1946 © 1963. Reprinted by permission of The Owen Estate and New Directions Publishing Corporation, New York.

Excerpt from *London Street Games* by Norman Douglas. Copyright Chatto & Windus, Ltd., 1931. Reprinted by permission of The Society of Authors.

Table from *Signs and Symptoms* by C. M. MacBryde, from Williams, R. H.: *Textbook of Endricrinology,* ed. 4, W. B. Saunders, Philadelphia, 1968.

Figure from *Love and Love Sickness: The Science of Sex, Gender Difference and Pair-Bonding* by J. Money. The Johns Hopkins University Press: Baltimore and London, 1980.

From "First Peace" by Barbara Lamblin. An Uncle John's Sports Art Publication, Perris, California. Originally published in "Stigma or prestige: The all-American choice" by Marie Hart. In *Issues in Physical Education and Sports,* edited by G. H. McGlynn. Palo Alto, Calif.: National Press, 1974.

Excerpts from *They Call It a Game* by Bernard P. Parrish. Copyright © 1977 by Bernard P. Parrish. Used with permission of Doubleday & Co., Inc.

Contents

PART V   CONSULTING PRACTICES AND ISSUES

PART I

MOTIVATIONAL THEORY I

1
The Motivational Model

INTRODUCTION

People both fascinate and puzzle, as well as attract and repel, one another. Not only do people display intricacies and complexities in behavior, but their capacities for good and for evil are sometimes unfathomable. In the world of sport we are able to observe and to study all of these emotions and motivations, which are generally enacted in relative privacy. Because of the communal nature of sport, even extremes in emotional and motivational behavior become part of the public domain. As we look ahead it therefore seems certain that the interests of the layperson, the sportsman and the sportswoman, and the psychologist will continue to converge upon the arena of sport. Sport, as known to most through little leagues, organized school activities, and contests for elite and professional athletes, forms a small but very prominent part of our society. But if we expand our conception of sport to the play activities of children and to the leisure activities of adults, we are examining a universal process. From the cooperative game playing of the Inuit to the leisure choices of the Brazilian poor, from the rule-making games of marbles among Swiss children to the sandlot baseball of American youth, from organized British cricket test matches to the 120,000 spectators and 50-million television viewers of a World Cup final—all are the domain of the psychologist in sport.

Some of the most puzzling questions about sports concern athletes' motivations for engaging in them. Why have some athletes such as Arthur Ashe, Pele, and Joan Benoit dazzled and inspired others with their talents? Why have some athletes such as Terry Fox (runner), Duk Koo Kim (boxer), and Sergei Shlibashvili (diver)* persisted in sport in spite of overwhelming odds against their success? What motivates the aggressive athlete: a Jack Tatum in his savage blocks on the football field? a John McEnroe fluctuating between brilliant performances and childish tantrums? a Brian Glennie or a Dave Williams enacting the role of hockey goon? Why were some athletes, such as Babe Ruth and Jim Thorpe, reliable on the playing field and unreliable off it? Why did Tom Seaver

---

*These three athletes died at ages 22, 23 and 21.

and Bill Tilden, outstanding athletes, appear to have little natural talent, at the early stages of their careers, while Steve Dalkowski, a pitcher gifted with natural ability, and Andrea Jaeger, after a brilliant early tennis career, were unable to sustain success? Why do female athletes from Babe Didrickson to Martina Navratilova often worry and confuse their followers and even themselves? What causes some athletes and even coaches (a Bobby Fischer, a Lance Rentzel, a Mary Decker, or a Woody Hayes) to continually struggle within themselves and with the society around them? The motivations of athletes are a fascinating study because they reflect the positive and negative values of the times, as well as the psyches of individual athletes. Two people engaged in the same sport may behave overtly in a similar manner, but each may express different feelings about his or her participation and may react differently to the stress of winning or losing. The study of the psychological motivations in sport examines and offers theories for these differences.

THE NEED FOR THEORY

In order to tackle the preceding questions, a framework is needed within which the behavior of athletes can be interpreted. It is therefore fitting that we begin this book with a comprehensive theory to provide a foundation for the psychology of sport. A theory should introduce ideas and possible explanations for phenomena when all the facts are not known or when the area is too complex to understand in full. The study of human motivation is such an area. Many researchers investigate facets of human motivation such as its hormonal bases, its neurophysiological bases, its learning bases, and its moral bases. Each may make some contribution to the understanding of motivation. Yet is is unlikely that any will supply all the answers. Theory must be flexible and comprehensive, casting its net widely in order to encompass the complexities of the human situation. It cannot pinpoint cause and effect because cause and effect interact in any specific situation. Even when one knows psychology, its theory and its concepts, the application of psychological knowledge remains a challenge and an art. What psychology and psychologists *can* provide is a repertoire of ideas and possibilities with which to interpret given situations and the individual and group behaviors that occur within them.

DESCRIPTION OF THE MODEL

In order to interpret complexities in motivation, a working model with four levels of influence upon motivation is proposed: the biological, psychological, social, and reinforcement levels. The model provides a framework for this book. It is flexible enough that it can cover a great variety of possible explanations for sports behavior yet it is specific enough to allow the introduction of some major

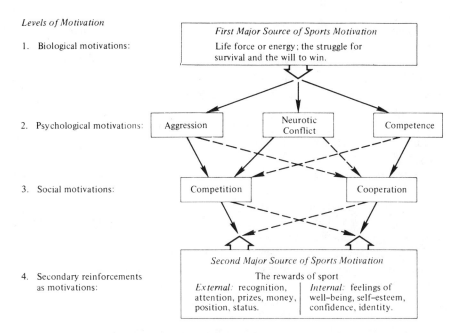

Levels of Motivation

1. Biological motivations:

First Major Source of Sports Motivation
Life force or energy; the struggle for survival and the will to win.

2. Psychological motivations: Aggression   Neurotic Conflict   Competence

3. Social motivations: Competition   Cooperation

4. Secondary reinforcements as motivations:

Second Major Source of Sports Motivation
The rewards of sport
External: recognition, attention, prizes, money, position, status.   *Internal:* feelings of well–being, self–esteem, confidence, identity.

Figure 1.   The Motivational Components of Sport.   Motivation in sport evolves from two major sources or influences: biological motivation and the reinforcements conferred through the sports enterprise.   Psychological motivation is represented in the three basic energy models of aggression, neurotic conflict, and competence.   The solid and dotted arrows indicate the greater and lesser degree of a connection thereafter.   Aggressive motivation and neurotic conflict are most likely to lead to competitive social motivation and, to a lesser extent, to cooperation.   Competence motivation is most likely to lead to cooperative social motivation.   Both the competitively and cooperatively motivated will be affected by the reinforcements of sport.   The external rewards will usually be most important to the competitor, however, and the internal rewards to the cooperator.

theories of human motivation.   The *biological level* of motivation represents the physical, constitutional, instinctive components of motivation.   The *psychological level* represents the channeling of energy from the previous level into various psychological styles particular to the individual athlete.   The *social level* represents the attitudes and feelings of the athlete toward others within the sport enterprise: other athletes, coaches, officials, fans, and even family.   The *reinforcement level* represents the rewards and punishments conferred on the athlete or participant from the sport environment.

DEFINITIONS

Some psychologists and theoreticians use the same constructs and words to mean different things, and this has led to much confusion in psychology.*

---

*For a recent attempt to clarify language and language issues in psychology see Reber's (1985) dictionary of psychology.

We therefore begin by examining the components of the motivational model and by providing definitions of them.

Life force or energy: This is the struggle for survival and the will to win as manifested in: being alive, pitting the self against the environment, striving for continued existence, striving for an optimal level of stimulation. Examples: a baby exerts effort to walk, cries when hungry; an adult struggles to achieve position within a group, executes acts for self-protection, desires to live as long as long as he or she can; the individual exerts energy in eating, exercising, sexuality, and generativity.

Aggression: Life energy is channeled into assertive self-expression in which the self is often pitted against other people and objects. This involves feelings of power, vivacity, anger, and strength. When frustrated, the individual lashes out physically and/or verbally, and often lacks self control. Therefore self-assertion may be inappropriate within the situational context.

Conflict: Life energy is channeled into opposing purposes and pursuits such as the desire to express impulse versus guilt for the expression of impulse. Energy is used to mediate the struggle between opposing purposes. Conflict can result in self-destructiveness, self-absorption, blaming others, complaints, worries, depression and inactivity, weeping, and other nervous symptoms.

Competence: Life energy is channeled into interacting effectively and purposefully with the environment. The individual expects to have the effect on the environment that he or she desires to have, and the expectations are realistic. Joy, pleasure, elation, and self-esteem accompany activity and interaction with the environment. Setbacks and failures are accepted as a realistic part of development from which new learning and new development may evolve.

Competition: Here the major social motive in contests is to win over others. The individual wants to defeat others, to be number one, to have rivals; sees the environment as competitive and resents others; sees others as trying to hold him or her back. The individual's own object is to win, often at all costs. The major theme of competition is the psychological perception of the environment as an adversary over which one must triumph or suffer belittlement as a consequence.

Cooperation: Here the major social motive in contests is derived from being there, from participating with others, from feeling part of the group, team, or club. The individual desires to raise the performance of all as a group experience; cares for others, emphathizes, congratulates others; looks forward to the next contest as an opportunity to partake in a new group enterprise. The major theme of cooperation is the psychological perception of the environment as supportive and interdependent with the self.

Reinforcement: Positive or negative incentives from the environment or from the self result from sport participation. Reinforcement is divided into external and internal reward (presence of incentives) and punishment (absence or withdrawal of incentives). External incentives may be money, praise, position, status, applause, adulation, free equipment, gifts, or products. Internal incentives may be feelings of health, happiness, self-esteem, self-confidence, well-being, or satisfaction in a job well done.

HOW THE MODEL WORKS

Sport motivation may be seen as evolving from two major sources: on the one hand a biologically based fund of energy, and on the other all secondary or environmental influences, each with positive and negative pulls. One individual may have an asthenic (thin and weak) body build and a low level of physical energy and even of physical health. He or she may therefore be quite uninterested in any sport participation. Compare this individual to one who is also asthenic in body build but who has vast quantities of mental energy. This person may find bridge or chess compatible with his or her endowments. Compare again this individual to a strongly built person who has a great amount of physical energy awaiting expression. The latter person is obviously a better bet in the athletic arena, other factors being equal, and given a sport that requires physical and/or competitive energy.

It is quite clear that all were not created equal on a biological level when it comes to sport. In some sports special physical characteristics are required — for example, the tiny man as jockey. In other sports muscle or aerobic capacity, coordination, endurance, grace, explosiveness, and various degrees of body fat are required to a greater or lesser extent. Recent estimates (Eysenck, Nias, and Cox, 1982, p. 48) are that for many sports, 70 to 90 percent of performance variance is constitutionally determined, leaving only 30 percent to be accounted for by other factors such as practice, psychological preparation, and luck.

It is not surprising to find Lois Retton, mother of gymnast Mary Lou Retton, describing her daughter's childhood as follows (as quoted by Ottum, 1984): "I swear that girl was so hyper you wouldn't believe it. I mean, energetic! First, she walked at an early age, and then she and her older sister, Shari, were running around here like little crazy people, doing tumbling and all, bouncing off the walls and breaking up the furniture. I finally sent them both off to dancing school." (p. 466). Similarly, Lydia Thompson, mother of Daley Thompson, describes her son's childhood (as quoted by Moore, 1984): "That child was a terror from the minute he was born, he never cried, but he never slept either. And by the time he was seven, he was a handful. He was still hyperactive. He didn't want to go to bed, he didn't want to do this, he wanted to do that. I couldn't keep up with him." (p. 198). He is described as being mobile and articulate by the age of fourteen months. These two athletes provide good examples of persons showing high energy levels even as young children.

Once the individual engages in play or sport these energies may be variously expressed and channeled. To summarize the individual differences occurring on a psychological level, we have referred to aggression, conflict, and competence as motivations. These refer to the degree to which the individual recognizes and relishes *force in sport* ("... when it came time to make tackles, I wasn't afraid, but actually enjoyed the bone-crunching contact" Tatum, 1979, p. 66); *self-destructiveness in sport* ("I started because I sensed it was all over for me ... I couldn't face it ... it got to the point where I was literally saturated with drugs and alcohol." John Reeves as quoted by Looney, 1983, p. 53); or *joy in sport* ("As far as my running was concerned, I was doing it because I got a big charge out of it. I loved to race. Running is a great activity ..." Bruce Kidd, former distance runner, 1979).

It is clear that an athlete does not show just one of these motivations to the exclusion of others. Tatum, for example, although the major feature of his play for the Oakland Raiders was his aggressive attack, at some times may have had conflict over his sport performance. Still, at other times he may have felt extremely competent. A player like Lance Rentzel who centered his autobiography (1972) on the theme of his neurosis as manifested in sport, clearly also had to have high levels of aggression to channel into football as well as being extremely good and intrinsically satisfied during some periods of play. Finally an athlete exuding competence, such as Wayne Gretzky, has been known to attack when frustrated and may also at times hold self-doubts with regard to his role and the whole sport enterprise. Thus the model, when we talk of psychological styles, is not intended to pigeonhole sports participants but is intended to describe their predominant modes or styles of action.

On the social level, the third level of motivation, we seek to describe how the athlete feels and thinks about others in his or her sports environment. Most specifically such attitudes are directed toward fellow athletes engaged in contests for the matching or testing of ability, strategy, and skill. We propose that competition and cooperation are the predominant attitudes. One can find athletes who fall into each of these modes of expression. Ken Landreaux, Los Angeles Dodger outfielder, illustrates the competitive attitude when he is quoted as saying: "Winning isn't as important as doing well individually. You can't take teamwork up to the front office to negotiate." (*Sports Illustrated*, July 9, 1984, p. 12). Notice the subtleties of that statement. The competitive attitude is expressed toward teammates. In contrast, Bill Bradley has written: "People on a meshed team will help each other personally ... A group of self-dedicated soloists, on the other hand, never ceases its internal competition." (Bradley, 1977, p. 114). The athlete who is motivated by social competition seeks to win out over others, whether they are teammates or official opponents, and is primarily motivated by the desire to defeat and to surpass others. On the other hand the athlete who is cooperatively motivated on a social level has generally affable feelings toward others. He or she sees other athletes as partners in the enterprise and as necessary dependents. The friends and social contacts made through sport participation are usually uppermost in importance to such athletes, even though they may also be champions.

Finally, the level of reinforcement refers to all those rewards and punishments conferred on the athlete by the sport environment through the fact of his or her participation. These may be divided into external rewards and punishments such as prize money or the absence of it and internal rewards and punishments such as feelings of well-being and confidence versus feelings of self-admonition.

It has been the writer's position (Butt, 1973a, 1976, 1979d, 1980c) that the constructive athlete, that is, the one who contributes most to the well-being of both self and others, is the athlete who is predominantly motivated by competence and cooperation on the psychological and social levels. Note that we are referring to the psychological predispositions of and the attitudes of the athlete; this in no way implies that the athlete avoids contests, excellence, or becoming a champion. In fact, it is our position that such psychological styles will be associated with increased and not decreased performance levels.

Accepting this theme does not necessitate avoidance of the complexities in athletic motivation. Of course, there are some sports that clearly require high levels of aggression (football, ice hockey, boxing) and there have been some very conflicted performers in sport (Bill Tilden, Jimmy Piersall, and Bobby Fischer, for example) who have been outstanding. What we are suggesting is that, other things being equal, the longest careers, the greatest well-being, and the careers most inspirational to others in sport are those of the competence-oriented and cooperative athletes. But the road to athletic glory and success is fraught with many traps for the athlete. In this book we will examine such pitfalls and consider how sport might be a more productive and constructive process for all.

Referring to Figure 1 on page 5, the solid and dotted lines in the diagram show the predicted associations between the motivations on the four levels. The solid lines indicate the stronger associations and influences while the dotted lines indicate the lesser lines of influence. It is clear from both observation and research that many complex interactions can take place within the motivational model and that the athlete's motivations may vary both across situations and across time.

The foregoing motivational model provides the basic framework to be used in examining the psychology of sport. The first two parts of the book are devoted to examining each motivational level in detail. The biological level will be discussed in the rest of this chapter. The psychological level will be examined in Chapters 2 to 5 in which aggression, conflict, competence, and play and leisure are discussed. The social level is discussed in Chapter 6 under the heading of competition and cooperation, while the reinforcement level, including both internal and external reinforcements, is discussed in Chapter 7. Finally, Chapter 8 examines attempts to measure and validate the motivational model.

THE STRUGGLE FOR SURVIVAL AND THE WILL TO WIN

From the time an individual is born into the world, energy is expressed and used in the process of living. This will to survive does not disappear unless the organism is extremely ill, disturbed, or alienated.

Individuals display different degrees of energy with regard to the process of living depending upon such factors as physical size and condition, constitutional makeup, and nutritional level. In the animal kingdom an active animal is a healthy animal. In the human species, especially in developed nations, where so much of life has become sedentary, one finds increasing sport participation and increased pleasure and determination in that participation. For many, sport has become a daily habit and activity. It is our thesis that on the most basic of levels this represents the desire to express energy assertively, to live with health, and to survive.

An athlete is often described as "highly motivated," as having a "strong will to win," or as having "a killer instinct." Sport participation, approached at the most basic of motivational levels, may be thought of as a representation of life, symbolic of the biological organism's struggle for survival. This is illustrated in Cleary's (1967) description of surfing, in which he portrays the surfer as engaged in a metaphorical struggle with death. The surfer seeks to dominate the wave and to survive his adversary by riding the most precarious part of the curl so that he experiences the symbolic thrill of potential annihilation while knowing the ecstasy of survival through his own will and effort. As we have become increasingly less concerned with everyday survival and with our biological past, sport may have come to symbolize a fight for life and an expression of will. Many athletes describe themselves as being consumed by the act of their sport participation. It demands all of their concentration and all of their being.

The career of the athlete from start to finish parallels rather closely a biological life cycle. There is the immature and awkward beginning, the rise to promise and reward, the pinnacle, and then the decline. An example of the struggle for survival in an athlete was demonstrated by the Canadian hero, Terry Fox, who died in 1981 having raised $24 million for cancer research through a cross-continental run on only one natural leg. The 22-year-old Simon Fraser University student, an all-around athlete and basketball player during his high school days, was diagnosed as having cancer in his knee at age 18. He eventually had to abandon his run in Thunder Bay, Ontario in September of 1980. The cancer had returned and spread to his lungs. He had eight months to live. Fox inspired a nation as a symbol of hope and the will to overcome.

Tekeyan (1976) describes the same flirtation with destiny in puzzling over the sport motivation of his lawyer son, a passionate and gifted participant. "That's the secret to Alan's ferocious drive. He is an athlete for the most primitive reasons — to seek and survive the danger of death. Every night when he comes home from the park or the gym, he is aching all over, but is exhilarated because he has again proven himself to be invincible." (p. 2). Jack Dempsey, heavyweight champion of the 1920s, a former hobo from the rocky mining country of Colorado, is quoted (Berkow, 1982, p. 15) as saying: "When I was a young fellow I was knocked down plenty ... I wanted to stay down. I couldn't. I had to collect that two dollars for winning or go hungry. I had to get up. I was one of those hungry fighters. You could hit me on the chin with a sledge-hammer for five dollars. When you haven't eaten for two days you'll understand." Boxing for Dempsey meant survival.

Most psychological theorists accept the assumption of a life force or energy, although some do not state it explicitly. Learning theorists (Hilgard, 1981), while accepting the notion of "biological drives," then have constructed their theories on the detailed analyses of acquired behaviors. Freud (1923), Erikson (1950), Maslow (1970), and others assume an evolution of motivation over the life span and use terms such as instinct, need, or drive to describe the biological forces behind the evolution. The overemphasis of North American psychology on environmentalism and learning theory has undergone correction since the publication of Wilson's (1975–1980) *Sociobiology*. However, earlier writers such as Wrong (1962) had called attention to the bias in the models that many social scientists were using in psychology and sociology. The sociobiological movement focused attention on inborn patterns of behavior and sought to reinterpret the competitive and cooperative behaviors that comprise a major theme of this book. Although the author does not accept all sociobiological assertions, it is clear that the biological substrata of human behavior need to be integrated into the theories proposed by social scientists.

THE RUDIMENTS OF STATUS

There is much information on the functions of status both in animal and in human groups. While personality theorists have tended to view this phenomenom as a study in power or achievement motivation, other theorists have considered status in terms of the survival of the group through the fittest emerging to positions of influence. Regardless of the label, there is a universal trend in living organisms to organize themselves into some pattern when in groups. This pattern often determines dominance in terms of the individual's rights to territory, space, mates, and food. On a mass level, for humans, it determines political structure. Some authors (for example Kirk, 1960) have argued that the necessity for structure inevitably leads democracies and revolutionary societies back to a conservative structure and organization. A hierarchy would therefore inevitably emerge from equality or from chaos.

What determines status and dominance in animal groups? One old result (Beeman, 1947) which still holds in more complex forms is that the level of testosterone or male sex hormone in either males or in females is linked to aggressive behavior and to status. That is, animals injected with testosterone, whether they be male or female, tend to ascend in the status hierarchy, for example, in the pecking order among chickens. Castrated males descend in status, a result known since Arnold Berthold reported in 1849 that roosters stop crowing and fighting after castration (as reported by Wilson, 1980, p. 124). The study of testosterone levels and human aggression has not resulted in definitive conclusions (Simon, 1981). But Whalen and Simon (1984, p. 266) suggest this may be due to the wide variance in "normal" levels of testosterone in human males.

A recent result of interest is the tendency of animals to engage in nondestructive play and the influence of that play on status hierarchies. Wilson (1980, p. 118) describes this as "dominance aggression." These animal sparring matches, formerly noted and described in detail by writers on ethology (Tinbergen, 1951; Lorenz, 1970), seem to have parallels in human sport activity. In children, games are engaged in for many reasons, but frequently the oldest children explain to, and enforce a set of rules on, the younger participants. If the younger can outperform the older at a given activity, then the status of the younger increases. Similarly if a woman can outperform a man at a given skill, the status of the woman is often increased and her skill admired. Some men, however, who may be less secure in the masculine role, may depreciate the high-performing female or avoid her altogether.

In animal and human groups there has always been some support for the notion that the biggest and the strongest dominate the status hierarchy. The fittest man would therefore be leader. Although many complex factors enter into human dominance and status (Bandura, 1977a), there is and should always be a place for the consideration of physical factors.

The struggle for status need not always represent a desperate division of food and territory. There are some societies in which the members have to be persuaded to accept positions of status, domination, or leadership because such positions are not sought after. Just as there may be many different manifestations of status within a community, achievement and power motivation may be expressed in other ways than by force. On the other hand, the advent of weapons and skill as vehicles of power maintenance may have released those who are physically weak from the cult of physical strength. Only some sports, and primarily those involving lower class males (boxing, football, and ice hockey) involve brute physical force tempered with strategy and skill. Other sports rely on physical force to varying degrees. Bridge, shooting, and archery require quite different skills and abilities. Women, in spite of having less physical strength than men, now theoretically compete with men for positions in the business community, in the military hierarchy, in political processes, and in space programs, even though women cannot generally compete with men of equivalent skill on the sports field. It is largely through technology, equipment, and birth control that the importance of physical strength has been diminished and the potential status of women has infinitely expanded.

Status hierarchies emerge not only from individual effort, but from group effort. Thus a group's ability to cooperate and to exert joint effort as a unitary force, from physical to moral, can advance the status of a group. Some of the outstanding achievements of the past, such as the building of the pyramids in Egypt, may have been based upon cooperative group effort (Mendelssohn, 1971). Status in groups emerges not only from competitive assertion, but also from cooperative assertion. The danger in competitive assertion for the purposes of status is that it may become destructive to both self and others. There is endless danger in the accumulation of weapons for purposes of physical domination. There is endless potential for inspiration and benefit in the advent of cooperative assertion in the name of group goals in cultural and community achievement. It is these two themes that will unfold in the present volume: assertion at the expense of others versus assertion in the name of excellence for the good and inspiration of all.

2
Aggression

INTRODUCTION

In the last chapter we examined the biological factors of sport motivation and assumed an innate fund of energy. Several theoretical schools have made more intensive studies of these life energies and their various forms of expression. Three are especially applicable to sport motivation. These are theories on aggression from the ethologists and sociobiologists, theories on conflict from the psychoanalytic and psychodynamic positions, and theories on competence from various socialization positions. Our purpose in applying these theories is to assist in the understanding of both individual differences in sport motivation and extremes in sport behavior. It is important to consider these categories as fluid and not static states. This means that it should be possible to assess athletes in terms of the degree to which they feel aggression, conflict, and competence motivations. Following are clear-cut examples of each motivation as illustrated in the statements of athletes.

On aggression: Rick McKinney, archer, (Levine, 1983), "I've made a target out of cardboard, and sometimes I stare at it for hours. I think mean, vicious thoughts: I'm going to kill that guy." *On conflict:* Tony Jacklin, golf, (Kahn, 1979), "I was a gibbering wreck through anxiety. I had never been as nervous in my life as I was at the beginning of that tournament." *On competence:* Kathy Whitworth (McDermott, 1983), "Anyway. I don't know of any other thing I'd like to do or enjoy so much [as golf]."

Examples are not always so clear cut and athletes may show a mixture of motivations over time or even at the same time. For example, Kathy Whitworth also described herself in 1973 as follows, "My nerves were completely shot. I shook so bad in the last tournament of the year that I couldn't sign my score-card. I knew then that if I didn't back off, I'd burn out. That was hard to face." She is clearly describing a state of conflict. Rick McKinney continued his 1983 quote on mental practice by adding that sometimes he thinks "positive thoughts ... I'm going to shoot perfect scores." He is thus rehearsing feelings of competence.

An athlete may be predominantly aggressive during the early stages of his or her career but evolve into a competence- or conflict-oriented athlete over time.

This depends upon how the athlete matures and how he or she is rewarded. There may also be input from significant other people such as from heroes, coaches, or fellow athletes. When a football or basketball coach believes aggressiveness is the way to succeed in sport and trains a team for aggressive play, one would expect the athletes to pick up on and to manifest this style of play. When another coach emphasizes team support and team morale, more cooperative motivations will be highlighted by the players. On a given day an athlete may play with extreme competence because everything is going well. On another day the athlete may be overcome by frustration (for example, due to a more difficult opponent, officiating, or a generally poor performance) and then become angry or aggressive in play. In describing the styles of athletes one should focus on their most consistent motivation, the underlying motivation that was determined not by the situation but by his or her personality. Thus we are suggesting three broad theoretical categories which reflect a combative, worried, or existential approach to sport. The subject of the present chapter is the aggressive or combative style.

TYPES OF AGGRESSION

Aggression may be defined as the energetic assault on animate or inanimate objects for a purpose. Note the key words. *Energy* is involved; there is *assault*, force and assertion; and a goal or *purpose* is involved. The purpose of aggression is to inflict pain, to dominate, to obtain, to outperform, to prevent. Aggression can be physical or verbal. Both types occur in sport: the physical aggression as the play unfolds and the verbal aggression as many athletes attempt to intimidate opponents on another level. Atyeo (1979) wrote an entire book which was basically a compilation of aggressive and violent incidents in sport.

For the purposes of this book it will be helpful to consider the various types of aggression that are manifested in sport. Six categories of aggressive behavior will cover most aggression in sport: (1) trait aggression, (2) socialized aggression, (3) game aggression, (4) strategic aggression, (5) situational aggression, and (6) post-game aggression.

Trait Aggression. Most sport attracts and rewards individuals who are high in biological aggression. Strength, speed, physical force, and the ability to overpower and outperform others are often sought after. These potentials are most common in persons of certain body builds and genetic endowments. We would predict, then, other things being equal, more innate aggression in athletes than nonathletes, particularly in given sports. An example of trait aggression is given by Tatum early in his autobiography (1979, p. 1) when he writes: "In college, and even in high school, I had developed a reputation as a devastating hitter. Whenever I'd hit a running back or receiver with a good shot, the man usually didn't get up. I've always had an affinity for controlled violence and contact sports."

Socialized Aggression. Through training and practice an individual can be taught to be more aggressive and to manifest aggression in preference to other styles of expression. Aggression is frequently viewed as part of the male role: it is expected, reinforced, practiced, and learned. Some have also advocated it for women. Campagnola (see Popma, 1980, pp. 16, 19) has called for female athletes to become "sexual stormtroopers" and to be considered as "independent, assertive and competitive." In an account of his playing for Medicine Hat in junior league hockey Don Murdoch describes this process of socialization (as quoted by Surface, 1977, p. 53): "They had the toughest goons going to run me off the ice ... But I got me a good right and left-hand punch both and dished it out, too. Fourteen fights and I won or broke even in them all."

Game Aggression. The expression of aggression is built into many games. As we have frequently mentioned, boxing, football, ice hockey, field hockey, and basketball are considered aggressive sports. But so are water polo, lacrosse, and car racing. Speed, body contact, equipment which can be used as weaponry, and a philosophy of violence can all lead to aggression in sport. Frank Kush (as quoted by Alfano, 1982) says: "Getting hit is football. Anyone who has been involved in football through high school and college should be used to it at this level. They should be able to take the punishment. Basically, we all have a fear of getting hit, which is why you have to hit. I have no compassion for anyone who is out for football who is concerned with being hit or hitting."

Strategic Aggression. Aggression as a strategy is used to intimidate another team or player. It is purposefully used, often within the rules of the game in order to gain advantage. Brian Glennie formerly of the National Hockey League (as quoted by McCabe, 1977, p. 37) says: "Hitting is my contribution to the hockey club. If I hit hard, it makes the other team worried and they don't play as well ... The real trick is doing it well every game."

Situational Aggression. This occurs when an incident or situation demands aggressive retaliation or assault. One player hits another back in order to get even. Thus an agitator, using strategic aggression, will often set up a situation which unleashes aggression in others. These others will lose their composure, retaliate, and a fight or a brawl will result. An example was reported by Cocking (1976), when Ted Green of the Boston Bruins clubbed Wayne Maki of St. Louis on the head with his stick, causing Maki to retaliate with a full swing to Green's head, fracturing his skull.

Post-Game Aggression. This category refers to aggression that continues or explodes after the athletic event, in either the athletes or members of the audience. Experience of and participation in aggressiveness in sport breeds more aggression (Russell, 1981a). The incidence of post-game fan aggression is perhaps best illustrated in the United Kingdom by the lower class soccer fans who regularly clash after games. Such fighting among fans after sport events has resulted in the deaths of fans, officials, and athletes, and in some areas has done much to lessen spectator attendance. Post-match aggression from players and coaches is also common, with incidents ranging from attacks on photographers and press to brawling in bars over women.

The many faces of aggression in sport, make it a complicated but fascinating field for the study of the nature of aggression. The latter is an area of study fraught with problems of both definition and individual prejudice (Von Cranach et al., 1977, pp. 253 ff.). In contrast, research on aggression in sport has met with success in terms of more definitive results and conclusions (Goldstein, 1983; Smith, 1983). The comparative success is due perhaps to the measurable and quantifiable indices of aggressive behavior available in sport research.

The illustrations of aggressiveness used thus far have been primarily from the saga of the male athlete. Aggression, as previously noted, is often thought to be more common in the male, but is also readily observed in the female athlete.

It is essential to all athletes that aggression be controlled and chaneled into skill in the sport. A John McEnroe, although displaying egocentric anger and aggression toward officials and spectators and fellow opponents when the ball is not in play, is usually able to muster up some control and to channel his anger and arousal into the game when the ball is in play. Again, Tatum (1979, p. 14) illustrates this point well: "Aggressiveness is as common to football as helmets and shoulderpads, but I had yet to learn how to channel my aggressive style of play into aspects of the game where it would do the team the most good."

In describing the athlete who has a high level of aggressive motivation, we are describing someone who is likely to manifest all the categories of aggression previously discussed. Such an individual is readily adaptable to a society and/or to a situation in which aggression is socially sanctioned. A hypothetical athlete highly motivated by aggression would be genetically and constitutionally predisposed to display aggressive emotion and aggressive behavior (strong, high energy level, combative, high male hormone if male, androgenized if female); would have a background that socialized aggression; would be attracted to games that sanction aggression; would be able to use aggression strategically; would be quick to respond to situational frustration; and, finally, would be inclined to show post-game aggression in social and family life. Situational aggression and post-game aggression may be moderated in a mature athlete. Other athletes would be less destructive if social values did not support their aggression and if punishments were levied against their violent acts and rewards removed from them.

THEORY OF AGGRESSION

What theories of aggression from the social sciences and other branches of study permit an understanding of aggression in sport? On the psychological level of motivation we want to examine individual differences in terms of how energies from the biological level are expressed. What styles predominate in given athletes? In order to examine aggression we begin with the controversial theory on aggression by Lorenz (1966) as updated by the sociobiological position (Wilson, 1980), the human ethologists (Von Cranach, 1977), and modern ethology (Barnett, 1981). When taking the ethological position in attempting to understand the biological basis of aggressive behavior, it is important to remember that Lorenz essentially founded the field by studying instinctual aggression. He theorized about the inevitability and adaptive functions of the *emotion* of aggression and *not* about the inevitability and adaptive function of aggressive behavior (Masters, 1977, p. 269).

Lorenz' theory of aggression is widely known and has aroused controversy for two reasons. First, he hypothesizes an innate source of energy (which is why we chose to use the theory in this book) and, second, he hypothesizes that this energy is action-specific. That is, aggressive energy can be directed toward several different targets, but it is not transformable. It must be expressed via a specific sequence of actions which are, in fact, mediated in humans by a myriad of factors (Bandura, 1977a). Ethologists have contributed greatly to the understanding of aggression because they started "at the beginning" in their studies with the biological basis of aggression. Through careful and systematic observation of animals in their natural habitat, they determined that fighting between members of the same species is common to almost all forms of vertebrate life. This intraspecies aggression serves evolutionary functions in that it allows the spatial distribution of the species over available territory, and allows for the mating of the fittest.

Equally important is their observation that fighting often does not culminate in a kill. Destruction of species members is unusual and the combats are largely ceremonial (Tinbergen, 1951, 1973; Lorenz, 1966, 1970; Wilson, 1980, p. 62). Wilson discusses this form of aggression under the topic of "dominance aggression." Injurious defeat between members is prevented by submissive gestures or signs on the part of the weaker combatant. An example is when a dog exposes its throat to a superior opponent, thus signaling the end of the struggle. Submissive gestures curtail the continued expression of aggression in an opponent. Although some researchers from different theoretical orientations have argued against this interpretation of animal behavior (Bandura, 1973, pp. 14–31), others (Rowell, 1974) have called for more attention to gestures of subordination and have researched such behavior extensively. In the human species it has been suggested that crying and smiling serve somewhat the same purposes.

They protect the young from onslaught and release protective behavior on the part of the caretaker.   In adult life a smile or an apology may also curb the aggression of another.   Ceremonial fighting in animals serves a useful purpose, then, in preserving the most efficient order of the species and in both preserving and allowing for the transition of status differences, as discussed in Chapter 1.

Although the results from the study of animal behavior cannot be applied directly to human behavior. the methods of ethology have been repeated on human subjects with the finding that the observations from animal behavior are sometimes paralleled in the human situation.   In addition, the generalizations and theory resulting from the animal work have stimulated speculation about the human predicament which has generated thought, controversy, and research. In his popular work Lorenz (1966, 1970) assessed the status of human aggression in the light of his animal studies.

Humans also have highly ritualized forms of sanctioned aggression, and the world of sport offers one of these (other examples are verbal aggression and the conquering of nature).   Relatively harmless ceremonial struggles may take place between persons, groups, and nations on the sports field.   Sometimes 100,000 spectators may be involved in the primitive animal experience of group aggression, which Lorenz has called "militant enthusiasm."   Here combat is waged symbolically, but is controlled by a highly systematized set of rules to which both sets of combatants subscribe in much the same way as animals spar with each other for status in the group.   It is noteworthy that in human sparring, aggressive instincts can become so aroused that the rules are constantly disregarded.   Members of an audience can also be aroused to overt physical combat with the opposing team or audience.

Because Lorenz takes the theoretical position that aggression is instinctive and largely unsocialized or unalterable by experience, he noted in the past that spectator sport offered one focus for the human's destructive urges — a position he later retracted in view of the more powerful arguments and research demonstrations that, in fact, aggression and destruction in sport lead to more of the same because of modelling effects, among others.   Further, the anthropologist Sipes (1973) demonstrated that violent societies sanction violent sport.   The catharsis theory, embraced by the instinct theorists, would of course predict the opposite.   Violent societies would have less violent sport and peaceful societies would have more, being more likely to drain off aggression through aggression in sport.

In general, the data support the social learning position.   Observing and participating in aggression breeds more aggression (Bandura, 1977a).   However, the controversy is not an either/or proposition.   Both can apply to certain individuals and certain situations.   It would be a foolish teacher of aggressive 14-year-old boys in a reformatory who did not build frequent sport and physical activities into their day.   Similarly, as will be illustrated in the next section, several aggressively oriented individuals have found socially acceptable outlets for their aggression in the world of sport. Although we rely heavily upon ethological theory to explain motivation in some athletes on a very basic level, it is necessary to appreciate other viewpoints that regard motivation as more alterable when various reinforcements become dominant. For the moment, the focus is temporarily on the most basic physiological side of human nature and upon motivation that is present in all to some degree. But, that readily becomes overshadowed by other facets of human nature in circumstances when the person interacts with, and is socialized by, the culture within which he or she develops. The effect of the ethologist's position, then, which argues for innate bases of aggression, has provided an impetus for those researchers and writers who have preferred to concentrate upon the environmental-social determinants of aggression.

Sports behavior occupies a unique position in the psychology of aggression. Just as all human beings appear to be equipped with innate aggressive responses and the energy to execute them, all athletes display drive and energy that are directed toward maintaining athletic rank or defeating an opponent. There are rare exceptions, such as when an athlete is physically sick, suffers from debilitating mental conflict, or deliberately "throws" a match or game for ulterior motives. This observation varies with different athletes and sports, but there is a common denominator: a will to win over nature or an opponent. In some sports the aggressive component is blatant, as in boxing, while in others it is more camouflaged by ritual and equipment, as in tennis. However, some boxers may not be motivated primarily by aggression once their energy finds outlet in the ring, whereas some tennis players may be. Thus, Schecter (1970) has commented that he finds himself liking most prizefighters, who are usually "the gentlest of men." Some have even described Sonny Liston as mild-mannered. In contrast, Hentoff (1967) describes his own tennis experience as providing an outlet for his frustrated need to express power and deadly instincts: "Better health through murder, and the corpses can so easily be replaced in tins of three."

Because biology is one source of aggression and an important one, it might be expected to be a strong motivation in the early careers of athletes before secondary reinforcements become established. Charlie Taylor, as described by Dowling (1970) provides a good example when he ascribes his early football motivations to having a fund of energy that he had to expend. Thereafter, motivation is probably due to the social environment of the sports world. That environment will often determine whether an athlete is led into a more constructive expression of energy through skill, or alternatively into an expression of energy which is primarily directed against others, including fellow athletes.

AGGRESSION AND INDIVIDUAL SPORT BEHAVIOR

In sum, individuals show variations in their levels of aggressive energy because of two factors. First, there are genetic and constitutional variations in the individual's potential for aggression. One individual may brim over with aggression, while another is passive, even lethargic. Second, as individuals are socialized by life experience, their energies may be redirected or transformed into other forms of expression. Athletes who are highly motivated by aggression may not have transformed their basic energies into more socialized activities. When athletic games require the expression of aggressive energy, they tend to attract individuals with high activity levels, a conclusion borne out by studies of athletic participants (Eysenck, Nias, and Cox, 1982).

How might an aggressively motivated athlete be expected to behave? He or she is likely to be impulsive, to respond at a more biological level to people and to games than most, to engage in much physical activity, and to strike out when a stimulus for aggression is present. The aggressive athlete will be active, eager, strong, highly motivated, and likely to seek to vanquish any opponent. This behavior would be characteristic of the athlete on or off the playing field. By focusing aggressive energies upon sport, however, the athlete will become socialized by realizing he or she must control and master the expression of aggression. As an athlete matures, the aggressive motivation becomes less obvious. Thus, the youthful individual who is able to discharge aggression through sport should eventually reach a happier adjustment than if he or she did not have that outlet, providing the sport is not one that itself encourages destructive violence. In the following paragraphs we will examine the biographies of two athletes who clearly illustrated high levels of aggressive motivation.

Althea Gibson, an outstanding tennis player and Wimbledon champion in 1957 and 1958, provides a vivid example of aggressive motivation in sports. Aggression as a theme appears early in her autobiography (1958). In accounts of her childhood she recounts that she learned correct fighting technique from her father, was tough, had a fighting temperament, and was afraid of no one. Althea describes some of her more memorable fights, probably remembered still in the streets of Harlem. The reader is left with the impression of a strong and forceful personality, quick to take offense and ready to fight. The fights often left Althea bloody and bruised, as did her physical encounters with adult figures of authority in her family. Significantly, she emphasizes that one of the problems she had to overcome in her early tennis competition was her impulse to cross the net and physically fight her opponent when she found herself losing a match. As she gradually realized this tendency, she was able to redirect her energies and accept the protocol of tennis. She dressed and acted like a lady while beating "the liver and life out of the ball." Her aggressive energies were thus channeled according to the rules of the game. As a postscript, it is of interest to note that Gibson did not fully develop as a player until her early thirities and perhaps could have dominated women's tennis for longer than, in fact, she did. She retired (after first attempting a career in singing), before sharing in the commercial windfalls of organized tennis, to take up professional golf. Gibson was the pioneer black champion in world tennis, long before the emergence of Arthur Ashe.

She suffered frustration and hardship in her tennis career because of her race. Later in life she was appointed New Jersey Athletic Commissioner.

World boxing champion Sonny Liston provides a second example of high aggressive motivation. In his biography of Liston, Young (1963) describes Liston's formative years. His father married twice and had 25 children. He often punished Liston physically (a factor that causes social learning theorists to perk up their ears). Liston ran away from his home in Arkansas when he was thirteen to seek his mother in St. Louis. It was then that his record of anti-social acts began. He was initially arrested for beating up other boys, and then for a series of armed thefts. He developed a reputation for mean aggressiveness. In the Missouri State Penitentiary, Father Alois Stevens suggested that boxing might provide Liston with the best outlet for his aggression, thus launching Liston on his boxing career.

Young describes Liston as naturally suited for boxing because anger and fighting were long-term features of his personality. Perhaps the most damaging incident in Liston's career occurred on May 5, 1956 when he was leaving a party and became involved in an argument with a policemen. The officer ordered a cab driver, illegally parked while answering a call from Liston, to move or get a ticket. Although Liston and the policeman gave slightly different accounts of the incident, it was clear there was a struggle over the policeman's gun and that Liston and the cab driver beat the officer, who required hospitalization. Similar incidents as this have occurred hundreds of times between professional athletes and others from various walks of life. The significance is, as it was in the Liston case, that although minor things like a traffic violation are daily occurrences, very few result in such physical violence. It was characteristic of Liston to strike out physically and aggressively in a frustrating situation. The other incidents involving male athletes today are often reported as having drugs or alcohol as precipitants. We contend that these incidents are also due to a high level of innate emotional aggression as well as socialized aggression through sport.

That two vivid examples of aggressive motivation happen to be of black athletes is not significant; rather, it reflects a combination of personal and environmental influences which is applicable to white athletes as well. Several have been previously cited. Both Gibson and Liston had early environmental experiences that reinforced the expression of aggression. These two athletes represent a channeling of basic life energy into aggressive motivation, and illustrate individuals whose tendencies to experience the emotion of aggression motivated them in sport.

Referring back to the types of aggression previously described, one must note that the athlete who is highly motivated by emotional aggression should not be confused with the athlete who has other primary motivations, but who displays aggression because he or she is placed in an athletic situation that demands it. Some sports require more aggression than others. Football, hockey, and boxing would be expected to attract more aggressively motivated individuals than curling, golf, and badminton. Yet the latter sports require their own forms of aggression. Indeed, even nonphysical sports have been described as fiercely aggressive. The psychoanalyst Fine (1967), in his analysis of chess, states that a major attraction for players of that game is to be able to enact their conflicts surrounding aggression. Cockburn (1974) says the same in his psychological analysis of chess. A chess player can adopt strategies other than direct aggression, however, while a football player or a boxer is required to express highly assertive behavior continuously. Training programs and match preparations are designed to arouse and to use aggressive energies. Thus the study of aggressive motivations is and will remain central to the study of sport.

SIGNIFICANCE OF AGGRESSION IN SPORT

Aggression, as formulated in the theories of ethology and sociobiology, has an adaptive function. It promotes the survival of the species through the preservation of the gene pool. Others have argued that aggression is a learned behavior even in the animal world (Altman, 1977; French, 1981) and that dominant mothers give their infants more freedom of movement and opportunity to test and practice assertion and aggression. There is no reason, however, to hold ourselves back theoretically by falling into the nature-nurture controversy — Biologists gave it up 40 years ago, although "social scientists have been slow to get the message" (Masters, 1977, p. 281). Having noted that the aggression construct is a complex one, that there are individual differences in the innate potential to aggress, and that aggression can also be learned or stimulated by specific situations, we are in a position to assess its overall significance in sport.

When aggressive energies are expressed within the rules of a sport and channeled into skill by a mature athlete, then one may witness a powerful and inspiring performance. An example is the competence orientation of the boxer Henry Cooper. Aggression of any type becomes destructive in sport when it is uncontrolled and used to deliberately diminish and cheat others while the rules of the game are ignored. It is significant that in sport, as in war, the generals or those who control the action (owners, politicians, coaches, and government officials) — that is, the leaders — rarely suffer physical injury from their aggression. It is those in the footranks that suffer both pain and injury, and even death. In sport, as in classical war, front-line casualties are usually lower class men. The damage done to this group through the sport of boxing is well documented (British Medical Association, 1984). The damage to football players is also on the record.

The fact of physical destruction through sport is further demonstrated by the thousands of professionals in the field of sports medicine who profit from treating sport injuries. The custodians of and owners in sport often brashly support violence, showing they have not thought through the consequences of personal injury to athletes, or do not care about it. At other times, even more brashly, they claim financial interest in the staged violence. Clarence Campbell, former president of the NHL, was notorious for this position. He stated in 1975: "If violence ceases to exist, it [hockey] will not be the same game. Insofar as it is part of the show, certainly we sell it ... You don't change a successful formula." However, in response to public outcry and the consequent positionings of politicians and the law, the rules of hockey have been altered to prevent some of the vicious brawls that were becoming common in the game throughout the late 1970s. In fact, most surveys show that "crowds" do not want brutality and permanent injury to players on the ice. The majority supports the execution of skill in the game, and this bodes well for some indication of civilized concern.

There are several variations on this theme with time, type of sample, sex, etc. For example, R. P. Bowles in *Protest, Violence and Change*, (1972, p. 128) reports that in 1970, 60% of Canadians did not like to see fighting, while G. W. Russell (personal correspondence) reported that 80% of women university students and 54% of men strongly disapproved of violence in hockey. Smith (1983, p. 112) reports that 61% of players and 87% of fans would like less violence in hockey. In the United States in 1984, *The Hockey News* stated that 67% of its readers who responded to a poll found the level of violence in hockey acceptable but 71% preferred the milder 1984 game to that of 10 years ago.

Turning to boxing, a sport in which the marketing of violence seems central, one may ask of the crowd: do they want to see blood or boxing skills? Given a choice, will a person choose violence, sadism, and pornography, or skill, eroticism, and art? How people respond to these questions provides a crude measure of civilization. That is, in civilized societies it might be predicted that most people would choose skill, eroticism, and art. Why then do some persons of comparative privilege persist in the sanctioning of the baser and more dysfunctional behaviors? Murdoch (Surface, 1977), talking of his early days when playing Major Junior A Hockey for the Kamloops Chiefs, said: "I wanted to shoot and be a hockey player. But the coach wanted me to be the head goon and specialize in beating up people. He got so many goons that the team couldn't hardly score and lost about five times as many games as they won." Paul Mulvey, a 23-year-old player from Merritt who was demoted by the Los Angeles Kings for refusing to carry out coach Don Perry's command to leave the bench to join an on-ice altercation on January 24, 1982, commented: "I'll be disappointed if the New Haven fans boo me for what I believe to be right. I realize Perry was respected by a lot of fans here but I hope they understand that I couldn't be a goon. I just want to get to the business at hand ... which is playing hockey." Perry was suspended for 15 days and his team fined $5000 by National Hockey League president John Ziegler. It is significant that ice hockey officials were forced to change their stance on aggression after the initiative was taken by a few players, fans, sports observers, experts, and general public opinion. But it was not until players were taken to court that hockey officialdom reluctantly consented to police its own.

The misunderstanding of people in sport on the subject of aggression is immense. Parents encourage aggressive play in their children, scouts look for aggressive athletes in their travels, coaches train athletes in the hopes of increasing their aggression. The idea is that a high arousal level produces high motivation and hence high performance. Yet the process of skill development in sport involves maturation and control. Aggression for aggression's sake should not be sanctioned. It is self-defeating and debilitating to others. The outstanding athlete enters competition with control and not with impulse. This has been demonstrated by the Soviet style of hockey, by the failure of rousing peptalks to produce winning behavior anywhere but in films, and by the fact that highly skilled athletes out-play aggressive ones on almost all occasions in all sports when the rules are enforced.

A sport organization should offer structure and constant monitoring to aggressive athletes and not condone violent outbursts. Management programs and therapies are currently available to assist in such behavioral change. If the athlete fails to respond to treatment, it is very doubtful that the public or official sport bodies will benefit from the time or the money invested in the athlete. Cultures other than North American have recognized this in their training programs. Because Western culture is highly individualistic and often violent, (1) we tend not to know how to "select" for the right kind of "aggression" in sport, that is, we fail to seek out highly assertive behavior which is non-destructive in intent and can therefore be more readily expressed by skill via training methods; and (2) we tend not to know how to "handle" destructive aggression when in fact it occurs. Smith (1974, 1979) has noted, for example, that many in the subculture of ice hockey, including parents, peers, coaches, and fans, see violence as a necessary vehicle for success.

In a significant program of research, Russell at the University of Lethbridge has conducted studies (1981a, 1981b, 1983a, 1983b, 1984) on aggression in both athletes and spectators. After a detailed examination of the many studies involving the catharsis versus social learning positions on aggression in sport, he concludes (1983b) that the latter position finds most support. He found (1981b) that spectators are more hostile after violent games, supporting Smith's (1976) result that 74 percent of outbursts involving soccer and hockey spectators follow extreme displays of violence on the field or ice. Furthermore, significant pre- to post-event increases in spectator hostility have been found at football (Goldstein and Arms, 1971), ice hockey (Arms, Russell and Sandilands, 1979; Russell, 1981b) and professional wrestling (Arms et al., 1979). Spectator hostility at the nonaggressive control sports of gymnastics and swimming remained constant over pre- to post-event testing. Russell (1979) found that the choice of N.H.L.

heroes by young hockey players was strongly influenced by the disproportionately greater attention given "local" teams and players by the regional media, yielding the theory of "media impact" and choice of hero. For reviews and extensions of the sports-aggression research area the reader is referred to Goldstein (1983), Russell (1981), and Smith (1983).

In conclusion, since the social learning position on aggression can be supported from sports studies as well as from the program of experimental work conducted by Bandura since 1963 (see also Bandura, 1969a, 1969b, 1973, 1977a) and others, one is justified in questioning the laxity of control surrounding the expression of aggression in many sports in both North America and abroad. Aggression in sport should unfold under rigid enforcement of the rules so that athletes are not hurt and so that youths are not misled. Sport officials should cease to endorse acts of violence and aggression which are destructive. There is no support for the notion that uncontrolled aggression improves sport performance when the rules of the game are enforced. There may be high levels of innate aggression in some athletes, and these athletes will be attracted to opportunities in sport. Good coaching, officiating, and training may help these athletes move from impulsive to controlled play and hence assist in their maturation and development. It is insufficient that sport activity provide a vehicle for impulse expression. It must also provide a vehicle for learning.

3
Conflict

INTRODUCTION

Two more energy models are useful in accounting for athletic motivation. Each, as in the case of aggression, may be significant in human development to the degree it is encouraged or discouraged. The two models are contained within the theories of neurotic conflict and competence. Both neurotic conflict and competence allow for innate motivations modifiable through experience. Those familiar with the athletic world may be struck by the different effects athletes have on each other and on coaches. Some athletes are excitable, unpredictable, and difficult to deal with, while others are mature, stable, and dependable. The former seem totally involved in themselves, while the latter are easy to communicate with. Neurotically motivated and competence-oriented athletes provide the Mr. Hydes and Dr. Jekylls of the sport world. In this chapter we examine the Mr. Hydes.

When we say an individual is in conflict we mean that he or she has not realistically integrated the various parts of his or her experience, which therefore act in opposition to one another. We propose that in the conflict-oriented or neurotic athlete, the innate energy of the individual is directed into maintaining and supporting the conflict that is central to his or her personal style. Freud (1922, pp. 141ff.) described the neurotically conflicted individual as a poor bet for friendship, love, or group participation. Why? The neurotic individual is so concerned with those problems central to him or herself that he or she has little left to expend on other forms of emotional investment. The conflicted athlete can, however, invest his or her emotion in sport because the sport is a vehicle for the expression of, and symbolizes, that conflict.

There is no shortage of sports literature highlighting the conflicting motivations of athletes, just as there is no shortage of athletes having conflicted adjustments. Beisser (1977) collected a series of case studies of neurotic athletes whom he had treated in therapy. One of the most widely read books in sport psychology, *Problem Athletes and How to Handle Them,* by Ogilvie and Tutko (1966), includes many cases of athletes with neurotic components in their motivations. In fact, if Freud's theory were applied in general, as Freud intended it should be, a neurotic basis would be found as the motivation for all sport.

In order to describe this consistent conflict or turmoil, we may use a simple stress and personaltiy model as proposed by Maddi (1967). It considers three features of neurosis or conflict. The first is *the degree of premorbidity* in the individual's personality and development or, in other words, the individual's personal vulnerability to maladjustment. The second is *the type of stress* to which the individual is exposed. The third is *the neurotic style* adopted. Neurosis is the result of conflict produced by a combination of the premorbidity and the stress. Thus it is the interaction between the personality predisposition and the type of stress to which the individual is exposed which heightens the conflict and results in the expression of the conflict. A good example of this is the case of a 35-year-old boxer seen clinically by the writer. An aggressive personality style was thwarted by the process of aging and failure in sport and this resulted in a clinical depression requiring hospitalization. The premorbidity was the aggressive personality style, the stress was aging and failure, and the resulting neurosis was depression.

TYPES OF CONFLICT

In further describing conflicted adjustments in athletes, Horney's (1966) personality styles are also valuable. She depicts neurotic styles as being due to three extremes in expression — the movement in an exaggerated fashion against, away from, or toward other people. Anger, withdrawal, and dependency are the featured personal themes. Sport could then symbolize for a participant a chance to move against other people and a time to vent hostility and anger toward them, a time to withdraw from people and have little contact with them, or a time to communicate with people in order to gain love and attention which cannot be found elsewhere. With success in sport, some persons who have shown conflict in the early stages of their careers may resolve that conflict and be able to mature and move out of their neurotic mode of expression. Others become increasingly conflicted with the length of time they stay in sport and may therefore suffer a breakdown or choose to drop out of sport.

Horney's general description needs to be expanded to include other common symptoms of conflict; thus to her three classifications of (1) anger, (2) escape, and (3) dependency we add four other patterns. These are (4) narcissistic and egocentric behavior, (5) obsessive thoughts and or behaviors, (6) depression and unhappiness or manic-depressive swings, and (7) anxiety or extreme nervousness.

Anger. The angry or surly athlete has a chip on his or her shoulder and continually thinks he or she is being put down, is being diminished, and is being cheated. The attitude can magnify with high achievement motivation and situational stress. The athlete may seethe, swear, and/or strike out physically at other athletes, officials, fans, or anybody else. The reader may wonder at the overlap between the aggressive athlete and the conflicted athlete whose behavior also features anger and aggression. The difference is that in the conflicted athlete it is stress that arouses the unrealistic, inappropriate, and the nonadaptive anger against others in order to protect the self-image or ego. The conflict within the angry athlete is that he or she cannot perceive realistically and protects the faulty perception with the assault upon others. The aggressive athlete, on the other hand, naturally seeks stimulation in order to increase arousal, has perceptions which may be quite realistic, and acts upon immediate and unsocialized impulse. Thus the frequent outbursts of a John McEnroe and many others like him, which feature manipulative use of anger and surliness, are most probably of the conflict variety. That is, they are usually dysfunctional for him and to others. They therefore serve to protect his own unrealistic perceptions and his own self-image.

Withdrawal. One manner in which to handle conflict is to deny it and to seek escape from it. This category of conflict motivation includes both self-imposed isolation and addictive behaviors. The heavy use of drugs and alcohol by athletes is a common method of escape from the people and pressures of the sports world. Frequently it is used by ex-stars as a process of weaning from youthful success. Jimmy Greaves, former England soccer striker, said of himself at age 31: "I became a walking vegetable. I can remember waking up in my car, not knowing where I was. I'd look at my watch and if it was dark I wouldn't know whether it was morning or night." Other escape mechanisms found in sport are compulsive fun-seeking and escape into films, discos, and the accumulation of material possessions. Often escape is symbolized in the sport itself. As cited on page 33 ff., Bobby Fischer provides an example of an athlete whose life has represented a series of graduated withdrawals into his own world and activities.

Dependency. The athlete who moves in the extreme toward others is excessively dependent upon the love and nurturance of others and will often not perform without them. He or she will "go to pieces" if abandoned by significant others. Sometimes this disintegration also extends to dependence upon the audience. The athlete may cease to perform or to try when the limelight dims (i.e., when other athletes are overtaking them career-wise), when placed in an arena that is not the major one for their event, or when an audience turns against them. Mary Decker is a good example of the dependent athlete as described by Moore (1984). Her dependency is illustrated by her need to perform within the protection of an emotional partnership and her inability to accept defeat and any subsequent, if temporary, fall from the limelight.

Narcissistic and Egocentric Behavior. The narcissistic athlete is entirely concerned with him or herself to the exclusion of others. The athlete will always do what is best for the self and puts egocentric interests ahead of others, even family, friends, and children. With success and maturity the athlete may outgrow this pattern. John F. Bassett, sportsman and entrepreneur, who died in 1986 at age 47 of cancer, provides an example of such change. When struck with melanoma in 1976, it reportedly changed his love of competition. He is quoted as saying: "All of a sudden I didn't care. I realized I had a beautiful wife, four great kids and winning and losing games wasn't life and death anymore." (Vancouver Sun, May 15, 1986.)

Obsessive Thoughts and/or Behaviors. Obsessional behaviors and symptoms include superstitious beliefs, dysfunctional training programs (self-destructive exercises, etc.), and hypochondriacal beliefs (obsessions with pain and injuries real or imagined). Athletes are often under extreme pressure to perform in spite of injury and often do so with chronic impairment (shoulders, knees, back, elbows). Thus, the ground is laid for prolonged stress to bring out obsessions with bodily well being and weaknesses. Jane Frederick of track, for example, admitted that she overtrains, worries, and suffers frequent handicaps through injury. Obsessional ideas can creep into an athlete's thoughts and some become bizarre to the point of hallucinations and delusions. Margaret Court, Bobby Fischer, and Chris Evert are only a few who have had such experiences.

Depression and Unhappiness or Manic-Depressive States. Extreme unhappiness and depression can arise in athletes who have a potential for affective mood swings. The athlete may withdraw, become unmotivated, and not care, or may suffer from periods of weeping and helplessness, low self-esteem, and self-doubt. In its extreme form and when the condition persists, suicide can result. Danny Thomas, for example, was named most valuable player in the Eastern League and was then called to the big leagues by the Milwaukee Brewers. He attempted suicide twice before killing himself at age 28 in 1980. His friends thought he could not take the pressure of the big leagues. His problems involved rape charges, hitting an umpire, drugs and alcohol, and marital difficulties. Many athletes across the years have both attempted and committed suicide. It is of course impossible to determine what part the sporting life plays in their affective swings and whether, given other life events, their actions would have been the same. In contrast to cases of depression, the athlete can show manic mood swings or swings in the active, assertive, and uncontrolled direction. Such manic swings can be as destructive as depressive swings to the self and to others. Jim Piersall (1955) of baseball provides an example.

Anxiety or Extreme Nervousness. Anxiety, either due to performance or due to events off the playing field, shows another type of conflict in sport. Uncertainty, lack of confidence, and loss of nerve can result in debilitating experience for an athlete. Tony Jacklin is quoted by Kahn (1979): "It got to the point where I knew I didn't want to be there. I was afraid to be around – it was awful. You don't want anyone to pull for you. You just want to disappear and for everyone else to disappear with you." Louise Brough, former Wimbledon champion, was known for continuing her competitive career late into her thirties and forties. At times she became so anxiety ridden that she could not toss the ball accurately for her serve. She was burdened with double faulting, and wept on the court.

The foregoing categories of behavior, and combinations thereof, are expected to be prominent in athletes who are motivated by conflict. We now turn to the theoretical background and to some explanations offered for conflict motivation.

THEORY OF CONFLICT

Conflict results from stress acting upon a type of premorbidity or vulnerability in a person. It culminates in a series of dysfunctional but adaptive behaviors. One wishes to understand the personal vulnerability and stress that ready the person for a conflicted style of sport performance. The theory that explains this in the most comprehensive manner is psychodynamic personality theory. Most dynamic theories of personality owe a debt to Freud for his controversial but useful explanations of unusual human motivations and behaviors. Freud offered a dynamic working model which still stands, although much adjusted, in the 1980s (see, for example, Silverman, 1976; Silverman and Weinberger, 1985). According to Freud's theory, the innate source of energy is modified as a result of an individual's experiences during the psychosexual stages of emotional development. The basic energy, or *libido,* consists mainly of sexual and aggressive drives from the *id,* that part of one's personality along with the superego not immediately accessible to consciousness. Pressures are exerted upon the id from the *superego,* the part of personality that has absorbed parental standards and social values. The *ego* suppresses or transforms these drives into socially acceptable expressions and thus manages the conflicts between the id and the superego through a series of *defense mechanisms.* Athletics is an acceptable expression of these mechanisms and, as such, is a direct form of sublimation. In the strict application of Freudian theory, each individual struggles for a balance between the demands of the id, the demands of the superego and reality. Thus, he or she is constantly in conflict. Society cannot tolerate the aggressive and sexual urges of the individual and still maintain order, yet these urges need some form of outward expression if the person is to experience equilibrium. Sport is a socially acceptable manner of expression.

In *Civilization and its Discontents,* Freud (1930) suggested that the higher the level of civilization, the more neuroses will be produced among its members, as civilization inevitably forces more and more restrictions upon the libidinal energies of individuals. This theory offers an explanation for the increase in sports activities in the leisure classes in the more developed countries. In current North American society there are high demands for efficiency and organization, and more and more claims are placed upon the average citizen to be precise, predictable, and nonaggressive. A society with such a social structure would hypothetically produce large numbers of instinctually frustrated people who would be attracted to sports participation. It is unfortunate that by the very nature of the social reinforcements offered, athletics tend to affect most those individuals who are neurotically inclined. Money, recognition, and status do not affect the mature, intrinsically motivated person as much as the immature, neurotically inclined personality. Thus, Gary Shaw (1972) writes that when he left a potential career in American football, his most significant aims were to develop his own goals, feelings, and sense of self. He sees this as a problem for most well-known athletes, and this, too, was the sentiment of Lance Rentzel (1972). Beisser (1977) describes this process as he saw it occurring in athletes with whom he worked in psychotherapy. He states that sport has different symbolic meaning for different athletes. Sport may be a way of expressing drives that otherwise would be unacceptable, or it may be a way of relating to a seemingly foreign or hostile environment. It may also represent either a healthy relationship with authority or a challenge to it.

The degree of neurotic motivation in an athlete depends upon the level of psychosexual development, or emotional maturity, the individual has reached, and it is represented by the quality of the sport performance. Freud (1905), it may be recalled, hypothesized that emotional development and adult adjustment styles were linked to the oral, anal, phallic, latency, and genital stages of psychosexual development. Applying orthodox analytic theory to sport, most neurotic athletic adjustment should stem from the phallic stage. This is thought to be the stage when Oedipal (and Electra) complexes arise over emotional attachments to parents, and as an outcome of the complexes the objects of the sexual aim are established. No one familiar with recent research results (see Chapters 11 and 12 for a full discussion) will try to explain all development of sexual identity by analytic theory. However it remains important in offering explanation of specific cases of strong emotional attachments to and problems surrounding relationships with parents. Such cases are not infrequent in the sport world. The early, strong, and sometimes symbiotic relationships of, for example, many female tennis players with their fathers and many male and female figure skaters with their mothers are of extreme interest. Thus we think the phallic stage deserves analysis because it is at this stage that emotions are expressed through outlets other than those specifically sexual, such as through identifications, activities, performance, attention-seeking behaviors, and peer-group games. Oral or anal stage fixations (such as extreme dependency or extreme compulsivity) are less likely to result in later athletic life styles, although conflicts stemming from these stages may interact with later Oedipal conflicts to further complicate the understanding of a neurotic style. It is during the phallic stage that the most intense and complex conflicts emerge and latency activities are established. Finally, at the genital level, physical activity might be used as a direct outlet for sexual frustration because sexual energies may be drained off by physical exhaustion. Freud's comprehensive theory offers both a general theory of sport motivation as well as an explanation for individual differences if it is pursued in sufficient detail.

More recent contributions to the psychology of conflict focus much less on intrapsychic processes and much more on environmental stress. That is, if one considers the model proposed — premorbidity plus stress equals neurosis — Freud concentrated upon the etiology of the premorbidity while more recent workers focus upon the stress or the environmental section of the model and on ways and methods to manage the stress. Chapter 16 is devoted to a discussion of stress in sport. The many behavioral and cognitive techniques that are used in order to deal with stress as well as practical suggestions for alleviating stress in sport are dealt with in Chapters 14 and 15. Some of the most important preventative work to be done in the field of sport psychology undoubtedly lies in working with parents and in educational settings in order to remove some of the debilitating stress placed on the backs of young children in sport.

Recent innovations and emphases add to but do not replace the contributions of Freud. His theory assists in the understanding of the development of individuals and how and why they react to stress and carry conflict in unique ways. Sport is an arena for major attempts by individuals to mediate and resolve conflict. The higher the level of sport excellence, the more the individual is placed under personal, social, and economic pressure to achieve. At the same time he or she may experience additional stress from a disrupted emotional life, constant travel, and a never-ending stream of new people, cities, and cultures.

CONFLICT AND INDIVIDUAL SPORT BEHAVIOR

The conflict-motivated athlete will be unpredictable and difficult to deal with because his or her athletic adjustment is a defense. Psychological defenses can break down under pressure, disappointment, or frustration, during which the individual may be temporarily indisposed. Such indisposition is frequently seen in sports contests when an athlete becomes unapproachable by sulking or by verbally or physically lashing out at others. Before a contest neurotic defenses are threatened, during it they are directly tested, and afterwards they may be temporarily shattered if the athlete has failed in his or her goals. If the athlete has won, he or she will usually be approachable, integrated, and receptive to the public. Two well-known sports personalities whose behavior may be interpreted as featuring conflict are Bobby Fischer, former chess champion, and Lance Rentzel, former football star. We chose these two examples of conflict motivation because much has been written about them, because they became international or national public figures, and because they represent very different sport pursuits.

Bobby Fischer's behavior over the years, as he single-mindedly made his way toward the world chess championship in Reykjavik, Iceland in the summer of 1972, shocked some and appealed to others. To the present day his interesting and frequently bizarre behavior continues to make media headlines. Born in Chicago in 1943, Fischer learned chess at the age of six by playing the game with his sister, who was five years older. Their divorced mother worked and studied to become a nurse. Fischer never knew his father. Fischer practiced harder and played more often than most serious young players. This singleness of purpose, along with his egocentricity and talent, eventually led to his chess achievements. Fischer's personal development was not so successful. Many hoped that his conquest of the chess world and his subsequent retirement from it would have led him to seek and develop a more balanced life. This does not seem to have occurred. Brady (1965), Fischer's biographer and supporter during his development, was forced to recognize the pathos of Fischer's position. To Brady, Fischer had paid highly for his expertise at chess by isolating himself in order to develop the independence and determination necessary to nurture excellence. Brady notes such idiosyncrasies as Bobby's lack of any identity other than "chess player" and his unusual habits and way of life, such as rotating his sleeping place among three beds in an apartment where he lived alone. Other than a few material possessions, mostly clothes acquired during his travels, Bobby Fischer had nothing but chess.

Fischer, of course, emerged as a success in the eyes of many because of his victory in 1972. Yet his personal attitudes, as described by Ginzburg (1962) in his controversial article "Portrait of a Genius as a Young Chess Master," revealed another side of the champion which has emerged most strongly during subsequent years. After failing to appear for an appointment on one day, Bobby, then 18, arrived an hour late on the second day, burst into Ginzburg's office and asked for food. Anger, insecurity, and compensation through chess were the major themes revealed in the interview, most of which was taped. Women, Soviet chess players, school, and even his mother did not fare well in the young chess player's estimation and all were disparaged. His plans for the future and, in fact, his identity were dependent on the fame and fortune of the world chess championship, for then the fatherless young man would have an identity, a powerful one, and he would use it. He would found a chess club, write books, and reform the world of chess by allowing membership only to those of class and talent. The rich would have to pay highly for the privilege of belonging. Bobby Fischer would have position, success, and power. He would be master.

Suspicious, bizarre, and egocentric behavior characterized Fischer's career in chess competition. So did his excellence, his mastery of the game, and his ability to dominate his opponent through psychological strategy. The adjustment that made this possible was built over the years through the process by which an isolated and insecure young man was able to become an equally isolated and confident chess champion with the will and the skill to "crush" others. By the early 1980s the 40-year-old Fischer had adopted a bizarre life style in Pasadena in which his withdrawl and passion for privacy reportedly approached that of Howard Hughes. His three obsessions were reported to be physical fitness, chess, and political philosophy. By the summer of 1984 Fischer was said to be in Los Angeles wandering from cheap hotel to cheap hotel, virtually penniless, very much a recluse, and still deeply involved in the study of chess. The enactment of basic personal conflict through the playing of chess is not a new feature of the study of chess players. As noted earlier, some would argue that the basic motivations of all chess players stem from a need to express conflict, both sexual and aggressive.

The second example of an athlete whose motivation features a neurotic component is Lance Rentzel, whose problem of sexual exhibitionism led him into psychotherapy. In his unusual autobiography (1972), he describes his conflicts. In 1966 and in 1970 he was involved in two incidents in which he exposed himself sexually to young girls. His prevailing mood prior to each incident was one of depression, futility, and self-doubt. His personal situation and that of the world seemed hopeless. Rentzel was driving in his car when these moods overcame him. He spotted young girls playing, became dissociated from reality and from any social judgment, and sexually exposed himself to them.

How do these behaviors relate to Rentzel's sport motivation? In the course of his psychotherapy with Louis West, professor in the Department of Psychiatry at UCLA, Rentzel examined his past development as it related to his adult life style and problems. He relates his self-explorations in his unique autobiography. He had been an able, gifted, and parentally indulged child. This social indulgence resulted from his achievements in school and in sport, and it continued later during his success at football. He notes the damage done by his excessive dependence upon the approval of others. He sees himself as playing a role both at home and away from it. He was appreciated not for himself but for what he achieved, leaving, underneath the success and bravado, an impoverished and underdeveloped sense of self. Against this sense of insecurity, Rentzel adopted a set of defenses, common to the athletic ego, that creates what is essentially a neurotic adjustment: a compulsive drive to compete and win, a desire to play a hero role, and a need to indulge in sexual exploits. All of these were needed to sustain the faltering sense of self, which depended almost entirely upon his ability to portray himself as he thought others saw him. When these defenses failed, Rentzel felt humiliated and defeated. He would then fall apart and lose all perspective. Many people experience such despair at some time in their lives and their reactions to it depend upon their individual strengths and weaknesses. That Rentzel tended to use an antisocial behavior to regain a sense of masculinity, identity, and power is probably due to early emotional experiences in his family and to an emotionally significant event at the age of 12 when he exposed himself to a young girl.

Stimulation from sexual exposure is aroused by the exhibitionist's momentary identification with the person to whom he exposes himself (Freud, 1913). Seeing himself through a little girl's eyes, the exhibitionist is able to feel himself a man and not a failure. He often chooses a small child with whom to identify because that serves as a balance between power and weakness. Exhibitionism, in a mild form, is characteristic of the adjustments of many athletes, and leads to extreme personal difficulty for many when they find themselves out of the limelight. Rentzel's sport motivation probably retained a neurotic core even after his therapy. As with Fischer, the neurosis represents the cultural values surrounding the sports person, as much as it does the individual athlete's attempts to adjust. Thus, there are two ways of coping with the problem of neurotic conflict in athletes. One is to suggest a change in the social values within which the athlete developed. The second is to work with the individual athlete to assist him or her to a better adjustment, as was the case in Rentzel's search for maturity. Now a businessman in his 40s, Rentzel votes Republican and says he will always see himself as a Dallas Cowboy.

In summarizing the Fischer and Rentzel stories, one might say that Fischer attempted to overcome his insecurity and regain his missing father, or a figure of authority, through his total identification with chess. Note that the object of the game is to trap the king, which is usually done by first overcoming the queen. By being better than anyone, competing with adults, and establishing his own set of rules, Fischer could seemingly create an absolute position of security for himself. This position, once obtained, was presumably not as powerful as Fischer hoped. Perhaps it involved too much negative backlash and too much compromise. Lance Rentzel's needs for emotional expression and self-acceptance were at the root of his conflict. His development had not permitted him forms of emotional expression that were in accord with his true feelings. Therefore, when his athletic adjustment failed him, he was driven to acts of exhibitionism.

The foregoing examples should provide the reader with an introduction to the understanding of conflict motivation in athletes via the study of case histories. We are now prepared to end the chapter with a consideration of the significance of conflict in sport.

SIGNIFICANCE OF CONFLICT IN SPORT

Many people in sport are not the happy, healthy, forward-looking individuals that coaches, the media, and sponsors would have us believe. Even American high school athletes have enormous pressures upon them to satisfy self, peers, parents, and coaches. Almost all coaches will be called upon to deal with conflict in their athletes, as will the athlete him or herself. The most important step in dealing with conflict in sport is to recognize when it exists. The denial of conflict has been part of the North American ethos for a long time, particularly on the playing field. It has been a very significant trend that athletes and those around them have begun now to publicize their vulnerabilities, fears, and failures. The number of athletes seeking help with problems of conflict in their lives is far beyond what is now public information since the files of clinicians are typically and strictly confidential unless the client chooses to publicize them.

Yet increasing numbers from the sport world have written or talked to the press about their lives primarily from the point of view of the conflicts experienced. Such candidness humanizes the dynamics of the sport hero, who for so long was presented to the public and to youth, in an unrealistic manner. Understanding the neurotic characteristics of athletes will help people to live longer and happier lives in sport, and out of it. It will also add to our knowledge of conflict, its origin, its development, and its management.

Parts IV and V of this book are devoted to the examination of ways of dealing with the problems of athletes. The area pioneered by Ogilvie and Tutko in 1969 has become a flourishing and fascinating field for clinicians as well as for physical educators, coaches, and medical personnel. Unfortunately the emphasis in much of this work is on forcing or helping the individual to adjust to a very chaotic and unreasonable environment. As we learn to understand better the neuroses of individuals we will also learn about the pathologies of the system that created them. Prevention is the key to the future.

4
Competence

INTRODUCTION

Competence refers to the effective interaction of the individual with the environment. The interaction and its consequent effect on the environment are both desired and satisfying to the initiator. Examples of competence motivation range from the very simple, in which the individual may be scarcely aware of what he or she is doing, to the very complex, in which the individual is attempting to master a new skill or set of skills. One carries a glass of water from sink to table in a competent manner if one does not spill it and places it neatly in the desired position. One serves competently in tennis by visualizing or deciding where in the service court the ball will land, the type of serve one will use (flat, twist, slice, reverse slice, etc.), and the speed with which one will serve. If all this is done, the serve is competently executed. However in terms of the motivational feedback, what represents competence for one individual may represent incompetence for another. A three-year-old child obtaining the glass of water will experience competence with a much different execution than would a waiter at Claridges. Or, the beginner at tennis will be more consciously challenged by merely putting the service ball in play than will the expert player who faces complex alternatives in deciding service strategies. In this style of psychological motivation, emphasis is on the energy that is used in the service of competence experiences so that one may consistently meet challenges and act upon the environment in the desired way. Both the infant struggling to pull him or herself up for the first time and the aging baseball pitcher struggling to control the ball and the game for one more time may be motivated by competence.

TYPES OF COMPETENCE

There are five major categories of human behavior through which competence may be expressed. Although one would not expect the average individual to rank equally high in all categories, that individual would have some experience with all categories. The fully functioning person, or the person with ideal adjustment as depicted in most North American personality theories, would be expected to display competence in each category. The five categories are (1) physical competence, (2) intellectual competence, (3) emotional competence, (4) social competence, and (5) spiritual or existential competence.

Physical Competence. The behaviors expressed in physical competence are speed, coordination, strength, reaction time, visual or auditory acuity and skill. These facets of behavior, and others, allow an individual to have a desired effect upon the environment in many athletic pursuits. Much athletic training is directed toward the tuning and development of these competencies, the aim being personal excellence and ultimately competitive excellence. Sometimes this aspect of competence is so cultivated and rewarded, to the detriment of the other forms of competence, that the development of the athlete is severely curtailed. Thus some black athletes who have entered universities on athletic scholarships have had their physical prowess used and their intellectual short-comings ignored, only to have to return to grade school when cast aside by the athletic establishment. Martina Navratilova provides a good example of an athlete with superb physical competence early in her career who had to hone both her emotional and intellectual skills through a kind of tutoring and support network before she was able to take her rightful position in the women's tennis rankings.

Intellectual Competence. Intellectual competence is the ability to use the mind to reach desired solutions or decisions. In sports this has to do with sizing up situations, strategies, taking in large amounts of information, and sometimes "instinctively" putting them all together in order to execute a game plan in view of the circumstances. It involves the retention of information, acting on the basis of experience, using the retained information, and being flexible enough to adjust its use when necessary. Bridge, chess, and any game involving the assessment of consequences and of predictive strategies are dependent on intellectual competence. Different positions, for example in football, vary in their dependence upon this competence. Many positions in football, basketball, and ice hockey may depend more upon instinctive reaction in that for the most part intellectual direction comes from players in key positions or even from the bench. Quarterbacks and pitchers are frequently known for their superior intellectual abilities and it is also well known in many sports that intellect plus middling ability will usually triumph over little intellect and outstanding ability. Bill Tilden was perhaps the classic intellect and strategist of tennis. His clearly written books on strategy are still in print and are better than most modern attempts to explain the subtleties of tennis.

Emotional Competence. Maturity, the ability to manage disturbing emotion, the ability to channel emotion into skill at the game, to remain motivated in the face of adversity, comprises the backbone of emotional competence as it relates to sport. Security, stability, confidence, and equanimity will be displayed in contrast to dysfunctional behaviors such as bitterness, blame, temper, and exploitation of others. The emotionally competent person will be responsible, loyal, know him or herself, and thus will be capable of sustained and meaningful commitment to other people as well as to sport. A very interesting plea for emotional maturity was issued by two senior athletes at the 1984 Olympics to Zola Budd, when she became the focus for the full wrath of a vengeful Mary Decker and her fans. Debbie Brill and Kate Schmidt wrote an open letter to Budd, printed in the Los Angeles Times,* which ran in part: "We feel like apologizing for Mary Decker's lack of graciousness, for the otherwise polite Coliseum crowd booing, while it was you who had the balance and strength to continue, and for entire nations that have stumbled and tripped over a seemingly simple issue — allowing a young girl to pursue her passion. But it is not our responsibility to apologize for anyone, we can only urge you to transcend the peculiarities of this last year, and go on to learn, grow, and benefit from all that sport has to offer — a very clear and measurable approach to life."

Social Competence.   Social competence is effectiveness in dealing with other people and with social situations. It reflects the ability to become part of a group, to contribute to morale, cohesion or performance within the group or in the achievement of group goals. The individual will derive intrinsic satisfaction from being part of a group. Relationships with others are usually good and satisfying, beginning in the family group with parents and siblings, and extending to peers and then to team members, coaches, officials, and opposing athletes and even fans. Kramer (1969, p. 5) describes such an experience when discussing a championship game against the Dallas Cowboys in 1967: "I forgot everything but the feeling of eleven men working together, trying to do everything in harmony. And I can still feel the pure pleasure of the scoring play ... " Walton (Callahan, 1983) has made a similar observation of basketball: "I love almost everything about the game, the life, the players, the crowds. Just being out there, the competition. I missed it." Coaches often have to work on the development of social competence in athletes.

Spiritual or Existential Competence.   This category of competence refers to the individual experiencing intrinsic satisfaction from the appreciation of morality, contentment, and the ability to be philosophical about victory and defeat. It includes the ability to see beyond one's own egocentric needs and contributions. The person will move away from isolation and individualism and toward concerns for the general welfare and for group prosperity. The person will show interest

---

*As quoted in The Vancouver Province.

in generations past, present, and future and will have confidence in humankind on the whole.   Examples of such experiences, often quite foreign to North Americans, are found in the autobiography of Japan's baseball legend Sadaharu Oh (with Falkner, 1984): "In combat, I learned to give up combat. I learned ... there were no enemies.   An opponent was someone whose strength, joined to yours, created a certain result.   Let someone call you enemy and attack you, and in that moment [you] lose the contest ... My baseball career was a long, long initiation into a single secret: that at the heart of all things is love." Another classic example is that of Eric Liddell. Duncan Wright, Scotland's greatest long-distance runner, said of him at Liddell's funeral in 1945 (Magnussan, 1981, p. 178-9): "Eric was greater than an athlete: he was a Crusade. He was without doubt the most glorious runner I have ever seen. Never has there been a greater need for a man with such a high moral and virile Christian character like Eric Liddell to be set as an example to our young people." Outstanding athletes who show spiritual or existential competence are often described as having something more than others.   They are inspirational to others.   Their peers will go to "watch them practice," and they will have the capacity to transcend both the pettiness of others and the limitations of their own abilities.

THEORY OF COMPETENCE

The third model of sport motivation is essentially constructive and found in both outstanding and lower level athletes.   The competence-oriented athlete is involved in sport for intrinsically rewarding reasons.   The athlete experiences feelings of self-fulfillment in the quest for excellence. The inherent satisfaction experienced is the reward of competence motivation, and it is essential to the development of all human beings.   White (1959, 1963) has been the major proponent of this model of motivation.   He argues for an extension of the Freudian concept of motivation in which the energy source is limited to the libido.   According to White, there are independent ego energies that originate entirely in the autonomous part of an individual's personality.   These energies are equipped with a drive toward *effectance,* which induces motivation to inter-act with the environment and to exert an effect upon it.   Each effort exerted by an individual has an effect upon the environment, which then feeds back into the experience of the organism.   The drive of effectance has been observed in the behavior of animals and young children as they learn the tasks they will be required to perform in the future.   Some of the first pleasures of life seem to involve drives other than the basic ones of hunger, thirst, and elimination.   Two such independent drives are related to curiosity and exploration.   Several years ago psychologists Butler and Harlow (1957) found that monkeys living in isolation could learn to solve problems in order to make interesting sights last. Rats and mice would explore mazes for apparently no other purpose than to satisfy that drive. Piaget (1936) has written about the behavior of his children, whose earliest pleasures stemmed from perceptual interaction with environmental stimuli. These, plus Freud's own undeveloped theories about ego drives, led White into his formulation of ego psychology. His theory of competence motivation asserts that the individual engages in continual interaction with the environment in order to experience the effect he or she will have on it. The experience may be stimulating, pleasurable, disturbing, or painful, but the drive for competence is hypothesized to be as vital to development as is the basic satisfaction of hunger or thirst.

The theory of competence views such experiences as a continuous extension of what a baby first undergoes in its initial perceptual interaction with the world. The development of self, of positive emotional experiences, and of feelings of well-being all depend on the early relationship between the individual and his or her environment, for these are not seen as separate entities but as constantly interchanging and affecting one another. The individual acts and reacts. Sport is one way in which this can be done within a clearly defined framework (the rules). The purpose of the activity is not to achieve a specific goal, but to experience the process of interacting with the environment and to deal effectively with the challenge. Lunn (1957) used the example of a golfer. If the golfer's object was merely to sink the ball in the hole, he or she could walk around the course with a bag of golf balls and drop each one in. A golfer prefers the difficult and challenging process of the game, however, precisely because it provides him or her with an expression of competence motivation. It lets the golfer relate to the world in an intricate and important way, and it builds the golfer's confidence and intrinsic pleasure when a shot is executed well. Athletic motivation is largely an expression of the search for feelings of competence. Ashe (1981) has expressed this in writing: "The ultimate connection between tennis and life is 'in the doing' – not the winning. Success is a journey, not a destination. The doing is usually more important than the outcome." (p. 208). White's (1959, 1963) major contribution to competence theory is that he provides a constructive theory of human motivation as opposed to the more limited and pessimistic positions emanating from the aggression and conflict theories. Further, this theory is based on an energy model that builds upon the assumption of biological motivation feeding into some of the complex activities and striving seen in human action.

Currently Bandura's work on self-efficacy (1977b, 1982, 1983) is prominent in the psychological literature and makes a contribution to the understanding of competence theory. However, it is less comprehensive than White's contribution because it is constricted by: results based on contrived experimental situations, molecularity in theorizing, and an overemphasis upon cognitive as opposed to emotional factors. His argument is that it is the self-perception of the performer that determines motivations and aspirations. Further, self-perception can be broken down into factors such as performance feedback and knowledge of standards by which one sets goals. The argument is that without external standards of self-evaluation and knowledge, the individual will not be motivated.

A comprehensive theory does not emerge from this work because it fails to speculate on or to integrate the importance of emotional factors in both motivation and performance. In contrast, those studying sport psychology have been unable to ignore the powerful affective components in sport motivation. As a consequence, theoretical attention is given here to the energy models of motivation and their relationships to inner experience and performance.

COMPETENCE AND INDIVIDUAL SPORT BEHAVIOR

The athlete whose predominant motivation for engaging in sport is competence is easily spotted. He or she is reliable, acknowledges the intrinsic value in sport, and sustains amicable relationships with fellow athletes and officials. Roger Bannister and Tom Seaver are two examples of athletes with strong competence orientations. Bannister's (1955) autobiography, *First Four Minutes,* provides an excellent example of a man who is motivated by competence from the beginning of his career. His outstanding feature is his inner motivation as he makes his way with dedication and sustained discipline toward becoming the first miler in history to break the four-minute barrier. Bannister's account tells of the challenge and the self-satisfaction he experiences in his achievements. He learns about those feelings as his career develops from that of a bean-pole school boy, to a socially conscious undergraduate, to an interested but not entirely committed Oxford medical student. Final commitment comes after an adventure in self-exploration which gives him the confidence to open new frontiers. The theme of his story is one of mastery and joy. Bannister runs because in racing he finds an inner sense of accomplishment quite apart from any of the external rewards. Bannister recognizes the higher values of sport and its potential for uniting people. He experiences what it means to have the support of fellow athletes, and how vital social atmosphere is to performance. At one point in his career Bannister finds himself enjoying races even when he has lost them. When he finally decides to set a new record in racing, it is a decision of personal commitment. For Bannister, the athlete's struggle is one of mastery over himself. It is not surprising that Roger Bannister is a proponent of personal fitness in spite of a car accident that has kept him from running since 1975, and continues to be active in British and international sport organization.

Tom Seaver (Devaney, 1974), American League pitcher, is another example of strong competence motivation in an athlete. When asked what motivates him, Seaver replies that the money, the glory of winning, and the breaking of records is secondary. What is essential for Seaver is that pitching excites and satisfies him. The achievement of skill and excellence in performance are his motivations. He derives satisfaction from a well-executed pitch into which he pours all his past experience of mental and physical development. To feel confident in situations of stress gives him his greatest satisfaction. His ambition is to sustain his competence year after year. In his character sketch of Tom Seaver, Jordan (1974) writes of Seaver's lack of vanity and lack of interest in personal publicity, and these are contrasted with his total dedication and self-discipline. Seaver works hard on every detail of his pitching, which, like Roger Bannister's running, has been a vehicle of self-exploration. In developing his superb level of competence, Seaver came to know himself and to balance his strengths and weaknesses. Out of this struggle emerged a confident and self-sufficient man. Bannister and Seaver are two athletes whose pronounced motivation is psychological competence. Their sports excellence was a long-term development for each of them, and it is reflected in their style of sport participation, and their relationships with others in the sport world.

At times all athletes experience feelings of competence during their sports participation. Tennis player Billie Jean King describes herself as "feeling beautiful all over" when she executes a shot exactly the way she visualized it. Basketball's Connie Hawkins talks about losing all sense of "time or pressure" when his game is flowing without flaw. Sandy Koufax described his love of successful baseball pitching as being able to do "everything you want out there." He talks about the ball being "light" and "an extension of your body." It is also significant that these strong feelings of competence need not only be associated with winning. Baseball's Jim Bouton reveals his feelings of joy when he satisfactorily controlled his knuckleball for ten straight innings. Even though the game was lost, his personal sense of achievement was his reward.

SIGNIFICANCE OF COMPETENCE IN SPORT

If sport is to maximize the process of human development, the significance of competence theory cannot be overestimated. It has fundamental significance in human behavior and outdistances aggression and conflict as categories of motivation because of its emphasis on positive development. Until White (1963) formulated the theory, which was based upon psychological research from experimental, developmental, and clinical psychology, many had thought that the job of socializing the individual was merely a matter of accepting biological needs and thereafter conditioning and controlling behavior. The individual was seen as dependent upon the interaction between his or her needs and a relatively autonomous environment. Competence theory, in contrast, stressed the interaction between the organism and the environment and, indeed, the predestined "goodness of fit" between actor and environment.

Competence theory provides a logical explanation of human motivation in that a large percentage of the human race lives quietly, peacefully, and predictably (barring political, economic, technological, or geographic disaster). Most individuals live without great destruction to self or to others and without distressing symptoms stemming from either aggression or neuroticism. Most live to enjoy, to learn, and to balance leisure with work.

We do not deny the neurotic and destructive tendencies shown by some people nor that self-abuse, abuse of others, and unhappiness exist. What we are arguing is that given sufficient opportunity to experience and develop competence, the socialization of most people is positive and their social participation is constructive. The experience of competence is as available to the infant who manipulates a plaything in a pleasurable manner as it is to a retarded individual who enjoys the experience of swimming, as it is to the quarterback who executes a difficult pass. The experience of competence must be judged by its intrinsic merit to the individual actor. It is a genuinely *psychological construct* and is not definable through external measures of achievement. The concept of competence has immense implications for society in general as well as for sport. It is therefore the key concept in, and the theme of this book.

We have thus far examined three psychological theories of human motivation which assume basic funds of energy that can be channeled into aggression, conflict, or competence. Although many athletes may be motivated by a mixture of the three, others have relatively clear-cut motivational styles at various stages of their careers. Competence provides the most constructive reason for sport participation. It is a motivation that should be encouraged in sport. Many are well aware that competence is the main feature of and motivator in sport. For such persons there is little need to encourage competence. It is already a natural process. However many others have lost sight of and touch with what should be the central feature in sport and therefore correction is needed. There are several ways in which this correction might be achieved. Coaches and teachers working with children in sport programs can foster and support a spirit of competence as soon as it is evident. Successful athletes who excel because of competence can be cited as examples for others to follow. Sports that demand abnormal training patterns, such as steroid regimens, and promote extreme aggression or neurotic conflicts can be discouraged. Finally, conditioning and learning methods developed in the study of behavior control by researchers such as Skinner (1971), Bandura (1969), Wolpe (1969), and others can and should be applied in order to encourage long-term benefits for those involved in sport.

Such methods are effective in some situations and less effective in others. Techniques to encourage behavior which is basically compatible with constructive growth (competence), should be more effective than those used to break a competence cycle in order to make a person more socially conforming. Note that a problem arises, as it does in therapy, if an individual experiences competence from destructive aggressive or neurotic behavior. It is our theory that if competence is encouraged sufficiently early in life, the ground is set for constructive participation later. If competence is frustrated, then power motivation and manipulation through aggression, neuroticism, or complete withdrawal may occur. The individual at that point may be difficult to rescue. But if the system is corrected to reward what is constructive behavior for all, the desperate and destructive behavior of some athletes will not be supported or reinforced, and hence may be corrected. Thus the tailoring of rewards and denials is justified to encourage desired behaviors and to discourage unwanted ones. This behavioral strategy is widely applied to the treatment of psychological disorders and undesirable social habits. The same principles can be applied to undesirable sport behavior.

To maximize competence motivation and minimize aggression and conflict in a sport program, it would be necessary first to define carefully which behaviors were constructive and which destructive, then to develop an accurate method of identifying athletes who display these behaviors, and finally to link a system of rewards and denials with the appropriate behaviors. Positive reinforcements can take the form of encouragement from a coach, material rewards, and spectator or peer group support. Negative reinforcements can be disapproval from a coach, denial of material rewards, peer group rejection, and spectator indifference or non-appearance. All individuals theoretically have the seeds of aggression, conflict, and competence within them. If competence is the most naturally occurring motive, then it should be possible to develop competence at the expense of the other two motivations, if the correct developmental and social environment is provided. The competence- or skill-oriented athlete will, in turn, provide for others the model of a constructive approach to sport, and will inspire spectators with expertise and mastery rather than con them with aggressiveness and antics.

PART II

MOTIVATIONAL THEORY II

5
Play and Leisure

INTRODUCTION

Two areas of study allow special insight into the significance of competence motivation. These are the play activities of children and the leisure activities of adults. Weisler and McCall (1976) have described play as universal behavior. So is the leisure of adults. Because of technology, advanced societies, sometimes referred to as the "post-industrial societies" are becoming increasingly involved in planning for the projected increase in leisure time for adult society. Indeed, this is the function of the government-sponsored Leisure Development Center in Tokyo. Life style predictions, community planning, and facility design projections all offer new fields of challenge for researchers. In contrast, the study of children's play has a relatively long history. It is central to the study of socialization and education.

THE PLAY OF CHILDREN

Play is experimental interaction with the environment for the purpose of intrinsic feedback and/or satisfaction. There has been much debate over the various definitions of play, games, and sport (as examples, see Sutton-Smith, 1966, 1979; Piaget, 1966; Denzin, 1975; Csikszentmihalyi, 1975, 1976; Barnett, 1976; Harris, 1980; and Bretherton, 1984). Hundreds of treatises and studies have been published and have occupied keen observers since the turn of the century. A good example is the small and concentrated book by Douglas, *London Street Games,* which started as an article in 1913 and was subsequently extended into book form and published in 1916, 1931, and 1969. The author does not document rules but rather aims to record the content of approximately 1000 games that the children spontaneously created and passed on through word of mouth. His little volume is a record of the historical universality of games and he applauds the inventive powers of children. He also records the lament of one observer who marvelled at the "stupidity of the social reformer who desires to close to the children the world of adventure, to take from them their birthright of the streets, and coop them up in well-regulated and uninspiring playgrounds where, under the supervision of teachers, their imagination will decline, their originality wither." (p. xi). The inventiveness and complexity of the content surrounding games is illustrated by the following skipping rhyme:

I am a little beggar-girl,
My mother she is dead,
My father is a drunkard
And won't give me no bread.
I look out of the window
To hear the organ play —
God bless my dear mother,
She gone far away.
Ding-dong the castle bells
Bless my poor mother —
Her coffin shall be black,
Six white angels at her back —
Two to watch and two to pray,
And two to carry her soul away. (p. 39)

Douglas notes that activity and laughter accompanied even serious lyrics. Piaget (1932) provided another milestone when he published *The Moral Judgment of the Child.* He followed in 1945 with the publication of *Play, Dreams and Imitation in Childhood.* The 1932 volume was based on his observations of the participation and rule development among Swiss school children as they played marbles. Through his careful observations he was able to describe the significance of play, rule making, and rule enforcement in moral development.

Competence expression and moral expression emerge through play and games. From the first attempts in infancy to perceive, touch, and affect the environment, the child moves to more complex experimentation with the environment — experimentation with objects, people, positions, role relationships, and ideas. Games are symbolic, repetitive, usually joyful, and involve social interaction and the management of success and failure of human relationships.

With the last activity, the management of success and failure, comes the second major feature of games — moral expression (the first being competence expression). Games not only satisfy the desire for competence and mastery but introduce the notion of social structure through rules, regulations, and form. Ross, Goldman, and Hay (1976), in their studies of the rudiments of play in children 12 to 24 months of age, noted that infant games involve reciprocity, turn taking, and repetition. Children's games feature mutual involvement in which one child makes overtures to another along with the anticipation that the second child will reciprocate. When the partner reciprocates a game is in progress. That 12-month-old children initiate a game to involve others is an important observation. Piaget (1932) has stated that children emerged from an egocentric style to a sociocentric style of play with age. It appears that he did not fully credit the young child with an intuitive sense of social reciprocity. He had noted that when younger children played with older children they tended to conform to the rules imposed by the older children. When children played with their peers they were responsible for working out the rules and abiding by them. In the former situation, the children learn to conform to rules while in the latter situation the rudiments of social morality may be found.

Through development of and experimentation with rule application in play, children learn why rules are to be obeyed, how mutual commitments to rules are maintained, and how defiant behavior can be brought into line. These ideas will be developed more fully in the following chapter on social motivation. For now it is important to note that children's play provides an example of the purest form of competence motivation which later emerges into the realization of and appreciation of social morality. Morality is learned through creating and adhering to a set of rules which are mutually agreed upon and which mediate the social interaction of the game. The rules make the game meaningful, give it structure, and make it fair to all. Note also that older children teach the rules of the game to younger children when age discrepancies exist in the group. This demonstrates the influence of status and dominance as discussed in Chapter 1. It is significant that children often prefer to play in groups with children of their own age and interests. It is the creation of the rules that is important and children will often tire of a game once rules are finally established and enacted.

There are hundreds of papers and articles on children's play, which cross age, social class, sex, and culture. Much of this literature has no theoretical direction. With the competence model to provide a basis for interpretation, the literature becomes more meaningful and significant. For example, the mere observations of Douglas (1931) become a probable reflection of the rhythms of and problems of lower class life in which the children grew up. Numerous observations from crosscultural perspectives become more meaningful when one considers the children rehearsing and learning to deal with changing cultural values. Ager (1974), for example, describes some of the changing styles of play among children in the Alaskan village of Tununak which was in the slow process of adaptation to Anglo-American culture. Sutton-Smith and colleagues (1979, 1984, 1985) have made oustanding contributions to the study of play and the cultural reflections of games and leisure activities. They have linked the styles of games played to the culture's level of development, geographical situation, and social class. The solitary play of kindergarten children, which Moore, Evertson, and Brophy (1974) found was linked to independence and maturity, also becomes more obviously functional when one considers the variety of skills besides social skills that the North American child must master. The study of play cannot be conducted on merely biological, structural, or social grounds. The psychological reasons for the universality of play must be considered and the missing link is the construct of competence and competence motivation. By using a functional approach and applying competence theory, many definitional problems are solved and the barrenness of endless experimental and objective accounts of play make sense. Harris (1980) discussed play as information seeking behavior which featured a weak commitment to the attainment of goals. This position would be much sharpened by a consideration of the intrinsic competence feedback provided by play at all age levels. Harris' separation of play from sport and the failure to broaden the concept of goal or reinforcement forces an artificial structure upon a continuous process.

The purpose of play is individual and social development. Free, undirected play is essential for the development of children throughout the world. At least part of every child's time needs to be spent in free play with self or with others, that is, in spontaneous as opposed to teacher-imposed play. It is unfortunate that in many developed nations, children's play is highly organized and adult centered. This leads to impoverished experiences with rule development through spontaneous play. It is doubly unfortunate that problems of health care and the supply of food and water cannot be solved in less developed nations so that educational programs could be developed in order to facilitate psychological growth. That is, children in both developed and less developed nations, for different reasons need more opportunity for spontaneous play. Weisler and McCall (1976) reach in the direction of White's competence theory when they call for new directions in research on play. Some major redirection may be needed in North America where, for example, studies suggest that the quality of interaction that the infant has with the parent(s) influences the style of play with peers. If there is poor child-parent interaction there is poor child-child interaction. There is a possibility that more early free play with peers might improve the child-parent relationship. A further concern in North America is the alarming stress placed on children by some parents determined that their babies will be super-achievers (*Newsweek*, 1983). Competitive parents who are known by their own achievements or lack of them want their children to join a meritocracy. This can lead to music, gymnastic, and art lessons for two year olds. The parents and profiteers of the movement need correction through educational programs. An appreciation of competence motivation would be as invaluable in parental education classes as it would be in the curricula of all sport coaching programs. Competence is needed as a platform from which to study and criticize the gradual institutionalization of children's play and leisure activities. This would lead to an examination of some of the complex interactions between competence, cognitive development, social symbols, and external reward — through institutions such as organized sport, television, comic books, and computers.

THE LEISURE OF ADULTS

Leisure refers to voluntary interaction with the environment for the purposes of rest, relaxation, escape, or pleasure. This defintion allows for the inclusion of much activity and inactivity under the heading of leisure, some of it constructive activity, some of it nonconstructive activity, and some of it inactivity with little other purpose than the experience of a state of rest. Leisure includes competence behaviors (of most interest here), relaxation or passive behaviors such as watching television or sleeping, and escape behaviors such as the use of drugs and alcohol. Note that leisure could be engaged in at "work" to the degree the person performs the activity for competence feedback and not for pay or other motives. As Csikszentmihalyi (1976) points out, many activities are performed within a complex web of both intrinsic and extrinsic motivations.

What people choose to do with leisure time depends on many factors, such as past experience, personaltiy, and level of arousal. Fiske and Maddi (1961) in their book *Functions of Varied Experience* describe arousal theory in which the individual seeks an optimal level of stimulation from the environment for his or her own comfort. Supporting evidence for this assertion is found in the research and theories proposed by Malmo (1959), Berlyne (1960), Eysenck and Eysenck (1969), Zuckerman (1972, 1979), and Farley (1985). Thus some will pursue violent and dangerous activities such as car racing or boxing while others will choose isolation and solitude in fishing or contemplation. The need for adventure, curiosity, stimulation and sensation seeking can all be cast within the arousal framework. And yet this does not allow for the importance of the quality of the feedback (or competence feedback) in performing the activity, a gap which Fiske and Maddi effectively cover by including a chapter by White (1961) on competence theory in their book. The main contrast between adult leisure and children's play is that children almost always play out of competence motivation. Adult leisure may or may not reflect on competence motivation. Indulgence in drugs and alcohol may fill leisure time but hardly involves competence feedback (although it may allow for the illusion of competence).

As with play there is an immense amount of literature on leisure. Journals are devoted to the study of leisure. Competence motivation, again becomes important because it allows us to interpret much of this new work, which again is surprisingly atheoretical. Leisure research would suggest that individuals seek an optimal level of arousal and activity and this may vary with several factors, such as personaltiy, culture, socio-economic status, age, work commitments or retirement, sex, addictive potential, and gullibility to trends and advertisement. As well as documenting some of these effects there are large numbers of studies on the influence of television, on leisure counselling, on leisure and aging, and on leisure and the environment. The fields of recreation, life planning, and the entire self-help movement in correcting unhealthy life styles all lend themselves to the constructive choosing and scheduling of leisure activity.

In "post-industrial" societies the planning of leisure time and leisure opportunities is very important. Japan provides an example of such post-industrial attitudes and work is being conducted at several centers. Work at the Leisure Development Center in Tokyo provides a main attempt by the Japanese government to plan for future changes in the work ethic, which has been deeply woven into Japanese culture and socialization. Technological innovation, success in the world economy, and an aging population have led to the prediction of massive amounts of free time in the future. And this imposition will be upon a population schooled in the importance of work and productivity.

The potential range of leisure activities is extremely varied. They could be aesthetic activities such as the tea ceremony, flower arranging, and cooking. They could be intellectual activities or artistic activities such as reading and writing or participation in any form of music or theatre. They could be physical activities such as swimming, jogging, or skiing. They could be escape activities such as gambling, drinking, or sex. In Western culture it may be noted that immense amounts of money are to be made by the provision of constructive and destructive forms of leisure. The same conditions exist in Japan except that the greater focus upon corporate welfare and planning does allow for the provision of more constructive outlets. The attempt in Japan is to steer people into competence-based activities (Secretariate of the 1978 Tskuba Conference, 1980) that preserve and continue the culture while steering people away from the more destructive escape activities. Thus some of the martial arts and sumo wrestling in Japan place high demands on the individual in terms of the discipline and traditional values that must be enacted in training and performance. It is interesting to note that whereas karate training in Japan is presumably controlled and used for the corporate welfare, it has been outlawed in the Soviet Union after a few years of immense popularity. The problem? The skills were being used for individual advancement through street crime and intimidation.

Medeiros (1980) of Brazil has emphasized the importance of leisure to lower class people, and the necessity of steering them away from destructive leisure choices such as gambling, drinking, and drugs. If people choose and are given the opportunity for constructive leisure activities, unlimited horizons for self-growth are opened. Education and insight, both of self and society, are to be experienced if a competence-oriented leisure ethic is adopted. Much of the Japanese effort has been made in a preparatory attempt to shift from a work ethic to a leisure ethic. The work ethic for the purpose of material advancement and show of responsibility is also deeply engrained in segments of occidental society. This is illustrated by Weber's classic treatise *The Protestant Ethic and the Spirit of Capitalism,* wherein he (1930) linked puritanism with the rise of North American capitalism.

The planning of one's leisure time and execution of the chosen activities is perhaps a major defintion of an individual's life and values. To spend time in front of a television set, although it may educate to some extent, hardly gives maximum competence feedback, but it is a statement of a person's life values. Similarly, the person who spends all of his or her time engaged in church activities makes another statement, while those who socialize with friends and relatives make another. Because sports and games reflect the culture where they are practiced, it is no wonder that so many in our developed cultures choose to balance inactivity with fitness, submission to the system with self-assertion, and the relatively limited social activity in many office jobs with the social excitement of group sport participation. Each of these choices emphasizes and keeps prominent a type of competence which is important to people in general. Thus the study of adult leisure shows the degree to which people are coping with life by seeking creativity and happiness through competence.

6
Competition and Cooperation

INTRODUCTION

A competitive situation implies a mutual exclusion of goals between parties while a cooperative situation implies a mutual interdependence of goals between parties. In studying these social motivations, we are more interested in how the individual feels in the situation than in how the situation appears outwardly. Thus our definitions for the chapter are that competition is *felt rivalry* or *felt exclusivity of goals,* while cooperation is *felt communality* or *felt commonness of purpose.* Both are used in a psychological sense and refer to how the athlete feels about and perceives others in his or her social environment. Note that competition and cooperation can be studied in terms of the *demands of the situation* in which the individual finds him or herself, and that the situation may call for either competitive or cooperative behavior (or a mixture of both). Or, competition and cooperation can be studied in terms of the *experience of individuals* and how they psychologically react to the situation. An individual can be placed in a competitive situation and yet *not feel* competitive nor be motivated by competition. Similarly an individual can be placed in a cooperative situation and yet *not feel* cooperative nor be motivated by cooperation. It is essential that the point be made at the beginning of this chapter that the *social motivations and feelings* of individuals may diverge from the *social definitions* or situations. There will always be a mix of competitive and cooperative motivations. For example, a very competitive child who wants to stand out and succeed over others may cooperate with teachers and special friends in order to achieve his or her goals. On the other hand, a competitive sport situation (in which there is a winner and a loser) may also contain elements of cooperation with rules and with teammates and opponents in observing certain limits in reaching the goal. A "competitive" athlete at any level may in fact be a skilled and competent individual who sees the athletic endeavor in a cooperative manner and is motivated by social cooperation. Ashe (1981, pp. 176–177) has written: "I associate killer instinct with a heightened emotional state, and I would not want to be known as somebody who had it ... I like harmony in everything. To me, there should be harmony among the crowd, court officials, the players and even the ball boys." Or, as Liang Boxi, coach of the People's Republic of China's springboard and platform divers is quoted (Wilkinson, 1982, p. 38): "The reason for our success comes from long, strenuous practice days, much patience, devotion of heart and soul to the task and a close harmonious relationship with themselves, each other and the coach." The point is that a situation, seen by one person as very competitive, may not be seen as competitive by another. What many North Americans see as a situation which demands competitive motivation may for others be largely a matter of cooperating with one's peers and raising one's performance through group support, team cohesion, and group identity. Bradley (1977, pp. 104 and 105) describes the importance of cooperation. Among his statements: Basketball "is a sport in which success, as symbolized by the championship, requires that the community goal prevail over selfish impulses ... The less conflict there is off-court, the more the inevitable friction of competition can be minimized, ... teams develop when talents and personalities mesh."

The topics of competition and cooperation as psychological motivations have been of extreme importance in the literature in the fields of sport psychology, the psychology of groups, education, crosscultural psychology, and conflict resolution. There is a long tradition of interest in this fundamental dimension which features at one extreme an individual who feels positional threat from others, and at the other, an individual who feels solidarity with others.

SOCIOBIOLOGY

At this point the sociobiological viewpoint may again be considered in order not to lose sight of the continual interaction in evolution between adaptation and innate disposition. Sociobiological writing suggests (Wilson, 1980, p. 162) that males, genetically programmed for maximum gene preservation and therefore interested in having a maximum number of progeny, must be competitive. This would be in order to preserve their status and breed with the most females. On the other hand females would be programmed to be more altruistic in order to confine themselves to the care and nurturing of one child or a small number of children in order to preserve their genes most adequately, having a possible progeny set of much lesser proportion than males. Although this theory may well have some place in the historical evolution of human behavior, the latter is also much influenced by adaptation; thus we should look to the validation of sociobiology in human behavior itself. But there one finds many noncompetitive males and many competitive females, as well as altruism deeply rooted in the behaviors of both sexes. Wilson (1985) has noted the essential nature of cooperation in the survival of a species. Earlier MacLean (1967) noted that the human animal not only evolves but evolves for the better, and his speculative theorizing is that the human brain, by the increased efficiency of the frontal cortex and control areas, not only becomes better positioned for the expression of morality and constructive social behavior, but will change and evolve as the times demand. Thus MacLean from his studies of comparative neurology and implant research has proposed that the empathic, altruistic, and cooperative association pathways within the brain are continually evolving.

THE FIRST EXPERIMENT ON COMPETITION

The following five sections of the chapter contain a review of significant literature on competition and cooperation. We start with some of the classic studies and move on to research carried out within the last decade. What was said to be the first experiment in the field of social psychology was carried out on the theme of competition. It was published in 1898 by Norman Triplett and was published in the *American Journal of Psychology*. The study was based on original observations from the field of sport, namely bicycle racing, followed up by observations of controlled behavior in laboratory conditions. The study became a classic and is much cited. It is as clear and readable today as it was in 1898 and features the printing of the original data from each subject. This is in contrast to much writing in psychology today, where it is impossible for the reader to judge the accuracy of data from the statistics reported.

Triplett, a psychologist at the University of Indiana, was a bicycle enthusiast. He noted that racers showed varying performances (as measured in time) when they raced alone, with a pacer, or in competition with another racer. By consulting the records of the Racing Board of the League of American Wheelmen, he found that racers were faster when with or against another cyclist than when alone. He theorized that the presence of other cyclists acted as a stimulant to the performer and proposed a *theory of dynamogenesis*. He then decided to replicate his study and test the generalizability of his theory by studying the same phenomenon in a laboratory. Forty children wound fishing reels against the clock either alone or in competition with another child. On average, the children in competition performed better than the children alone. However, in examining the individual results, this trend is found to be less conclusive. In fact, only half of the children performed better in competitive conditions. One-quarter performed more poorly and one-quarter showed no difference in performance between the two conditions. Further, the younger children performed better under the noncompetitive conditions, while the older children performed better when competing. It is interesting that the age effect occurred in children ranging in age from 10 to 12 years, as the observation that competitiveness is related to increased age in North American children is a constant one in current literature. There were many possible offshoots to Triplett's much cited early experiment. The follow-up work during the early 1900s and beyond focused upon performance levels in audience and nonaudience conditions rather than upon the psychological and social effects of competitive and cooperative conditions. The former theme led into the important area of social facilitation research (Zajonc, 1965), which showed that dominant (well-learned) responses were enhanced by an audience while non-dominant (poorly learned) responses were lessened by an audience. Bond and Titus (1983) used meta-analysis of 241 studies to confirm this effect while Michaels et. al. (1982) confirmed it in a sport setting. Good pool players became approximately 9% more accurate in their shots when watched by four observers while players who were below average dropped 9% in accuracy under the same conditions. Worringham and Messick (1983) supported the general effects of social facilitation when they found solitary joggers, both male and female, increased their speed when running past a woman, seated in a park for the purposes of the experiment. It is unfortunate that the study of audience effects, although important in its own right, so out shone the study of cooperation and competition as a follow-up to the Triplett work. The latter topics did not receive much attention until picked up by Deutsch in 1949.

However, Triplett's work did leave us with three important observations on competition and cooperation: first, he demonstrated the importance of competitive and noncompetitive conditions as independent variables in psychological studies; second, he demonstrated that some people perform well in one condition while other people perform better in another; and third, he demonstrated that age and experience tend to be associated with ability to handle competitive situations.

PSYCHOLOGICAL STUDIES

Another classic study in psychology was publisheed by Deutsch (1949). College students had to solve a variety of problems under both competitive and cooperative conditions. Instructions for the competitive condition were: "To motivate you to contribute your best efforts, we will have a reward for the individual who comes out with the best average." For the cooperative condition the instructions were that effectiveness in solving problems would "be evaluated by ranking you as a group in comparison with four other groups who will also tackle the same problems." The incentives were college grades. Deutsch notes that pure competitive and cooperative situations are difficult to create, but that relative differentiations were achieved in the two situations. When compared to the cooperative condition, the members of the competitive groups were self-centered, directed their efforts at surpassing others, and showed group conflict. In the cooperative condition the subjects were coordinated as a group, receptive to each other, and demonstrated insight and understanding in their behavior. They were more productive as a group and arrived at solutions to problems more quickly.   Thus, the cooperative condition produced better group coordination and a higher level of performance. Where group members competed for mutually exclusive goals the atmosphere was disruptive and destructive. Hostilities developed and the competitors became insecure. Deutsch concluded his study with a strong recommendation for the encouragement of cooperative atmospheres in groups.

Since 1949, Deutsch and his associates have devoted much time to the continuation of the study of competition, cooperation, and conflict and its resolution. Recently (1982, p. 40) he has continued to report the results of relevant studies, including one in progress, which compared groups interacting on equality, equity, and winner-take-all bases. The equality (cooperative) groups were more productive than the other two and their autobiographical roles were afterwards described as "nurturant, affiliative, cooperative and altruistic." The winner-take-all (competitive) groups were least productive and described themselves as being more "aggressive, ruthless, selfish, rougher, unsharing, and changeable." The equity groups fell in between on both performance and self-description. On the basis of this and other work on the competition-cooperation dimension over almost 40 years, Deutsch calls for a planned reduction of competitive situations in society. The resolution of conflict can be accomplished by communication, coordination, shared goals, and the control of threat.

Using the results of a different experiment, Mintz (1951) came to similar conclusions. His subjects were given an individual performance problem. They were given strings attached to cones that extended inside the narrow neck of a bottle that was slowly filled with water. The subjects first were given competitive instructions in which monetary rewards were promised, and so they perceived the situation "as a game in which each participant could win or lose money." Then they were given cooperative instructions in which the "incentive offered was membership in a group of people who were going to show their ability to cooperate effectively with each other." In the first situation, chaos resulted and cones jammed at the bottleneck. In the second cooperation took the place of competition, task achievement was higher, and more subjects reached their goals. Based on the results, Mintz concluded that subjects could become inefficient in their behaviors as a result of the reward system that motivated them.

Another program of research was carried out by Sherif and Sherif (1969, pp. 221–266), again with parallel conclusions. The Sherifs' subjects were 11- and 12-year-old boys, divided into two groups, who participated in a research program at a summer camp. The initial conditions were designed to produce group solidarity; then, unknown to the subjects, other conditions were created to produce intergroup competition. Baseball, touch football, and tugs-of-war were arranged, and once the games were under way group conflict was deliberately induced. For example, refreshments, some more appealing than others, were put on a camp table as one group of boys arrived first. The more appealing drinks and foods were being devoured when the second group arrived. The conflict bordered on open warfare. Name calling, fist fights, and a sense of exaggerated chauvinistic feelings developed on each side. When the conflict seemed irreconcilable, Sherif and Sherif set about reducing the competitive attitudes between the two groups by introducing a common task requiring a united effort. These tasks were called "superordinate goals." Some examples: the mile-long pipeline for the camp water supply was secretly broken by the researchers and the boys jointly searched for the leakage; the food supply truck was deliberately damaged so that all the boys had to work cooperatively in order to solve their mutual problem. The result of these cooperative efforts was the development of friendship and communication between the groups.

Sherif and Sherif came to the same essential conclusions as Deutsch and Mintz. Competitive social motivations create atmospheres that produce personal and social disruption and less than optimum performance levels. Such atmospheres can be changed if individuals combine their efforts in striving for mutual goals. It is of interest to note that not only would these experiments be ethically suspect and perhaps not conducted during the 1980s if ethical guidelines were followed — but that these experiments, unknown to the Sherifs, were funded by the Central Intelligence Agency. The CIA was apparently interested in how to induce intergroup conflict. The Sherifs did not begin to study the resolution of conflict in their experiments until it became a practical necessity. After one series of experiments the boys were so agitated that the researchers did not feel they could send them home in their aroused state. It is very clear that much research needs the trial of time and historical perspective to be fully assessed.

Many recent studies on competition and cooperation have focused upon the origins of the two motivations in children and on the encouragement of cooperative atmospheres in classrooms and other social situations (Crockenberg and Bryant, 1978; Johnson and Johnson, 1978; Johnson, Johnson, and Skon, 1979; Johnson and Johnson, 1979; Leet, 1979; Orlick, 1979; Hertz-Lazarowaz, 1980). The overwhelming conclusion is that cooperation is the most productive and constructive atmosphere (Cook and Stingle, 1974; Bryan, 1975; Slavin and Tanner, 1979). Other researchers (Senior and Brophy, 1973; Banerjee and Pareek, 1974; McGuire and Thomas, 1975; Crockenberg, Bryant, and Wilce, 1976; Johnson and Ahlgren, 1976; McClintock and Moskowitz, 1976; McClintock, Moskowitz, and McClintock, 1977; Johnson, Johnson, and Anderson, 1978; Ahlgren and Johnson, 1979) note that age and often sex in Western societies are related to competitiveness: the older participants and males are usually more competitive. Only Barnett, Matthews, and Corbin (1979) reported no findings for these trends while McClintock and Moskowitz (1976) found sex differences but not age differences. As a culmination to these studies Johnson et. al. (1981) carried out a meta-analysis of 122 North American studies which examined the effects of different goal structures on achievement. The result: the cooperative atmosphere is strongly superior.

One is again reminded of the significance of the in-depth observational studies of games which are conducted in the ethological as opposed to the experimental tradition. Ross, Goldman, and Hay (1976) found that children show agonistic behaviors in their play but that they also show cooperation in spontaneously expressed games which feature turn taking, reciprocity, and repetition. Children as young as 12 months direct such cycles by initiating them to their peers, adults, and older children.

In the field of sport psychology many have introduced the idea of cooperative games as a way of developing cooperative orientations in children (for an example see Orlick, 1978). This clearly is a statement on the failure of schools and institutions to honor the directions chosen by children in their own play activities, when given free rein. That their cooperative cycles can be broken by the imposition of singular, unproductive, competitive activities in which they must compete for external reward or adult favor seems puzzling and unnatural. Perhaps this socialization, in the past, prepared children for their later life in which they, particularly males, were expected to compete for status and position. At the present time such socialization seems dysfunctional in that the more leisure time people have available, the more time they will have for natural, intrinsically guided activities. The more studies conducted, the firmer seems the conclusion that when the general good is considered competition cannot be supported. In the United States immense efforts have recently been directed toward the rediscovery of intrinsic motivation and cooperation. This has been followed by criticism of and calls for correction in education and in social values.

EXPERIMENTAL GAMES

Another research area in the study of competition and cooperation is that of experimental games. These are studies that adopt an economic view of human nature, studies which Lerner (1982) has severely criticized. They are used here in order to examine results in terms of the significant themes of this book. In these laboratory studies participants were asked to play a variety of games with or against a partner for specified rewards. Psychologists have investigated how the participants' choices in the game are affected by such variables as personality type, motivation, variation in reward structure, and pregame strategy. The accumulated research in experimental game behavior was compiled by Wrightsman, O'Connor, and Baker in *Cooperation and Competition: Readings on Mixed-Motive Games* (1972). This book was a predecessor of Derlega and Grzelak's *Cooperation and Helping Behavior: Theories and Research* (1982). The shift in the titles of these volumes over the ten-year period is significant in terms of the recognition of the importance of cooperation. The Wrightsman et al. survey included studies done up to December 1970. Additional articles have accumulated since then, most critical of the failure of experimental game research. Again, there are lessons to be learned from the failures of the past.

The studies must be considered with qualifications: whether laboratory results are applicable to life situations; the variations of populations, procedures, places, and time; and the constant fact of the changes that go on in a person as the result of the research when it is in progress. Hence, the conclusions of Wrightsman et al., based on 1,000 papers, were limited. Much of the debate in his summary is a product of laboratory situations created rather than a product of how people act in life situations. In interpreting these and other studies it is necessary to look for consistencies in methods and in areas of psychological investigation, and for programs of study where results have been replicated. Such a study, which used the Prisoner's Dilemma experimental game (see Figure 2), was reported by Kelly and Stahelski (1971). In this game the participant's choices affect his or her own as well as the opponent's reward.

The game was repeated a number of times and one of the unexpected results was the low number of cooperative choices made by participants, even when a competitive style of play resulted in losses for both players. This result has been much replicated in research with North American participants using the experimental game model. Over a period of time in the Kelly and Stahelski

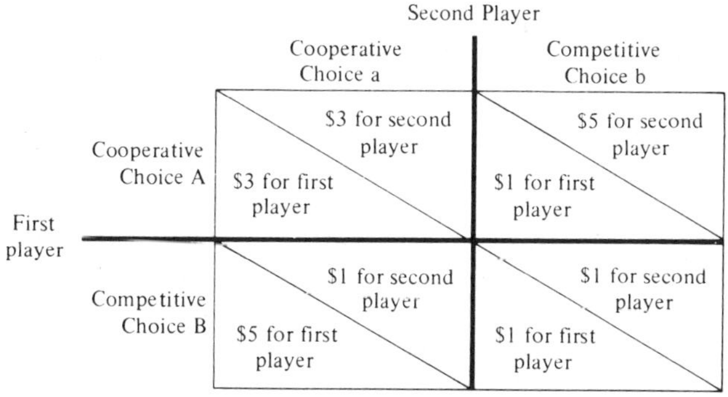

Figure 2. The Prisoner's Dilemma Experimental Game. The first player may choose A (the cooperative choice) or B (the competitive choice). His or her payoff is contingent upon the second player's choice which may be a (cooperative) or b (competitive). If the choices are Aa then both players receive $3. If they are Ba then the first player receives $5 and the second player $1. Conversely if they are Ab, the first player receives $1 and the second player $5 and if they are Bb, both players receive $1. The choices with the greatest payoff for both players over repeated trials of the game are Aa (the cooperative choices). In fact, a feature of experimental game behavior is a large percentage of Bb responses with a competitively oriented player usually imposing his or her style upon a cooperatively oriented player, to the detriment of both. The values in the above matrix are examples only.

work the number of cooperative choices rarely reached more than 50 percent of the total choices. In the next crucial step of their studies, they paired participants who were basically competitive with participants who were cooperative in their pregame philosophies; over a series of games the competitive players forced a competitive atmosphere onto their trusting opponents, and a negative spirit dominated the games. The competitors had more influence than the cooperators even though the latter were more aware of the interaction that was occurring. The cooperators knew they were being forced to change their style and compete while the competitors perceived only the conflict of the game and were oblivious to the cooperative overtures being offered. The competitors' defenses limited their perceptions.

These results are substantiated by other surveys in experimental games that suggest that competitors tend toward the expression of authoritarianism, aggression, isolationism and egocentricity, distrust, and autonomy (Vinacke, 1969). In the situation where a competitor is partnered with a cooperator, the important finding is that the personality of the competitor prevails and the cooperator responds to the situation. Kelly and Stahelski conclude: "It is simply that his [the competitor's] experience has been severely biased or limited by his tendencies to be aggressive, egotistic, exploitative, and rivalistic in interpersonal relationships." These results were confirmed by Kuhlman and Wimberley (1976).

In spite of the above conclusion Pruitt and Kimmel (1977) attempt to counteract this dismal outcome by introducing a "goal/expectation theory." They note that in some studies when games progress past 50 trials (in fact somewhere between 30 and 60 trials) the majority of participants turn to cooperative choices once they realistically realize their long-term goals. The problem in real life and in sport is that the benefits of cooperation are not as clear cut. As long as the competitor can win and impose a competitive atmosphere, the spoils of victory will be his or hers. The benefits of cooperation, although they exist, are much less obvious because competition is overtly rewarded.

CROSSCULTURAL STUDY

Mead (1937) edited *Cooperation and Competition Among Primitive Peoples,* a major anthropological survey. Although she drew no conclusions on the superiority of one system over the other, she did note the features of competitive societies as: a social structure dependent upon individual initiative for its continuation, individual attachment to property, conformity to a single success scale, and strong ego development. Cooperative societies feature a social structure that does not depend upon individual initiative or power over others, belief in an ordered universe, slight emphasis on status, and a high degree of security for the individual. In later anthropological writings, a repeated theme has been concern for the survival of cooperative societies. Although they possess social and psychological strength, they have little to protect them from encroachment by groups with competitive norms.

In his study on the cooperative behavior of Blackfoot Indian and non-Indian Canadian children, Miller (1973) reached similar conclusions. He found there was a higher level of cooperation among rural Indian children than among urban children. Blackfoot Indian children lost their high level of cooperation, however, when they integrated into the white school system. Further, urban children in white segrated schools were more competitive in game responses than urban children attending integrated schools. Miller has also argued that human potentials are wasted through environmental cultivation of competition. Those who do not win also fail to develop a necessary sense of worth as individuals and fail to exert their rightful influence as members of society.

Similar conclusions have resulted from the research program of Madsen and Shapira (Madsen, 1971; 1977) among Mexican and Anglo-American children in Mexico and California. The Anglo-American children showed high degrees of competitive motivation that increased with age and urban living. Nelson and Kagan's (1972) study again replicated those already cited and further stated that cooperative and competitive styles of behavior in children develop out of early childhood experiences. Depending upon the system in which the children must eventually live, any imbalance between the two might be to their disadvantage.

More recent studies support the foregoing conclusion. Children raised communally and in the country are more cooperative than children raised in the city (Pareek and Banerjee, 1974; Richmond and Vance, 1974, 1975; Plattner and Minturn, 1975; Pareek and Banerjee, 1976; Madsen and Shapira, 1977; Knight and Kagan, 1977; Toda, Shinotsuka, McClintock, and Stech, 1978; and Alvarez and Pader, 1979). These results have been further demonstrated crossculturally in the kibbutz (Shapira, 1976), in Africa (Munroe and Munroe, 1977), and in India (Jain, 1978). To make the argument fully international, one may note that in New Zealand, Thomas (1975, 1978) found his effects were reversed by socioeconomic status. Marko (1978) reported from Czechoslavakia that his students valued competition, while Nieciunski (1978) reported from Poland that cooperation is learned with age.

A great many variables, including political climate, can determine the outcome and conclusions of studies. There is little doubt, for example, that many North American institutions have difficulty in realizing the benefits of cooperative atmospheres because they have never questioned the competitive ethic.

Politics aside, the trends in the foregoing research are relatively clear cut. Economics and development seem to lead to individualism, isolation, and competitiveness; to the lessening of cooperative behaviors and styles; and to rule by the competitive ethic. The swallowing up of one system by another as first noted by Margaret Mead is a process with extreme impact upon the social fabric and the mental health of the people within. Such changing systems and the consequent effects upon mental health, as people try to adjust to the new value frameworks imposed upon them, are described in a recent book edited by Nann, Butt, and Ignacio (1984). In this volume, authors representing world perspectives comment on rural and traditional values as opposed to materialistic Western values. Many authors, for example from Africa, Egypt, and the Philippines, call for the continuation of their communal and traditional ways. Most people throughout the world are not sympathetic to Western values and it is fitting and necessary that we re-examine them. Even the president of the American Psychological Association (Spence, 1985) has noted the destructiveness of the competitive ethic and called for re-examination. It is significant that an international theme of such importance and proportion is played out in the psychology of sport and that we are able to re-examine some of these values through the study of sport.

PERFORMANCE AND SOCIAL MOTIVATION

The question of the effect of competitive and cooperative motivations upon performance was much debated ever since a few early experimenters concluded that competitive situations increased performance.

Triplett's (1898) study, discussed on pp. 58–59, is one such experiment often cited in which half the participants performed better under competitive conditions. The assessment of Miller and Hamblin (1963) is as explicative as any to date. They conclude that when the experimental task requires a high interdependence of performers, then cooperative motivations lead to higher performance. When the task to be executed involves no interdependence, then competitive motivations may lead to a higher performance. The nature of the task, therefore, becomes crucial in the claim by some that performance levels are increased or decreased by competitive motivations. However, the most comprehensive review to date (Johnson et al., 1981) concludes that cooperative goals as opposed to competitive goals strongly enhance performance.

There are two important points to be made. First, there are very few situations in life in which people are not interdependent. Humans are social animals and are always reliant upon and intertwined with others in conducting their lives. On individual, group, and even international levels, people are becoming increasingly aware of this and of the need for cooperation. Second, we are arguing that in sport, also, performers are in fact frequently interdependent and that performance levels will be raised by cooperative psychological motivations even when contests are being staged.

The competitive sport model, as perceived by many, is not, therefore, a good representation of life, nor does it provide good training for life. However, we will be claiming throughout this book that sports people can be linked by superordinate goals or constructive values. When this occurs the athletes will usually be motivated by competence. Their appreciation of the values in sport will change the function of the sport in which they are participants. It also leads to the constructive application of the sport model to life in general. It should be noted that we are not suggesting that sport contests be eliminated but that the competitive psychological motivation for engaging in them and the social perception of them as competitive be reduced.

Rabbie (1982, p. 138) has suggested that winning and losing need to be assessed in terms of the goals and perceptions of the actors. He cites experiments by Deutsch and others to argue that losers sometimes feel morally superior and are satisfied with their goals in terms of moral satisfaction. However, much does depend on how a situation is socially defined. If two athletes, for example, are competing for a legitimate winner-take-all prize in golf or tennis, there is clearly no interdependence in goals. Thus it is very difficult for spectators, and athletes, to see past this overt social definition of the situation to the covert interdependence.

THE SIGNIFICANCE OF COMPETITION AND COOPERATION IN SPORT

Although a few still extol the benefits of competition, most experts (Deutsch, 1969, 1982; Zander, 1981; for example) argue strongly for the importance of cooperation from both theoretical and research bases. They note the higher base rate of cooperation over competition in all kinds of social life, and more importantly, the greater need for it. Researchers from Maclean (1962) to the sociobiologists (Wilson, 1980) have suggested that altruism, empathy, and concern for others are as rooted in ingrained biological processes as are agonistic behaviors. Most recently, the child developmentalist Kagan (1984) has supported this notion by arguing that the development of conscience and morality may be ingrained, and Kohn (1986) has summarized the case against competition.

On the side of competitive motivations and situations, some argue that they build character, self-confidence, team solidarity, and democratic values. The former arguments unfortunately tend to hold only for winners, and the effects of competition, if not staged absolutely fairly, lead to much cheating and dishonesty. On the side of cooperative perspectives and situations lie solutions to the important questions facing humankind today. The distribution of resources, the control of pollution, the saving of endangered species, the regulation of nuclear industries, the guiding and policing of giant corporations, the control of terrorism and conflict — all involve problems of interdependence.

The ideal of cooperation is not new but merely more widely supported by research data in the 1980s. In several of his books Russell (1930, 1932a, 1932b, 1961) called for its encouragement as illustrated in the following passage (1932a, pp. 103–104): "Competition is not only bad as an educational fact, but also as an ideal to be held before the young. What the world now needs is not competition but organization and cooperation; all belief in the utility of competition has become an anachronism and even if competition were useful, it is not in itself admirable, since the emotions with which it is connected are the emotions of hostility and ruthlessness."

If the issue is so clear cut, the reader may well wonder why North American consciousness lags. The answer is that the interpretation of the competition-cooperation theme strikes at the very heart of social values. Lerner (1982) has adeptly pointed out that it is the accepted economic model of man that has led to the exaggeration of the importance of competition in North American psychology. Quoting his conclusions (pp. 275–276): "The economic model of man is a tragically persistent, distorted image of human motivation that portrays each of us as continually engaged in the attempts to maximize our 'profits.' The main evidence that supports the model has been generated by the appearance of these 'economic' norms in the belief system of subjects who participated in essentially role-playing — that is, norm-expressing — exercises under the guise of social psychological experiments."

The importance of competition has often been upheld by the value commitment of writers instead of by understanding as best we can, the total world system and its effects upon individuals. Two examples of this occur in the best-selling books by Michener (1976) who realizes and states his biases, and Lasch (1979), who tries to justify his biases and does not give evidence of realizing them. The competitor often looks at a situation through distorted lenses, perceiving cooperative intentions in others as a camouflage hiding a competitive agenda.

Lasch (1979, p. 23) provides us with an excellent example of such distortion in his own perceptions as he seeks to rationalize the weaknesses of what he calls the American narcissist: "Fiercely competitive in his demand for approval and acclaim, he distrusts competition because he associates it unconsciously with an unbridled urge to destroy. Hence he repudiates the competitive ideologies that flourished at an earlier stage of capitalist development and distrusts even their limited expression in sports and games. He extols cooperation and teamwork while harboring deeply antisocial impulses."

Lasch's insights may be insulated by his privilege. It is no wonder that persons of lesser life experience and increased molecularity in training are following suit. The issue is that when individuals see their social interactions as competitive — whether in terms of profit, wins and losses, or who comes out ahead on limited or artificial pragmatic dimensions — the depth of their emotional experience of life is lessened as well as their empathy and ability to help others. It is our contention, however, that to perceive people as competitive is often an inaccurate perception of the essential motivations within people. Such a perception overlooks the influence of situations on how people behave in terms of the rewards and punishments conferred on them for their competitive behavior, and further ignores the question of good and evil in human nature, of social constructiveness and destructiveness, of seeking solutions to social problems, and of seeking to avoid destructive conflicts (the latter two can only be achieved through cooperation). It is significant that the same misinterpretation often occurs in the sport world. That is, cooperative social motivations are incorrectly cast within a competitive framework.

Several incidents from the world of sport allow us to illustrate this point. In one incident that took place at the Crystal Palace in London and was widely reported in the British press, two British runners, Frank Clement and Brendan Foster, finished the 1500-meter race tied for first place in 3:38.5. The athletes deliberately paced each other in a joint effort, and chose to finish together. In spite of their efforts, first place was awarded to Clement on a photo-finish decision. The Canadian skater Toller Cranston once declared during a pre-contest interview that his one goal was to perform well for himself and for his coach. Within minutes after the interview, Cranston was introduced by the television announcer as the champion who would have to skate for his life to maintain his ranking in the competition. Shaw (1972) described in detail the pressures to surpass and to isolate himself from his fellow athletes, in spite of his need for their friendship, in order to qualify for the University of Texas football team. Each of the situations features a competitive social norm being imposed upon the performances of athletes. The norm is not only conveyed to and forced upon the athletes involved, it is also imposed upon the sport fans and enshrined in the record file. Athletic contests are structured so that athletes are encouraged to compete with each other for a position to which a reward is attached. The reward may be a championship, a ranking, a team position, and often money and prizes. If athletes do not intend to behave competitively, as in the situations above, their intentions are usually ignored, and their behavior is interpreted as competitive.

When competitive norms are forced upon situations, some unfortunate consequences often result. The University of Miami caused much strife when it refused to forfeit an illegal football victory it had been awarded over Tulane after scoring the final and winning touchdown after five downs instead of the four allowed. A national hunt jockey in Great Britain was taken to a hospital in a dehydrated condition after collapsing from abuse of the "p-pill", a drug taken by jockeys to reduce weight. Other reports alleged to be the tragic results of anabolic steroid regimens: a 14-year-old boy lost his hair; a shot-putter developed a fatal kidney disease; a discus thrower developed a hormonal imbalance. A last example is provided from the All-American Soap Box Derby. There, the winner was disqualified for cheating and forfeited his first-place trophy and a $7500 college scholarship. Officials discovered that an electromagnet gave his car an unfair starting advantage. The car was rigged by the boy's adult relatives. These incidents illustrate the extent to which athletes will go in order to win. In each case above the goal was more important to them than the means of attaining it.

A brief survey of any sports arena will document the social and psychological destructiveness of competitive motivation or felt rivalry. The problem has been identified in many sports (for example, basketball, ice hockey, and tennis) time and again. Take the following example from men's tennis. Fred Perry is quoted by Grimsley (1982): "They, the players, are continually taking out of the sport and never putting anything back ... They are strictly individualists today, self-centered, with no recognition of authority and no feeling for the roots and traditions to which countless people have contributed over the years. They seem to feel the game belongs to them. It belongs to itself. It belongs to history." The problem is that when the goal in sport is only to win and preserve status, with no broader appreciation of the significance of sport, serious consequences often result.

First if an athlete does not win or is not winning there is frustration, aggression, and regressive behavior. Second, if an athlete fears that he or she may not win then the avenue of cheating is opened up as a viable possibility in meeting goals. Third, losing becomes a diminishing and depressing experience for the competitively motivated athlete in that he or she has lost out on the desired outcome. Losing does not become the learning, inspiring, or challenging experience that it can be for others. Losing is seen as failure rather than as an event which can egg an athlete on to higher performance through reanalysis, examination of significant stages in the contest, improvement in strategy, and increased understanding of the game.

It has been found that a primary support group leads to more cooperative behavior in experimental games. Madsen and Lancey (1981) found this to be the greatest predictor of cooperative behavior. It therefore makes good sense to provide athletes, whatever their level of performance, with a tightly knit and understanding group of supporters. This group may be made up of coaches, parents, psychologists, managers, and/or friends. It is notable that many professional athletes, when they are able to afford it, travel with a primary support group. Martina Navratilova's entourage of Renée Richards, Nancy Leiberman, and various other apointees, (who changed over time) clearly served a significant function in providing psychological support for the champion.

Team cohesion is a second area of research which demonstrates the importance of the cooperation variable in sport. Again, Bradley's (1977) classic article on team spirit and performance in basketball should be required reading. Research (Zander, 1974; Browne and Mahoney, 1984; Carron, 1980, pp. 245-50) clearly backs up his observations that team cohesion is related to high morale, group members liking one another, and high performance in most sport situations.

Zander (1974, p. 68) echoes the concerns of both Mead and Miller for the over-emphasis societies place on certain modes of expression at the expense of equally worthwhile, and perhaps even more worthwhile, modes of expression. Quoting Zander, "our society does not run on individual achievement motivation alone. I fear that our beliefs that it does have led us to assume that people who can't cut the mustard on their own initiative can't cut it at all. We have designed our schools, businesses, and public agencies primarily for individual achievers, and lost the valuable contributions others could make in different circumstances." This observation has been well documented in research on sport, where having individual achievers on a team who cannot put team welfare above their own frequently leads to poor overall performance. Straub (1975), Ball and Carron (1976), Lefebvre and Cunningham (1977), Bird (1977), Nixon (1974), Wid-meyer and Martens (1978), and Carron (1984) have all examined various aspects of team cohesion and its relationship to performance. Good relations, support between athletes, and common concern for one another will not replace skill, effort, and competence in play. But even among skilled, competent teams few will succeed unless team spirit emerges. Rabbie (1982, p. 137) notes that winning efforts will tend to result in higher morale and that morale declines when performance begins to decline. We must here go beyond such studies and observe that most championship careers, of teams and of individuals, have at some time featured plateaus and setbacks which have been weathered and overcome. Team and individual spirit hold during periods of difficulty. Studies of team cohesion constantly support the importance of cooperation in sport.

A further set of studies refer to the athlete's basic reasons for staying and continuing in sport at both professional and amateur levels. Many elite athletes and most young athletes report that their major reason for continuing is the camaraderie they feel with their fellow athletes, the friends they make and have made, and the social support they feel from sport. The statements of well-known athletes support these observations (for example, see Kramer, 1968; Cooper, 1972; Sheehan, 1980).

If a cooperative atmosphere prevails in sport through such feelings among athletes, then learning takes place more readily. Not only are athletes and coaches more willing to give information and to pass on what they know to others, but those others are more receptive to learning due to the trust provided within the cooperative atmosphere. It is important to note again that we are not arguing against the staging of sport contests in which there are winners and losers. The argument is against instilling in sports people that the overriding goal is to win and to defeat others. Athletes of cooperative motivation can per-form well and brilliantly in spite of the competitive perceptions of others. These others are misinformed. The cooperative athlete can reap all the benefits of growth, happiness, and greater skill development in spite of the competitive at-mosphere. Why then be concerned about the latter? The problem is that there are serious and negative consequences when the competitive structure in sport is imposed upon it.

Athletes compete for artificially limited goals. Children are conditioned to accept as superior the status of "the winner," and those who win are rewarded with prizes and privileges. This one-sided attitude results in negative effects on four levels.

First, the character of the competitive athlete becomes increasingly undesirable as he or she develops an intense egocentric orientation with rigid psychological defenses and insensitivity. Obsession with his or her own winning status dominates the athlete's being.

Second, the performance level of all is lowered when a competitive atmosphere pervades the game. There is reason to argue that this includes the winner too. If an athlete's only wish is to beat his or her opponent, then he or she will be satisfied with a performance that does just that, even if it is not his or her best.

Third, when the "winning-is-everything" philosophy prevails, the door is open for cheating. Fixing games, using anabolic steroids, and using tricks to distract opponents or belittle officials become vehicles to achieve victory and its prizes. The world of sport reinforces these behaviors and very often cheating goes undetected or ignored. Coaches, athletes, owners, and fans may in a variety of ways contribute to these undesirable norms.

Fourth, competition breeds more competition at the expense of other forms of interaction. The most powerful encouragement for competitive behavior comes from the system itself, which forces those who are cooperative into adapting like attitudes or losing out altogether.

One theme of the studies reviewed in this chapter has been that competing and conflicting parties can be brought together through the introduction of strong and overriding values or goals to which both subscribe. By definition the parties then become cooperative, and the positive effects of such an outcome have been well documented. Some athletes are basically cooperative and contribute toward a cooperative social atmosphere even when competitive norms exist. They do this because they are able to view sport as having value over and above their own egocentric involvement. Although this cooperative social motivation can occur in athletes motivated by psychological aggression or neurotic conflict, it most frequently occurs in individual athletes motivated by competence.

Those athletes who are oriented toward competence tend to appreciate the skill, expertise, and esthetic qualities involved in the sport. They appreciate the efforts and good play of their opponents, therefore, as well as their own. Seeming competitors are invisibly united by their recognition of, and subscription to, excellence. When athletes have this kind of orientation, it is quite common for opponents to be found in good humored opposition, in acts of goodwill toward each other during play, and in postgame discussions reviewing the intricacies of the game they have played. There is not the backbiting, the ill feeling, and the interpersonal dislike that characterize a competitive game in which each athlete is out primarily to defeat the other. With competence and cooperation encouraged as sport motivations, sport can be socially and psychologically constructive instead of destructive. Athletes then tend to contribute to raising rather than lowering the performances of their opponents, cheating is never considered, and excellence in performance rather than winning becomes the major aim. It is a tragedy that society so often imposes competitive interpretations and structures upon excellence that is developed out of competence and cooperation.

7
Internal and External Reinforcements

INTRODUCTION

North American psychologists have focused more effort on the study of rein-forcements as determinants of human motivation and behavior than on any other topic. This work comes from the long tradition of learning theory research that was launched independently around the turn of the century by both Thorndike (1898) in the United States and Pavlov (1902) in the Soviet Union. The tradi-tion was continued by J. B. Watson (1913, 1919), E. C. Tolman (1932), K. Lewin (1935, 1936), E. R. Guthrie (1935), C. L. Hull (1943), and B. F. Skinner (1953a). The movement was popularized by the work and writings of two psychologists whose names became household words, J. B. Watson and B. F. Skinner. For the classic text on the history and evolution of learning theory in North America the reader is referred to Hilgard (1981). Although some ridiculous claims were made about the importance of stimuli in establishing and maintaining human behavior,* there is also no doubt about the power of reinforcement to influence human styles, choices and behaviors.

A reinforcement may be a reward or a punishment and it may exist in an internal or an external state. In this chapter we will describe both positive and negative incentives in sport. Since behaviorists (Skinner, 1953b) have demon-strated the importance of positive reinforcement over negative reinforcement, the discussion is weighted toward the positive. As many theorists and researchers (White, 1963; de Charms and Muir, 1978) have demonstrated the important yet neglected features of internal reinforcement over external reinforcement, this discussion emphasizes the internal. Thus the theme of this chapter is *positive internal reinforcement as essential in sport motivation.* This emphasis is a natural outgrowth of competence theory. It contrasts with most applied behavioral techniques in sport which highlight external reinforcement. See for example the books of Rushall and Siedentop (1972) and Martin and Hrycaiko

---

*Note the pioneer, J. B. Watson, giving advice to parents in 1928: "Treat [children] as though they were young adults. Let your behavior always be objective and kindly firm. Never hug and kiss them, never let them sit on your lap. If you must, kiss them once on the forehead when they say good-night. Shake hands with them in the morning."

Incentives

	Positive	Negative
Internal	Joy in hitting, running, catching, throwing	Frustration due to constant fumbling
External	Travel, attention, prizes	Coach abusive

Incentives

Figure 3. Examples of Incentives or Reinforcements in Sport.

(1984). The emphasis should not undermine the fact that both internal and external reinforcements may be either positive or negative (see Figure 3).

Taking a 12-year-old boy as our example — in the first case he continues in the activity of baseball because he revels in the action, the exercise, and the fun he has handling a bat and ball and participating in the plays (positive internal). In the second he continues to play because he likes the trips, uniforms, winning, and the attention and status resulting (positive external). In the next case he stops playing baseball because he never gets any hits and fumbles the ball when it comes to him even though he tries hard and puts in extra practice time (negative internal). Finally, he stops playing baseball because his coach hurls verbal abuse at him (negative external).

Internal reinforcements are those reflected by the enhanced or diminished feelings of the actor without observable material mediators. These feelings may be extrapolated to states of pleasure, self-confidence, and satisfaction. External reinforcements are those which lie outside of the actor such as money, prizes and perks.

Psychologists have carried out an immense amount of work on internal and external motivations and reinforcements, and related concepts. The work concentrates on how individuals perceive their own control and influence over events in their lives and how this in turn affects the way they behave in and perceive various situations. The social significance of these orientations has received attention in the fields of education, the care of the elderly, and sport. The following sections provide a summary of some major areas of psychological study.

LOCUS OF CONTROL

Rotter (1966) developed a theory of and a scale to measure locus of control or how persons perceive their own degree of control over potential reinforcements. Do they perceive themselves as reinforced by outside influences or luck or do they determine their own reinforcement by virtue of their personal characteristics?

Rotter assumes that locus of control is unidimensional construct. He believes all people are much influenced by the manner in which they perceive potential reinforcements or events. The dimension ranges from those who attribute events to chance or the actions of others to those who attribute them to their own actions. Put another way, some people see themselves as acted upon while others see themselves as acting in order to influence outcome. Much of the research to date has stemmed from the original scales of Phares (1957) and Rotter's (1966) modification. It has been suggested that persons high on internal control are more competent (Naditch and Demaio, 1975) when incentives are high and adjusted (Wolk and Kurtz, 1975). Although Rotter and others caution against the valuation of internal locus of control as "better" than external locus of control, in fact, much of the research done supports this assertion. In his book, Deci (1975) argues in accordance with the basic theory that if reinforcement is perceived as controlled from without, then intrinsic motivation is reduced.

The locus of control variable has been related to styles of: cheating, aging, parent-child interaction, and political conviction, to name but a few of the correlates. When the concept of competence is applied to the interpretation of internality, it may be theorized that anxiety, depression, and helplessness are related to external loci of control, as documented by Seligman (1975). The person who does not experience competence feedback is, indeed, helpless.

ENDOGENOUS AND EXOGENOUS ATTRIBUTION

Kruglanski (1975) proposed a theory of endogenous and exogenous attribution, the main distinction being that endogenous attribution represents behavior that is seen by the actor as an end in itself while exogenous attribution is behavior seen by the actor to be a means to an end. Thus a tennis player performing for the love of the game would continue to play if prize money, travel, and attention were taken from him or her, while the exogenous attributor would cease to play the game. Kruglanski has noted that for activities in which money is central to an activity, as in the playing of stock market games, payment increased intrinsic motivation. However, when an activity was performed merely to gain money, payment decreased intrinsic motivation. Extrapolating to sport, the attributions an athlete makes may have considerable effect on his or her motivations. Such attributions may vary with sport, social class, or level of professionalism — to name but a few possible correlates.

PERSONAL CAUSATION

De Charms and Muir, (1978), in his program of research on personal causation, notes that there is damage to children in schools and training programs when intrinsic motivation is not encouraged. Token economies, rewards, and "bribes" lead to the lessening of actions previously carried out spontaneously for adventure and pleasure. Langer (1975, 1983; Langer and Rodin, 1976) has demonstrated the same effect in the institutionalized aged. When given choices over their daily decisions measurable improvements in well-being emerge even to the point of longer life in one study (Rodin and Langer, 1977). In spite of the urgency of applying the results of internal and external reinforcement studies (for an example, see de Charms and Muir, 1978), the application of the results has lagged behind the proliferation of studies. The studies continue to be funded and to test out psychological minitheories with little action or generalizability on the applied front. Jackson and Paunonen (1980) for example, have pointed out the multidimensionality of the control variable (personal causation) and have called for more sophisticated conceptualizations.

One finds, in fact, that sport psychology is farther ahead than general psychology in examing the applications and implications of intrinsic motivation and personal causation. Thus, while academic psychologists call for a shift from behavioral and cognitive psychology and criticize the positivistic philosophy and sterility of method to which psychology has become bound (de Charms and Muir, 1978; Sampson, 1981), writers in sport psychology have been turning to the inner athlete and to the examination of intrinsic motivation in great numbers.

THE INNER ATHLETE

Some of the many widely read books on the experience of the inner athlete are: *The Inner Game of Tennis* (Gallwey, 1974), *The Inner Athlete* (Nideffer, 1976a), *The Joy of Sport* (Novak, 1976), *Inner Skiing* (Gallwey and Kriegel, 1979), *This Running Life* (Sheehan, 1980), and *Powers of Mind* (Smith, 1975). Ryan, Vallerand and Deci (1984) have summarized recent research on intrinsic motivation in sport. The theme in sport is one of increasingly turning to self-exploration and adventure through sport as well as to new horizons of excellence.

In sport, we find an unparalleled opportunity for the experience and expression of competence (as therapists are quickly discovering). We also find outstanding examples of persons treated as pawns through a very high reward system. This can affect both behavior and motivation in sport. Halberstam (1981), who followed the Portland Trail Blazers for a year, noted that both professional basketball players and management observed that the arrival of Madison Avenue and high salaries have not made the players happier. In fact, their self-perception and identity is often wound up more with salary than performance: "The big salaries, older players believed, had gradually altered the athlete's self-perception and had made what they did less joyous and less of a sport." This was accompanied by a loss of community feeling, cooperation, and loyalty to the team and its members. Due to over-scheduling and low motivation, players are noted to concentrate on playoff games while playing lethargically in most of the regular season.

The salaries of concern in the NBA range from a reported $60,000 to $2.5 million (paid to Earvin Johnson of the Los Angeles Lakers) in January, 1985. The Detroit *Free Press* cited 11 players as being paid more than $1 million a year. It is no wonder that we find *Sports Illustrated* citing Mayor Ed Koch's defense of his salary boost from $80,000 to $120,000 in 1983: "Is the mayor of New York being overcompensated? Well, ... how do you like the fact that Dave Winfield probably makes $2 million a year? I'm not suggesting I should be comparable to Dave Winfield, but ..." (Aug. 12, p. 14). The likelihood is that Koch will keep his job and remain highly motivated because of the great amount of control, relative autonomy, and personal influence accompanying his position. So will Dave Winfield, depending upon the degree to which he is able to gain inner satisfaction and competence, as well as money, in executing the sport at which he excels.

Most athletes need a mixture of internal and external reinforcers for a balance in their motivations. In being guided too much by the external motivators, the athlete may give up some of the existential feelings needed to continue to be motivated. By being entirely guided by internal reinforcement, the athlete may become disgusted by the outside world of payoffs that offer him or her little satisfaction. Such an athlete may choose to withdraw from a sport in order to pursue other forms of challenge. Eric Heiden provides a good example. After winning five gold medals at the 1980 winter Olympics, Heiden rejected the promise of fame and financial reward, proceeded to Sweden to study and took up bicycle racing. Heiden is clearly the model of an existential athlete who the young would do well to emulate. It is a pity that the world of sport could not integrate him better in terms of reward. And yet, as in many intrinsically motivated persons, their actions and life styles, and not their status, power, and domination are messages to those who follow them.

BEHAVIORISM, COGNITION, AND COMPETENCE

An understanding of various psychological theories is helpful both in interpreting the sports world and in applying psychology to sport in order to maximize performance. Some take a behavioral approach with athletes and place total emphasis upon outside reinforcements in determining motivation. Such naive manipulations can only have short-term effects unless combined with other types of facilitation. A cognitive approach, for example, analyzes the individual's perception of his or her sport performance and allows for differences in perception among athletes in terms of exchange theory and the meaning of reward. An emphasis upon competence, or an affective approach, deals with the developmental and emotional needs of the athlete in terms of confidence, pleasure, growth, and maturity. In applying the latter theory the individual is never a pawn to the pressures of increased performance levels, but is always an integral part of the quest for further growth and challenge which may be represented in performance improvements.

The athlete generally seeks to sustain the child's enthusiasm and motivation in continuing sport but with excellence becomes increasingly courted by external reward. Since it has been suggested that the greater the external reward the less the internal satisfaction from the activity, the professional athlete is placed in a quandary. How does he or she sustain the original motivation? What are the options for the advanced athlete who faces being "bought off" by external reward? There are several. One is to seek ever-increasing rewards in the form of money and benefits so that one is assured of a continuing market value. This may be done not on the basis of sustained or improved performance but on the basis of market exposure and image promotion. Many veteran athletes continue to endorse products on the basis of past reputation. Another option for the athlete is to develop the internal side of his or her motivation so that the sport performance becomes refined and a creative expression of self. Many psychologists working with athletes have as their major goals the heightening of human awareness and self-knowledge in order that such internal motivation can continue to find expression. Another option is to escape from the pressures and boredom of sport through fast living and to increase motivation artificially by, for example, playing under the influence of drugs (Mandell, 1974). As demonstrated by many sport careers cited elsewhere in this book, this pattern becomes an exercise in self-destruction. A fourth option by which the athlete attempts to adjust from too much external pressure and too little internal desire is to turn to religion as a motivator. This would presumably put the individual in touch with his or her spiritual and subjective desires in a world fraught with pressures to produce and to perform for external reasons. It is significant that several sport scientists have sought to develop this dimension of athletics (Snyder and Spreitzer, 1983, p. 262ff.). A final option for the athlete is to maintain a level of skill as a profession or business and to collect one's checks while at the same time inspiring and exciting spectators. The athlete then performs out of previous competence and the resultant self-confidence which has been developed, maintained, and then sold. This is not meant to be as cynical an adjustment as it may seem, and in fact it probably characterizes the performances of many outstanding artists as well as athletes. The individual is professional, confident, skilful, and objective about his or her own abilities. He or she performs consistently and predictably. He or she may have outstanding rapport with audiences and on occasion be spurred on to inspirational performances by that rapport. Little further psychological growth will take place directly from sport, although it certainly may take place as a by-product or from other life experiences. The athlete will no longer question or challenge the values or the arena in which he or she performs. Such motivation occurs in the mature performer when sport becomes either entertainment or pure business.

ACHIEVEMENT MOTIVATION REVISITED

Achievement motivation is a strong theme in North American psychological writing, with the names McClelland, Atkinson, and Veroff most prominent.

More recently Horner (1972), with the concept of fear of success in women, added both controversy and content to the literature. A major characteristic of this writing is an extreme dependence upon the North American value system or, more specifically, the philosophy that it is of value to achieve highly, to gain reward from society, to forge ahead, and to improve position within society. From McClelland to Horner, the research is founded on the premise that all should seek mastery and improved status whether they be men, executives, women, or blacks. By measuring the imagery projected by participants in a program of experimentation lasting over years, McClelland (1961) made many significant observations which give us insight into sports achievement as well as into other endeavors. Some of these observations follow: (1) High achievers set realistic and obtainable goals. (2) High achievers are competitive and highly motivated. (3) High achievers seek out situations in which to demonstrate excellence. (4) Some women are motivated by a fear of failure rather than a desire to succeed. (5) Parental style of reinforcement has much to do with the development of high need achievement. (6) Need achievement and need affiliation are often incompatible with one another. (7) Achievement imagery in art and cultural products within a culture can predict the economic and technological development of that culture years later.

Note that all of these conclusions relate in some way to individual advancement in a material culture where status is largely economically determined. Even observation 7 refers to the advancement of some and not all members of the culture. McClelland and associates spent much time and effort in studying and suggesting ways to increase achievement motivation in un-Americanized societies. And in his excellent review of McClelland's work, Maddi (1976, pp. 501–521) also shows this bias:

> If enough parents in a society bring up their children this way, then there will eventually be many citizens choosing a way of life involving the challenge of competition with a standard of excellence. Following Weber, McClelland contends that the challenge is most vivid and salient in entrepreneurial activity, which activity is basic to economic development. (p. 509)

McClelland, (1973, 1985) however, has changed his orientation in recent years more toward the identification of competence, skills, and values in various situations in order to chart success. Others too, have increasingly questioned the crosscultural application and cross-age comparative validity of these results (Maehr, 1974; Maehr and Nichols, 1980, Spence, 1985). Maehr and Kleiber (1981) have suggested a whole new trend in the study of achievement motivation which they believe will lead to its reformation. This will occur as the population in the United States ages. Life after forty, they suggest, is more directed to preserving what one has and caring for the welfare of others than toward acquisition and establishing a way of life. The authors suggest that in aging the individual becomes intrinsically motivated and therefore the concepts of competence and self-actualization become more relevant than McClelland's achievement motivation, which relates to competitive mastery.

Some suggest that life in the quick paced North American society, whether it be in business, politics, or sport, does little to enhance longevity or quality of life. Further high achievement motivation may well be related to Machiavellianism, power striving, and other less desirable traits. The more internally motivated, competence-oriented individual may not only live longer but may live with more dignity and constructiveness in terms of others' welfare. This would be a worthwhile topic for further investigation, since some studies of the elderly suggest that egocentric and self-contained individuals do live longer.

In conclusion, we suggest that unpleasant side effects are not likely to emerge if an individual's achievement arises from competence motivation. Competence-oriented persons performing at an outstanding level are motivated by enjoyment and pleasure in their skill or art and therefore can appreciate fully interdependence, the need to help others, and the benefits of the cooperative spirit. Several such athletes have been cited so far including Lidell, Cooper, Bannister, Sheehan, and Bradley. If their skill is highly valued by society, such athletes may well become wealthy and materially advantaged due to monetary reward. But even if their activity is not highly valued and reinforced economically, and there are many such examples, the athlete's quality of life still may be higher than that of the materially advantaged person. This is because the reward and reinforcement for their skill is internal.

PRACTICAL IMPLICATIONS FOR SPORT

If an athlete tries to perform well in a sport because of its satisfaction to him or her as a person, because of the delight and joy in the game, and because of an appreciation of the esthetic and structural perfection possible from the game, then the athlete is experiencing internal reinforcement. If, on the other hand, the athlete performs because he or she wants to be recognized by others, wants to please his or her parents, or wants to please a coach, then the reinforcements are external. North American parents and some coaches need a massive overhaul of perspective in terms of the pressures they place on young athletes to compete and win in order to gain external reward. The problem is that external reinforcements can be powerful reinforcers even though they are unlikely to be permanent or constructive in terms of the athlete's development. Intrinsic and extrinsic motivations converge in the person of the coach, be he or she parent, partner, or official coach. Some coaches are ineffective because they emphasize external sources of reward and serve only in capitalizing on the individual's existing alienation from him or herself. Such coaches are fanning the flames of neuroses in their athletes, of whom only a small number will succeed.

It is only if the athlete is successful in his or her own terms that he or she will be happy and fulfilled. The pursuit of competence is a superordinate goal that can be shared by both coaches and athletes. The coach who has a deep appreciation of the sport for immediate and personal feedback rather than for such ulterior motives as status and money will pass on an understanding of internal reward. The extrinsic factors will be pleasant but quite secondary. This kind of coach may well gain as much satisfaction from teaching the developmentally disabled as Olympic champions. Of course, society will place most demands upon him or her for the latter, but his or her efforts and dedication will be in sport and not necessarily where society places most reward. The best coaches and teachers are frequently found elsewhere than in the major leagues.

8
The Measurement of Sport Motivation

PSYCHOMETRIC POSITION

In this chapter we examine attempts to measure some of the concepts proposed so far in this book. The author, having spent much time in both clinical work and on the study of psychometric problems, approached the task of measuring sport motivation with some definite opinions on the limitations and potential of such psychological measurement. First, consider and accept that personality and motivational assessment will be accompanied by error in measurement. The determinants of personality and motivational styles are complex. They are further complicated because situations as well as personal styles interact to produce action and behavior and because one is attempting to measure entities which are continually in a state of flux. The problem is that some fairly sophisticated psychometric theories and techniques, having emerged from the field of ability and intelligence testing, were extrapolated to personality measurement. But a response to a general knowledge question, for example, which has a definite answer provides more precise data than a response to a true-false type personality description.

The field of intelligence testing has a long tradition behind it. Various abilities, even if defined in terms of specific cultural values, can be measured and measured fairly accurately. This is because the tests are behavioral, questions can be graded in terms of difficulty, and therefore interval measurement can be made along a dimension represented by degrees of a specific ability (Fiske, 1971, p. 137 ff.). When measuring personality or motivation, however, items usually do not represent different degrees of a dimension but rather a frequency of acts or endorsements. This is categorical and not metric measurement. However, the standard concepts from intelligence testing can still be applied in personality and motivational testing. Two such concepts are reliability and validity.

Reliability refers to the internal consistency of scales. Thus, if one is using a questionnaire it refers to the correlation between any two halves of the test or to the correlation between the test given at time one and again at time two. There has been much discussion over the meaning and value of reliability. If one wished a perfectly reliable test one would ask the same question over and over again (or at least very close approximations thereof) while hoping that the participant's mood did not fluctuate in the meantime. This would be the same as measuring a person's height in centimeters where split-half reliability would be perfect but the stability coefficient (over time) would show slight variations dependent upon the time of the second measure. (People are shorter when their height is measured at night than in the morning when they have just arisen). One can see that an item in personality measurement provides quite a different unit of measurement than does a centimeter. In personality measurement, there is no sense in asking the same questions again and again. Thus one asks different but related questions. One wants some reliability in a measure but not perfect reliability. If the items in a test were unrelated, they would form no test and tap no trait. The actual amount of desired reliability in a measure is debated among researchers. In addition, it is important to note that reliability indexes are a partial function of the number of items in a test. Thus short scales will automatically have less reliability than long scales.

The *validity* of scales, on the other hand, is an important concept in testing because it indicates whether the test measures what it purports to measure. Thus an intelligence test must correlate with some kind of ability; a scale on aggression must correlate with aggressive behavior, acts, or fantasies; and a cooperation scale should in some way predict or indicate a participant's true actions toward and feelings about others. Scales and measures should predict to some extent exactly how an individual is likely to behave in a given situation. If a scale has validity it will automatically have some reliability. For details on types of reliability (namely, split-half, stability, and parallel forms) and types of validity (namely, concurrent, construct, convergent, discriminant, face, and predictive) the reader is referred to one of the standard texts on psychological testing (such as Cronbach, 1984; Anastasi, 1982).

A critical and significant article was published by Burisch (1984) on the status of psychological measurement. The conclusion was that many of the sophisticated analyses used should be re-examined since many may have the status of the emperor in the "Emperor's New Clothes." That is, they have little meaning and use, although it is difficult for those invested in the field to admit it. Burisch points out that very simple rating scales are, on the average, more valid than are most lengthy and sometimes complex questionnaires (p. 225). The overall conclusion: simplicity in measures is best.

THE SPORT PROTOCOL

The Sport Protocol is a questionnaire instrument developed by the author for the purposes of first, exploring the theory in sport psychology described thus far, and second, assisting those who wish to think about and understand their own sport styles and motivations. The use of questionnaires has always been of value in psychology because a great amount of information can be gathered efficiently in a short period of time. Since the Sport Protocol measures were to be used for the purposes of theory testing and providing information for discussion to sport participants, it was decided to use a questionnaire method and to keep the scales very short and simple. The Sport Protocol takes half an hour or less to administer. It consists of the scales and questions listed in Figure 4. In the subsequent sections of this chapter we describe its use and development for research purposes. Its clinical and counselling use is described in Chapter 18.

---

1. Sport motivation scales. Total score plus five — 5 item scales. (See Butt, 1979d.)
   1. aggression
   2. conflict
   3. competence
   4. competition
   5. cooperation

2. Background information (life data, attitudes, perceptions of coach and parents, etc.).

3. Affect scales. Total score plus two — 5 item scales. (See Bradburn, 1969; Bradburn & Caplovitz, 1965)
   1. positive affect (happiness)
   2. negative affect (unhappiness)

4. Activity (Initiative). Total score plus three — 5 item scales. (See Gough, 1964; Cochrane et. al., 1965)
   1. lack of fears
   2. force
   3. insensitivity

5. Socialization. Total score plus five — 5 item scales. (See Gough, 1964; Butt, 1973)
   1. family stability
   2. control
   3. security
   4. confidence
   5. social concern

6. Murray's constructs. Six — 6 item scales.
   1. achievement
   2. succorance
   3. autonomy
   4. affiliation
   5. endurance
   6. leadership

Figure 4. Meausres Contained in the Sport Protocol.

THE SPORT MOTIVATION SCALES

The Sport Motivation Scales were developed to measure the five motivations of aggression, conflict, competence, competition, and cooperation. Their development was first described by the author (Butt, 1979d) in a paper titled "Short Scales for the Measurement of Sport Motivation." The initial item pool was written on the basis of rational criteria; that is, items were based upon the theoretical descriptions of the motivations included in the first edition of *Psychology of Sport* (Butt, 1976, pp. 1–60). Rational item selection refers to the process by which a construct such as aggression is defined, described, and finally represented by a pool of relevant items. Fifty items were originally written for the sport motivation scales, 10 items per scale, with the intention of selecting the best 25 items for the final scales, 5 items per scale. This would be in line with the successful 5-item *Affect Scales* of Bradburn and Caplovitz (1965) upon which the present scales were modelled. Once the items were written they were administered to groups of athletes and university students. Test and item statistics, test-test correlations, test-criterion correlations, and factor analyses were carried out in order to ensure the inclusion of the best items in the scales. Split-half reliabilities ranged from .43 to .75 while stability coefficients after a two-week time lapse ranged from .50 to .80. Validation indexes ranged from correlations of .18 to .67 with other test measures, yielding construct validation measures. Other validation indexes fell in the .20's when the scales were correlated with coach ratings of performance level and measures of actual performance level.

The correlations between the three psychological motivations and the two social motivations were as predicted for both males and females. The results are given in the first studies (Butt, 1979d) reported in Table 1 (p. 89). As predicted by the theory, aggression and conflict correlate higher with competition than with cooperation. The correlations of competence with cooperation are greater than with competition. This is true of both male and female groups.

OTHER SCALES IN THE SPORT PROTOCOL

There are six additional sections to the Sport Protocol besides the Sport Motivation Scales just described. Section 2 of the Sport Protocol is on Background Information. This includes a number of items on family background, quality of relationship with parents during sport development, ambition in sport, and attitudes toward the coach. These questions yield important clinical information about the athlete which may be used in a follow-up interview as well as criteria with which to correlate other scores and variables.

Section 3 is composed of Bradburn and Caplovitz's (1965; Bradburn, 1969) Affect Scales. Here two indexes of five items each measure the number of happy and unhappy feelings the participant has experienced during the last month. These successful indexes of mood have been widely used in the psychological literature.

Section 4 is made up of three scales of five items each, all of which purport to measure the instrumentality-expressiveness dimension of personal style. This dimension, formerly known as the masculinity-femininity trait, has come increasingly to the forefront with the advent and the study of gender and sex roles. The items tap three constructs: lack of fear, force, and insensitivity. They are all scored in the instrumentality direction. The three facets of the present scale were based on a factor analysis of Gough's (1952) Femininity Scale, carried out by Cochrane and Strodtbeck (1965). In our studies to date these scales have not shown the degree of reliability one would expect, so we consider these still in the experimental or trial phase. Users may wish to use other measures of instrumentality-expressiveness.

Section 5 of the Sport Protocol is comprised of the Socialization Scales, which are five-item indexes that describe the degree to which the individual has internalized social mores and values and hence how well he or she is integrated with the general society. These indexes were based upon a factor analysis of the Socialization Scale of Gough and Pederson (1952), which later became part of the California Psychological Inventory (1964). The factor analysis was carried out by Butt (1973b). Five forms of emotional integration emerged from the analyses: family stability, behavioral control, security, self-confidence, and social concern.

Section 6 is comprised of 6-item measures of selected needs from Murray's need typology: achievement, succorance, autonomy, affiliation, endurance, and leadership. The variables were chosen as of interest in sport because of their frequent examinations in both the psychological and sport literature.

Finally, the participant responding to the Sport Protocol is asked to rate his or her level of accuracy in responding to the questions. Their answer of "very accurate," "accurate," or "not accurate" allows an initial reading of the participant's confidence in his or her self-description.

SUPPLEMENTARY TESTS

The Sport Protocol is a preliminary research and screening instrument. It can also be used as a basis for further discussion with the participant during which consensual validation can take place; that is, the individual can explain and follow up on any responses he or she has made. There are occasions on which more information is wanted by the individual or group involved, at which time it is advisable to use additional scales and/or tests. For descriptions of these other instruments, the reader is referred to Chapter 19.

PERFORMANCE INDEXES

A significant advantage for the psychologist working in sport is the plentiful supply of relatively clear-cut performance measures of actual behavior in sport. There are knowledgeable ratings available from coaches or teammates who interact with the athlete daily. The ingenious researcher can and will find a variety of measures far beyond what one usually finds for participants in studies who are not in sport. In our studies to date we have used the following performance indexes: rankings from sports records, coaches' ratings of morale and performance contributions, peer ratings of performance and morale contribution, times for performance (in timed sports — running, swimming), winning and losing records, dropping out of sport, making a team versus not making it, goals scored, fouls, and position played. Others have used penalties, penalty times, styles of play, passing patterns, and off-field behavior.

A REVIEW OF STUDIES

Approximately 1000 participants have responded to the Sport Protocol in our various studies and probably 1000 have participated in the studies of other researchers who have used the instrument. It has been translated into five languages other than English. These are Japanese, Dutch, Spanish, German, and French.* The instrument has therefore been used with participants from many nations with varying results. Taken as a whole and allowing for the inevitable measurement error and the notorious instability of the correlation coefficient, the work has been both productive and revealing. The following discussion reviews the results of the studies in which the Sport Motivation Scales have been used. The results are summarized in Table 1.

In the initial group on which the scales were developed (Butt, 1979d), comprising both university students and a competitive swimming club, the theory was supported. Similarly in a cross-Canada study of 132 male and female figure skaters (Butt, 1979c), the theory held as an accurate description of sport motivation. These figure skaters ranged in age from 9 to 21 and in ability from provincial participants to national champions. Not only were the correlations of competition .36 and .39 with aggression and conflict, respectively, and the correlation of cooperation .31 with competence, but the pattern of correlation with other constructs repeated those found in the Butt (1979d) study.

In examining 115 male ice hockey players in British Columbia at the Junior, Midget, and hockey school level, Stevens (1981) replicated the results.

---

*Only the Sport Motivation Scales have been translated into French and not the whole of the Sport Protocol.

Table 1. Testing the Sport Motivation Model Via the Correlations of the Psychological Motivations (Aggression, Conflict, and Competence) with the Social Motivations (Competition and Cooperation) Across 10 Studies. Decimals are Omitted.

AUTHOR(S)	ATHLETE GROUP	N AND SEX	SOCIAL MOTIVATIONS	PSYCHOLOGICAL MOTIVATIONS		
				AGGRESSION	CONFLICT	COMPETENCE
Butt (1979)	Mixed-swimming club & university	(1) 67 males	Competition	25*	44***	06
			Cooperation	03	04	35***
		(2) 121 females	Competition	43***	42***	12
			Cooperation	26***	13	33***
Butt (1980)	Figure skaters	(3) 132 males & females	Competition	36***	39***	04
			Cooperation	01	-08	31***
Stevens (1980)	Ice hockey	(4) 115 males	Competition	35**	41**	-07
			Cooperation	03	-02	22**
Wrisberg et al. (1984)	Gymnasts	(5) 181 females	Competition	29***	40***	13
			Cooperation	-20***	-04	09
	Professional baseball players	(6) 110 males	Competition	32**	33**	19*
			Cooperation	15	05	31**
Butt & Redgrove (1978)	Mixed-London school children	(7) 50 males	Competition	14	28*	-03
			Cooperation	16	-45***	12
		(8) 42 females	Competition	40**	27*	26*
			Cooperation	-04	-01	23
Butt (1979)	Mixed-Japanese university athletes	(9) 80 males	Competition	45***	28**	44***
			Cooperation	33***	-01	29**
Butt (1985)	World class field hockey	(10) 209 females	Competition	44***	47***	13*
			Cooperation	10	12*	09

$*p < .05$, $**p < .01$, $***p < .001$

Competition correlated .35 and .41, respectively, with aggression and conflict, while cooperation correlated .22 with competence. When the groups were divided into the four subgroups, the correlations jumped around for some of the groups, particularly for the competitive Junior team. Stevens found differences between the three levels of hockey players on the motivation scales, with the younger players being less aggressive and less competitive. Wrisberg, Donovan, Britton, and Ewing (1984) found similar results with 181 age group gymnasts and 110 professional baseball players. For other groups with much smaller numbers, the results were unstable. In all but one of the ten studies, the expected correlational pattern held for aggression and conflict. They were correlated highly and significantly with competition and to a lesser extent with cooperation. The only exception is found for the correlation of aggression to competition and cooperation in British males. Thus there is one exception out of 19 correlational comparisons. Competence is correlated to cooperation and to a lesser extent to competition in five out of ten studies.

As one moves up on the sport ladder and participants become more trained in the competitive ethic, the relationships between the motivational variables that are predicted theoretically become less stable. In some cases the instability may reflect measurement error (due to translation or unreliability, for example) or to genuine variations in the correlational patterns with different socialization practices and experiences in competitive sport. Thus two lines of research are suggested. The first is improvement of the measures. The second is following up on the complexities of motivation within the groups studied. The writer has already begun to extend the motivational scales. Others have worked on the theoretical complexities of the motivational model. For example, Wrisberg et al. (1984) have made several interesting suggestions for alterations in the above theory, while Fabian and Ross, (1984) have worked exclusively on the complexities within the competition variable in developing a more detailed inventory for the assessment of competition.

It has been noted that studies with sufficiently large numbers of participants which do not support the theoretical model tend to be those carried out on groups with a highly developed competitive ethic. With June Redgrove, formerly of Middlesex Polytechnic, the writer carried out a study with 50 male children and 42 female children from a North London school. The male data replicated the correlational pattern only for conflict, while the females replicated only for aggression and conflict. Eighty male university students from Tskuba University in Japan showed the theoretical predictions for aggression and conflict but not for competence. Competence was more highly associated with competition (.44) than with cooperation (.29). There were similar patterns for world class women field hockey players (n = 209), who replicated for aggression and conflict but not for competence (Butt, 1985). In some individual field hockey teams aggression correlates highly with cooperation. This was seen in one of the teams in which coaching strategy had emphasized aggressive play as a positive asset and therefore had strongly encouraged aggression.

In an eight-month study following the training schedule for a world championship of the Canadian national women's field hockey team, the Sport Protocol documented affective changes over four testing times. The team became less happy with the duration of their training but the 15 players who made the team recovered their original level of happiness as the world championships approached (Butt, 1980b). The total of 29 athletes declined in feelings of competence, security, and morale during their strenuous training. Negative affect increased, while ratings of the morale contributions of teammates decreased.

The studies have confirmed that competition is generally associated with unhappiness and discontent, while competence and cooperation are associated with contentment, stability, and satisfaction with one's life. Some studies (Butt, 1979d; Butt, 1979c, 1980a) have confirmed the association of competence with higher performance indexes, but this tends to be true of specific coaching and team situations. The two top teams in the international field hockey study (Butt, 1985) had very low motivational profiles, indicating controlled motivation and energy used in the service of executing skill in sport.

In other studies Fabian and Ross (1984) found construct validity in using the competition scale in that it correlated with the new competition scale they developed. Meuris and Bougard (1982) found no differences between team position played and scores on the motivation scales in Belgian soccer teams. In contrast, Butt (1980a) found differences between forwards and defense in the international field hockey study.

The foregoing review of studies has given some idea of the use of measures of motivation in psychology of sport research. Overall the Sport Protocol has proven to be a useful instrument in describing and documenting affective processes, motivations, and socialization in sport. It can be used to clarify the conditions under which the motivational theory proposed applies or does not apply. Thus far it appears to be valid when used with participants who are developing in sport and aspiring to national and international status. The motivational profiles of athletes tend to be heightened as they climb the sport ladder but level off and probably decline with maturity and success. We have recently been looking at the relationship between the psychological motivations and basic energy level in the model and the social motivations and measures of internal and external reward preferences. If the Sport Protocol is to be used with more precision, there may be a need to increase the length of the Sport Motivation Scales in order to ensure adequate distributions of scores when working with small groups of participants. That is, when there is poor measurement it is usually because the items have failed to spread out the participants. Thus there is little variance and little chance of finding the real correlations of the scales with other variables. That is why the successful studies have tended to include diverse talents and diverse ages as well as sufficient numbers of participants to gain a reasonable spread or variance in scores.

In this chapter a quick questionnaire method has been described for studying the motivations of athletes. It has provided some confirmation of the theory of sport motivation thus far proposed. The instrument may be used by others, not just to validate the theory but to explore it, revise it, or to take from it what seems useful in creating theoretical extensions, further studies, or in counseling athletes. The latter use is the topic of Chapter 18; the former uses have been reviewed in this chapter. However, such cross-sectional work is merely preparatory to the longitudinal studies which need to study athletes and sport participants over the course of their development.

PART III

THE NATURE OF AND THE ADAPTATION OF THE ATHLETE

9
Personality of the Athlete

INTRODUCTION

Personality refers to the unique expression and character of the individual. It must be studied within the social context in which it develops. Personality is not an isolated phenomenon separate from the environment, although it is often perceived in that way. Rather, personality is expressed through the complex and interdependent relationships formed between the individual and his or her environment. Given genetic and constitutional characteristics, perhaps the most important molding of human personality occurs in the interaction between parents and children. Close to this in importance is the transference of that interaction to leaders and idols. It is through identification with significant figures that young people first relate to the culture around them.

Personality evolves from a number of influences that may be divided into three broad categories: physical, personal, and sociocultural. Physical influences are the inherited biological characteristics that cause people to differ from each other. Personal influences are the unique events experienced by the individual that cause lasting effects. Sociocultural influences are internalizations from the environment that surrounds the individual. These influences are absorbed from parents, educators, social institutions, and media, and are the product of the society in which the person grows. If a society is highly competitive and sanctions the expression of aggression, comparable behaviors will be supported by parents and educators and reflected in the child's development. Thus, when a child performs well in a socially sanctioned activity, such as sport, he or she will usually receive reinforcement and support from parents and others. The careers of most athletes reveal that they were strongly reinforced early in life and encouraged to devote their energies to sport.

Human personality converges with social role, and, in order to fill the role of athlete, the individual must have or develop certain qualifications. Thus, the following questions are raised. What type of person is attracted to competitive sport? What effect does long-term involvement in sport have on the individual? What kind of personality emerges, finally, as champion? This chapter seeks to answer these questions.

IS THERE AN ATHLETIC TYPE?

We have at time of writing, three excellent review papers of the literature on sport and personality. These are by Folkins and Sime (1981); Eysenck, Nias, and Cox (1982); and Browne and Mahoney (1984). These reviews provide important illustrations of some of the difficulties and differences in the approaches used to try to answer the question: is there an athletic type?

Folkins and Sime use an atheoretical approach and look solely at studies in which they list positive changes in mental health versus no change in mental health following regimens of physical activity. As in the vast literature on the efficacy of psychotherapy in inducing personality change, they criticize the descriptive nature of the studies and come to the conclusion that physical activity results in positive changes in self-concept and thus improves mood and affect when used with depressive and mentally retarded participants. They detect no changes in personality traits as a result of physical fitness training. Thus they largely replicate the conclusion of Carl Rogers (1961) on changes in personality in psychotherapy. Psychotherapy does not change pathologies or symptoms so much as it changes self-concept and causes philosophical acceptance of difficulties in living.

In contrast, Eysenck et al. start with a theoretical position which includes the assertion of a biological basis to personality styles. They emerge with a firm conclusion that athletes will tend more frequently than others toward extraversion due to the wealth of information proposed in the theory on the extraverted style. Thus Eysenck et al. line up with those writers who have earlier proposed a set of characteristics more common to athletes than to nonathletes: Kane (1972), Ogilvie (1974), Butt (1976), Morgan (1979).

Why then do other writers (Kroll, 1970; Rushall, 1972; Martens, 1975; and Carron, 1980) conclude that there is no evidence for an athletic type? As Butt (1976), Morgan (1978), and Eysenck et al. (1982) have pointed out, there are trends in many studies, even with the limited instruments available, that many athletes group in measurable quadrants on major personality dimensions. In order to arrive at this conclusion one must begin with a knowledge of personality variation, a theory, and the realization that simplistic statistical methods applied to data filled with error rarely yield clear-cut results. One must consider the complex interactions between personality and the intervening variables contained in athletic participation and performance. Schwartz, Davidson, and Goleman (1978), for example, have pointed out that to understand the effects of physical fitness training one would in fact have to include its interaction with personality type. Thus for those overburdened with cognitive anxiety, relaxation therapy might be a superior activity while for persons experiencing somatic anxiety, exercise may be a more useful activity. There would be similar interactions expected between types of sporting activity and personality type or predisposition.

In the third review by Browne and Mahoney (1984), the field of sport psychology is reviewed for the first time in the *Annual Review of Psychology*. The authors try to give a state-of-the-art resume of this newly emerging branch of psychology. They note (p. 609) that "extraverts are more socially inclined, more adventurous, take higher risks, and in general are more involved in sports — at least in those where there is a high level of incoming stimulation." They predict a productive future for the study of the significance of extraversion in sport. The interaction of athletic participation with perceptual style (for example, tolerance of pain and ability to control dysfunctional anxiety levels) and with general well-being over time are noted. Aerobic activity has been found rather consistently to relate to positive psychological effects and lowered physical tension. The authors observations converge neatly with the theoretical position of Eysenck. They call for longitudinal studies, particularly on children's issues in sport, in order to tackle some of the difficult interactions between personality and sport activity.

The study of personality in sport is complicated by more than the interactions involved between various personality styles and traits. It also involves the following six factors.

1. The type of individual who is attracted to a specific sport may not be the one most naturally suited to it once the selection process of the sport takes place by coaches, sport organizations, and the social and cultural values which surround the sport. Thus, on the one hand those best suited to a sport may not be encouraged to remain in it. On the other hand those encouraged to remain in a sport by external or extraneous factors (work well with a specific coach, have socioeconomic support from family) may not be the most naturally suited for it.

2. Personality changes may occur over time as the individual is socialized by and adapts to the intensive subculture of sport. To study personality in sport at one point in time, as most studies have done, is almost self-defeating. There will be little comparison across studies. Longitudinal studies of the athlete entering sport, being socialized by sport, and aging in sport are essential for the future understanding of how personality unfolds in sport.

3. The sex and sex roles of athletes complicate the comparability of results due to the extreme types of both male and female found in many, if not most, sports. One is dealing with small sections of the general population the members of which are often under extreme role strain (see Chapter 11), and, further, one is using questionnaires (with their huge margin of error) to gather information. Hence it should be no surprise that sex and sex-role effects can skew results.

4. Individual versus group sport differences further increase error variance in studies of sport. The socialization process and demands on athletes are

clearly different across many types of sport. The individual versus group sport division is one of the more obvious.

5. Position played skews the results in studies of personality by sport. There are different demands upon athletes fulfilling specialized roles in a sport. The goal keeper versus the forward, the quarterback versus the corner linebacker, the enforcer versus the goal scorer all have different roles which demand different skills, abilities, and approaches to their jobs.

6. Finally, studying sport at different performance levels yields noncomparable results. There are many changes in role demands and personal adjustment as the athlete, regardless of age, climbs the sport ladder from local, to national, to international competition and from there to the professional level.

THE PROBLEM OF PREDICTION

The study of psychology has several purposes. Two contrasting aims are "to predict and control behavior" and "to understand and to explore behavior." One can seek to understand and to explore without assuming the final result will be prediction and control. In sport psychology many studies have been carried out with one or both purposes and the attempts at prediction have resulted in considerable controversy, including the alleged abuse of test results (Browne and Mahoney, 1984, p. 610). Studies have been undertaken on the personality of athletes in which the final aim was the selection and placing of athletes in programs or on teams. Morgan (1979) is correct in noting that accurate prediction of athletic potential via personality traits or factors is impossible. This is because of the error present in personality measurement and because of the complex interaction between what the individual brings to the sport and what the individual must develop in order to cope with the sport. However, given the appropriate prediction problem, the social and institutional sanction to solve it, and a supportive political atmosphere, there is little doubt that a high level of accuracy could be achieved in predicting athletic success in various sports.

The problems of prediction have to do with *placement,* where the potential of any given individual must be accurately assessed. If we try to predict whether any given individual in a sport program will be successful or unsuccessful, we will have extreme difficulty. Note that coaches, sport organizations and individuals, however, must constantly make such predictions in deciding who will be allowed into a sports program or who will continue in it.

The problems in which prediction can be accurate have to do with *selection,* where we must choose from a large number of individuals those with most potential for a limited number of places. Let us say we have 10,000 people to choose from in order to develop a top level team for any sport. The assignment is to choose 100 for intensive training. Then the art and science of prediction could be very accurate. A combination of tests would be used based upon top level performance norms and criteria. These might include constitutional measures, motivational measures, personality measures, physiological and reaction time measures, social measures, and of course performance measures. Appropriately weighted combinations of these indexes should lead to a high level of predictive accuracy. The weighting used may be clinical (intuitive) or actuarial (statistical), or a combination of the two. In any case, a high level of performance can be expected from a team selected in this fashion.

Methods such as those just described are used in some countries for the selection of athletes for high level training programs (Riordan, 1981). In the Western world, however, such selection and prediction is philosophically incompatible with political rights and beliefs and thus this use of testing is sometimes called unethical. Athletes and their supporters want the freedom and the right to compete for and to persevere in their quest for the few top positions in sport and in elite training programs on the basis of their own decision and not on the basis of tests administered, which may even be biased against a certain individual or individuals. Note that in placement problems one is seeking to predict accurately for each individual, while in the selection program one merely wants to capitalize on the overall group trends and perfect accuracy for any one individual is not needed.

The above program calls for testing of many variables other than personality. It is naive to expect that performance in sport can be predicted by personality alone, even if it is predicting the outcome of a championship performance. Constitutional factors, physiological factors, performance record and experience, sociological background, and mood can all contribute to the balance or imbalance that determine the outcome of any legitimate athletic contest.

THE EARLY YEARS

It has been pointed out that conclusions in psychology should be reached by looking for consistencies in results across independent studies and methods. We have so far concentrated on review papers which have come to conclusions about the relationship of personality to sport. Other reviews, written from different perspectives have come to the same conclusions, but so have several pioneer researchers in the psychology of sport.

Kane (1972) concluded that the male athlete was characterized by extraversion and emotional stability. That is, he scored highly on trait measures of dominance, social aggression, leadership, tough-mindedness, stability, and confidence. Kane's survey of female athletes revealed a similar profile, except that the women tended to score lower on emotional stability or emotional control.

Ogilvie, Johnsgard, and Tutko (1971) came to similar conclusions in examining the relationship between personality and athletic ability. They describe the male athlete as emotionally healthy and tending toward extraversion. They further describe him as tough-minded, self-assertive, and self-confident, with a high capacity to endure stress and a low level of anxiety (p. 235). Their conclusions on the personality of the female athlete differ somewhat from Kane's in that they describe the female personality as being parallel to the male except for lower extraversion and higher emotional stability. Women are more tough-minded and independent and are better equipped to handle stress than men.

Morgan (1972), in his unique program of research at the University of Wisconsin, came to similar conclusions. The entire freshman class at the University of Wisconsin completed the Minnesota Multiphasic Personality Inventory (MMPI), and Morgan and his colleagues, following the athletic and sports participation of the students over their four years in the university, were able to refer back to each student's MMPI. They completed many excellent studies and reports, and generally concluded that the athletes were extraverted and vigorous. They had lower levels of tension, depression, and fatigue than the general student population, from which they consistently differed in a positive way.

An illustrative study from the early years that investigated the relationship between personality and athletic ability was reported by Werner and Gottheil (1966). It was carried out at an American military academy and compared 340 cadets who were athletic participants to 116 who were not athletic participants before entering the academy. The time span of the study was from entrance through to graduation four years later and the Sixteen Personality Factors Questionnaire was used to make the comparisons. Significant differences regarding several personality traits emerged. The athletic group described themselves as sociable, dominant, aggressive, enthusiastic, group-dependent, and conservative, and a higher proportion of the athletic participants graduated than nonparticipants. The study did not find significant changes in either of the groups over the four-year span.

Both Booth (1958) and Schendel (1965) did find suggestions of change over a period of time between athletes and nonathletes. Using the MMPI Booth generally concluded that athletes showed more masculinity of interest and that older athletes scored lower on the anxiety and social responsibility scales. Schendel used the California Psychological Inventory to observe differences at various educational levels. High school athletes showed more socially desirable traits than nonathletes, but college comparisons yielded the opposite results. At that level, athletes were less conscientious, less tolerant, less aware of others, less adaptable, and less independent. The athletes again showed more masculinity of interest.

In studies of female athletes, Peterson, Weber, and Trousdale (1967) used the Sixteen Personality Factor Questionnaire to investigate the personality profiles of athletes selected from the American Athletic Union and the 1964 U.S. Olympic teams. They concluded that female athletes tend to be emotionally aloof and more serious than the average female. They were also intelligent, conscientious, aggressive, and persevering. Using Edward's (1963) Personal Preference Schedule, Thorpe (1958) studied a group of female physical education instructors and students at Florida State University. The instructors were reported to be higher than the norms on the need preferences of deference, order, dominance, and personal endurance, and lower on autonomy, succorance, nurturance, heterosexuality, and aggression. Black (1956) studied female students using the MMPI, and found the "most athletic" to have a more masculine interest pattern as well as more confidence and energy, and to be freer from concerns about health and from anxiety, insecurity, self-consciousness, and sensitiveness.

In studying the psychological patterns of several national champions and college wrestlers, Johnson, Hutton, and Johnson (1954) used projective techniques. They found several common traits: aggressiveness, lack of emotional inhibitions, self-assurance, and the need to achieve. Other studies have shown that athletes in group sports tend to be extraverted and self-confident, while those participating in individual sports are more inclined to be introverted, stable, and confident. Yet they also indicate that the individual, as well as the team athlete, may move toward extraversion and stability the longer they pursue sport.

Taken as a whole, the early studies of personality and sport present a constellation of traits found in both male and female athletes: dominance, extraversion, enthusiasm, confidence, usually aggression, resiliency, and a high activity level. There is confirmation of the tough, assertive, uncaring, and low-insight profile of the competitor, as suggested particularly in the work of Eysenck. This does not, however, negate the positive psychological benefits of confidence and feelings of well-being that characterize those who are physically fit.

Of additional interest is the general status of the female athlete's personality. On the basis of the preliminary studies reviewed, the personality of the female athlete may be closer to that of the male athlete than to that of the average female. Although some (Dyer, 1982; Snyder and Spreitzer, 1983) argue and present studies to show (based often upon captive female athletic participants) that there are no masculine traits in the female athlete, one need only search the literature to find numerous studies which suggest that the more androgynous or instrumental the female athlete, the more successful she will be as an athlete (Myers and Lips, 1978; Butt and Schroeder, 1980). After a review of the literature on the personality of the successful female athlete Williams (1978) comes to the same conclusion.

In the preceding discussion we have examined some general trends in studies on the personalities of athletes. The reader should realize that there are many athletes who completely contradict the trends noted. A Bobby Fischer, a Michael Gross, and an Eric Heiden clearly do not fit the mold. Nor do the conclusions undermine the importance of the strong situational factors in sport that influence behavior.   In addition, there are variations within a sport and between sports.   For example, Mandell (1974) has examined the relationship between position played and personality within football, while others have looked at differences between sports, (Johnson, 1972; Schorr, Asley, and Joy, 1977.)

In summarizing the material discussed thus far, it is possible to place the personality traits of athletes on two major dimensions: extraversion versus introversion, and stability versus instability, as illustrated in Figure 5.

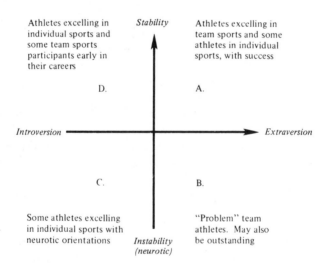

Figure 5. Summary of the "Athletic" Personality.   The greatest concentration of athletes may be expected in quadrant A, representing the social ideal of extraversion and stability. Many football, baseball, and hockey players belong here as, for example, Gordon Howe. Quadrant B includes those extraverts who have had to deal with emotional problems.   Good examples are Jim Piersall and Reggie Jackson of baseball, and many football and hockey players who have had to cope with problems of expressing physical, personal, and sexual aggression when away from the sports arena.   If their emotional problems are overcome, these athletes may also move in the direction of quadrant A.   Quadrant C includes those athletes who are introverted and unstable, and who are found most often in individual sports.   Bobby Fischer in chess, Bill Tilden in tennis, and Doug Hepburn in weightlifting are representative.   With success in sport some of these athletes will also move toward stability and perhaps toward more extraverted behavior.   Most will move only to quadrant D, however, in which athletes are introverted and stable.   Connie Hawkins of basketball provides an example of such movement.   Most athletes in quadrant D will tend to be in individual sports.   Roger Bannister and Rod Laver provide examples.

THE CURRENT STATUS OF PERSONALITY IN SPORT

In review, programs or research reviews which focus upon physical fitness, sport, and personality emerge with two major findings. The first is that physical exercise programs tend to result in improvements in self-concept and mood. Thus the quality of life of the retarded, of heart patients, of depressed patients, and of alcoholics seems significantly improved (Ledwidge, 1980; Browne and Mahoney, 1984). The second major finding is that athletes as a group tend toward extraversion and stability (Kane, 1972; Ogilvie, 1974; Butt, 1976; Eysenck et al. 1982). These observations are important for both practical application and for the general advancement of knowledge about personality. It is of interest that in spite of the empirical and theoretical support for the athletic personal style, some writers still report studies and argue that none can be detected. For example Carron (1980, pp. 27–28) use Hardman's (1973) review of 42 studies of athletes who responded to the Sixteen Personality Factor Questionnaire. Not only is this a notoriously unstable instrument to measure personality (Buros, 1978, p. 678 ff.), but in addition, many of the sports groups cited have very small n's and many of the sports included are individual sports which are far from the group athletic norm. They include table tennis, karate, golf, and swimming. Added to these factors, the data are almost entirely British and Britons score lower on extraversion than do Americans.

In spite of this cross-national difference, the British psychologist Eysenck argues for the same theoretical framework as do Ogilvie, Morgan, and Butt. Within Eysenck's theory (see Eysenck and Eysenck, 1969, 1976 for background and Eysenck, Nias, and Cox, 1982 for its application to sport) the extraversion-introversion dimension is biologically based and has to do with the excitability of the central nervous system. The extravert has low electro-potential (low cortical arousal) and therefore seeks strong stimulation from the environment. The introvert has a high level of electro-potential (high cortical arousal) and therefore seeks to withdraw from strong stimulation. Hence extraverts will be more attracted to rough and ready (sensation producing) sports than will introverts. Howard (1976) subjected sporting activities to factor analysis using the Personality Research Form and found different correlations to different classifications of sport. Extraversion was highly correlated with action-oriented seasonal competitive sports in high school students (football, softball, basketball, and tennis). Other studies (Morgan and Costill, 1972) have found distance runners to be introverted.

Similarly, Eysenck's theory allows for clarification of the stability-instability dimension which he claims is related to the autonomic system (activity of the limbic system). Since neuroticism (instability) has drive or motivational potential, Eysenck claims that in younger athletes too little or too much is dysfunctional. A middling amount of nervousness should be optimal. However, he notes (p. 10) that if neuroticism is dysfunctional, it will be lower in high-level performers, that is, they will tend toward stability.

The last dimension which Eysenck adds to the "big two" is psychoticism, or poor superego formation. This refers to an antisocial attitude characterized by egocentricity, coldness, nonconformity, aggression, impulsivity, and hostility versus cooperation, empathy, and concern for others. Eysenck et al. hypothesize that if sport requires and rewards the former traits, individuals who are high on psychoticism will enter and flourish in sport. He notes the frequent relationship between Machiavellianism, cheating, and success in sport, and argues for the presence of high psychoticism scores in both male and female athletes. Thus the theoretical profile for the prototypical athlete in Eysenck's theory is a person who is extraverted, stable, and antisocial. Further, he claims this pattern may not be affected by constructive sport socialization to the degree commonly expected because (p. 3) 75 percent of the variance in these traits is due to genetic influence and only 25 percent is due to environmental influence.

Eysenck et al. note the extreme interrelationships and interactions between (1) personality, physique, and competition; (2) personality and sexual behavior; and (3) personality and the effects of drugs. In the first observation, the authors expand on Sheldon's constitutional theory on the relationship between body build and temperament and extend it to body build and sport. In the second, they note the high rate of and variations in sexual activities of extraverts as opposed to introverts. This point will be reviewed in Chapters 11 and 12 on the sex roles and sexual behavior of athletes. Finally, they note the importance of dealing with personality when trying to understand the influence of various drugs. Personality predisposes an individual to react to drugs in predictable ways. Amphetamines produce a very small but measurable improvement in the performances of swimmers, shot putters, and runners when given in small dosages. In large dosages, however they produce sham rages in animal subjects, as they have been observed to do in football players. (Sham rage is continued and prolonged or heightened aggression.) This is often followed by periods of decline and depression. It is obvious to anyone reading the sports pages that drugs on and off the playing field are becoming an increasing problem. Even young athletes have struggled to overcome problems of substance abuse. Diver, Greg Louganis and jockey, Steve Cauthen provide two examples. To many athletes the use of drugs, both for recreational purposes and as ergogenic aids, is accepted as part of the subculture. Zimmerman (1983) has described the use of drugs in American football:

> The problem is, the NFL always has had a kind of a drug culture. Heavy drinkers, even problem drinkers, were good ol' boys a few seasons back. Then the needles, the painkilling shots, joined alcohol as an accepted drug against the ever present pain of postgame Mondays. Then came anabolic steroids and amphetamines, often dispensed with the full knowledge of the club. A way of life was taking hold: Pop it, drink it or shoot it and you'll feel

better.   Cocaine was the natural offspring, particularly with young people who had money to toss around.

There are those athletes who have tried to leave the drug culture. After arrests, convictions for peddling, institutional treatment, and drying out periods, many have returned to family life and religion as sources of stability. Their adjustment is rarely smooth. The association of extraversion with sport, with sexual activity, with sensation seeking, and with increased psychoticism (antisocialness) after drug usage is important in understanding some of the problems in the personal adjustments of athletes.

How is the immense drug problem in sport to be dealt with? One way is to stress education programs for and counselling of young athletes before they become exposed to the drug subculture. A second way is to crack down on the drug users and peddlers within sport and to treat them clinically or through legal channels. A third way emerges from the theme of this book — to encourage and stress the experience of competence in sport at all levels and the internal satisfaction that goes with it. Artificial aids and destructive substances are incompatible with the experience of competence. Many in the athletic world are becoming aware of the hazards of a life style that features a constant assault on the environment* at any cost, therefore, a fuller understanding of personality and the traps within sport should lead to fewer casualties. Just as persons with biological predispositions to mental illness must avoid certain types of stress, so should many athletic types avoid the hazards hidden in the world of competitive sport.

---

*Due to the demands for aggressive behavior.

10
Pathology of the Athlete

INTRODUCTION

In the last chapter we noted that persons who are extraverted and highly assertive tend to be attracted to competitive sport. Morgan (1980) has estimated that 20 to 45 percent of the variance between athletes and nonathletes may be accounted for by personality traits. Others stress the low correlations between personality and physical activity criteria and conclude that only 5 to 10 percent of the variance is accounted for. In either case, even with the lower figures, the findings have both theoretical and practical significance. Personality emerges as an important contributor to individual variations in sport performance and sport behavior.

In coaching, working with teams, counselling, or working on sport regulation and organization, it is important to recognize the prototypical athlete. In many competitive sports one will be working with highly assertive, asocial, outgoing, and sometimes destructive behavior. One might also expect incidences of acting out sexual behavior and a high level of sexual activity in athletes. Behavioral problems may be expected when athletes are under extreme pressure. Drug taking, externalization, problems with authority, gambling, and risk taking may all accompany an extraverted style. Note that there are always exceptions to the norm. In the lower echelons of sport or in sports such as bridge, badminton, or the biathlon, one would expect many exceptions. What is important is that many competitive sports require action, onslaught, and aggressive behavior and the athlete with a predisposition to such behavior will be attracted to them.

To the degree the athlete is characterologically immature, irresponsible, and unstable, he or she will show pathology particularly when under pressure or frustrated. In any team, the presence of one or two unstable athletes will cause many problems. An example occurred with a notorious Canadian ski jumping team which was disbanded entirely due to drunkenness, foul language, and misbehavior. The chairman of the Canadian Ski Association jumping committee explained that one team member arrived in Thunder Bay from Europe "in such a drunken state that he didn't know whether he was in Canada or Austria. Many of the team members made complete asses of themselves in Europe, especially in front of other teams and fans who turned out for the competitions. On a couple of occasions some of the jumpers made only one jump and never returned to the tower for their second jump. They left the coach waiting and wondering what happened to them. Another time one of the jumpers didn't even bother making any jumps, then walked down the hill laughing at everybody." (*Vancouver Sun*, p. 26, Mon. Jan. 26, 1976).

Variations of such incidents are very common in the sports world. Extraverted, unstable individuals may court trouble and manifest egocentric and dysfunctional behavior. The extravert at best (when stable) may also relish fast driving, hard drinking, and intensive experiences in living. A consumer-oriented society and commercial sponsors relish a Joe Namath, a Vitas Gerulaitis, or a George Best as long as they do not show outright delinquency or criminality and damage the image of the sport. All three have walked the line between fast living and self-destruction. As long as the life styles of athletes support consumerism, they can be of value to sales far beyond what their sports skill would warrant. This is due to their ability to command the attention of the media and the public by frequent exposure. But immaturity and irresponsibility, when combined with extraversion or a high need for stimulation and risk-taking, becomes the premorbid personality disposition of the athlete. When such potential is nurtured and reinforced by the sports world, the tenuousness of the athletic adjustment becomes increasingly apparent.

CHARACTER AND ATHLETICS

When the traits of dominance, extraversion, enthusiasm, confidence, and resilience result from competence motivation and stability they indicate a healthy and constructive adjustment to a career in sport by the committed athlete. Gordie Howe of hockey reflects this process of adjustment in saying: "I am going to stick with hockey as long as I can. It's the only business I know. It's my life. I'd be lost in anything else." (Vipond, 1971, p. 17.) So does American football player Jerry Kramer, who writes: "That's why I'm going to keep playing professional football. I know now that for me the main lure of football is the guys, my teammates, the friendship, the fun, the excitement, the incredibly exhilarating feeling of shared achievement." (Kramer, 1969, p. 235).

Those who must deal with athletes at a human level, however, often find the athletic life difficult to adjust to and fraught with egocentricity. Traits of egocentricity appear even in the competence-oriented Howe and Kramer before competitions. When playing a home game in Detroit, Howe would rise at 10:00 A.M., eat two scrambled eggs, attend the team's meeting at the stadium, have a brief solitary leisure period at home (TV), eat a ground round steak dinner at 2:00 P.M., sleep for two hours, and leave for the stadium (Fischler, 1969).

This typical example of a pregame schedule leaves little time for tending to the needs of family or friends, as the game dominates the player and those associated with him.   In his autobiography (1969), Kramer describes "putting the girls" (their wives) in a room together the night before a game while he and a teammate shared another room because, as players, they were inclined to be ill-tempered on the eve of a game.   Once again the athlete's family must adjust to his needs because he faces a competition.   Ken Dryden (1983, p. 19) comments on the demands of professional hockey, where life rhythms are defined by the games: "It is a high-energy life lived in two- or three-hour bursts, and now, after eight years, I don't know how to use more. I am not very good at off-days."

The three athletes cited were all known in sport for competence and consideration of others.   In less mature sport personalities, egocentricity and lack of consideration for others can become deeply ingrained and destructive.   The biographers of Babe Ruth (Sobol, 1974; Creamer, 1974) have given a portrait of just such an outcome, where an extraverted, fun-loving, competent sportsman did not develop self or social responsibility.   Ruth was selfish, egocentric, and lacked insight into the personal needs of his first wife; later he was babied and dominated by his second.   The relationships between male athletes and their wives are not equal domestic partnerships.   Shirley Young, wife of George Young, who ran on four United States Olympic teams, described her life as follows (Dolson, 1975): "I'm not a clinging dependent woman. If I wanted a ditch dug, I'd just go out and dig it."   Young was once going off to a competition.   His wife asked him where he was staying.   He replied: "In a motel," and drove off.

A behavioral adjustment that frequently precedes contests is anxiety in reaction to threat and, hence, increased defensiveness when competitive stress is at its height.   Often, there is heightened egocentricity and emotion that vents itself in bragging, bantering or pre-game rituals for the purposes of increasing or decreasing arousal levels.   Some of this behavior is based upon superstition, but much of it is due to extreme anxiety brought on by the challenge of the game and the threat of loss.   If anxiety and compensation become dominating personal styles, the athlete will not be psychologically well adjusted.   The continuation in sport will be accompanied by increasing symptoms of uneasiness.

The degree of an athlete's adjustment can best be determined by his or her reaction to losing.   The athlete whose sport is a constructive expression of self will show no disintegration upon losing.   The performance is congruent with the personality because it is a testing of competence, and the athlete performs for the intrinsic satisfaction found in it.   The athlete whose sport is an expression of needs for external support, such as winning, money or gaining status, will show signs of disintegration upon losing that are manifested in anger, weeping, sulking, and self-imposed isolation.

When an athlete storms off the playing field after a loss, he or she is generally showing the defense mechanism called rationalization, or, as the attribution theorists (Greenwald, 1980. Lau and Russell, 1980) would explain, the loss is being attributed to external factors. On the other hand, when a win is explained, the athlete usually attributes it to internal factors such as a fine performance. Egocentric and defensive behavior does not occur only in insecure or immature "sport brats." Let us note that the same rationalizations associated with a potential loss of status can affect the outwardly secure and privileged as well. Witness the accusations of the New York Yacht Club after losing the America's Cup to the "Australia II" captained by John Bertrand. The possibility of surrendering the Cup after 132 years proved too much of a blow for the august American followers of the sport and its organizers (Levitt and Lloyd, 1983, *Upset*). Among other things they tried to disqualify the "Australia II" because of its controversial new design.

Other individual defenses besides rationalization (attributing to the loss to external factors such as injury or other people cheating), are projection (blaming someone else such as an umpire or an opponent), denial (pretending one didn't really want to win), and compensation (escaping from feelings of failure by excesses such as drinking or sexual exploits). With these defenses the athlete avoids dealing with loss and failure. They protect the ego, but in a destructive way, because the athlete does not face the situation realistically nor grow from the experience of it. Immature behavior, whether it is an expression of negative feeling (fighting, spitting, swearing, crying, screaming, vomiting) or positive feeling (hugging, kissing, holding of hands, pouring champagne over heads), is tolerated in sport far more than elsewhere. The social behavior expected of an athlete resembles in many ways that expected of a young, ill, or irresponsible person. Athletes are rewarded to an extreme for good behavior (winning) and punished (often inconsistently) for misbehavior. The athlete is not expected to appreciate and internalize the reasons for rules and regulations; he or she often functions under a system of fines and penalties levied that force him/her, like a child, to behave. This is not a sound way to develop children and it is an even poorer way to develop athletes.

The confusion in the sport system over the recent spate of drug problems is a good example of the external control of athletes and their failure to regulate themselves independently. The imprisonment of athletes for drug-related offenses, the introduction of drug abuse programs for athletes, the use of detectives in order to spy on athletes to identify problems — all indicate the failure of internalized control and a failure of constructive socialization practices in sport. The athlete has not been socialized for his or her own maximum welfare nor for the maximum welfare of sport. The athlete has not found the optimal compromise between need structure and the means of fulfilling that need structure from the sport system. Rather, the athlete has been bought off by large sums of money and external reward which he or she is frequently incapable of handling. The athlete's life style then may become congruent with the aims of promoters and consumerism rather than with his or her own needs for health and happiness.

Sport engaged in for competitive social motivations may well have a negative effect upon character. We should therefore be concerned with the effects of "competitive" sport for several discrete reasons. The *first* is that identificatory learning is an important influence in the socialization of youth and the athletic "hero" is a prominent figure to youth. When antisocial behaviors are rewarded or tolerated from such "heros" those behaviors may well be copied and continued. The *second* is that situational determinants of behavior (such as in sport) are becoming increasingly important as the older values of religion and community continue to decline. The *third* is that the vast media exposure of competitive sport, particularly on TV, has a powerful influence in transmitting the values held so highly in that field. The combination of these has led people to identify more and more with staged competition. It is not surprising, therefore, that psychologists, philosophers, educators, and athletes have questioned the value of competitive sport and its effect upon personality and character. Sports such as football and hockey have received more cirticism than others, but there should be concern about any sport situation in which competition is forced upon the players and the viewing public.

Singer (1972) has questioned the effects of varsity athletics upon character. He noted studies that concluded that athletes and varsity letter winners showed poorer attitudes toward fair play and sportsmanship than nonathletes and non-letter-winners. It seems that the better the athlete, the poorer the character development. Singer questioned whether sport produced these qualities or whether those possessing the qualities tended to do better in sport. He also took into consideration the conflict between the competitive attitudes of athletes and the social ideals of sport.

McMurtry (1971) of the Philosophy Department at the University of Guelph, Canada, a former professional football player for the Calgary Stampeders, wrote that football forced him to suppress his natural instincts and feelings and re-channel them in a way that was destructive and foreign to him. Mechanized, stereotyped plays replaced his need for enjoyment in spontaneous physical outlet, and hatred replaced friendship. Wilson (1964), a first-ranked British tennis player, wrote in his autobiography that the farther along he went in the tennis hierarchy, the less he enjoyed the game. The spontaneous pleasure of playing disappeared because of the demand to play so often and to win each time. His energies had to be focused on competition instead of on the development of competence. Bruce Kison, baseball pitcher, was reported by Jordan (1974) as saying that when he arrived in the big leagues he quickly absorbed the social norms of the older players: to be brash about women and mainly concerned with maintaining his position. Kison states that he protected himself against the aspiring young player who was actively seeking to replace him. Jim Brosnan, another pitcher, rates professional baseball as a selfish game (as reported by Schecter, 1970) and his advice to his son, if he aspired to a baseball career, would be: "be selfish." LaVerne Barnes (1973), who was married to Emery Barnes (now a politician) of the Canadian football league, describes being married to a football player as: "living with a self-centered, boorish, emotional, immature exhibitionist, and trying hard to keep a sense of humor." Dryden (1983) also notes the decline in the game of ice hockey in which he sees individual virtuosity eliminated as the game is "taken over by coaches, by technocrats and autocrats who empty players' minds to control their bodies ... " (p. 132). It became popular for some writers to call such critics of sport "radical" or "narcissistic." In fact these critics are much too diverse for such easy labels and their opinions are backed up by the work of many concerned social scientists. Thus their views are best taken seriously as an important critique of sport.

Increasing numbers of observers and participants in organized sports are calling attention to the behavioral norms of the sport world and their effects upon personal development. In general these observations confirm the results of the predominant personality descriptions of athletes noted in Chapter 9 and the effects of competition noted in Chapter 6. The athlete finds in the competitive sport world an environment that encourages the personal expression of independence, self-confidence, dominance, egocentricity, selfishness, and limited insight. This total athletic profile is not a positive one. It is not a personality structure that will lead to constructive handling of problems in personal or in social life. The structure is a product and a pawn of a power-oriented, winner-take-all philosophy that will serve only to preserve the values of individualism and competitiveness at the expense of the development of other more essential human qualities.

THE FUTURE

Writers have begun commenting upon the "hall of shame" in sport. They refer to the long and continually lengthening lists of athletes involved in traffic offenses, drug charges, thefts, rapes, gambling, alcoholism, ergogenic aids, aggressive attacks, wife abuse and murder. It is becoming less common for writers to focus upon the competence-oriented, well-behaved, or more gracious athletic participant and articles such as O'Hara's (1983) analysis of three 'gentlemen' tennis players: Brian Gottfried, Tim Mayotte and Peter McNamara — are too rare.

The psychological development of athletes, as considered this far, should provide a good understanding of constructive personal adjustment in sport as opposed to destructive adjustment. In the personality of any athlete, one expects to see a complex combination of body type and temperament, personal dispositions, and socialization experiences in sport. The athlete's adjustment will be affected by experiences of success and failure in sport and all of the hardships, joys, and frustrations of obtaining his or her current level of skill. An eleven-year-old girl gymnast is forced to live hundreds of miles from her family in order to undergo the desired coaching and training. An eight-year-old hockey player is forced to undergo the pressures of striving to make the team and then to make it off the bench. A professional athlete is sought after as a hero and pursued by fans, companies, agents, and benefactors with material luxuries — all of which he or she feels unable to handle. In spite of the complexities in the interaction between breakdown in athletes and the demands of sport, one is able to make some summary statements about the vulnerabilities of athletes to breakdown which we expect will hold up under future scrutiny.

One will find two types or styles in sport: the extraverted style and the introverted style. Because the world of organized sport tends to emphasize external reward and hence competitive dominance, one expects the extraverted style to be attracted to and to be sustained more often in sport than the introverted style. The extraverted individual has a low level of arousal and therefore seeks high activation. He or she displays risk taking and assertive behavior. Being less subject to internal controls and socialization processes, one would therefore predict a high number of behavioral and acting out problems in athletes at most levels. These difficulties may be expected to increase as the athlete advances in the sport structure to the degree that structural controls are weakened. Travel, free time, money, lack of discipline, and the lures of large cities are some examples of events which might weaken the usual structures in the athletes' lives. To the degree the developing athlete can be confronted with good coaching, structure, and guidance or education; to the degree competence and skill are highlighted in training; the extraverted athlete can move on to a stable adjustment and make major contributions to the world of sport. However there is much evidence this is not being done.

Although the study of personality traits in sport is unable to predict athletic success, it provides a very significant factor in athletic success when combined with a knowledge of the personalities of the coaches, the other team members, and the overall strategy of the sport organization in which the athlete must function. The fact that sports staff, coaches, and athletes are all gaining increased insight into the nature of the problems involved in athlete recruitment, motivation, and adjustment at all levels bodes well for the future of sport. In another ten years, perhaps, the competence-oriented athlete who is physically gifted, as well as stable and socially constructive, will move to the forefront of sport. Lessons are being learned from some of the destructiveness and pathology surfacing in the current crop of athletes. Athletes, coaches, and the public are increasingly aware of the problems and will become more so. So are officials and organizers. The future therefore promises increased knowledge of the effects of both competition and competence followed by slow correction in the sport environment for the benefit of both athlete and sport.

11
Sex Roles in Sport

SOCIAL ROLES

Special behaviors are expected of people who occupy social roles. Whether the role is that of bus driver, teacher, husband, wife, leader, or athlete, it is expected that norms will be met. A bus driver is expected to be competent, to keep his vehicle on schedule, to be courteous to passengers, and, usually, to get along with his fellow drivers. If any of these expectations are not met, the driver may be suspended and no longer allowed to fill the occupational role. In a similar manner, the role of athlete carries with it a set of social expectations that are defined by a developmental and excellence continuum. The minor league hockey player has a set of expectations to meet just as does the high school or university athlete. Bouton (1970, 1971), who in many ways deviated from the prescribed role behaviors for an athlete of his status, described the incidents that led to his gradual alienation from the baseball community: at the time he was playing a player should not be a loner or an "oddball," read too much, violate the "sanctity" of the locker room by writing books, speak to "censured" reporters, or pubicly make fun of teammates. Glenn Burke, formerly with the Los Angeles Dodgers (1976) and Oakland Athletics, left baseball when made to feel an outcast because of his homosexuality, which he felt strongly conflicted with the behavioral norms of his peers. "I worried about what they'd say or do. I didn't think they could cope with it. I'm not a troublemaker. I don't pick at people. I don't cause trouble. What I do is my business. I quit for my friends, who I thought might be uneasy. I was making them uncomfortable." Similarly, the nonconformist Bill Johnson for a time was kept off the U.S. national ski team and, once he made it, was removed in 1981 for refusing to conform to dry-land drills. He annoyed teammates with his egocentricity and temper, and they referred to him as the "Hatchet Man" (Johnson, 1984a). Johnson succeeded by winning the Olympic downhill in February 1984, and his subsequent adjustment to the team has been problematic (Johnson, 1985b).

Because the role of an athlete is a highly valued one in many cultures, there is a great deal of emulative and imitative behavior especially from males who aspire to it. Jordan (1974) wrote: "Since sport is a universal male experience, all men, whether they wish to or not, must likewise make their peace with it." Some do so through fantasy, some as spectators, others by means of a hobby-like approach that uses all the newest equipment if not any of the expertise and skill. Some establish a negative identity with both sport and instrumental behavior through early experiences of failure and/or nonparticipation.

What are the general social expectations of athletes? They are that the athlete be aggressive, competitive, independent, skillful, youthful-looking, mature, strong, and masterful. In short the athlete is expected to reflect the North American ideal. In other countries there are variations upon these expectations, but the mastery, skill, and strength expected of athletes remains constant in all nations for most sport.

Occupational activity and other social roles are often aligned with the major male-female role division in almost all societies. Maleness and femaleness, and the social expectations attached to each, have been a focus of fantasy and examination since human beings began recording thought. Never has the biology and sociology of sex differences been subjected to so critical and searching an analysis as in recent years, however, and we are fortunate to be able to make use of these results in the present chapter.

THE WOMEN'S MOVEMENT

The current feminist wave in North America was marked by the publication of *The Feminine Mystique* by Betty Friedan (1963). This book examined the unrest and emotional conflicts of women, particularly middle class, college-educated women who ended up in the suburbs. These women who raised children in isolation from the mainstream of society were devalued in terms of minimal overt reinforcement from the society in which they lived. The incongruence between personality and the ultimate role in which women found themselves caused a dynamic explosion of concern and discontent, energizing the women's movement of the sixties and seventies.

Factors other than discontent contributed to the movement. One was the advent of birth control, another was the fact that both social and political power were no longer determined by strength alone, and a third was that a general revolt against authoritarian and paternalistic structure occurred during the sixties. Alternatives were needed and women were prepared to provide them. The movement has had, and will continue to have, major impact on the youth in North American society, both men and women.

Social scientists participated in the movement, recorded the movement, and sometimes watched from the sidelines as the phenomena of a major social change unfolded. It was obvious that traditional femininity was being forsaken. Many females were seeking equality, freedom, independence, and social rewards — money, position, and status. These had previously, except for the extremely wealthy, positioned, or talented women, been the rights of males. How were women best to succeed in their bold new step? The answer: by identifying with men, by having a male mentor, by thinking like men, and by seeking the same rewards as men. Hennig and Jardim (1977) in *The Managerial Woman,* document the closeness to their fathers of 100 outstanding women achievers in the business community. These women describe themselves as tomboys as youngsters and half had not married. A brief survey of the back-grounds of women in many sports reveal the same prominence of fathers. Some sports are exceptions, such as figure skating and gymnastics, in which a female aesthetic ideal is projected. However, in other sports, for example tennis, a survey of players past or present will show the importance of male mentors and particularly fathers. In tennis Lenglen, Bassett, Rinaldi, Jaeger, Evert, Temesvari, and many more were initially coached by ambitious fathers who were often tennis coaches. The mothers tend to play a background role, at times supportive, at other times absenting themselves due to discontent. Successful women are often schooled by men to defeat other women.

THE CONCEPT OF ANDROGYNY

The psychological literature was inundated with articles on the concept of androgyny after Bem (1974) introduced an androgyny scale for the self-report measurement of masculine and feminine traits. Bem's basic innovation was to measure masculinity and femininity as independent traits instead of as a uni-dimensional trait with masculinity at one extreme and femininity at the other. She argued that participants showing strong masculine and feminine traits were androgynous and were psychologically more open, adjusted, and competent than those persons constricted by either the masculine or feminine sex role. Bem initially contended that equal scores on masculinity and femininity regard-less of strength yielded androgyny. She later adjusted this contention and defined a person as androgynous if he or she had scores above the group mean on both scales. Persons taking Bem's scale rated themselves on traits which later studies have shown fall into three categories: socially desirable/undesirable male traits such as independent-dependent; socially desirable/undesirable female traits such as emotional-unemotional; and sex specific traits which are not related to social desirability such as aggressive-unaggressive (masculine) and cries easily (feminine) (Spence, Helmreich and Stapp, 1975).

Later the same research team (Spence, Helmreich, and Holahan, 1979) argued that androgynous and masculine subjects of both sexes have higher com-fort ratings, independent of type of task, than did feminine and undifferentiated subjects. They concluded that this showed the importance of instrumentality and expressiveness per se and suggested that researchers could well drop the concepts of masculinity and femininity and instead use the terms instrumentality and expressiveness regardless of sex. They argued (Spence and Helmreich, 1980) still more strongly for this when they suggested disengaging instrumentality and expressiveness from the whole concept of sex roles, masculinity, femininity, and androgyny. Although this ideological separation may not be realistic, it may be useful in trying to liberate instrumentality from masculinity and expressiveness from femininity. However, most men still score higher on instrumentality and lower on expressiveness than do most women when representative groups are measured. There is variability and overlap between the sexes yet it remains that generalized tests of well-being and competence are related to instrumentality and expressiveness and that both men and women high on instrumentality (masculinity) emerge most confident and adjusted. That is, masculine men and masculine women (to use the old terms) score better on various measures of well-being than do androgynous men and women or feminine men and women.

Thus the concept of androgyny and its benefits, initially proposed by Bem (1974, 1975, and 1977) and supported by Block's work on gifted Californian participants, (1973) has undergone considerable evolution and criticism. Not only have the psychometric properties of the androgyny scale been thoroughly criticized (Pedhazur and Tetenbaum, 1979; Myers and Gonda, 1982) but so have its theoretical underpinnings. Locksley and Colten (1979) suggest the concept of androgyny is an arbitrary one because sex is a structural feature of situations and an ongoing organizational presence in life experience. Linking the freedom from a sex-related measure to individual mental health and adjustment and treating it as a personality trait is not realistic. In fact, dominant and submissive attitudes are dictated by the social structure. Thus the authors do not believe such concepts should be linked to sex identity and to sex roles when they are socially arbitrary. The authors suggest that research should investigate how people deal cognitively with being perceived in social space largely as a result of their sex; how they cope with the fact that prestige, power, and reward are allocated largely as a fact of sex. Locksley and Colten's politically astute position is backed by important features in instrumentality-expressiveness research. Again, these are that more men than women score highly on instrumentality and that more successful than unsuccessful women score highly on instrumentality. That is, social rewards are more likely to go to men and women who show instrumental or masculine traits.

This is surely true of the sports world today. Sports performances for the most part require strength, assertion, dominance, competitiveness, and force. Butt and Schroeder (1980) used the Block (1973) design to study the sex-role socialization of female athletes and concluded that the best athletes were instrumental in orientation and highly socialized. Myers and Lips (1978) found that masculine men and androgynous females were most outstanding in squash.

The results of such studies are relatively consistent in spite of the results being influenced by the instrumentality-expressiveness scale used, the overall distribution of scores in the participants, the socioeconomic status of the athletes, and the type of and level of development in the sport(s) under study.

In recent years, the relationship of instrumental and expressive roles to sports roles has been greatly examined. There has always been confusion in the sport world, for example, over the female expressiveness in male figure skaters just as there is confusion over the instrumentality or masculine traits of many women basketball players. This area of confusion is most noticeable with regard to masculine women, who vastly outnumber feminine men in sport. This is because most sports were developed by men and later adopted by women. The treatment, management, and socialization of female athletes has always been ambivalent, and this ambivalence reflects the general society's problems and uneasiness with women who achieve in a man's world. As more women achieve in sport or in other walks of life, the social strain and ambivalence toward them should lessen.

THE FLUCTUATIONS OF AND INVARIANCE IN SEX ROLES

McIntosh (1971) has studied the close relationship between a society and its sport. The way games and sport activities are played vary with the social values they reflect. There are games that predominantly reflect manners, aggression, skill, mental and physical ability, and status differences. Sport is a form of social ritual varying in importance in different cultures. In some it has replaced other rituals. In the North American culture, athletic events have been described as masculine initiation rites. Indeed, the convergence between conceptions of the traditional male role and the athletic role is striking. Sport generally expresses the predominant values in a society. In North America and Western Europe, particularly, those values are male-oriented, as are the leadership roles and the power positions. Individuals gain and hold such positions by aggressive competitiveness and by association with a privileged group. Most social institutions are organized around males who are encouraged to be dominant and authoritative to their subordinates but submissive to directives from above, in other words, bureaucratic. In contrast the universal role assigned to females is socioemotional. Females are expected to satisfy the needs of others for nurturing, to care for the children and to keep the home. Females are socialized to be cooperative, expressive, and responsible.

Traditional roles, of course, have always been challenged. This has been particularly true of sex roles from the 1960s to the present time. Youth — women and men — have questioned their social positions and have taken steps to change or defy those structures imposed upon them. Fashion and style to some extent reflect the rebellion and the triumph of free choice over discipline. Thus the homosexual male community sets many fashion trends for both heterosexual men and women. Popular heroes have frequently ridden the wave of gender blending in the arts and entertainment. Tiny Tim, Boy George, and Michael Jackson provide some examples. They have been followed by trends in the 1980s such as 10-year-old boys wearing earrings and ponytails. There is also greater equality between the sexes, supported in legislation, and what appears to be an increase in the incidence of same-sexed relationships or homosexual life styles. In spite of these trends a large proportion of men and women live in traditional family arrangements and follow traditional sex roles. Even so-called liberated women living with men with or without children do the majority of the household tasks in spite of spending the same number of hours working outside the home. Thus traditional sex roles, in spite of being examined, experimented with, and to some extent liberated, are still deeply entrenched in society. They are part of the social structure in which we live, the mores and manners of everyday life, and the psychology of the sexes.

On the basis of the foregoing, it is clear that if a North American male pursues the role of an athlete, he becomes a study of role congruence. As long as he competes and wins, he is filling the North American ideal and will be rewarded materially and socially. For the female athlete the traditional role relationship is quite different. The sex-role stereotype for women, begun at an early age with emphasis upon her need for protection and submissiveness, domestication, and beauty, obviously clashes with the athletic role for the traditional woman. This makes the female athlete a study in role conflict. The male athlete can further secure his social identity by engaging in sport as a lifelong activity. The female athlete has typically either extended her social identity into the conflicting arena of sport, often to the benefit of her mental and physical health, or she has dropped her traditional feminine identity and sought a new identity in the role of athlete.

THE MALE ATHLETE: A STUDY OF UNSTABLE ROLE CONGRUENCE

The current body of knowledge about sex roles is richer than ever before, and one result has been a serious questioning of the implications of the male role stereotype. This questioning includes criticism of the value of the athletic ideal as it stands today. Those experiencing the athletic ethos have witnessed both its positive and negative features. Positive features tend to be the adulation and material rewards heaped upon the athletic hero. But with changing social values there are also strains attached to the role.

Stein and Hoffman (1978) examined the role strains of the male athlete and summarized seven major themes. The *first* was the ambiguity and anomie which resulted from conflicts surrounding the achievement of individuals as opposed to the cooperation needed for team membership. As the athletes advanced in level of competition they wanted to perform, and not sit on the sidelines. The camaraderie previously experienced subsided as such conflict grew. The athletes also found a shift in their own values over time. They gained less satisfaction from the competitive sport experience and found their peers often associated such competition with being dumb, having few social skills, having low political awareness, and being a bully. A *second* strain occurred in men who did not have the personality traits to back up the role expectations of the athlete: competitiveness, assertiveness, leadership, and confidence. This mismatch between personality and the goals prescribed by the role produced internal conflict. A *third* strain resulted from the inability to realize the goal of winning. Although some athletes played very well in their individual positions they felt strain if their team did not do well.

A *fourth* strain increased with the passage of time. The external rewards emanating from the athletic role diminished in value over time. The glory and prestige of performing in the big game began to lose its appeal. The scholarships for winning games and the enjoyment of practicing and of playing well did not compensate for the lack of personal enjoyment and role constrictions (for example being subjected to bed checks or practices seven days a week). A *fifth* strain resulted from the role conflicts of being an athlete while at the same time trying to meet other time commitments and other emotional involvements. The toughness, independence, nonemotionality, insensitivity, blocking of pain, and focusing upon the details of winning — while admired in high school — became increasingly questioned in university by both the athletes and the females with whom they associated. A *sixth* conflict resulted from role overload. The role of athlete increasingly impinged on other role demands, for example, those of friend, student, political activist, or other club member. Finally, the *seventh* strain developed around the experience of intrinsic anxiety over physical injury. Several athletes interviewed played with injuries, even broken bones, and several had operations in order to continue playing. Playing with pain and discomfort were expected by athletes. It was the norm to which they attempted to adjust.

Many have concluded that the idealizing of the "he-man" image in sport has made the athlete a pawn of a system that must be reexamined, a contention with which many athletes would agree. The question is: what happens to an athlete who is under continued pressure to conform to a "he-man" image which belies his true feelings and desires? Horney (1945) stated that by sanctioning the aggressive personality, society applauds it for being free of inhibitions, strong, and assertive. Yet that same personality is often emotionally impoverished, incapable of expressing love and affection, incapable of experiencing the subjective side of human nature, and incapable of enjoying the activities of others. Such imbalance in personality development does not serve the individual or society well. It was an important breakthrough when athletes began to criticize the dehumanization of the process they were forced to undergo in training. The conclusion Block (1973) reached in her review was that extreme sex-role typing leads to less personal maturity and individuation. This supports the athletes' own observations and fears that long-term sports involvement can be personally destructive. Block observes that an individual can achieve greater maturity by merging the major social traits of both sexes. Maccoby (1966) also concluded that development can be impeded by extreme sex-role typing. The expressions of aggression, mastery, and hyperactivity, typical of total male identification, lead to cognitive inattention and a lack of discipline. In contrast, the passivity of total female identification leads to cognitive deficits and a lowered ability to manipulate and deal with ideas. These findings, when considered along with the previous results on the athlete's personality, support why many athletes are concerned with their psychological identity and growth if they remain in the sports system.

Reports of role strain are not confined to university athletes, they are also present in elementary and high school athletes who have made a major role commitment to sport. The most frequent reason for considering dropping out of sport is its confinement; it often leaves little energy for development in other life activities. The young athlete usually enters sport seeking competence or because competence is promised. The competitive role demands levied by the athletic organization, parents, and coaches often go far beyond the athlete's competence development and begin to infringe on the possibilities of competence development in other areas (school, social, intellectual, artistic.)

Role conflicts are also apparent in the lives of professional athletes, as any survey on the adjustment problems of professional athletes will show. While the majority of male athletes used to survive, or seemed to survive, the excessive drinking, womanizing, and immaturities of the role through role conformity and group socialization, this is no longer obviously the case. There are now many serious repercussions from the role in terms of physical and psychological injuries. Alcoholism, drug addiction, and behavioral problems are rampant. Depression and suicide are not uncommon. Severe injuries occur too frequently (even to the point of quadriplegia). Injuries too frequently result in death. Boxing is notorious for its growing list of athletes who have died from injuries during competitions. The problems facing athletes who have peaked and are in their declining years are receiving renewed attention, as are the younger athletes who have suffered early heart attacks. On the one hand, aging boxers may injure themselves by fighting far past their prime, while on the other hand some young athletes drop out of sport early, missing some of their prime years. Ali and Frazier provide examples of the former while Heiden and Borg are examples of the latter. All of these reflect the difficulties and stresses associated with the role and life style of the respective sports.

Even though sport participation may thwart the male athlete's psychological development, he is socially supported in his role; his adjustment conforms to the mainstream of society. He may face some challenges from those who think along nonsexist lines and question the role ideal he epitomizes. He may be thrown into personal conflict when he himself begins to question and reject the athletic role. He may suffer from manifest conflict and adjust by reasserting his identity with the masculine role, thus increasing his dependence upon psychological defenses and heightening future conflict.

But the most serious conflict for male athletes is when time, the strongest opponent, begins to make headway. With age a decline in physical ability sets in, and the athlete experiences the passing of his image as the young, strong, competitive ideal of North America. A. E. Housman (1859-1936) immortalized the male athlete's conflict with age in his poem, "To An Athlete Dying Young;"

The time you won your town the race
We chaired you through the market-place;
Man and boy stood cheering by,
And home we brought you shoulder-high.

Today, the road all runners come,
Shoulder-high we bring you home,
And set you at your threshold down,
Townsman of a stiller town.

Smart lad, to slip betimes away
From fields where glory does not stay,
And early though the laurel grows
It withers quicker than the rose.

Eyes the shady night has shut
Cannot see the record cut,
And silence sounds no worse than cheers
After earth has stopped the ears.

Now you will not swell the rout
Of lads that wore their honors out,
Runners whom renown outran
And the name died before the man.

So set, before its echoes fade,
The fleet foot on the sill of shade,
And hold to the low lintel up
The still-defended challenge-cup.

And round that early-laureled head
Will flock to gaze the strengthless dead,

And find unwithered on its curls
The garland briefer than a girl's.*

The athlete is applauded for avoiding his athletic decline through death. Decline is not integrated into the athletic image, nor are diminished strength, immobility, and physical inactivity a part of the American ideal. In some countries where the role of the aged is a valued one such as in Japan, the athlete will face personal but not cultural conflict as he ages, for the culture has an equally valued role for him to assume in his later years. The adjustment is more difficult in North America, as the following lines illustrate:

Yeah, you're down and you're out, boy,
All the playin' is done,
You tried and you failed, boy,
And you ain't anyone...**

The athlete past his performance prime can salvage his identity by maintaining his promotional image, taking on business interests, keeping up former athletic associations, or guiding his children into athletic careers. Some former athletes maintain their link with sport by following it closely in their later years. Some completely turn their backs on it. Others may pursue different sports for pleasure.

The main buttress of the professional male athlete's ego is money. He is not used, he is bought, although he claims to be used if he is not paid handsomely. To the sports world the male athlete is also a social ideal. Through him people can be placated, inspired, conned, and aroused. They all want a piece of him and he sells these pieces symbolically. The successful male athlete is smothered with money, products, sex, and the unrestrained emotions of his fans. If he has been on the receiving end long enough and has managed his affairs well, he will be a wealthy, established man by the end of his playing days. He can then face his physical decline with status and security, and with the restless ease of a man who made it materially if not psychologically. However, this isn't always the case. Many athletes have "blown" their earnings along with their athletic abilities, and have ended up as broken men on alcohol or drugs. The end of the road for the male athlete presents him with his most difficult social role adjustment, since the years of his earlier career do not prepare him for this strain.

However, any athlete has two fortes with which to ease his physical decline into age: one is the sense of competence and self-confidence which he may have

*In L. Untermeyer, *Modern British Poetry* (New York: Harcourt, Brace, 1950), 94–95.
**Robert Coover. *The Universal Baseball Association, Inc.* Random House, Inc. 1968.

built up over his years in sport, and the other is his cooperative feelings for others whom he has met in sport. His sense of competence may continue to be expressed in veterans' or masters' events if it remains specific to the sport in which he has specialized. It can also be channeled into other fields of endeavor if he is inclined to business, hobbies, or social welfare. His sense of cooperation with fellow athletes and friends will be a positive and relatively permanent legacy from his sport career. Good examples of this type of adjustment in later life are various Australian Davis Cup team members, most of whom trained under coach Harry Hopman. Noted for their competence, team spirit, and camaraderie, players such as Sedgeman, Hoad, Rosewall, Emerson, Newcombe, and Stolle have persisted through the years. In contrast to some others in tennis who seem to conduct their lives solely for material purposes, the Australians have enjoyed the playing of tennis as well as the material advancement. That is, they continue their involvement in the game through their tennis ranches and schools but also continue to play for pleasure and social reasons and in tournaments even in advanced years.

We suggest that some of the horrendous problems so clearly evident in the aging American athletic hero could be alleviated if the system were to encourage competence motivation and cooperation in the early years instead of the individualism, egocentricity, and competitiveness that have been so dysfunctional to so many. Both professional leagues and sport associations are becoming increasingly aware of the problems of their ex-athletes and career, personal, and drug counselling are formally offered. Although some programs help in dealing with the problems created by sport, the problems addressed by these programs can only be dealt with fully by helping athletes before and not after they have entered the major leagues.

THE FEMALE ATHLETE: A STUDY OF ROLE CONFLICT AND CHANGE

The role conflicts of female athletes occur much earlier than those of the male and are not easily resolved. The female athlete will experience all of the role strains experienced by the male athlete and more. In spite of attempts to correct the inequality of opportunity between male and female athletes, extreme disparities persist in Europe, the United States, Canada and other occidental nations. Female athletic participation is largely determined by socioeconomic status and family tolerance of the athletic role for the female. Thus the prominent woman in sport is from a privileged home, giving her both financial and personal freedom, or she is from a lower or middle class home in which the family (usually the father) strongly endorses physical education, fitness, and/or sport involvement for women. Thus the backgrounds and attitudes of the parents are the crucial variable in determining the involvement of the female in sport.

Formerly it was common that one or both parents worked in physical education or one or both parents themselves were athletes. Increasingly, parental attitudes are mediated by the high reward system for Olympic medalists and for sports such as women's tennis and golf. However, in perspective, there is less social and material support for the female athlete than for the male athlete and fewer women pursue athletic careers.

Through constructive participation in sport and exercise women can experience the development of self. Self-image is enhanced. Snyder and Kivlin (1975) compared female collegiate athletes to nonathletes and reported that the athletes showed more psychological well-being and more positive attitudes toward almost all of their bodily features such as posture, body build, legs, and waist. Further, when Snyder and Spreitzer (1977) compared the well being of groups of female students engaged in: (1) no sport, (2) sport, (3) music and sport, and (4) music, they found the students participating in one activity (sport or music) were higher on well-being and intellectual ability than nonparticipating students. But the students participating in two activities (sport and music) showed the highest ability and well-being of all. Furthermore their participation was mediated by parental encouragement. The well-being associated with female athletic participation is well documented in other supporting studies (for example see Vincent, 1977). It is to the advantage of women that attitudes have changed since the 1950s, when many considered it unladylike to engage in sport.

In spite of these changes, there is still a stigma attached to the role of female athlete. Women who depend upon the role of athlete for their major identity carry a triple burden. *First,* like her male counterpart, she will behave in an increasingly agentic, assertive, competitive, and independent manner, which may well cut her off from some of the expressive skills most women possess. *Second,* for many women athletes there is something of a vacuum as they move up the competitive ladder. That is, there are many more promising female athletes than there are professional positions to fill. *Third,* if she makes it to the professional ranks and has the opportunity to reap the financial and social rewards, the female athlete must often pretend to be what she is not for the purpose of her public and her sponsors. This duality usually has to do with presenting a public image which will appeal to a broad base of women for the purposes of selling cosmetics, clothing styles, sport equipment, and youth products. Such sponsors are rarely amenable to overt masculinity in female athletes. The question of whether outstanding female athletes are indeed more masculine than other women will be dealt with more thoroughly in Chapter 12 (pp. 139–144).

Within the traditional framework of social values, the woman pursuing an athletic career is pursuing a male role. The role of athlete and the role of female are opposed. The aggressiveness, strength, competitiveness, and independence of the male and female athlete are in sharp contrast to the submission, sensitivity, weakness, and dependence prescribed for the female position. How does the female athlete resolve this conflict?

The female athlete may not enter the field of sport with the breadth of identity common to most women of her age. She is often much more dependent for her identity upon her immediate family. To the extent that the family screens her from stereotyped roles and values, she may not even be aware of the cultural conflicts between her athletic pursuits and her femaleness. In this way the family acts as a buttress for the developing female athlete. Hall (1973) found that family attitudes were one of the most significant factors accounting for female athletic participation. Snyder and Spreitzer (1983, pp. 67–73), among others, have confirmed this result. As the female athlete becomes increasingly aware of her dilemma, she often seeks to resolve it by trying to fulfill the expectations of both roles. Chi Cheng, track champion, conveyed this attitude when asked how she dealt with the public's perception of masculinity in female athletes; she replied that she took every opportunity to "show off" her femininity in public. She said that athletes are like other women in bed even though the public perceives them as masculine (Hart, 1971). American distance runner, Vicki Foltz, when asked about femininity hang-ups answered (Rohrbaugh, 1979, p. 30): "Yes, I have lots of hang-ups. You wouldn't believe it. I always worry about looking nice in a race. I worry about my calf muscles getting big. But mostly I worry about my hair ... I suppose it's because so many people have said women athletes look masculine. So a lot of us try, subconsciously maybe, to look as feminine as possible in a race. There are always lots of hair ribbons in races." In summary, to avoid being stereotyped and considered masculine, some female athletes go to great lengths to exhibit their femininity. Some women genuinely fill both roles, the female and the athlete. For others the flaunting of femininity is a display only of outwardly appearances, as the individual remains closely identified with her family and maintains an immature sexual identity. Others seek to fulfill only the requirements of the athletic role and present the well-known image of the female "jock," denying all femininity. These three types of adjustment may be called: (1) the feminine type, (2) the hysteric type, and (3) the instrumental (or jock) type. To these two more types can be added: (4) the liberated type and (5) the image maker. The liberated type is comfortable and confident with herself and will be herself regardless of situational demands. The image maker will manipulate the media and/or be in the hands of a promotional agent. She will present herself to the public in keeping with the demands of sponsors, her tour, and her most marketable image.

These five adaptations reflect psychological adjustments that are apparent in the woman's behavior. In the first case, the feminine type, she behaves like an athlete when performing, but elsewhere reveals typical feminine behaviors. Margaret Court is ostensibly an example in that she combined a career of tennis champion with that of wife and mother. When she first won the Wimbledon championship as Margaret Smith in 1963, she spoke of her lack of fulfillment in the role of world tennis champion. She retired shortly thereafter to open a boutique in Perth, Australia, and after marrying Barry Court she made a tennis comeback. Such women, who psychologically need to fill the traditional female role, may be "good competitors," but usually they will express their displeasure in the singular pursuit of athletic goals. Chris Evert is another appropriate example of a female tennis player who has attempted to fill both the athletic and female roles. It is of interest to note that both Court and Evert have suffered serious emotional setbacks during their lives which caused them to question either their careers, their mental stability, or their marriages. Their difficulties demonstrate perhaps the conflict inherent in fulfilling both the female and the athletic role.

In the second adjustment, the hysteric type will superficially conform to the feminine role. In this case, the sexually immature athlete, the "girl" will often be excessively coquettish and flirtatious. She pays lip service to the demands of femininity, but her heart is in her athletic career. Athletics may psychologically represent for her a way to gain attention, privilege, and the admiration of people who are significant to her. Her behavior fills a narcissistic-exhibitionistic need. Until she matures she will be unlikely to take on a full feminine role. An example of this adjustment is another female tennis player. She reports that she always experienced a high degree of stimulation from undressing in front of a man and seeing him aroused. She would go no further in her sexual exploits. Her enjoyment of performing in tennis tournaments brought her somewhat the same sense of elation. She continued entering tournaments into her fifties and beyond, always giving minute attention to dress and appearance.

The third adjustment, denial of the female role altogether, was formerly accompanied by social stigma. The woman would busy herself in the athletic subculture, often teaching physical education in a school where there were no men to challenge her role. An example is Leila Lombardi, racing car driver. Fox (1975) described her American racing debut. Lombardi dressed, acted, and drove like a man. When she was eighteen the priest in her Italian village called her attention to the female role she was expected to fill. She did not fill it and instead isolated herself from social expectations and developed competence and an identity of her own in racing circles. In tennis, golf, basketball, pool, and wrestling there are circuits of play which offer a professional life to many such "masculine" women. In body structure, manners, style, speech, and action, these outstanding female athletes frequently epitomize stereotypical male and not female role presentation. A recent development in women's sport has been the legitimization of the athletic role for women, causing many instrumental or "masculine" types to evolve into the "image making" type, or adjustment number five.

Adjustment four, the liberated or independent type, is clearly the adjustment to which most modern women would aspire. The independent women is the ideal result of the women's movement. She is someone above and beyond her gender role identity. She does not role play and has absorbed few of the sex structures to which Locksley and Colten (1979) refer. She may be raising a family with a husband or lover or by herself. She may work outside the home in athletics or other lines or be a full-time performing athlete. She is independent, free, and unfettered by social role prescriptions for the positions she occupies. It is quite difficult to find examples of individuals who are fully liberated from sex-role prescriptions in spite of the expectation that one would find great numbers in the athletic movement. Germaine Greer (1984) and others have turned to the theme "biology is destiny," and if one accepts that position, to be fully liberated, one would have to be liberated from one's own sexuality. The other alternative is the androgynous type of adjustment where the individual shows the qualities of both sexes. However, many androgynous persons are hardly vehicles of ideal adjustment and, as previously cited (p. 115–117), optimal adjustment seems to accompany masculine styles since most social reward will result. Thus in suggesting possible examples of independent or autonomous athletic women, one can only judge by life style and career. The following are possibilities: Debbie Brill, high jump champion; Jane Frederick, former Olympic pentathaloner; and Joan Benoit, marathoner. All of these athletes, by outward appearances, seem thoroughly themselves and have given long and loyal service to their sports and competitions.

The fifth adjustment, which we have called "the image makers," refers to those athletes who have stepped from the athletic ranks in a blaze of glory into commercialism, sport as entertainment and profit. The career of Billie Jean King provides an example. She emerged from a lower-middle-class Californian background to tennis and media supremacy. She believed tennis competence should be rewarded with money, and she rose to a position of leadership with two tides: one of women's rights and the other of commercial backing for competitive sport. Ms. King accepted the competitive and material ethic of the (male) role and strove for a small number of women to do likewise. Though some would wish to cast BJK as the "liberated type," she is perhaps better classified as an "image-maker" in view of her subscribing to the public institution of marriage while her personal behavior involved a "lesbian marriage" lasting many years. Always "instrumental" in mannerism, attitude, and competitiveness, BJK seemed to hide behind the conformity of marriage until unmasked. When Seligson (1984) asked BJK, during an interview when she was 40 years of age, why she didn't downplay the Barnett lawsuit, she replied: "I could have. I thought it was the right thing to do at the time. Even though I knew I was going to blow my image." The image makers are torn between their conflicting desires to please others while at the same time to do well for themselves. They are encouraged by commercial sponsors to present themselves in a manner acceptable to the public.

Athletes falling within the feminine, hysteric, and image making types are often complimented and appreciated for their femininity as much as for their athletic performances. A "good looking" woman may obtain recognition from the sport world even if her athletic ability is not outstanding. A female athlete who desires success may play upon her own femininity even though she does not experience it. It will attract fans, impress officials, and encourage sponsors. McDermott (1982) writes how relieved women's golf organizers were in 1981 when they found they could use Jan Stephenson's image to salvage the sport just after BJK's lesbianism had "almost knocked a wheel off the apple cart of women's sports." Stephenson, who got support from both golfing parents, is perhaps closer to her father who reportedly writes to her almost every day. She says she "wouldn't do anything he (her father) wouldn't be proud of." Although her looks are being used to prop up the image of women's golf, Stephenson revealingly says: "If you took me away from the golf tour, I'd be just another pretty face." She also summarizes the conflicts between professional sport and the usual female choices of life style, expressing at the same time her highly conservative attitudes: "I've considered giving up golf for a man but golf's part of my life, so I have to compromise. I compromise my whole life for golf."

The role of the female athlete has been thrust forward into public and professional attention in recent years. It has become a frequent subject in symposia and in sports articles. Many of these feature detailed examinations of the sex-role position and problems of female athletes (Hall, 1978; Harris, 1980; Popma, 1980, Oglesby, 1984; Bredemeier, 1984). The apparent changes notwithstanding, the female athlete stands on the threshold of freedom and her future development is still in question. The conflicts of the female athlete over the past decade are made vivid in Barbara Lamblin's poem "First Peace:"*

i was the all american girl, the winner, the champion,
the swell kid, good gal, national swimmer,
model of the prize daughter bringing it home for dad
i even got the father's trophy

i was also a jock, dyke, stupid dumb blonde
frigid, castrating, domineering bitch,
called all these names in silence,
the double standard wearing me down
inside

on the victory stand winning my medals
for father and coach
and perhaps a me deep down somewhere
who couldn't fail because of all the hours
and training and tears
wrapped into an identity of muscle and power
and physical strength
a champion,

not softness and grace

now at thirty-one, still suffering from the overheard
locker room talk, from the bragging and swaggering
the stares past my tank suit
insults about my muscles
the fears, the nameless fears
about my undiscovered womanhood
disturbing unknown femininity,
femaleness

feminine power.

The pain and confusion of conflict suffered by the young athlete become the
legacy of the mature one. Note that the major conflict is between the expectations of those close to her, father and coach, and the lack of understanding
from society at large. In the poem the answer to the conflict was "feminine
power." How is feminine power to be interpreted?

To the extent that women athletes are skill and competence oriented, the
movement of women to the forefront of the athletic arena will be a good thing
for sport and for the personal development of the athletes. There are many
studies demonstrating high self-esteem in female athletic participants (Vincent,
1977; Snyder and Spreitzer, 1983; Balazs, 1975; Lerch, 1976; and Colker and
Widom, 1980.) If women athletes are oriented toward competitiveness and
aggression, their presence will be damaging to sport, for it will help to sustain
sport within its old limited and destructive mold. Although such participation
may lead to feelings of achievement and material success for these women, it
will encourage the same limited identity exhibited by the male athlete. Unfortunately, many successful women athletes have made the latter adjustment.
They have faced difficulties and conflicts in achieving their positions, and now
want the same recognition and status they see given to men.

It is not only in sport that women must think carefully about the path they
will follow. Women have always held the major responsibility for some of the
most crucial and significant functions in society. The socialization of children,
childbirth, childcare, offering emotional insight, comforting, and keeping of the
home are only some of the important but unpaid tasks women have carried.
Lott (1973) and more recently Greer (1984) are two of the many researchers
and thinkers asking for a reconsideration of what roles women need to be
assisted with, as opposed to liberated from, in that they must be acknowledged
as not only essential but top in terms of social priority. The skills and insights

---

*Quoted by Marie Hart, "Stigma or Prestige." From Barbara Lamblin's *My Skin Barely Covers Me.* An Uncle John's Sports Art Publication, Perris, Ca. 1975.

honed through the female role need not only to be supported, but also applied in positions of cultural and political leadership.

PERFORMANCE AND SEX GAPS

Women have about 53 to 60 percent of the muscular strength of men, 70 to 80 percent of the lung ventilation and oxygen intake, and about 50 percent of the improvement in muscle strength after training. In sports requiring strength, speed, skill, and endurance, women's performances are approximately 70 to 80 percent those of men. There are counterpositions on the above figures which were reported by Zaharieva (1971). First, some, such as Shaffer (1972) call attention to the strengths of the sexes in discrete areas. If one concentrates upon the above measures, men are stronger, but if one concentrates upon susceptibility to disease, child mortality, and life expectancy, women are stronger. Thus, many sports — tennis is one   favor the strength of men. Secondly, another group, such as Scott (1974) and Wilmore (1974), argue that over the centuries women have been docile and sedentary. Now that women are becoming increasingly active and competitive they are closing the gaps in previous records. For example the 1974 100 meter dash record was 9.9 seconds for men and 10.8 seconds for women. Twenty-five years earlier it was 10.2 for men and 11.5 for women. If we look at the closing of the gap from 1928 to 1984, there is some indication that the closing of the gap may have peaked. In 1928 the difference was 2 seconds, in 1960 it was 1 second, while in 1984 it was 1.04 seconds. However for the marathon the difference in 1976 was 28 minutes 24 seconds, in 1980 it was 16 minutes 29.6 seconds, and in 1983 it was 14 minutes and 30 seconds. Dyer (1976a, 1976b, 1982) is a strong proponent of social factors limiting the performance records of female athletes. By examining records crossculturally and over time he notes the gaps collapsing between the sexes and states that he can envisage the day when no gaps will exist. He claims that at the least it will be possible to equate such social factors as opportunity and encouragement so that the question of physiological differences can be accurately tackled. In this writer's view, it is doubtful that this will ever happen. Competitive equality may be possible for tasks which favor female physiology. However, it is probably impossible for those which do not in view of the inherited constitutional differences between the sexes as reported in reviews by Bardwick (1971), Hutt (1972), and Maccoby and Jacklin (1974).

It is important to emphasize that there are immense differences in the physiologies required in different sports. As Dyer points out, in many ways swimming, for example, favors women due to their advanced maturity in adolescence and due to additional body fat (26 percent in the average woman student, 12 percent in an average male) in long distance events. Boys in adolescence have not developed the strength they will ultimately have in adulthood. On the other hand in sports such as football or tennis, it is difficult to conceive of women ever overtaking men in serious competition. Strength, weight, and aggression are required in these sports and in almost all sports in which men outrank women. It is conceivable that given a quirk of nature, yielding an atypical physiology, a woman could match a man at the top of his sport prowess. But this has never occurred to the writer's knowledge. The collapsing of some records for women may be due not only to their increasing adaptation to sports in which they have little experience and social support but also to steroid use and other strength-gaining devices which may soon be illegal and better policed than they are today. When women train hard and decrease body fat to below 10 percent of body weight for any sport, they are likely to cease menstruating (Bonen and Keizer, 1984). This is common in marathon runners, track athletes, skiers, tennis players, and ballet dancers − to name but a few. Thus to be "in shape," many women become less feminine, that is, they give up the reproductive cycle (which resumes when hard training ceases and body fat increases). In conclusion, there is no way a functioning female, even though outstanding, will be able to compete against an outstanding male in most sports.

What awaits the female athlete, psychologically, after her arrival at the top of the sports circuit? First, she will usually play in an all-female group. Many of her fellow participants will be extreme personality types because they subscribe to an atypical role described previously. The world of professional female athletics is "cutthroat." In order to meet the competitive role requirements, the participants often express even more extreme personality traits than male athletes. They are competitive and often "supercontrolled" emotionally while on the sport field. In off-competition hours they tend to maintain that adjustment, yielding a "superbusiness" type, or they otherwise compensate in becoming a type that impresses one as bored and confused with much emotional "spilling over." This may be displayed in anger, tears, jealousy, or various sexual activities. The reader is referred to Rita Mae Brown's (1983) novel for an inside sketch of women's tennis, with which she was very familiar. Brown had just finished a lengthy relationship with Martina Navratilova. There are, of course, some women athletes who show strong competence motivation and provide a stabilizing influence on their sport. However, the female competitor in professional athletics has tended to take on the worst attributes of the male athletic role. The cooperation, compassion, and broader communal identity of the female tend to become submerged. Unfortunately, one must conclude that, save for a few, the professional female athlete has not merely been bought for a time. She has sold out.

12
Sexuality in Sport

LEVELS OF SEXUAL DIFFERENTIATION

The relationship between sex-role behavior and sexual behavior is not clear cut. There is, however, a tendency for individuals who fill extreme male or female role positions to manifest the sexual behavior expected of that role. But since sexual feelings and behaviors are usually private, whereas sex-role behavior is public, the two need not always converge. Thus social scientists now refer to *gender identity* when describing a person's feelings of maleness and femaleness. *Sexual preference* refers to a person's attraction to males or females and this can be heterosexual, homosexual, or bisexual.

There are many levels of sexual identification, so that even the qualities of maleness or femaleness may be defined at different levels. The same individual may be identified as male at one level and as female at another, and this has caused difficulty and controversy surrounding the admission of some athletes into female events at the Olympics. Hampson and Hampson (1961), MacBryde (1964), and Money (1973) have researched and published studies concerning these levels. Figure 6 is adapted from MacBryde's book.

One would expect indexes taken on any individual at each of these levels to be highly interrelated, which is true. Yet they need not be, and individuals with hermaphroditic, bisexual, and homosexual adjustments result. Hampson and Hampson (1961) have contended that the critical period for gender role learning occurs around two or three years of age for children in a hermaphroditic group. Children who had their sex roles reversed after three had lasting difficulties readjusting to their new role assignment. More recent opinion has been that gender identity and gender role dispositions are far from neuter at birth. Money (1980; Money and Ehrhardt, 1972) has noted the extreme importance of chromosomes, antigens, and fetal and pubertal hormones. His model for the development of gender identity and gender role is reproduced in Figure 7. Note the feeding in on the right of prenatal antigens (H-Y antigen), and later, pubertal hormones. Adult gender and role identity evolves as the result of a complex and continuous interaction between biological and social factors.

Of especial interest to sport behavior is a syndrome described by Money and Ehrhardt (1972, pp. 95–114) as *fetally androgenized genetic females,* the

Level	How it is Identified	Origin
1. Chromosomal sex	Direct chromosomal count of cells grown in tissue culture	Parental germ cell
2. Nuclear sex	Buccal smear, sections of peripheral tissue	Sex chromatin
3. Gonadal sex	Histologic appearance	Medullary and cortical components of primitive bipotential gonad
4. Genital ducts	Pelvic exploration	Mullerian ducts, Wolffian ducts
5. External genitalia	Inspection, urethroscopy	Genital tubercle, urethral folds, labioscrotal folds, urogenital sinus
6. Hormonal sex	Secondary sex characteristics	Secretory cells of testes, ovaries and adrenals
7. Gender role	Social comportment, mannerism and dress, direction of sex drive	Neuter at birth

Figure 6. Levels of Sexual Differentiation. Although the above levels of sexual differentiation are usually consistent within a given individual, they need not be. Level two, nuclear sex, is currently used in Olympic sex tests. The greatest number of deviations for consistency on the levels occur with level seven, gender role. Although individuals adopting the dress and mannerisms of members of the opposite sex are now treated more tolerantly than when the above levels were described, those adopting homosexuality or lesbianism are still considered to deviate from the social norm. Historically this has not always been the case in all cultures. Note that Van Wyk considers gender role to be neuter at birth. Today, after much debate and study, most of those working in the area of sex roles and sexual development would choose to divide gender role itself into several levels or types of expression, which also could be disparate. (Adapted from J. J. Van Wyk in O. O. Williams, *Textbook of Endocrinology.* 4th ed. (Philadelphia: Saunders, 1968), 516. Reproduced in C. M. MacBryde, ed., *Signs and Symptoms: Applied Pathologic Physiology and Clinical Interpretation* (Toronto: Lippincott, 1964, 24. Reprinted by permission.)

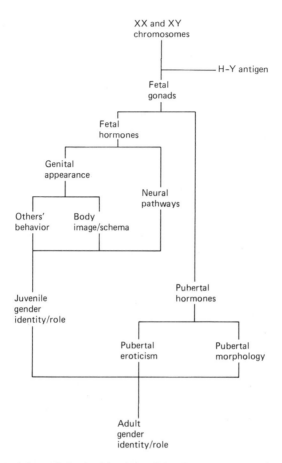

Figure 7. The Aetiology of Gender Identity and Gender Role. From Money (1980) with permission. Money and Ehrhardt's model features the influence of prenatal hormones (H-Y antigen) which feed into development between the chromosomal and fetal gonads components. Following the prolonged influence of fetal hormones on the physiological and social components on the left, pubertal hormones emerge at adolescence (on right hand of model) and influence adult gender and role comportments.

syndrome of progestin-induced hermaphroditism. Due to drugs administered to mothers during the 1950s to avoid miscarriage, the authors were able to study 10 cases of prenatally induced hermaphroditism in individuals who were genetically female. The drugs caused masculinization of the clitoris, a condition corrected surgically when the masculinization is incomplete. No further surgical or hormonal treatment is necessary because at puberty the girl's own ovaries function normally, feminizing the body and inducing menstruation, although it may be late. To this were added 15 cases of fetally androgenized genetic females, the female androgenital syndrome in which the adrenal glands do not function. The dysfunction begins in fetal life. This causes the release of androgen and again the masculinization of the external genital region but not of the internal functions. When such a condition is discovered, surgical and hormonal intervention allows these children to be raised as girls. Cortisone therapy, which was developed in the 1950s, is used.

The authors were thus able to study 25 fetally androgenized females. They were interviewed in depth and compared with 25 matched control participants. When the study was carried out the children ranged in age from 4 to 16 years. The 50 mothers of the girls were also interviewed. Certain behavioral patterns characterized the girls in the experimental group, and these included: tomboyism as a long-term way of life, high energy expenditure in recreation and aggressive activities, liking of utilitarian and functional clothing rather than feminine clothing, avoidance of childhood sexual play, choice of masculine play objects and rejection of dolls, rejection of plans for maternal roles and motherhood, preference of career goals as opposed to marriage goals, little interest in romance and boyfriends, and no apparent indication of lesbian tendencies. The conclusion: "tomboyism is the sequel to masculinizing effects on the fetal brain."

Biological factors may have a profound influence on an individual's comportment and style of life. In addition, human behavior is immensely influenced through the process of socialization. When the foregoing is extrapolated to the athlete, two possible conclusions emerge. The first is that the extreme role stances are inherent in the athlete's biology. The second is that role stance could be developed over time due to the socialization of athletes and the demands of the life style which the athlete is adapting to. There is no doubt that the extreme training regimens which the athlete shoulders, such as specialized weight training, aerobic and physical conditioning, and constant and continued activity, could lead to physical changes within the person. A good example of this, discussed in the preceding chapter, is the female athlete's cessation of menstruation when she trains to below 10 percent body fat. Menstruation will resume when lighter training is adopted. In the case of the male athlete, training is toward greater muscle mass, strength, and aerobic activity. Many athletes try to increase performance by taking testosterone derivatives, steroids, growth hormones, etc. The conclusion: induced androgenization and high levels of performance in many sports are related.

SEX AND THE MALE ATHLETE

Eysenck, Nias, and Cox (1982, pp. 22 to 26) have compared sexual activity to sport since many men, they report, associate sex with fun and pleasure rather than with serious commitment. Omitting the long-term emotional commitment which many people like to associate with love and sex, the fact is, write Eysenck et al., that there are extremely different styles of sexual behavior associated with personality types, and the personality type that characterizes athletes also characterizes those of high sexual activity.

The research program included a number of specific predictions about extraverts with regard to their sexual activity, namely: (1) they will have intercourse earlier than introverts; (2) they will have intercourse more frequently than introverts; (3) they will display more varied sexual behavior outside of intercourse; (4) they will use more different positions in intercourse than introverts; and (5) they will display longer precoital lovemaking than introverts. These predictions stood up in studies by Eysenck (1976), Zuckerman et al. (1972), and Giese and Schmidt (1968) in both males and females. Thus Eysenck concludes: "there is no doubt about the greater heterosexual activity of extraverts along the lines predicted." (1976, p. 26). Upon reexamining Chapter 9 on personality, and the predictions of a high degree of extraversion and stability in outstanding athletes, one may conclude that a high degree of sexual activity among athletes is expected.

HOMOSEXUALITY AND THE MALE ATHLETE

In recent years the terms "latent homosexuality" has been applied to male athletes moving in exclusively all-male groups. Their compensatory interest in sexual exploits has also been noted along with a narcissistic interest in their own bodies and physical development. Although these characteristics do exist, they should not be categorized as homosexuality. The athletic role is, rather, an extreme form of social adaptation encouraging a skew toward shallowness, drive, and a striving for superiority. Sexuality, in terms of biological stimulation and physiological consummation, with women as objects, is compatible with such a role. The cultivation of sexual bonds with other males, even on a fleeting basis, would be incompatible. The emotional bonding between male athletes may be more often a sign of desire for physical and emotional contact with others without aiming for sexual consummation. The male athlete, then, somewhat warped by an extreme role identification, makes his emotional and sexual adjustment as best he can. For most this means a pursuit of the values he holds important — activity and achievement — while neglecting the potential development of the more subjective and emotional sides of his personality. Many male athletes have observed the "use of women" as part of their athletic role, as illustrated in the writings of McRae (1974), Shaw (1972), Rentzel (1972), and Meggyesy (1970).

This does not imply that there is no homosexual behavior among male athletes. Indeed, self-love and egocentricity may partially lay the groundwork for some homosexual behaviors. Many taunts occur in sport over so-called deviance, that is, of self-love and egocentricity. A prominent example was when Daley Thompson, 1984 Olympic decathalon gold medalist, baited American sprinter Carl Lewis by wearing a T-shirt to his victory press conference with the slogan: "Is the world's second greatest athlete gay?" The slogan referred to the rumored, but denied, sexual orientation of Lewis, whom the American press had long touted as the world's greatest athlete. After withdrawing from professional baseball, Glenn Burke (see p. 113) claimed at least a dozen top players were homosexual. He felt driven out of baseball because of the nonconformity of his homosexual orientation to baseball norms. David Kopay (1977) wrote about his perspectives as a homosexual playing in the National Football League. One of the greatest tennis players of all time, Bill Tilden (Deford, 1975a, 1975b), had a history of homosexual behavior before being arrested and convicted in California in 1946 and 1949 of soliciting minors. He died in 1953. Tilden was treated with intolerance after his conviction of homosexuality, in contrast to the nonchalance with which Europeans have treated their tennis players who were similarly inclined. For example, Germany's successful player, Baron Gottfried von Cramm, was long admired until the Nazis jailed him on an alleged homosexual morals charge, which ultimately prevented his admission to the United States. He nevertheless lived an eventful life until killed in a car accident on the Cairo to Alexandria highway in 1976 at age 67.

In some sports, figure skating for example, homosexuality is thought common. When top performers are homosexual there is concern for the socialization of younger boys coming up in the sport. It is reported that figure skating judges grade down for overtly homosexual gestures in competition. This poses an interesting conflict in view of the association of male homosexuality with creative and artistic freedom and the life styles of many creative artists. In our (Butt, 1979c) studies of figure skaters, the men involved in figure skating rated themselves as close to their mothers. This resulted in the hypothesis that mothers were dominant in the homes and therefore a female aesthetic prevails which the boy portrays in his figure skating. In figure skating one finds a similar ethos to ballet, in which many male dancers since the outstanding Nijinsky have been homosexual. Note the concern shown by the press and, reportedly, President Reagan, when his son wanted to become a ballet dancer. Many parents would have theirs sons beaten up on the football field to be sure of their sexual identity even at the expense of their physical survival.

PRENATAL HORMONE SECRETION – THE CASE CONTINUED

To what degree is sexual comportment and sexual preference dictated by environmental and social influences and to what extent is it inborn as a result of biological influences such as prenatal hormone secretions? Homosexual orientations may, more often than not, be present in a child at an early age and therefore an early predisposition is assumed. In a recent study based on 1,500 participants in the San Francisco Bay area Bell, Weinberg, and Hammersmith (1981) concluded that there is little evidence for the analytic theory that poor emotional relationships with parents (for example, a weak father and a dominating mother in the male) cause homosexuality. Using path analysis for both sexes, an important factor in predicting homosexual adjustment in adulthood is gender nonconformity in childhood. That is, the boys tended to be indifferent to or to dislike boys' activities. The girls were tomboys and preferred boys' activities in childhood. Although gender nonconformity does not always predict adult homosexuality, the authors conclude that such behavior does seem to flag an early predisposition far outweighing the more common analytic and sociological theorizing. Gender nonconformity is not a necessary prelude to homosexuality because some homosexual men are masculine in childhood and beyond and some homosexual men are feminine. Therefore at least two styles of homosexuality are suggested.

The first style is *homosexuality* per se, which exists when an individual acts out sexual behaviors (and roles) typical of his or her own genetic sex. But the sexual behavior is directed toward a member of the same sex in preference to the opposite sex. In this style one finds masculine men loving other men and feminine women loving other women.

The second style of homosexuality is *inversion,* in which the role behavior and sexual behavior is more typical of, the opposite sex. The individual is strongly identified with the gender identity of the opposite sex. Therefore strictly speaking (if one accepts the identity which the person has adopted), the individual is not psychologically involved in homosexual behavior. He or she is much more accurately described as inverted, or turned into the opposite, a term which we have borrowed from Havelock Ellis (1910), but used more specifically than he has.

With male athletes, one would expect to find less homosexual behavior than in the general population. This is because inverted types, except for sports which portray female artistic impressions, are all but excluded from participation in sport which requires the strength, speed, and bulk of men. Inverted male styles are much more compatible with art, music, ballet, theatre, hair styling, design and fashion — occupations which, in fact, support some of the common social stereotypes of "homosexual" men. Such styles are more explainable by the fetal brain hormone theory than are homosexual styles. Green (1974) studied feminine boys over time and found half had become bisexual or "homosexual" as adults. More recently Gladue, Green, and Hellman (1984) gave volunteer groups of homosexual men, heterosexual men, and heterosexual women doses of estrogen. They measured the blood level concentration of luteinizing hormone which facilitates ovulation in women before and after the estrogen doses. There was little change in the luteinizing hormone level of the heterosexual men, but the level in homosexual men became elevated and fell between that of the heterosexual men and the women. Thus hormonal responsiveness was related to homosexuality, or what we would prefer to call "inversion".

Animal studies suggest the viability of the fetal hormone theory, although no consistent hormonal differences between homosexual and heterosexual persons have been demonstrated. It is important therefore to consider both the alternatives of (1) "neuroendocrine responsiveness" described above and (2) that a hormonal effect could have operated at any critical and limited period during development and therefore be undetectable at other times. Feder (1984) critically discusses the effects of hormones on the brain and their implications for human behavior. Reviewing the effects of hormones on sex role, sexual orientation, and gender identity, he concludes that a deterministic relationship has not been demonstrated. He does note that hyperandrogenization of 23 women in the United States treated with corticoids in adulthood yielded 10 with bisexual fantasies and 4 with bisexual experiences. None were exclusively homosexual (Ehrhardt et al., 1968). Feder (p. 189) also notes that plasma androgen level is associated with social rank (Eberhardt et al., 1980) and that social factors, such as rank, may alter the secretion of androgen. Sexual behavior in men is known to be partly dependent upon androgen (p. 189).

In conclusion, because of the congruence between hormonal activity level, gender role conformity in childhood, personality development, and the role expectations of male athletes, one would predict a high degree of heterosexual activity and a low degree of homosexual activity in male athletes. This is in spite of the well-documented cases of homosexual male athletes some of which have been noted. This conclusion is further supported by the virtual absence of homosexuality of the inverted variety in many sports. These conclusions are theoretically based and, given the present state of knowledge, seem to be the most reasonable speculations. The field awaits definitive study both through frank interviews with representative athletes from all sports and through further investigation of the hormonal influences on behavior across time.

SEX AND THE FEMALE ATHLETE

The sexuality of the female athlete has recently become of great public interest. The lesbian interests of Billie Jean King (1982) and Martina Navratilova (1985), the desires and success of Richard Raskind (Richards, 1984) in becoming a woman, the widespread use of masculinizing steroids and ergogenic aids, the cessation of menstruation in women during hard training, the failure of some female athletes to pass sex tests, and the publication of Stella Walsh's hermaphroditism are just a few of the landmarks that have increased attempts to understand the sexual adjustments of women athletes.

The female athlete occupies an extreme social position. In the past there was no firm social role attached to her athletic position but she pleased society best when she looked and acted feminine over and above her athletic pursuits. Her excellence at sport was then tolerated by the public. Recent developments have legitimized the athletic role for women. The feminist movement, television coverage and sponsorship of women's sport have made possible lucrative careers in golf, skiing, skating, and tennis. On the other hand women's basketball, ice hockey, volleyball, and field hockey have not fared well commercially. There are few outstanding careers in track (notable exceptions are Decker and Benoit), although several women do support themselves on the track circuit. Rowing, trap shooting, squash, and badminton also produce few lucrative career opportunities. Yet there are outstanding female athletes in these sports, some of whom are fighting for the legitimacy already won in other sports.

Nevertheless, the roles of dedicated female athletes tend to confuse as well as charm the public. To any outsider observing women's sport at close range, the inevitable questions will surface: "Who are those women who compete and live together on closely knit tours, or crash their way into coed basketball or hockey games? Are they lesbians who hate men, or rejected heterosexuals who want to get back at men? Are they rebelling against their parents' orderly ways of life, or being pushed toward fame by stage mothers and fathers? Do they sneer at sexiness, glamour and marriage — or secretly covet a 'normal' life?" The above quote from *Newsweek* (June 3, 1974, p. 52), reflects a typical conservative view from outside of women's sport. As one moves closer to the inner circles, perceptions and views on women athletes become more varied. Female athletes have "hangers on" just as there are "groupies" or "Bimbos" who follow male sporting circuits. Athletic women have also been conveyed to the public via commercial sponsorship and have become much sought after by sponsors and commercial interests. There have always been a group of men and women who admire and desire strong women and who will side with women's issues as husbands, lovers, sponsors, friends, or circuit personnel. A good example of this is Britain's Teddy Tinling (Deford, 1984), a prominent designer of tennis clothes, who continued to play an important role in parts of the women's tennis circuit.

In the current climate the female athlete may be commended for her athletic feats, but she will be doubly praised by the heterosexually biased media, sponsors, most fans and organizers if she also displays feminine traits. These traits do not include promiscuity, but rather the display of feminine mannerisms, appearances, and emotions. The built-in role conflicts of the female athlete have already been discussed (see Chapter 11, pp. 123 to 130). In societies where much is expected from and attributed to sexual identifications, behaviors, and roles, one must ask how the female athlete, who is often atypical on these dimensions, perseveres against the tide.

In recent years there has been a great debate about whether participation in sport is associated with masculinity in women. In the language of the social sciences: are instrumentally oriented women drawn into sport? And does involvement in sport make women more instrumental in behavior and outlook? The answer to both of these questions is "yes." As long as the status quo model in sport as conveyed in hockey, basketball, rowing, running, tennis, and so on prevails, then strength, speed, skill, and competitive assertion will be important. Thus larger, stronger, and more masculine women who are trained to the same criteria as male athletes will be the best. They will tend to rise to the top of the competitive ladder and will tend to reach the highest status among female athletes. Thereafter they will reap rewards similar to that of the male athlete. A woman following the traditional expressive role will find it difficult to fill the role of athlete, particularly if she has strong emotional commitments outside of sport. Note that we are not stating that an expressive woman *cannot* make it in the sport world if she is well trained, determined, and coordinated, but that it is *easier* for an instrumentally oriented woman to do so. Further, we are saying that most women will develop more instrumental characteristics the longer they remain in the world of competitive sport.

CLOSE RELATIONSHIP TO FATHER AND FAMILY SUPPORT

The female athlete tends not to identify with the role set by society at large, but to be conditioned and protected by a close association with her father and to have family support. Note that in instrumental sports the close relationship is usually with the father; tennis is an outstanding example. In expressive sports, such as figure skating and gymnastics, the close relationships is probably more frequent with the mother. It is significant that many female athletes were trained by their fathers at the beginning of their careers. The mother traditionally plays a background but supportive role, which allows the female athlete to develop outside the usual sex-role structure and its expectations. This often engenders immaturity in her. There may be very little opportunity for the development of her sexuality because sexual feelings are repressed. The female athlete remains "father's little girl," and, though she may be flirtatious and provocative, she will shy away from the sexual consummation of a relationship. Such "little girl types" fare well in the athletic world. Many play their designated feminine role while being competent athletes, thereby complying with the social commitments set down. The social world of the female athlete may well be described as adolescent because it tends to be devoid of mature commitments and responsibilities to other people and to the world at large.

Although the above comments are based upon the observation of the socialization of female athletes in the Western world, they also apply to some athletes in the Eastern bloc who were likewise initiated into sport and trained by their fathers (for example, Martina Navratilova). However, in some Eastern nations there are additional insulations for promising young women athletes. Dyer (1982, p. 226) describes the role of the East German sports school which inducts promising young athletes between the ages of 8 and 11. First, they are selected on the basis of a specific sport's need for physical characteristics and physical maturity. Second, they are selected on the basis of the intensity of their motivation and interest. Third, the environment of the sport school is controlled and thus the young girl is well insulated from any notion that her pursuit of sport interferes with the portrayal of femininity. East German female athletes have been outstanding for their achievements in sport. At least one reason why this is so is that they are not subjected to the sex-role conflicts that so often confront young women in sport in the West.

LESBIANISM AND THE FEMALE ATHLETE

A question frequently asked about female athletes is: are they all lesbians? Many men cannot conceive of a top female athlete who performs "like a man" unless she is also masculine in her sexual inclinations. As has been discussed, a close association exists in many minds between masculinity and athleticism. This is automatically applied to the female athlete who gains the reputation of "butch" or "jock." There is little allowance made for the fact that, in an athlete emerging from a strong background of competence, the athletic performance is solely an expression of her competence as a person and has nothing to do with her sexual preferences. It is not true that all top female athletes have lesbian leanings. However the question remains: Is there a higher incidence of lesbian behavior and orientation among athletes than nonathletes? The answer is yes. There is a tendency for lesbian patterns of sexual adjustment in sport growing out of the unisex groupings, the social expectations that tend to make some female athletes inaccessible to male companionship, and the fact that lesbian types are drawn into sport by the masculine role prescription, and are inclined to foster lesbian-type relationships among their peers. For these reasons the pursuit of athletic careers has often been considered out of bounds for average women even when they have shown athletic talent.

It is reported that many mothers despair of their daughters travelling alone on the tennis circuit, so common are the seductions of younger players by older ones. From time to time exposés are published about the amount of lesbianism present on the tennis or golf circuit, let alone the less commercial sports for women such as field hockey, basketball, and volleyball. The commercial sponsors of sport, courting increasingly large numbers of liberated women who can presumably identify with freedom, strength, and competitive zeal — and buy products to match — are still a long way from endorsing a Sapphist society. The products peddled through sport are still traditional ones: Avon and Bonne Bell beauty products, feminine lines of cigarettes and fashion. Thus the publicly expressed love affair between Navratilova and Rita Mae Brown at Wimbledon in 1980 was much frowned upon, reportedly even by Billie Jean King, who accused Navratilova of selling out women's tennis. King's much publicized affair with a "secretary" who allegedly waited on her hand and foot was not to surface until months later.

It is generally not publicized that many professional women athletes travel quite openly with female companions. On the other hand, from time to time extreme scandals surface. The firing of the women's basketball coach, Pam Parsons, from the University of South Carolina provides one such example. The team's 1981 record showed a seven win and no loss record and a number two national ranking when veiled charges were made involving lesbianism, recruiting violations, and drug use. Said Parsons: "In men's basketball, they want coaches who produce, in women's sports, they want women they can mold, women who will roll over and die. And I won't die." (Lieber and Kirshenbaum, 1982, p. 30). Parents became increasingly concerned about the plights of their daughters in sport. As one mother is reported in the Lieber and Kirshenbaum article (p. 37): "What would you say if Pam Parsons came into your home, all dressed up, with pretty clothes and makeup and a nice hairdo and said, 'In a year from now you won't even know your daughter?' You'd think, 'my little tomboy is finally going to learn to be a lady.' Instead ... ." As previously mentioned, the Ladies Professional Golf Association was supposed to have uttered a collective sigh of relief when Jan Stephenson proved a suitable pin-up girl in 1981 after Billie Jean King's long-term lesbian affair had almost overturned the apple cart of women's sports.

King (1982) has since written an interesting but self-serving book ghosted by Frank Deford, explaining her lengthy lesbian affair, decrying labels, and apparently trying to rescue women's tennis from its lesbian scandals. She also shows herself to be amazingly concerned about image, her place in history, and the view of female athletes by the public. In Chapter 15 the authors spend much time explaining the immense concern that straight athletes such as Chris Evert have with displaying their femininity and their immense self-consciousness of the jock image. King shows the same defensiveness with a remarkable rationalization of the lesbian culture on the tennis circuit which in places she denies and in places, acknowledges. She particularly resents the double standards in comparison to male athletes (p. 191): "In so many ways, too, we're damned if we do, damned if we don't. If we're athletic, we're mannish. We're alleged to be aggressive broads, and any real competitive fire we exhibit is antifeminine." On lesbianism she says (p. 188): "I can only tell you that, from all my years in sport, from everything I know, reports of the incidence of homosexuality are, like Mark Twain's death, greatly exaggerated." And yet she also says, "On tour, you'll see the gays and the straights and the bis all hanging out together, going out for dinner. Doubles teams can often be made up of girls with different sexual preferences." (p. 189). She also sees the need to add (p. 192): "The lesbians I know would never think of proselytizing younger players, in a shower or anywhere else."

Turning from the specific and well-documented case of King to a general discussion of lesbianism in women's sport, it is amazing that so many writers and researchers have avoided and continue to avoid the issue. Although studies need to be done and researchers have tried to do them, it is significant that definitive studies have not been funded and carried out. When they are done, as eventually they will be, the results will be very revealing of female groups which have adopted the material and competitive ethic of the male world. Arguing on a theoretical level, we predict a considerably higher incidence of lesbian activity in female athletes than in women in general.* This is because a higher number of athletes than nonathletes have always been tomboys and this is predictive of, though not deterministic of, inversion. Second, if body build is examined, top women athletes will be more androgenized than the average female. Third, there are cases of hermaphroditism in female athletes and several have failed to pass sex tests. Fourth, the role to which the female athlete aspires is an assertive or instrumental one.

Note that the two styles of homosexuality previously discussed, homosexuality and inversion, also apply to the description of female adjustments and both of these styles would be expected in high level female sports. That is, the men's sport circuits are more or less devoid of effeminate (inverted) males but the women's circuits are not devoid of masculine (inverted) women. At least some of such masculine women will also be inverted in sexual choice; that is, they will play out a male role in having sex with women. On the other hand, what we have described as homosexuality will also be present in female athletes, in that there will be women, identified with their own sex, who will prefer to have sex with other women. Women's sports studies could lead to an advance in knowledge about individuals in society. So far both commercial sponsorship and the culture of sport have colluded against such advancement.

DISCRIMINATION AGAINST FEMALE ATHLETES

Unless the female athlete is of high status she is often discriminated against if she indulges in heterosexual affairs, or if she indulges in homosexual attachments. Her treatment in the former case is not unlike that of the biblical adulteress who was stoned by villagers. Athletic officials are often highly judgmental.

---

*For a somewhat similar discussion of sexual orientation in the general population, the reader is referred to Brown (1986).

Female athletes are usually out of bounds as sexual partners, so if a woman athlete should "play around" she at once becomes a target of scorn by those who may unconsciously desire her. Similarly, by attributing lesbianism to female athletes on an even wider scale than is actually the case, the male ego protects itself with: "These women are excellent athletes, far surpassing the usual male performance; therefore, because males should outperform women, they cannot be real women and therefore cannot be courted as sexual partners."

It is unfortunate that women have also been known to use these "sour grapes" arguments against other women athletes. When the U.S. women's swimming team came in second place to the East German team in the 1976 Olympics in Montreal, they mocked the East Germans for their lack of femininity. Shirley Babashoff and teammates chose the standard reply to interviews: "I don't want to look like that," referring to the "muscle-bound, steroid stuffed mastodon in a one piece suit." As the writer (Joe Gergen) pointed out, Babashoff at five foot ten inches and 160 pounds was hardly a sylph.

Concerns about sex-role image dominate the world of the female athlete and can be observed readily by examining the photographs of female athletes in the major media. The frequency with which female athletes are photographed with significant men in their lives is outstanding. King is seen in photos with her husband Larry prominently on display. Carling Bassett was frequently photographed with her late father or boy friends, Mary Decker with her husband, and other female athletes with their male support figures. The message seems to be conveyed that competent women in sport are backed and directed by men. This is ironic in that for competent women to emerge in any sport system, they must be free of domination and strive for equality. This is why the women's tennis and golf circuits are independent from the men's. Thus the men and women who support athletes successfully (coaches, family, and friends) are rarely dominating. If they are, counteraggressions and stormy relationships can be predicted between the athlete and her coach, father, boyfriend, or husband. The female athlete will achieve most if she functions with guidance and freedom so that she can mature at her own rate and not feel she is being molded, put down, or fettered by social expectations of sex-role or other constraints.

Fortunately, the competence feedback in sport supports most athletes past the sociopsychological pitfalls of sex-role conflicts. However, these conflicts remain important and controversial issues deserving detailed examination. This chapter is largely theoretical and speculative and attests to the need for detailed clinical interviews with athletes in order that the demands of their role, their behaviors, and their adjustments can be better understood. Note that to the extent the female athlete is extraverted, outgoing, stable, and stimulus seeking, she is likely to seek the same physical activities and outlets as the male athlete. This also applies to sexual behavior, whether heterosexual, homosexual, or both. Suzanne Lenglen (Pileggi, 1982) provides an example of such a style. Perhaps the most famous and controversial tennis player of all time, the young French woman was trained by her father. Outgoing and sociable, she drank heavily and had many sexual affairs while maintaining world supremacy in her sport. She loved the attention and publicity of being the best. When she fell from the limelight, she faded fast and died in relative deprivation in 1938. She never married.

The top female athlete today is more highly selected and emerges through much tougher competition. Today, more often than in the past, she is singular and ascetic in purpose. Given the large numbers of women athletes that find themselves and their lifestyle unsuited to juggling a relationship with a man, it is predictable that increasing numbers will end up with female partners.

Great strides have been made in professional women's sports as a result of the efforts of the women athletes themselves and the advent of television and commerical sponsorship. There are many role models of outstanding female athletes now prominent in sport which were not in evidence a few years ago. Not only can young women see examples of successful women athletes at the present time, they also realize that the successful woman athlete now has vehicles for the expression of her competence in events that were not available to her in the past.

However, not all of the attitudinal change that is necessary to support women's sport has gone smoothly. Girls are still not allowed on boys teams if the boys teams do not accept them. The United States Supreme Court ruled in 1981 that 12-year-old Karen O'Conner had no right to try out for her junior high boys' basketball team. This decision reversed that of a District Judge given in 1980. In 1977 an Ontario Human Rights Commission Board ruled that a 10-year-old girl was wrongfully refused player registration by the Ontario Minor Hockey Association. A Divisional Court overruled the Commission by stating that the Human Rights Code had not been broken because the minor hockey league is not a service available to the public.

The fitness movement has been criticized, especially that part of it portrayed on television programs, where women perform scantily clad. The argument is that the programming is sexist in that the women performing are being exploited sexually while the women at home are being introduced to the trivia of fitness (costumes and paraphernalia). Although there is little doubt that a change in the image of the women would be beneficial, the positive values of such programs cannot be underestimated if they encourage women of all social positions to exercise.

Colleges and universities have attempted to equalize the resources for women and men's sport, but many have had difficulty in doing so. In the United States the demise of the Association for Intercollegiate Athletics for Women was controversial. The body began in 1971 and was responsible through to 1982 for 47,332 women's athletic teams and 195 national championships. In 1981–82 the National Collegiate Athletic Association began to organize tournaments.

The latter organization, which controls men's intercollegiate sport, has extended its control over women's sport. This (and Title IX) has resulted in increased federal funding for women's sports and a 500% increase in athlete participation since 1973 — but a 50% drop in the number of female coaches. Thus women's sports are being increasingly controlled by male administrators and male personnel (Acosta and Carpenter, as quoted in the New York Times, December 15, 1985.)

Positive trends are noted in the inclusion of provisions for equality in the laws of some Western nations. In the *United States* this is enacted in Title IX of the Education Amendments of 1972: "No person in the United States shall, on the basis of sex, be excluded from participation in, be denied the benefits of, or be subjected to discrimination under any educational program or activity receiving Federal financial assistance." In *Canada* Section 15(1) of the Canadian Charter of Rights and Freedoms applies: "Every individual is equal before and under the law and has the right to the equal protection and equal benefit of the law without discrimination and, in particular, without discrimination based on race, national or ethnic origin, color, religion, sex, age or mental or physical disability." In *Great Britain* the Sex Discrimination Act of 1975 outlaws discrimination on the basis of sex and yet in a section devoted exclusively to sport it states that women can legally be barred from: "any sport, game or other activity of a competitive nature where the physical stamina or physique of the average women puts her at a disadvantage to the average man." This clause has been used to prevent young girls from participating in "boys'" sports. In Canada and the United States the same ruling is generally given by judges when girls attempt to play on boys' teams. Although many women are making significant strides in the world of sport and many myths about the female athlete are being dispelled, there is still a need for detailed examination of the issues. Treatises such as *Sport and Gender* (Hall, 1978), *Fair Ball* (Hall and Richardson, 1982) and *Women in Sports: A Status Report* (Acosta and Carpenter) have an important place in seeking further equalization of athletic opportunities for women and men.

In spite of the positive changes, there is still considerable conflict over the role and position of the female athlete in society and in sport. This was shown, for example, in the U.S. power lifting championships when women power lifters faced compulsory testing for steroids whereas the same testing for men was voluntary (Todd, 1983). Furthermore, while there is extreme public debate and conflict over the rights of women weight lifters to take steroids, there is only private debate and the acceptance of the rights of the male athletes to do the same. Pat Todd (Todd, 1983, p. 75) demonstrated that she could be a champion without using steroids and reaped considerable backlash of negative publicity for drawing attention to the issue. Yet the time is ripe for such leadership from women. Women athletes are in a better position than men to change the directions of sport toward competence and grass roots development. They are also more able to lead sport away from the destructive treatment of individuals in training and in coaching programs. It is ironic that although women are discriminated against in sport, this very discrimination in some ways makes it easier for women to break through the negative structures strongly entrenched in men's sport.

A final assault on the identity of the female athlete takes the form of the Olympic sex test. Female participants are expected to have their integrity as well as their sex investigated before they are allowed to perform. As Franks (1973) wrote:

> The sex tests, required of all female entrants to determine hormone levels, were humiliating — as well as painful. One American swimmer described the testing room as "full of those bug-eyed doctors looking you up and down as though they were dying to say, 'Flat-chested, eh? Well, we'll see...'" Bona fide womanhood was established by pulling out a strand of hair (which often took more than one yank to get) and examining the cells in the root.

Since sex can be determined on a number of levels and the Olympic committee has chosen chromosomal criteria, a number of individuals who are legally female and consider themselves female may be barred from competition. The criterion is usually that in order to compete, a woman must have more than ten cells in every 100 with Barr bodies. Most women have Barr bodies in approximately twenty cells out of 100. A Barr body is a densely staining mass signifying the presence of the second X chromosome. Consider an athlete such as Renee Richards, legally a woman, who was prevented from competing in several international tennis tournaments because she failed such tests even though she claimed to have passed them on some occasions (Richards, 1984). Should she have been allowed to compete?

Let us assume that there is a physiologically marginal person competing in the women's events at the Olympics who psychologically identifies herself as female. Since the test results depend very much upon the level of sex test chosen, the result of any individual falling in no-man's-land should depend upon that individual's psychological identification and choice. To subject this person, and large numbers of other young women, to such an assessment is unnecessary and demeaning. One must feel sympathy and respect for the many athletes who left the Olympics in past years rather than take sex tests. Their rights as individuals were violated as well as their rights as athletes.

Is sport better off or more just without the entry of marginal women? If accurate tests were conducted, how many female athletes should be barred? After all, the tests place an individual on a continuum, and the cut-off criterion is quite arbitrary. We have suggested in this chapter that female athletes form a unique group in which genetic and hormonal differences from the norm are very likely to be found. If one removes an Eva Klobukowska or a Stella Walsh from competition, what kind of athlete replaces her? Perhaps one who is equally atypical, but whose physiological quirk is not so easily identified. It is clear that it would be cheating if a man masqueraded as a woman in order to enter women's events. However it is quite a different case when the individual genuinely identifies with women's events, is legally recognized as female, and has no wish to cheat or defraud. Sport organizations should accept the law of the land and recognize that for many persons maleness and femaleness are not clear-cut categories. In other words, sex tests should not be used in sport.

The difficulties that confront female athletes will not be resolved easily, for they are built into the greater social structure that encompasses the sport world. Spectators want to view that which sustains a norm because it appears to be legitimate; thus, they often search for femininity in a female athlete in place of competence. The competence of female athletes can be appreciated just like the competence of male athletes, if an audience focuses on the skill manifested in the sport and not on the less relevant dimension of sex and competitive partisanship. A spectator with sexist perceptions will focus upon feminine expressions in female sports and masculine expressions in sport in general. That spectator will expect the female athlete to be pretty, graceful, and delicate, and will have little interest in the perceived role reversals of a superstrong and competent female or a slight and graceful male. These role reversals serve no integratory ego function for the observer. It has been the female athlete's traditional legacy to be perceived as a freak. The present generation of athletes, however, will not leave their successors with the same stigma. The question for the present crop of female athletes is whether they will passively accept the status quo and reap the material rewards it offers, or whether they will be able to combine their competence with a different set of values and social meanings — those of community, cooperation, and mutual concern among athletes. With the latter choice the female athlete could carry to the world at large a new and powerful message: that excellence in sport does not necessitate greed, selfishness, and winning at any cost. Rather, excellence in sport can lead to the health and growth of the athlete, to the community of athletes, and to the inspiration of all. Leadership in this direction will be easier for women than for men, if women choose to assume that leadership.

PART IV

HELPING THE ATHLETE

13
Referral

THE EMERGENCE OF SERVICE IN SPORT PSYCHOLOGY

Referral to a sport psychologist or sport consultant is becoming increasingly common. A person may self refer, or be referred by a third party such as a coach or general practitioner. Still others become interested through team-sponsored workshops which introduce sport psychology and then follow up with individual sessions. There are two broad reasons for referral. The first is for education. The individual (or group) wants to know how best to develop healthfully, live fully, and achieve optimally. The second reason is for treatment. The individual has a problem which requires outside help. In the first case the person is seeking preventive information and self (or group) enhancement. In the second case the individual seeks intervention or treatment from the psychologist. These two themes, prevention and intervention, will unfold side by side in this section of the book.

Interest in the applied psychology of sport has expanded during the 1960s, 1970s, and 1980s (Salmela, 1984). Prior to the 1960s, little work was done and few books were available on the subject. Instead, coaches and athletes developed their own miniature theories of personality, motivation, and performance, and applied them to the athletic field. The few isolated people working in sport psychology after the initial experiment by Triplett (1898) did not have a great impact on social thinking. Perhaps the most important contributions were in sociology and in the study of children's play and its significance. The study of cooperation and competition was launched by Deutsch (1949) but his findings were too seldom applied with institutional support. In the 1960s the serious examination of both the athlete and sport began. Ogilvie and Tutko (1966) published their landmark book, *Problem Athletes and How to Handle Them,* in which they accepted the status quo attitudes toward sport and yet showed extreme insight into the clinical problems of athletes. Goodhart and Chataway (1968) published *War Without Weapons,* an insightful sociological and political analysis of sport. Morgan and colleagues (Morgan and Johnson, 1977, 1978; Morgan and Pollock, 1977; Nagle et al., 1975) conducted programs of research into the personality styles of successful athletes in their landmark studies at the University of Wisconsin.

The 1960s and 1970s also saw the flourishing of what is now known as the radical critique of sport. Some of these were Marxist critiques of capitalistic sport. Examples are Edwards (1969, 1973), Hoch (1972), and Scott (1971). Such writings made an important contribution to the analysis of sport and that tradition continues today; for example see Cantelon and Gruneau (1982). More numerous critiques of sport were written by professional and other athletes who had questioned, probed, and criticized the sport system. Examples of athletes who have contributed greatly to the examination of sport and its effects upon athletes are: Bouton (1970), Meggyesy (1970), Rentzel (1972), and Shaw (1973). The first edition of the present volume was even erroneously classified in the radical category by Lasch (1979). In fact, many books marked a new way of looking at sport and predicted the extreme problems in adjustment common in athletes today. The books had in common the questionning and analyses of the value systems underlying sport and how they affected athletes as individuals and as the members of groups.

The 1970s and 1980s saw increased commercialization and government intervention in sport and in elite athlete development. They also saw greater interest from the Western world in the Eastern bloc's use of both science and psychology in sport. Eastern teams often travel with psychologists, choose their teams with psychological factors as additional criteria to sport skills, and generally have been farther ahead in the use of psychology in sport than the Western nations.

Increasing 'problems' with athletes have arisen in the West when they organized themselves into players' associations, unions, and advocates of athletes' rights. A major demand was that they no longer be treated like chattels by the sports establishment. Winning and becoming prominent in sport no longer meant honor and status for a lady or a gentleman. Instead, it meant money and fame for children from all walks of life provided they developed their talents sufficiently to get to the free lists, the scholarships, the professional contracts, and eventually to the advertising subsidies being offered. Governments were interested in the status and recognition accompanying gold medals from the Olympic Games and became increasingly willing to sink funds into the psychological preparation of athletes. Athletes, striving for success, began trying everything that would help them increase performance, including psychological techniques, and very often teams, leagues, or governments would pay for it. Many psychologists were willing to volunteer their time in order to engage in and develop a new, and dynamic field. Today there are a plethora of people working in sport psychology and many more who use their services.

A host of professional and ethical problems are raised by the application of psychology in sport. These are dealt with in Chapter 20. The intervening chapters are not intended to prepare the reader for the practice of sport psychology. Such practice requires lengthy training in psychological, clinical, and practical techniques under qualified supervision and usually a Ph.D. degree in psychology. However, to omit the application of psychology to sport in this book would be to omit a major section of the field as it exists today. The following chapters are therefore intended to inform the reader, as fully as possible, of the state of the art within the space constrictions of this volume.

WHO IS THE CLIENT?

The clients of the sport psychologist are diverse. They may be individuals, parents, coaches, teams, clubs, organizations, and governments.

Individuals. An individual of any age may become a client. Thus a child, adolescent, university student, adult, or aged person may all present themselves for some form of consultation. This necessitates a good deal of knowledge from the psychologist in life-span developmental psychology, as he or she must be informed of the natural progressions and conflicts experienced by individuals during development and aging.

Parents. Parents frequently make the first contact with the sport psychologist. They may consult alone or bring along the child for whom they have concerns. These consultations can range from a parent giving his or her fifteen-year-old child five consultations as a Christmas present in order that he or she can explore some psychological methods for helping field hockey performance to the mother of a gymnast who brings in her teenaged daughter because the latter has been sexually acting out during road trips and failing to get along with sport organizers.

Coaches. Coaches are the most frequent clients of sport psychologists. The coach must deal with people on all levels of sport organization. Because the athletes they coach are not often the personality type which is reflective enough to seek psychological assistance, it is often the coach who initiates the search for advice on psychological applications in sport.

Teams. The psychologist is sometimes hired to consult with a whole team and to offer support and diverse services should the team as a whole or specific members of the team need them. The psychologist then becomes part of the specialized support system for the team and often reports back to team members, to coaches, and to higher management. The psychologist may help with problems of drug and alcohol abuse, team morale, team organization, time management, and goal setting, to provide a few examples.

Clubs. Clubs may hire a psychologist for members to consult or for general group psychological services. For example, a golf, tennis, or country club can hire a psychologist to provide individual services. Often, the psychologist is hired for group rather than individual consultation. For example, a swimming, gymnastics, or soccer club may wish consultation on and assistance with program planning, program organization, and program evaluation.

Sports and Other Organizations. League, state, provincial, and municipal organizations may hire a psychologist to consult on programs, problems, and how to optimize resources. Referrals here can range from youth sport organizations to national or professional organizations. The National Football League, The National Basketball Association, or a multinational organization or company may refer their members for problems ranging from drug or gambling addiction to life style counseling.

Governments. Because of the prestige of winning teams and winning medals, governments are increasingly adding to sport sponsorships and are paying psychologists to work with teams and athletes, organize programs, and consult in program evaluation. There is still much too little attention given by governmental sport agencies to the human repercussions of their elite training programs in North America. The marriage of elite sport programs to business and corporate interests for the purposes of image enhancement and profit has resulted in goals which do not emphasize competence development in athletes. The resulting problems have drawn increasing numbers of sport consultants and sport psychologists into the process.

WHAT ARE THE REASONS FOR REFERRAL?

Due to the novelty of the field of clinical sport psychology, many referrals approach the sport psychologist with little more than a vague notion that the psychologist will help them to improve their athletic performance. The idea prevails that if other people are being assisted by a psychologist, then it is time that the client is as well. Or, put more bluntly: "The East German team has one (a psychologist), so it is time we had one too. What do you want us to do?" Or, "John Kelson, our pitcher, says you helped him so I'm here too." Thus the psychologist is often left to educate the client as to what assistance is available so that he or she can help to decide on the course of action and degree of commitment to psychological treatment and/or training. Referral can be broadly broken into seven categories: life style consultation, developmental problems, maximizing performance, competitive stress, program organization, program evaluation, and clinical problems.

Life Style Consultation. The sport psychologist may be asked questions about healthful life planning. With preventive fitness programs coming increasingly into vogue for individuals, corporations, and other organizations, life style consultation is popular. Reportedly, corporations save five dollars and twenty cents for every dollar spent on life style consultation for their personnel. Victims of illness, who have recovered from heart attacks, cancer, or other stress, are seeking counseling to prevent further breakdown. Some healthy and fully functioning people of all ages wish to plan a more healthy life style and often do so with expert consultation. These services are offered by a wide variety of personnel in fitness centers, in preventive medicine clinics, and in recreational offices, as well as by life style counselors and sport psychologists in both public and private service.

Developmental Problems. The most frequent referral from parents, and often from general practitioners, is in regard to some developmental problem in a young person. Is the child with the right coach? In the right sport? How much should the child be pushed? Is the child showing negative effects from sport? Negative effects of frequent concern are temper tantrums, acting out behavior, low motivation, and difficulty relating to authority. Sometimes these questions may be clear cut and easily answered. At other times the presenting developmental problem may be a beacon for more deeply seated problems within the child.

Maximizing Performance. Psychological principles as applied in sport are becoming increasingly known, heard about, and read about (for examples, see Klavora and Daniel, 1979; Suinn, 1980; and Nideffer, 1981). As the sporting community and public hear more about the practice of sport psychology from these sources and, perhaps more frequently from the media, people are increasingly seeking out the psychologist in order to explore how psychology can enhance performance. They want to perform at the highest level possible and realize that psychology offers a large uncharted area which might help them advance. It is this outlook that has made sport psychology increasingly acceptable and sought after. It has changed the image of the sport psychologist from that of "shrink" to "expert helper." It is also probably the most frequent reason why the services of the sport psychologist are sought.

Competitive Stress. This is significantly related to maximizing performance, the previous reason for referral, for there are negative consequences for athletes who push themselves too hard and too fast or who are pushed by others too hard and too fast. The result is an overload of stress with concomitant symptoms and disabilities. Reactions to stress are probably the most frequent form of breakdown among athletes and competitive stress is often extreme in athletic programs. For this reason, Chapter 16 is entirely devoted to the topic.

Program Organization. Agencies which most productively use the services and information of sport psychology often do so by seeking help on how to organize and develop programs. The sooner the consultation takes place the better, for then the psychologist can offer many ways in which to avoid the pitfalls inherent in poor human organization. Indeed, with proper planning, much energy, discomfort, and money can be saved. Parents, little league coaches and organizers, clubs, and professional organizations would all do well before launching new programs to seek consultation on efficiency, on maximizing the healthful motivations of the participants, on avoiding both physical and psychological injury, and on the management of morale. This in all likelihood, is the most important contribution psychologists can make to sport because early detection of problems may eliminate many of sport's psychological casualties.

Program Evaluation. The evaluation of programs, once they have been initiated and developed, is becoming increasingly important as the public calls for accountability from organizations such as schools, municipalities, and government. Increasing numbers of sports programs are being organized for the welfare and growth of the persons involved in them. Such programs, once in operation, can be accurately guided and/or corrected by a constant monitoring of how the participants are affected by their involvement. Program evaluation is essential for the maximum benefits of programs to all participants and for maximum value to those who are paying for the programs.

Clinical Problems. In some cases there is psychopathology in the athlete, official, or program participant, necessitating clinical treatment and a clearly defined intervention in order that the state of psychopathology not worsen. These cases are treated within a clinical model, as would be any case of psychopathology that required a clinical psychologist. Adequate interviewing, assessment, diagnosis, and treatment plans should be made along with deciding whether the individual will remain in active sport participation or drop out until the problems recede.

EXAMPLES OF REFERRAL PROBLEMS

Combining the sorts of persons who are referred to the sport psychologist with the reasons for referral, one emerges with a seven by seven categorization of the situations the sport psychologist will deal with most frequently. Although not exhaustive, Figure 8 shows examples of each type of referral for each group. The examples shown in the figure give an overview of the great variety of tasks facing sport psychologists. Most of the examples are cases of actual referrals. However, several of the governmental referrals have been created for the purposes of this book. Such referrals from an overall regulating agency should be encouraged as ways in which the understanding and treatment of human problems arising from all nature of athletic programs could be advanced. In fact, such assignments are common in some countries, (for example, The GDR) but much less common in the United States and Canada, where elite training programs are overseen by specific sport bodies which may wish to preserve their organizational structures. Such programs too frequently exploit athletes, while leaving them to handle psychological and social problems that arise from sport involvement. This is the result of the increased bureaucratization of the various sports associations. Often concerned with only reaching performance criteria, such associations are rarely the most objective assessors of the psychological, social, and organizational problems which arise for athletes.

HOW IS A SPORT PSYCHOLOGIST SELECTED?

As with most professions, competent practictioners usually become known by word of mouth. Someone knows the psychologist because he or she has seen the psychologist for services, or knows the psychologist from his or her writing, public lectures, or teaching. Media releases are becoming increasingly important in spreading professional reputation to the public. This is unfortunate, as the background and the claims of the interviewer are seldom screened, and many outlandish pronouncements have been and continue to be made by persons erroneously calling themselves sport psychologists.

Physicians and lawyers are an additional source of referrals since they often require an expert in psychology and sport to consult on medical and legal problems. As in several branches of psychology (for example: product liability, personal injury, custody issues and eyewitness testimony) psychologists in sport will be increasingly called upon to give evidence as expert witnesses in legal proceedings (Blau, 1984). Psychologists also refer to one another when a client requires a specialized technique or other help which not everyone specializes in.

Most professional associations have lists of psychologists who specialize in sport psychology and in addition will tell any client whether the psychologist is certified to do clinical work. This certification is based upon state and provincial government law in the United States and in Canada which screen professional psychologists who are trained and competent in offering psychological services. The legislation is designed to prevent untrained persons from calling themselves psychologists and offering psychological services. The problems of untrained psychologists in the practice of sport psychology are considerable and will be dealt with in detail in Chapter 20.

REASONS FOR REFERRAL	CLIENTS		
	1. INDIVIDUAL	2. PARENTS	3. COACHES
1. Life style consultation	A 25-year-old lawyer, new to a large city, requests an assessment of what turns out to be his rigorous, compulsive, and exhausting sport pursuits.	Two parents bring their 8- and 10-year-old sons for an assessment of the family goals, diet, sleeping, and long distance running schedules.	A coaching association hires the psychologist to give a day long workshop on stress management for coaches.
2. Developmental problems	A 14-year-old boy is referred by a physician for acting out behavior particularly anger, temper, and kicking the boards and ice during figure skating training.	A 15-year-old boy becomes very upset he did not make the high school basketball team. He refuses to see the school counsellor. His father makes an appointment-ment for him with the psychologist.	A competitive tennis coach seeks the answer to why his most promising proteges leave his program at age 13 and 14.
3. Maximizing performance	A provincial level field hockey player makes one appointment to talk about techniques he might use to enhance his sport performance.	A mother pays for five sessions for her tennis playing daughter to help her improve her play. The sessions are a birthday gift.	Two coaches from a competitive swim club ask how they can improve the performances of their athletes.
4. Competitive stress	A university table tennis player at state level competition complains his performances have fallen off and that he blows large leads.	Parents are concerned over the eating habits and intense motivation of their 12-year-old daughter on the tennis tour.	A coach seeks the psychologist's help in lessening the competitive pressure placed on 5- and 6-year-old boys in pee-wee hockey training. Parents and other coaches are stressing winning and leave half the boys in tears every game.
5. Program organization	An Olympic hopeful has his coach and a psychologist draw up a three-year training and competitive schedule including goal setting, time management, training, and school schedule.	The parents of a university elementary school request the formation of an athletic program which emphasizes participation and cooperation.	A coach with a hockey team in a slump and with low morale asks for assistance.
6. Program evaluation	A weightlifter wants to know if his training schedule will be equally effective without the use of anabolic steroids.	The parents of children in a competitive swim club think the program is too tough and ask the coach if they can have it assessed.	A national field hockey coach asks for an assessment of an 8-month training schedule leading up to a world championship.
7. Clinical problems	A baseball player suffers from nervous tic and anxiety which is interfering with his performance.	A mother brings her 15-year-old daughter who has been acting out sexually and defying the authority of coaches and officials during gymnastics tours.	A gymnastics coach wants the psychologist to hypnotize a talented gymnast who is blocking on difficult vaults and fails to complete them.

Figure 8. Referral Problems in Sport Psychology: Some Examples.

CLIENTS (CONTINUED)			
4. TEAMS	5. CLUBS	6. ORGANIZATIONS	7. GOVERNMENT
A coach asks for five educational sessions for his junior hockey team on how to avoid drug and alcohol abuse.	A country club engages a psychologist for a summer-long educational program which interested members sign up for.	A corporation engages a psychologist to counsel its management on preventive life styles.	A government agency has the psychologist write a pamphlet on life style management for touring elite athletes.
A basketball coach asks what he can do about lesbianism on his teen-aged girls' basketball team.	A club badminton pro hires a psychologist to give three sessions to the club junior team on how to prepare for and do well on tournament trips.	A little league has the largest drop out rate over several years.	A national tennis center cannot recruit adequate talent for its programs.
A hockey club for boys 10–13 requests consultation on how the boys can get the most out of their hockey–both for their personal growth and for improving play.	All of the members of a competitive swimming club are assessed in order to make recommendations on how performance level can be raised.	A professional football team owner hires a psychologist to improve performance through the treatment of drug and alcohol problems.	A national sports body hires a psychologist in order to have recommendations on how to improve the cooperation and motivation of Olympic trainees.
A basketball team cannot play together and is in a slump in spite of their being two "stars" on the team.	A national soccer squad consistently fails to live up to national expectation. The coach is given one more season to turn the club around.	A Pop Warner football league cannot keep officials due to lack of parental discipline.	A psychologist is recruited to carry out studies on athletes who have left national team status.
At a staging camp for figure skating teams, their team organization, communication, and potential frustrations are discussed with the assistance of a psychologist.	A golf club wants its competitive development program planned.	A representative of a day care center calls to have the psychologist assess equipment at the school. Parents are suing over an injury to their child which was suffered while playing on a swing. Potential court case.	A government plans a 10-year developmental program for talented 12-year-olds from three major sports. Psychologist is asked to assist in planning.
An evaluation of "on the road" programs and travel arrangements for a girls' basketball team is requested.	A tennis club has spent $25,000 the previous year on a developmental program. They now want it assessed.	A youth organization asks for the evaluation of winning and losing teams over a season.	The government requests that the 10-year developmental program described above be evaluated.
A psychologist is hired as the clinical consultant for the players on a profesbaseball team.	A hockey club asks for a psychological assessment of a player whom coaches think is a malingerer (feigning injuries).	A lawyer calls to have his client assessed. Client is appealing a conviction and fine for $25,000 for having injured another player by striking him in the face with his stick in a commercial hockey league. Potential court case.	A national sports association requests intervention for problems with substance abuse among its athletes.

Figure 8. Referral Problems in Sport Psychology: Some Examples.

Finally, governments and various sports associations usually have lists of qualified practitioners who have worked with or are qualified to work with national teams and high level or elite athletes. How the psychologist operates after the referral is made depends upon the presenting problem of the client, the questions being asked by the client, and the goals which are set through discussion with the client.

14
Maximizing Performance

INTRODUCTION

In the last chapter it was noted that most referrals to the sport psychologist involve quests for increased sport performance. In previous chapters, two themes have been developed with regard to sport performance: the destructive and the constructive potentials of sport in contemporary life. Sport is destructive or constructive depending on whether the involvement leads to personal growth, well being, and maturity of character or whether it leads to human problems, disturbance, and diminishment of character. It is unfortunate that the search for excellence contains the potential seeds of destruction. We have argued throughout the book that excellence growing out of competence motivation is not destructive to self or to others. However, as people attempt to maximize performance there is as much potential for harm as for good to be done. It is tragic enough when athletes ruin themselves through unrealistic sport striving but it is doubly so when the destruction is helped along or supported by parents, coaches, doctors, psychologists, or others who have a blind adherence to the competitive ethic. When quests for status and victory result in greed, jealousy and abandonment of the proper care and concern for developing athletes — then sport organization should be seriously questioned.

Consider the following incidents. In Canada parents give up custody of their 14-year-old sons so they can play in the Metropolitan Toronto Hockey League. A 23-year-old basketball player in Chicago had to go back to school with 12 year olds to learn to read in spite of having had 16 years of schooling, including four years at Omaha's Creighton University while playing basketball (Menaker, 1982). Canadian swimming teams have been notorious for their ignorant and immature chants calculated to unnerve other teams before competitions. Young athletes aged 12 and 13 are asking for drugs from their physicians in order to improve sport performance (according to Dr. Wayne Hildahl, chairman of the Manitoba Medical Association's sports commission, 1982). There is also the case of the American tennis father who reportedly struck his 16-year-old daughter in front of a crowd of 3,000 in Buenos Aires for hitting a poor shot.

On the other hand there are counterforces operating to correct some of the destructive trends within sport. In Boulder, Colo., a father sued the manager of his son's baseball team for being a poor role model for his 14-year-old son. Parental reaction to the player abuse in football has led to its public examination and censure. Mewshaw (1983), travelled the men's professional tennis circuit and called for a return to the basic values of fairness in sport instead of the greed and favoritism which prevail there. Some sport officials (women's international field hockey) still proudly state that people take precedence over economics in their plans and programs. Social scientists and other professionals increasingly argue against the abuse of children in sport (Butt, 1979b; Martens, 1976; Tutko and Bruns, 1976).

Given this tangled web of conflicting values and purposes, there is still legitimate concern among athletes, parents, coaches, and sport organizers at all levels on how to improve performance. This is justifiable as long as the welfare of the athlete(s) and of society is kept in mind. There is, however, much misinformation and ignorance surrounding increased sport performance just as there is much genuinely helpful information.

MISCONCEPTIONS

1. Equipment. Please note that in this section we are not arguing against the fact that sports equipment has been improved since the early days nor that there have been significant "break-throughs" from time to time. What we are arguing is that a new gimmick, such as graphite tennis rackets or carbon soled sneakers, can enjoy a lucrative market run, because aspiring sportsman believe it will improve their performance. In fact, once sports equipment has attained a certain level of quality and reliability, minor changes usually have little to do with performance. At best a "placebo" effect takes place. It is the athlete's skill that counts and not his or her equipment.

The evolution of equipment design from the old to the new in skiing, tennis, golf, or any other sport is an interesting phenomenon, rather like the evolution of the automobile. Increased performance, in the long term, is achieved. But the foisting of new designs, gimmicks and gizmos on the playing public to the tune of billions of dollars a year has everything to do with marketing and little to do with sports performance.

The relationship of paraphernalia to ego in sport is often intimate. The time enthusiasts spend examining equipment, comparing it, and discussing it is a type of *in vacuo* preening which has little to do with performance. Further, in addition to being over estimated as an aid in trying to "get better," equipment is also frequently blamed for an athlete's poor performance and is sometimes even destroyed in a fit of temper.

In summary, new equipment may increase motivation temporarily, enhance self-image or enjoyment, and attract the interest of others for conversational purposes — but it rarely has measurable performance value over the previous year's model. If performance increases were measurable one can rest assured that the equipment manufacturers would carry out studies and bombard the public with the results.

2. Lessons. * Lessons are another source of improvement according to many sports people. Almost anyone who claims to teach a sport can, with the backing of the humblest club, association, or past success (or, better still a newspaper feature) draw adherents. Sometimes they draw crowds without any of these. Many aspiring sport people ignore the fundamentals of performance development. They don't practice, or study the performances of experts, or even bother to analyze their own performances. Still, they seem to think that a few hours of lessons will provide a footing for their aspirations in sport. In fact, such short-term lessons impart only the rudiments of technique, and sometimes not even that.

Technique must be practiced and developed over a period of time. It can rarely be picked up solely through lessons. Few teachers of sport have the ability and flexibility needed to meet the individual demands and skills of pupils who present themselves for coaching. Most teach a standard technique that may ill-suit the pupil because it ignores each student's uniqueness, thus diminishing the contribution he or she would make as an individual to the sport. Sport performance must be an expression of self if the person is to develop to the maximum.

In spite of this, lessons are still the most usual method through which individuals seek improvements in performance. There have been few studies done to determine how much lessons improve performance levels or at what age, from which coach, how many lessons, and so on. In a nutshell, the problem is that the standardized techniques most coaches impose reflect the coaches' lack of personal involvement with their pupils. If we study outstanding performers, we see that many execute their sport in ways that would defy the average teacher. The development of timing, coordination, and skill through long hours of concentrated practice are not things that can be easily, or speedily taught. They grow and develop from within when an individual's motivations for engaging in sport are given the right environmental surroundings and support.

Persons giving lessons naturally wish to be known as pros, and often they seek out promising athletes who have already achieved a significant level of performance in their sport. The pro then gives lessons to the promising junior, who was bound to develop with or without lessons. The pro may then imply that the outstanding athlete developed from the same set of lessons given to others when, in fact, the athlete has developed for quite different reasons. These other reasons will be discussed later in the chapter.

---

*This section should be read in conjunction with the section on the coach (pp. 168–172). The argument is that lessons given within a superficial context have little effect while lessons given within the context of a constructive coaching relationship may have much effect.

3. Short-Term Psychological Techniques. With the immense recent interest in psychological techniques for improving performance in sport, the opportunity is ripe for practitioners to jump into the sport world with promises of enhanced performance through the use of the latest psychological gimmicks. As will be discussed in a later section, it may well be the practitioner who administers the technique rather than the technique itself that enchances the performance of the athlete, if enhancement does occur. Many of the techniques available are much the same or overlap. They are currently seen as new and innovative and therefore are interesting and make for lively discussion. This may give them *placebo value.* Such placebo effects may be sufficient to spur people on with the power of suggestion rather than create any substantive or lasting effect on their performance. The problem is that any improvement will be short lived. This treatment phenomenon is well known in fields other than sport, particularly in drug therapy and psychotherapy.

Since Eysenck (1952) published his now famous paper on the efficacy of psychotherapy, this topic has been debated and researched. The individual's improvement in treatment may be due to spontaneous remission or positive anticipation. In some cases there may be no improvement or there may be an actual decline in the condition. All of these possibilities have been noted in the voluminous literature on both drug therapy and psychotherapy (for examples of reviews see Garfield, 1981). Drug therapy and psychotherapy continue to be used because clinically and socially they seem to have extremely positive effects for some people under certain conditions. Researchers have argued, using "meta method" techniques (Smith and Glass, 1977; Smith, Glass and Miller, 1980), that overall positive effects are measurable and this has been confirmed in recent NIMH studies. If this is so, then the conditions under which positive outcomes occur are of great importance.

Most worthwhile psychological techniques seem to work best when they give the client social support while he or she is learning good habits. The client has to work hard over time in order to establish the good habit and reap the benefits thereof. The same social support, exertion from the client, and long term quest for good habits are very likely the ingredients necessary for performance improvement in sport.

Schilling (1980) of Switzerland wrote an interesting speculative paper on the many psychological techniques which came into vogue and were in great demand before each Olympic year. He cautions that athletes may think that so much can be gained from psychological techniques that they ignore other important elements of training and of sport execution. After hearing so many claims for sophrology, autogenic training, biorhythmics, methods of personality deployment, transcendental meditation, and acupuncture, Schilling advises caution and asks for the experimental evidence if, indeed, these techniques are working so well.

One laudable and yet aborted attempt to measure the efficacy of a technique was Suinn's (1980b) performance assessment of his visual-motor-behavioral rehearsal technique (VMBR) in a skiing program. Suinn established his control groups before applying VMBR to a group of American Olympic skiers. However, the coach was so pleased with the technique that he decided the experimental group members would race for the most part while the members of the control group would not race in the championships. Thus final performance comparisons could never be made between the experimental and the control groups. Suinn's study, although not completed, marks the direction for future work. Some fine studies await execution on the performance increments, if any, associated with equipment innovations, lessons, and psychological techniques.

ESSENTIALS

We now turn to three enduring and essential ingredients for the development of athletes: a healthy relationship between parents, or parent substitutes, and their children; a unique relationship with a coach or coaches; and confidence in a support group.

1. Parents and Their Children. A healthful and supportive relationship is needed between youth in sport and parents, or parent substitutes. This is a relationship in which the parent encourages the youth to fulfil his or her potential, all the while knowing the difference between encouraging and pushing the child beyond his or her capacity. The effects of parent and child interactions on achievement and performance have been demonstrated experimentally by McClelland (1961) and by Sears (1965) and colleagues. McClelland assigned tasks to children in the presence of their parents. Some parents were tense and demanding, interfered at once, and steadily imposed their own egos upon their children's performance. Other parents were more relaxed. They encouraged, joked, made suggestions and generally supported the child's performance. Not only did the latter group perform better in the experimental task, but their character development was also affected. Sears has shown children of relaxed, supportive parents to be more honest, self-confident, and mature. The positive parent-child relationship is complex and takes many forms. It is easier to describe destructive relationships than constructive ones, and this is what we shall do.

In every sport organization involving young people there is a special type of person. This is the "sports parent" — "the baseball father" or "the tennis mother" — who pushes the child onward in the sport. This parent is always present, constantly lobbying for favors for his or her child. The parent sometimes encourages the youngster and sometimes criticizes, and will often go to any degree of self-sacrifice to further the child's interests. Whatever the style, however, the parent's main interest is to maximize the performance and benefits of his or her own child. This is often done with little concern for the opinions of the official representatives of the organization sponsoring the sport, for the other children involved, or for the very child the parent is pushing.

Such parents do themselves, their child, and the sport a great disservice. They are victims of their own competitive strivings, and are often quite oblivious of the needs of their child. The parent overidentifies with the child. If the child also identifies with the parent, then a closely knit and "successful" team may develop, but it is necessary that the child assume the parental ego, for he or she is not free to develop one of his or her own. The parent then dominates the child. These parents can impede the development of the child's character to an extent that the child will have a difficult time overcoming the damage later. Or, they may alienate the child from themselves all together as the child grows to resent being pushed and cannot psychologically accept the advantages extended to him because of favoritism. Such parents seem dedicated to preventing the world from interfering with their child's potential progress as they see it. The irony is that the parents themselves are unmistakable barriers to their child's advancement, even though they see themselves as the child's protector. If a developing athlete is to be successful, he or she must trade on his or her own abilities and, what is more important, must develop the psychological resilience necessary to accept losses and setbacks. There are surprisingly numerous parents who fail to realize this.

2. The Coach. Next to the athlete, the key person in maximizing performance is the coach. Not all athletes have coaches, but it is doubtful whether they will achieve top performance levels without them. The few athletes who do achieve are exceptional. Roger Bannister, the first four-minute miler, had no coach as such, but was surrounded by a small, close group of people with whom he trained, and at least one person has claimed that Bannister did have a coach of a sort. Examination of the lives of "coachless" athletes generally reveals that they have been able to create and follow their own role of excellence. In other cases, there is always someone who, although not officially a coach, fills the role at crucial times during the athlete's career. A coach differs from a teacher or a pro in that he or she has an ongoing personal relationship with the athlete that has deep psychological import. Without an emotional relationship, the coach could not invest him or herself deeply enough in the athlete, and without a deep trust in the coach, the athlete could not have enough faith to make the necessary sacrifices that bring achievement and success. Without the coaching relationship, it is difficult for an athlete to develop to his or her full potential. The contributions of the coach are essential and unique.

Acquiring skill and developing potential into the full flower of excellence is usually a long and painstaking course that is travelled by the young and talented. To travel the difficult road requires help, faith, and knowledge from another, but most of all it requires a relationship of mutual trust so that both may take personal risks.

Strauss (1973) has made a thorough study of the coaching relationship from an interactional perspective. The mutual trust must be such that identification takes place between the two, one that can best be described as a form of love relationship. This relationship, according to Strauss, is similar to a courtship in which one party has firmly in mind where the relationship will go and what may be accomplished. Initial contact is made, the parties are attracted to one another, each feels the other one out, trust develops, and together they proceed along a much-travelled road but in a manner unique to their own relationship. The relationship continues until one outgrows the other, or the goal is achieved. Then there is a parting of the ways. As in love, there may be other "coaching" relationships for both. The coach may have other protégés and the athlete may move on to other coaches, but the special relationship between the two will never be duplicated. The relationship has a beginning, an overture, a testing period, a working period, a climax in performance, and an ending, as each completes his or her part of the task. The good coach vigilantly concentrates on the needs of the trainee. The good coach also has a keen sense of his or her own limitations, and while continuing to offer emotional support will pass the trainee on to a more advanced coach after all that he-she could do has been done.

Society tends to frown upon intimate emotional relationships between individuals of different ages. Yet in schools, sport programs, and camp situations, this is precisely the kind of relationship that must develop if young people are to advance quickly along the path to excellence and even to achieve adult adjustment. To encourage psychological health in a society there should be more relationships across ages, not fewer. In most coach-student relationships this is the case. However, those who enter into such intense emotional attachments need structural support and a very strong commitment to the task of coaching, lest the relationship become an active, sexual one. Social perception in the sport world is ambivalent about coaching relationships. The sports culture will immediately notice, comment upon, and criticize what is obviously an emotional relationship between an unknown coach and a developing athlete. At the same time it will reward and eulogize a coach who has spent a life fostering such relationships and producing excellence in sport or in other activities.

That such relationships frequently become sexual is demonstrated by the number of girl athletes who have married their coaches. Nancy Greene, world champion skier, and Chi Cheng, world champion sprinter, are examples. Many more, of course, have sexual experiences of various sorts with coaches. Suspected homosexual episodes are also not unknown, as illustrated by the following item.

Coach is Charged in Morals Case

Mamaroneck, N.Y.—A 52-count indictment charging the coach of a national championship Pop Warner Football League team in Mamaroneck, N.Y., with sodomy, sexual abuse, sexual misconduct and endangering the welfare of minors has been handed up by the grand jury of Westchester County, it was learned today.

[The coach], 28, of Mamaroneck was charged with engaging in "deviate sex acts" with certain members of the Mamaroneck Lions, a team of boys between the ages of 11 and 13 who have won all 38 games in the past four years under [his] direction.*

Probably the greatest tennis player of all time, William Tilden (Deford, 1975), was suspected of homosexual relationships with his protégés in the twilight of his career. It would, of course, be more likely that pairs of the same sex in coaching relationships keep the relationship emotional rather than actively sexual. For many the thin line between the divisions is often confused. One can expect codes of ethics for coaches to grow out of such dilemmas in the future as official bodies attempt to control what have sometimes been very difficult emotional and sexual rites of passage for young athletes.

Good examples of a coach's constructive use of emotional power and technique are illustrated in the confidence, decisiveness and vision of the following coaches. Linda Brauckmann, coach of Karen Magnussen, world skating champion (as described by Magnussen and Cross, 1973) states that she neither wants nor needs to be in the public eye. She knows who she is: she is a skating teacher who works hard at it and is good at what she does. She knows she can never surpass, by teaching, the degree of talent present in her trainees. She realizes she could be the best skating teacher in the world, but without the talent of the skater ... "you're nothing." It is the skater, therefore, and not the coach who should reap the recognition. The skaters are the performers and the executors, not the coach. She continues that she has never encouraged Karen Magnussen to be competitive and to skate against people. "I always told her to skate for herself. If she was the best, she would win. It was as simple as that." Anatoli Tarasov (1972), former head coach of the Soviet National Hockey Team describes his ideal of what the coach must project for each individual hockey player training with him. In feeling the coach's genuine concern for him, the hockey player gains the confidence necessary to attempt to fulfill the ideal the coach projects. Tarasov stresses the relationship between the coach and the athlete as being crucial to the athlete. The first principles of good coaching command that the coach have an empathic understanding of the athlete's character, an insight into the various paths of development that are possible, a genuine regard

---

*A report from the *New York News,* March 5, 1974. Name of coach omitted by this author.

for the person of the athlete, and the ability to communicate all of this. It is also necessary that the coach be a technical expert at the game, but this alone will not make a good coach. An ideal coach is usually idealistic, genuine, and a natural psychologist. His or her primary concerns are with the welfare of athletes as people. Wooden (1973) former UCLA basketball coach, substantiates the essential positions of Brauckmann and Tarasov. He, too, stresses the importance of athletes doing their best rather than winning against others, competence in development, and cooperation in team membership. The personal and psychological development of the individual is put ahead of achievement in the sport itself, because the wise coach knows that excellence at sport grows out of personal confidence and competence in other areas. Wooden also agrees with Brauckmann's appraisal of talent, and says that a coach is unable to achieve outstanding results unless his trainees have the necessary talent.

The emphasis on competence and character development by these three coaches contrasts sharply with the position often taken by one of America's most famous football coaches, Vince Lombardi. Dowling (1970) quotes a speech made by Lombardi to the Green Bay Packers at their training camp before what was to have been his last season:

> I've never been with a loser, gentlemen, he began, and I don't intend to start at this late date. You're here to play football, and I'm here to see you play as well as your God-given abilities will allow. And that means total dedication. I want total dedication from every man in this room, dedication to himself, to the team, and to winning. Winning is a habit, gentlemen. Winning isn't everything, it's the only thing. If you can shrug off a loss, you can't be a winner. The harder you work, the harder it is to lose. And I'm going to see that you work, I'm going to see that you execute, I'm going to push you and push you and push you because I get paid to win and so do you. Football is a violent game. To play you have to be tough. (pp. 45–46)

Lombardi's men were to serve him in the name of victory. The three coaches already mentioned saw sport as a process of growth for their athletes, and the athletic performance as the province of the athlete. Lombardi emphasizes the external goal of winning and the win belonged to him. He had little faith in the abilities and motivations of his players, and hoped that by forcing them to the utmost he could make them win. Even though sensationally successful within the American football system, Lombardi must be judged a failure on a psychological and social level. This judgment is made despite his success with some individual athletes who operated on the same level. Those athletes went along with the physical and psychological sacrifice he demanded and accepted the same limited set of values: proving oneself superior to others through force, and reaping the material profits of winning. However, Lombardi was also deeply involved emotionally with his athletes.

A coach may urge a trainee, as Lombardi did many times, toward a performance that has a detrimental effect upon the trainee's character development. This occurs when the coach shows no concern for the trainee's personal welfare and concentrates only on the sports performance. It is not surprising that many athletes drop out of sport as a result. They feel used. This was the case with one potential world champion athlete. Her coach stated: "All I care about is that she breaks the world record and that's all she cares about. I'm not interested in her character." This young woman became disillusioned, started using drugs, and became involved with a young man who was not interested in her potential athletic greatness, all probably a direct reaction to the poor quality of the coach-athlete relationship. Timing is essential in coaching relationships. The intense identification of athlete with coach will not last indefinitely, and the coach must move at the correct tempo. The coach must neither frighten nor overprotect the athlete. He or she must not move too quickly or too slowly. He or she must be a personal, as well as a sports, mentor. He or she must always balance the welfare of the individual with excellence at sport. An individual who has the potential but not the psychological resilience necessary to survive the competitive market place of sport, may be protected by the coach or may even drop out of the sport with the coach's blessing.

An example of a successful athlete-coach relationship is provided by gold-medal Olympic swimmer Alex Baumann and his coach, Jeno Tihanyi, a professor of child growth and development, as described by Gasher (1984). Having coached the 22-year-old swimmer since he was nine years old. Tihanyi also supported him through the experiences of his brother's suicide (Baumann's brother had also been a former national team swimmer), the boycott of the Moscow Olympics, a severe shoulder injury, and ultimately, the death of his father. Tihanyi describes the relationship with Baumann as one of complete mutual trust. Mechikoff and Kozar (1983), provide an interesting book on the perspectives of high school and college coaches from the United States, including many insights on the applications of psychology by coaches.

3. The Support Group. This is another essential ingredient in the competent athlete's development, and is well illustrated in the case of several professional athletes. Their performance level is often improved, not by a single coach, but by a network of support from other significant people in the athlete's entourage. Martina Navratilova is given to travelling with a group as a support team. At one time this included Nancy Leiberman, a former U.S. basketball star who acted as her trainer-motivator, and Renee Richards, the tennis-playing transsexual who provided strategic support and for some time acted as coach.

For some athletes and teams the support system is provided by the team itself, which is the reason that morale is so crucial to team success. The many papers on team morale and overall performance levels are a substantive body of literature (see p. 67 and 73), which show the importance of the whole social network and emotional atmosphere in the athlete's training and development. In the competitive world of individual sport it is often necessary for the athlete to operate in a cocoon wherein careful nurturing allows for the high level of exertion and performance. This nurturing is provided by the support group, variously made up of coaches, spouses, lovers, family, and friends.

The early description (1924–1933) of the Hawthorne effect (Roethlisberg and Dickson, 1966), showed how the attention of management and peer group identity in the Western Electric researches was associated with enhanced performance on assembly line jobs. Since then, it has been known that attention and support from significant people boosts performance.* Janis (1982, 1983) suggests the same concept after reviewing the literature on the efficacy of psychotherapy. He carried out a series of experiments in the field in order to test his hypotheses on the importance of social influence processes occurring during counselling sessions. The desired performance changes were, for the most part related to adjustments in terms of job retraining, reduction of smoking, and reduction of eating in the treatment of obesity. Janis describes in detail the process described by Strauss ten years earlier (see pp. 169) but from a different point of view. He breaks the counselling process into three phases: (1) *building referent power,* which includes gaining the respect of clients by giving positive feedback and insight along with the opportunity for cognitive restructuring; (2) *using the referent power,* which includes reinforcing the social support networks and plans of the client to overcome the difficulty or problems; and (3) *retaining the referent power* and promoting internalization after the counselling ends, which includes building self-confidence in the client and fostering personal responsibility. Although Janis's comments are somewhat mechanical in that he ignores the emotional aspects of the exchange (he seeks to promote the "science of counselling"), he does describe in cognitive terms what Strauss described in the coaching relationship. Both conclusions transfer readily to the athletic situation in which the quality of the social support system, provided by coaches and other significant persons, is crucial to the athlete's development and performance. In the end, enhanced performance is related to security and maturation, which in turn allow the individual to take risks. Risks allow the athlete to break free from old habits and structures and to strike out with an inspired new confidence in order that talent and promise can be expressed in maximized performance.

NONESSENTIALS

In the search for higher performance levels many athletes believe in an array of methods for increasing performance which may or may not have value and

---

*For an important critique of these studies, the reader is referred to Bramel and Friend (1981).

which can have damaging effects which far outweigh any psychological advantage. In this section we will examine three very different examples: the pep talk, ergogenic aids, and superstition and anchoring effects.

1. The Pep Talk.   The pep talk is often considered to be a main strength of the coach.   The athletes are presumably "psyched up" so that their motivation to win is increased.   There are many records of pep talks in which the coach, highly aroused himself, may yell, shout, swear, or criticize his team's abilities.   He or she may even become violent, all in the name of winning.   In urging athletes to win by superficially psyching them up, the coach is merely manipulating their emotions at the last minute.   The constructive coach gives what he or she can long before the athletic contest begins, and this has been internalized into the athlete's cognitions and character.

Such an athlete requires no pep talk, nor does the coach need to give one. Karen Magnussen and her coach again provide an excellent example. Brauckmann tended to review some small but unimportant technical points with the skater before a performance.   Then, Brauckmann would wait patiently for her pupil at the gate of the rink.   The coach-athlete relationship was very clear.   Brauckmann had done her coaching and Karen Magnussen was skating.   With a respected coach the pep talk can be helpful if it enables athletes to focus upon the task or raises or lowers arousal levels appropriate to the task before them.   When the pep talk is used to arouse aggression and hate toward the opponent, we suggest it is unscrupulous.   Even in football, not all successful coaches or players use pep talks.   Unless proven otherwise, we conclude that athletes should be very skeptical of short term pre-game arousal techniques, especially when they are controlled by someone other than the athlete.   Studies are much needed on the phenomenon of the pep talk in terms of who uses them, under what conditions, and with what real outcome.

2. Ergogenic Aids.   The competitive ethic elicits much self-destructive behavior from athletes.   One course of self-destruction comes with the use of amphetamines, pep pills, and steroids, or any other assumed booster such as in sodium bicarbonate overloading, commonly described in the athletic world as ergogenic aids.   A few years ago amphetamines were widely used in sport, although this was not public knowledge.   Today the harmful effects of amphetamines and other substances are widely known and officials in sport are now concerned with controlling their use.   Athletes who get up for a contest by artificial means are prevented from developing the psychological strengths to do so on their own. Further, these aids limit the athlete's ability to decide whether he or she wants to get up for the performance because the pills will artifically increase arousal anyway.   Ergogenic aids are a way of ignoring intrinsic mental and physical messages.   They are not ego-enhancing, they are ego-deflating, and they serve to alienate the athlete from his or her own motivations and ability to make decisions.

The same may be said of the long-term use of steroids, which build the body's muscular system and, therefore, increase strength. Steroids are used by football players, weightlifters, boxers, competitors in heavy field events, and others. In 1973 Hopkins suggested that the East German women's swimming team was being trained on steroids, which had caused the exaggerated physical development among the teenaged members of the team. At least one defector from East Germany who swam for the team, Renate Vogel-Heinrich, has substantiated these suspicions. Increasing numbers of high school coaches in North America are suspected of recommending steroids to their athletes, and there are physicians who not only advocate their use, but openly prescribe them (for example, see Todd, 1983).

At writing, the sport world is becoming increasingly aware of and alarmed by the use of drugs. Athletic associations are being forced to take firm stands against their use and athletes themselves are lining up on both sides of the controversy. *Sports Illustrated* has reported the controversy in many magazine articles (as examples see Zimmerman, 1983; Neff, 1983; Johnson, 1985a). The early publication by Morgan (1972) was farsighted indeed in his review of the use of ergogenic aids in sport.

One of the alarming facts of drug use in sport is the extent to which athletes will go in order to escape detection. Thus blood doping is advocated by some. If an athlete's own blood is removed, stored and re-injected just before the contest, this can hardly be considered the injection of an artificial substance. To escape detection from urine tests, athletes have been known to urinate through artificial bags and penises. In the case of strength increase through steroids, some try to avoid detection by ceasing the drug regimen long enough before the contest to escape detection but close enough to maintain the advantage. Still other athletes will play the odds and, since all athletes are not tested in all competitions, manoeuver themselves into the untested category. Increasingly, however, the use of artificial substances can be detected through more accurate and refined tests.

Moreover, liver defects, stroke, heart problems, and the androgenization of male and female athletes have all been linked to steroid use. Some athletes have taken a strong stand against the drug era and should be applauded for their efforts.

The use of drugs to gain unfair advantage in sport contests shows a pathology of values. Strong stands from official bodies are needed and are becoming increasingly common. Athletes using artificial substances should be disqualified from competitions as well as from public and official support. They should be helped and reeducated to become less self-destructive and more appreciative of long-term constructive values in sport. Some athletes will argue that they must use ergogenic aids because the competition does. There is always the suspicion that one's winning opponent has gained unfair advantage through some new or powerful potion. Although the temptation is great, we believe the athlete must win on his or her own constructive terms and not on the terms of others. Because detection techniques are being improved yearly, because there is not conclusive evidence that artificial aids increase all performance, and because many of them have dangerous side effects, no athlete should be prescribed drugs and artificial aids to sport performance. If athletes become hooked on drug regimens they will become walking labs for drug technicians. Competitions will then take place between technicians and not between athletes.

3. Superstition and Anchoring Effects. Superstitious behavior is very common among athletes. Pele was one of the most superstitious of stars, obsessed with the number 10, which he constantly wove into his life, routine, and career in sport. Phil Esposito was reported to have an array of superstitions, including one against seeing crossed hockey sticks in the dressing room before a game. This was certain to signify defeat. In tennis, many players, John Newcombe among them, wore copper bands or bracelets to ward off injuries and control arthritis. Tony Roche was known to wear the same pair of tennis shorts for two years because he believed the shorts were lucky for him. Many athletes have a favorite piece of clothing, or will walk in a certain pattern on the court or the field. They will wear charms to ward off injury, go through pregame rituals, and indulge in special movements before performing. If athletes believe that through these rituals, performance will improve, then they, in truth, believe in magic. Sometimes institutionalized means are used, such as Vince Lombardi's mustering his team for a pregame prayer as part of the game preparation.

Superstition and religion in sport are forms of self-suggestion requiring a process of disassociation so that encouragement and support can emerge in one's self-interest from a projection of one's own mind. Sometimes these projections are simply objects supposed to bring luck. At other times they are projections of past protectors such as parents, guardians, coaches, or religious symbols. When such projections foster cooperation, communal thinking, and appreciation of life, strong religious or spiritual values are constructive (see for example the case of Oh, pp. 41). More often, in sport, they foster a sense of being the one the Almighty favors. Thus the individual obtains his sanction through duties, charms, or tokens of luck, and gains support in preserving his or her place in a competitive world. This conception of the world is no more than a reflection of the competitor's inner self, and it is unfortunate that the conception is such a powerful one for as long as it is the experience of true religious feeling will elude the competitor (Jung, 1933).

Superstitious behavior is sometimes used in the psychological techniques pre-scribed for athletes. The notion of "key words" to facilitate sport performance is one such example. If a basketball player is having difficulty on free throws or an archer is releasing shots too soon, then it is possible to train the individual to associate a "key word" with the moment of release of ball or arrow. The basketball player may think, say to himself, or say aloud "sink," and the archer may think "rose" at the crucial time. This trick may help the athlete focus on the task and control unwanted anxiety or distraction at crucial moments. Many athletes claim to have been helped by this small technique. Yet there are other methods of helping an athlete over a block, through the development of self-confidence and skill, so that the athlete believes in his or her own capabilities rather than in the "key word" technique.

The problem with pep talks, ergogenic aids, and psychological techniques such as key words is that they all provide anchoring effects which are external to the athlete. Because they anchor the individual externally they create a potential for distracting the athlete from the hurdles and challenges which must be met directly with increased self-confidence if the athlete is to achieve maximum potential.

TEN GUIDELINES FOR IMPROVING PERFORMANCE

It is inevitable that athletes and coaches want to know how best to foster constructive improvement in sport. How can the coach and athlete realistically satisfy their strong desires to concentrate on sport and to experience maximum levels of achievement? How can they escape the traps, fads, and false promises which so frequently present themselves in the world of sport? The following ten points are offered as guidelines. These are intended to encourage competence in athletes and to give them a solid base upon which to develop both character and excellence at sport. These guidelines apply to both professional and amateur athletes and, for the most part, to all levels of skill development.

1. The athlete should develop a clear understanding of, and feeling for, the intrinsic value of the sport in which he or she participates. This is most easily developed when the athlete is introduced to the sport by a coach who communicates the joys, challenges, and rewards the sport holds. If athletes understand that the sport in which they participate is greater than themselves and will continue longer than they will, and if they have a clear picture of its organization and rules, and understand that it places the highest value upon the development of competence, then the athlete will be able to concentrate fully upon developing his or her own competence and appreciating the competence of others. Many athletes become frustrated because they are led to believe the sport is ripe for their own exploitation. They become aware of the external rewards of sport and set out to attain the top by any means available, thinking only of themselves and their success. A deep feeling of identification with the value and esthetic qualities of the sport will allow the athlete close communication with those who share that appreciation.

2. The developing athlete should be provided with coaches and athletic models who fulfill the ideals of the sport and the sports community. The models provided, deliberately or by accident, for a developing athlete will have an important effect upon his or her athletic adjustment, for the athlete will take on the qualities, behaviors and values of those with whom he or she identifies. If they are mean, rude, and bitter, the athlete will likely absorb those qualities, just as if they are mannerly, fun-seeking, or fancy-dressers, he or she will emulate those. The important point here is that coaches and models must be selected for traits other than sports skill alone. The current sports scene has so many destructive characters within it, that probably the most discerning young people drop out, their reaction being: "I don't want to be like that and, therefore, I will never play like that." The less discerning will adopt, and identify with, the model as sanctioned by society, and proceed, therefore, to take on the qualities of the model whether or not those qualities and behaviors are constructive or destructive to themselves or to sport in general. Any sports program should give special attention to the characteristics of both the coaches and athletes it supports, for the transmission of false and destructive values in sport occurs at this level more than at any other level in the development of the athlete.

3. The atmosphere and opportunity for regular and adequate training must be provided. A golfer must have frequent and regular access to a course, a tennis player to a court, a swimmer to a pool, and a skater to a rink. Athletes participating in team sports must have organized practices and training in adequate facilities. In many cases, athletes have become frustrated in their athletic careers because of the absence or unavailability of facilities. Given his or her enthusiasm, the athlete should not be frustrated by being unable to gain access to the facilities so badly needed for development. Practice and regular training are essential to athletes.

4. The atmosphere and the opportunity for regular and adequate mental practice and mental discipline must be provided. Mental practice can help immensely in developing sport skill. This is discussed fully in Chapter 15. Because of this, an athlete will improve most quickly if he or she regularly spends time in mental rehearsal when resting, traveling or relaxing. He or she can think of strategies, imagine games in progress and rehearse his or her reaction to various tight or pressure situations. Mental practice also takes place when the athlete sits down with fellow athletes and coaches to talk sport or review style, techniques, strengths, and shortcomings. All of this allows the athlete to perfect his or her skills, to become more rounded, and to gain in confidence.

5. In team sports, which include almost all, since even individual sports are often organized around teams, the team spirit and dynamics can be optimized by careful selection and balancing of a group, which in turn will increase the performance level of all. It is very easy for a group to be sabortaged by the consequences of too many conflicting individual needs, or by a single team member bent on performing better than the others by any means. The psychological duress such individual motivations can cast over a team can render the team stagnant insofar as improvements in performances are concerned. Sometimes if cliques are present on a team and the status of the members is not flexible, performance also may become stagnant. If team members are constructively bent on representing themselves, their team and their sport in the best way possible, then a skillful leader should be able to correct flaws in a team structure. With careful selections of teams and attention to group structure, performance levels can be raised all around. When this philosophy is adopted, some positions on a team might be filled by athletes who are chosen more for their ability to encourage others than for their own performance.

6. The athlete should have clearly in mind his or her goals in maximizing performance. How good does the individual want to become? Does he or she want to play on the school team, the national team, make the Olympics, or be Olympic champion? Most very successful athletes have a dream and, hence an image in their minds of the things they would like to do and the goals they would like to accomplish. To have an ultimate goal that one would like to achieve but is not neurotically attached to increases motivation and acts as a guide for the individual's activities. This is true of personal as well as professional goals. A plan will give direction. It will prevent floundering and indecision, and when new channels for development and opportunities arise the athlete will be poised to take them.

7. The athlete should be provided with social and personal support for as far as he or she can go in the athletic hierarchy. The athlete's climb to the top of a world sports' ladder is demanding, full of pitfalls as well as challenges, and can be lonely. For this reason the athlete should not, unless he or she prefers it, have to train for competitions without group support. The athlete should not have to travel to competitions without the company of interested supporters or fellow athletes and should not be encouraged to leave his or her groups of origin behind as he or she improves in athletic skill; rather the athlete should be continually encouraged to refer back to them for a mutual sort of support. During his or her passage to ever more difficult levels in the sport's hierarchy, the athlete must not be made to feel that he or she is giving up personal attachments and sources of support. The athlete needs to feel that his or her old psychological environment is still supportive. He or she also needs new groups and coaches with whom to identify. Very often athletes cannot move smoothly from group to group as their athletic skill improves. The mechanisms and pathways are often not present within the sports organization in which the athlete develops, so that, for example, he or she moves forward to late adolescent excellence and then meets a vacuum when reaching out to develop further.

   8. Discussions should be conducted by the coach before championship events so that the athlete can adequately organize specific championship goals. The athlete should go into an important contest fully motivated and believing he or she will do well. The athlete should look forward to the achievement of a new level of competence and the chance to test his or her ability. There must be no holding back on how the individual feels on a given day (the athlete feels positively), no complaints about the conditions (because the athlete has prepared for them) and no threat if he or she does not win (for others will then have done better and for that the athlete appreciates and respects them). But the athlete must know what he or she wants and is striving for. In high level sports, contestants are often quite evenly matched and the athlete with the most purpose, the best thought and planning and the highest level of aspiration will perform best.

   9. Before major meets, championships or tests, a careful study of the prospective opposition and the setting for the contest should be made. This is an extension of mental rehearsal, but used in preparation for a specific event. The site, climate, atmosphere, and conditions of the event should be thoroughly familiar to the athlete. So, too, should the style, strengths, weaknesses, and records of the opposing team, person or entrants. In some events, such as track and field, the other participants are perhaps less interesting than they are in direct contact sports such as boxing, tennis, or team sports. Still they are important in all sports. The athlete should go to the contest with a full knowledge of the situation and what he or she will face. When there are too many unknowns he or she may be distracted from full concentration and performance. Step by step, before and after the event, the coach and the athlete are well advised to prepare for all likely or even unlikely circumstances to be faced.

   10. Last and most important, an athlete cannot be forced to perform at a level beyond his or her degree of personal and social maturity; sometimes a coach or others may just have to wait. It is very unwise to push an athlete who is having trouble with motivation, erratic performance, or dedication to practice. Many developing athletes are in the process of resolving adolescent personality conflicts and other problems of identity and purpose. The athlete has to come to the coach. It is not enough that a parent bring the athlete to the coach or that someone else is "baby sitting" and planning the athlete's future career. The potential athlete, himself or herself, must decide.   Sometimes athletes will develop very slowly within a sports program and get pushed either up or out. Neither is the answer.   The athlete should be understood by a coach; problems should be dealt with if possible, but otherwise the athlete should be allowed to develop at his or her own pace.

15
Treatment Techniques

INTRODUCTION

Numerous psychological techniques are applied in sport psychology. It is therefore fitting that this chapter be devoted to outlining and describing some precursors to the currently used techniques as well as ten categories of technique used in sport psychology.

In sport, as in other fields, definitive studies have not been made to demonstrate significant differences between the various schools of treatment or technique. Janis (1982), in the paper discussed in the preceding chapter, attempted to specify the changes which take place in clients as a result of interventive counselling and the factors which sustain that change thereafter. He saw the major mediators of change in *the social influence process* and in *the social support network* of the client when he or she leaves therapy. In spite of the immense amount of time, energy, and money psychologists have expended on the evaluation of change, it is quite probable that one can look to sport psychology to provide the landmark studies of the future. The performance criteria and possibilities for controlled studies are significantly better from the field of sport psychology than from the field of psychotherapy. This is because the performance criteria (the dependent variables in any outcome studies) offered in the study of sport come close to a researcher's dream.

Why then has psychology and sport taken so long to be seen as a unified area of study? In many ways sport has not needed psychology, and psychologists have tended to be ignorant of sport. This is no longer the case. By reporting that sport did not need psychology, we mean that good athletes are usually prototypes of optimal psychological concentration. Many have developed excellent psychological focus and habits in conjunction with the development of their other skills in sport. As an example, Joan Benoit's coach of 1984, Bob Sevene, described her as using no conscious mental training. She does not spend significant time visualizing a race before she runs it nor does she need to see a race course before she runs. Instinctually, she runs to better her own performance, and rarely thinks of "beating" someone else.

However, with the large sums of money, various investments, and career status often at stake in major sporting competitions, not all athletes are as able to concentrate on competence. Athletes and their mentors are increasingly turning to professional psychologists and others in the quest for a competitive edge. This is a beneficial trend to the extent that most qualified psychologists have gone through long training in which the basic ethic is respect for individual welfare. A danger lies in the degree to which practitioners are caught up in the drive for success at the expense of the athlete's welfare.

If psychologists concentrate on the growth and welfare of the athlete, a very bright future can be expected for psychological applications in sport and from the resulting research and writing. An important body of knowledge should emerge from the many studies that are now planned and in progress on the comparative merits of the techniques to be described in this chapter.

THE PRECURSORS

1. Hypnosis and Suggestion. Hypnosis as a source of behavioral change has been much studied and argued without substantive support from research studies of its efficacy. Still, many athletes have performed under hypnotic induction. Parrish (1972) cites his use of self-hypnosis in football. He was presumably able to count himself in and out of a state of suggestion before a play, during which he intensified his plans and motivations. Although Parrish claims this worked well on some occasions, it usually worked when it closely followed one of his formal lessons in the technique. Thus, he abandoned the technique as unreliable.

Attempts to study the outcomes and the efficacies of hypnosis have produced inconsistent conclusions. It seems that some subjects in some studies have had their performances raised by hypnosis while others have not. In general, the more expert the athlete, the less his or her performance will be affected by hypnosis. However, personality factors such as susceptibility, self-confidence, and field-dependence might be expected to interact with the hypnotic suggestion to determine its effect. Hypnosis, like any other pheonomenon, has a "placebo effect" in that people expect and hope for positive effects and are, therefore, psychologically receptive to experiencing positive change in performance. Thus, some temporary change occurs because of the psychological set of the subject and not because of the objective effect of the technique. The same positive but temporary change is observed after the use of new drugs, new forms of psychotherapy, and new teaching techniques. The subjects will usually sink back to their earlier level of performance with the passage of time.

The word *hypnosis* often carries magical connotations and, in fact, does not have to be used at all. Barber (1970, 1974, 1980) has probably carried out more studies than anyone on the phenomenon, and he concludes that what is commonly known as a hypnotic trance is nonexistent. Barber personally demonstrates the power of self-suggestion by setting the flame of a match to his own hand, after preparing himself not to react. According to Barber, what is observed in hypnosis is a demonstration of the extraordinary powers of attitudes and emotions. Barber's position is borne out by the results of London and Fuhrer, (1961) who also conclude that the strength of "hypnosis" in influencing performance stems from the motivational instructions given, not from the magic of a hypnotic trance. Moss (1965) concluded that the presumed effects of hypnosis upon performance are a much exaggerated phenomenon.

Any process induced in an athlete through a hypnotist or the use of suggestion must be aimed at ego-building rather than ego-defeating, if it is to be successful. The athlete himself, captain, group leader or coach, must aim toward encouraging permanent habits, attitudes, and skills in the subject, which will become part of his or her everyday repertoire. Thus, Riecke (1969) suggests using hypnosis not just to "achieve maximum effort during competition" but to "improve all of the qualities necessary to make a champion athlete ..." He suggests using hypnosis to contribute to the development of five essential factors: (1) to increase motivation and to foster an intense desire to train, (2) to "correct errors in technique," (3) to be able to manage annoying factors in the environment, (4) to encourage the expression of a "fierce competitive attitude at the proper time" and (5) to assist the athlete in removing his mental limits.*   Riecke is a former weightlifter, and knows well the psychological barriers the athlete must overcome. Hypnosis is not the best way to go about removing them, however, and the sooner the athlete stops thinking in terms of hypnosis and starts thinking about the process of acquiring good mental traits or habits, the sooner he or she will develop mastery and the skill he or she desires to perfect.

There is another classic way in which hypnosis is used in sport: to treat injuries. This brings up quite a different set of considerations from hypnosis used to increase performance. In treating injuries one is trying to eliminate a given sensation in a localized part of the body, which may be caused by both subjective and physical factors. In contrast to the attempt to increase performance, here one is trying to assist the athlete to acquire a set of mental characteristics with which to meet temporary problems.

The use of hypnosis to treat sport injuries has been studied by Ryde (1971). He accumulated the results of 250 cases after nine years of study. In these cases hypnosis was used to treat sports injury where "the loss of function was due mainly to muscle spasm and anxiety." He reported that his results were inconclusive, and that the purpose of his work was to provoke interest in the technique. Some individuals were not helped, as in the case of a sprinter suffering from leg cramps: hypnotic induction was attempted immediately at the onset of the cramp, but failed to have any effect. In contrast other individuals seem to have been helped immensely through hypnosis, as in the case of a runner, aspring

---

*Cited by permission from *Hypnosis Quarterly,* Vol. XIV, No. 3, 1969, p. 7 ff.

to an Olympic team, who overtrained after a month's layoff caused by illness. He experienced pains in his calf muscles. After hypnosis, on the day prior to a race, the pain disappeared. He established a new record (unofficial) for his age group during the race, after which the pain resumed. Ryde also describes a case in which the condition was "non-traumatic," that of a table tennis player with a "painful limp from a withlow on her R. hellux." One hour before a national championship the pain was reduced by hypnosis, after which she was able to play well, losing by a narrow margin. Ryde concludes:

> There is about 40 percent symptom removal from all subjects in my hands in selected cases. This rises to just over 50 percent when hypnotized subjects only are considered, excluding those subjects who achieve some degree of relief. These results do not form part of a controlled trial and so lose some of their value; it must be borne in mind that some of the patients who were undergoing prolonged hospital treatment also showed an instantaneous symptom removal. These results contradict all my previous learning and experience, for there is an apparent alteration in the natural history of disease.

There are many professionals who actively explore the use of hypnosis in sport and in other fields. Pulos (1979) is one advocate of its use in sport for the purpose of developing good habits over a long term. The applications and study of suggestion and hypnosis in sport remain an important field for investigation, the potential results having implications that reach far beyond the sport world.*

MENTAL PRACTICE

A frequently posed question in sport literature is whether mental or physical practice is most important in the acquisition of skill. There are numerous studies on this question. One major review of the literature was published by Mohr (1971). She reviews 39 studies, of which 24 contrasted mental with physical practice. Of these, 19 concluded that mental and physical practice were equally important, four concluded that physical practice was superior, and one found mental practice to be superior. Feltz and Landers (1983) reported the most recent review of mental practice effects, concluding that there are perhaps special conditions under which mental practice is most effective. They did not address themselves to the relative merits of mental and physical practice.

Why is mental practice valuable? Just as physical effort and practice may influence pathways of association in our bodies and our minds, so too pictures in our minds also may influence physical capabilities by stimulating the same

---

*For reviews of research on hypnosis the reader is referred to Hilgard and Hilgard (1983) and Kihlstrom (1985).

pathways. For example, an individual who has no mental image of how to shoot a basketball is unlikely to be able to perform one well. The person who has watched others can transform a mental observation into physical action. If the basketball shot is visualized over and over and is combined with continuous practice on the court, then that makes for the best chance of developing a shooting skill. The importance of mental practice is recognized in strategy sessions that go on in almost all sports, including the training of football, tennis, and golf teams. Any sound training schedule will allow time for this means of improving skill. Most major athletes will attest to using mental imagery techniques. They will not be facing new situations, in championship contests, for in their minds they will have been there many times before. The acceptance of mental practice and the appreciation of its importance forms the basis of many of the treatment techniques now in vogue.

TREATMENT AND TRAINING TECHNIQUES

In order to do well in sport, there are five types of discipline or categories of training required. The first is *physical skill training*. This involves practicing the sport, doing drills or playing practice games, matches, or simulating competitions. The second is *physical fitness training,* which includes activities such as weight lifting, working out on exercise machines, running, diet, sleep regimens, and so on. This is a highly developed area and one in which advocates of machinery and technology have a field day. Over the last 20 years, there has been a proliferation of equipment for both training and assessment of physical fitness. The third area is that of *cognitive training,* which is currently in vogue and essentially the subject of this chapter. The fourth area involves *affectional training,* or emotional training. This involves the quest for emotional maturity in the athlete but often it is elusive. This is not only because many sports training programs ignore this phase of development but also because the modal personality structure of the athlete (described in Chapter 9) in some ways make the achievement of emotional maturity difficult. The fifth and final type of training for optimal performance involves how to use, benefit from, and cooperate with a social support network, or *social support network usage.* North Americans tend to focus upon the individual in training programs to the exclusion of that person's social embeddedness and dependence. One may safely predict that in the future there will be continuing and important emphasis upon social support networks and how to create them, sustain, and evaluate them.

The remainder of this chapter will examine ten of the most frequently used forms of cognitive, behavioral and affective training. Since all of the techniques have features in common, any categorization will mean some overlap and repetition. The overall purpose of the techniques is to correct dysfunctional thought, behavior, and/or emotion in order that the athlete be able to reach full potential.

Almost all of the techniques try to deal with competitive stress, distraction, anxiety, and fragmentation of motivation. They are used both for overarousal and for underarousal, that is, for "burnout" or for low motivation.

1. Positive Thinking. One of the oldest techniques for self-improvement comes from the old Coué assertion: "Every day in every way I am getting better and better." If stated to oneself in the mirror each morning, life reportedly improves. The idea of positive thinking was picked up by Dale Carnegie with his series of self-help books, such as the famous *How to Win Friends and Influence People*. In the same way, current psychotherapists strive to help their clients overcome dysfunctional thought patterns and replace them with functional ones. Two examples are Beck's (1967) psychology of and treatment of depressive conditions and Ellis, (1973) goals for clients in his Rational Emotive Therapy.

In Beck's work the primary focus is on having depressed patients give up their negative patterns of thinking for more optimistic ones. The major thrust of Ellis's technique is that the client give up catastrophic thoughts which might have to do with expectations of rejection, low feelings of self-worth, fears of being thought pushy, stupid, and so on. The client is given assignments in which he or she is sent out to execute certain acts which seem threatening or impossible. With the new mode of thinking, the client will not crumble if the actions fail because the catastrophic thinking has been altered. There is a strong emphasis upon mental rehearsal and positive thinking in these techniques. *Psychocybernetics* (Maltz, 1966, 1974) is a popular variation on the theme in which mental training and mental imagery, featuring positive expection, are given top priority. *Thought stopping* (Cautela and Wisocki, 1977) was another innovation encouraging the athlete or client to stop negative thoughts when they come into mind. A positive thought is then substituted for the negative one and the client learns to regulate and eventually eradicate negative thinking. *Discriminant cue analysis* trains the athlete to note the differences between times of high level performance and low level performance. By comparing and contrasting the two situations, the athlete learns the cues and triggers for the successful outcome and will be trained to focus upon them in the future. Positive thinking techniques should be introduced into the training programs of all athletes, with or without a formal trainer.

2. Competence Training. All psychotherapies have within them the goal of increasing the self-esteem or self-confidence of the client. In order to achieve this, the client must become sensitive to the feedback and pleasure experienced when he or she influences or interacts with the environment in a desired manner. A sense of competence will develop when plans, ideas, and actions are executed successfully in the way the individual intended. Intrinsic feedback will be paramount and self-confidence will transfer to similar future situations. Bandura's studies (1977, 1982, 1983) on self-efficacy and the expectation of success address themselves to the issue of competence. So does Morgan (1981) in his studies on effort sense and motor memory. The individual with effort sense uses both psychological and physiological self-knowledge to make accurate predictions of his or her ability to execute specified tasks. Attribution theory (Heider, 1944, 1958) is closely allied with the development of competence and can be applied widely in sport settings. For an athlete's competence to grow, he or she must be able to attribute success to efforts, intentions or motivations of the self rather than attributing it to external factors such as luck, equipment, favoritism, or ergogenic aids. There is a tendency for most athletes, and people in general, to attribute successful outcomes to their own efforts and unsuccessful ones to outside factors (Greenwald, 1980; Lau and Russell, 1980). Rhodewalt, Saltzman, and Wittmer (1982) have found some athletes to be *self-handicapping*. These athletes do not go all out in preparations for important events, presumably so that failure can be attributed to lack of preparation and self-esteem therefore can be protected. Protecting self-esteem through faulty attribution will interfere with the development of competence. Press interviews after major competitions will usually support the attribution prediction that external factors will be blamed for losses more frequently than internal factors. Wins are attributed to the good performance of the interviewee.

Several of the following techniques attempt to focus the athlete upon his or her own execution in sport in order to highlight internal experiences. If athletes suffer from poor motivation or "burnout" the first question is why the athlete is not experiencing sufficient competence feedback from sport to maintain motivation. If the athlete is inclined to be playing for others, (a parent or a coach, for example), for money, or for other external reasons, then it is not surprising that motivation falters. The emphasis on competence training is an essential theme of this book and it is the author's focus in both research and consulting in the psychology of sport (Butt, 1976, 1979, 1980).

3. Meditation. Since the 1960s there has been a mushrooming interest into the powers of mind as practiced by Eastern religions and sects. For many, meditation seemed to have release value from the pressures and strife of everyday life. It provided contemplative and spiritual techniques which encouraged concentration on the subjective mind as described in the teachings of Chinese, Japanese, and Indian philosophies. The Way of Life, the Buddhistic ways, and the ways of yoga and transcendental meditation became major tools in the quest for equanimity of young North Americans. On the heels of the meditation movement came the applications of subjective psychology in sport. Gallwey's (1974; Gallwey and Kriegel, 1979) books on inner tennis and inner skiing were matched by Nideffer's (1976) book on the inner athlete. The techniques had been more formally spelled out by Benson and Klipper (1976) in *The Relaxation Response*. Meditation of any type involves reflection on the spiritual or subjective side of one's nature and the loosening of the mind, body, and spirit from the structures which usually encase them. The quest for freedom and inner peace may well be necessary for a true feeling of accomplishment. Thus it is not surprising that athletes should try to tap inner resources while reaching for outstanding achievements. That meditation should be adopted by some athletes as a corrective process is a significant trend worthy of study.

4. Relaxation. Relaxation and its many variations is a much used introductory technique in sport psychology. It is used to ready clients for cognitive restructuring, for mental practice, and for visual motor behavioral rehearsal.

Relaxation-tension contrasts, progressive muscle relaxation without tensing, differential relaxation, and *relaxation activation* are all variations of how to produce a restful and often preparatory state in clients. They are used not only in sport psychology but also in prenatal classes, with the elderly, in various study programs, and in the control of obesity and smoking behavior, to name a few applications. Sequences are repeated verbally and are printed in several books (Bell, 1983, pp. 50–52; Suinn, 1980, pp. 310–313; Nideffer, 1981, pp. 176–177). Easily obtainable are the relaxation sequences on numerous tape cassettes. (For example see Joseph Barber, 1981, "Natural hypnosis induction" and T.X. Barber, 1978, "Philosophical Hypnosis.") If relaxation is practiced every day for two or three weeks the individual will probably be able to relax specific muscle groups at will. The new skill can be used to reduce anxiety and tension before practice and competition or to control nerves at other stressful times. As Nideffer (1981) points out, one does not want to induce relaxation in an athlete who needs vast amounts of concentrated energy to perform his or her task just before a sport contest or performance.

Classic work on the theory and application of relaxation techniques can be found in the books by Wolpe and Lazarus (1966) and Jacobson (1976). Groups of athletes, for example in workshops or training programs, will usually respond very well to relaxation techniques, in fact, sometimes too well in that it is common for athletes to fall asleep during them.

5. Affective Control. Since 1908 the *Yerkes-Dodson law* has been used to explain the relationship between arousal (emotion) and performance. It found that arousal and anxiety are related to performance and achievement criteria in the shape of an inverted U curve. With a low level of arousal animals and humans do not perform particularly well. As arousal (motivation) becomes greater, performance improves. As arousal rises still further, performance begins to fall off as the high tension presumably interferes with the execution of the task.

Anxiety is a fact of life. It often occurs as the result of stress. It can also occur because an individual has developed a disposition for anxiety reaction over time or because an individual has an innate or genetic predisposition to manifest

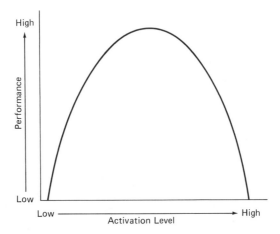

Figure 9. Performance as a Function of Arousal Level. There is a curvilinear relationship between performance level and arousal or activation level in the shape of an inverted U. This applies to any given task and also to sport performance. There are variations in the progress of the curve but not in the inverted U shape.

and/or to react with anxiety. The U-shaped curve describes observations of animals and human subjects across groups. Individuals can reflect infinite variations on this theme. Some athletes will perform best when under extreme arousal while others will appear either to be burned out or to have lost control of their ability to perform. Thus any treatment for affectional control must take account of individual differences as well as the situational demands of the sport performance. Any techniques used to "hype" athletes are of dubious merit because if athletes are performing out of competence motivation they do not need to be aroused for a contest by external means. Their excitement and anticipation of competence will summon enough energy (energy which White, 1963, called *effectance*) to perform. Malmo's (1959) drive theory is applied by many practitioners in sport. Problems of motivation arise from a lack of control of affect and energy. Thus the control of drive is an important area in applied sport psychology. Problems can often be cast in terms of overexcitability on the one hand versus blandness and boredom on the other. Although individuals may be predisposed to these two reactions it is important to note that they may also be reacting to the demands of the sport situation which can be unrealistic and debilitating. If the athlete does not have the desire or the ability to change in accordance with the demands of sport, alternative activities and commitments should be considered. The careers of many athletes have benefited from an extended period away from sport. If the athlete has severe emotional and motivational problems in sport, treatment may move from the educational into the clinical sphere.

When affective fears and anxieties are specific, then a specific cognitive or behavioral technique may be applied. This would occur in a case in which an athlete wants to stay in sport but is bothered by a specific phobia, anxiety-arousing symptom, or situation. For example, an archer constantly releases the arrow involuntarily, a tennis player cannot toss the ball accurately for the serve in tight match situations, or a baseball player is overcome with a nervous twitching when he approaches the batting situation. The study of anxiety in North America has almost always been confined to an examination of the individual — his or her nervous system and noncoping behavior or negative cognitions. In fact, problems of too much or too little arousal may be due to the society in which the individual finds him/herself. There is often either too much pressure on the individual to achieve and perform or too little social support and meaning for what the individual does. Successful sport programs mediate this unrealistic environment through the presence of a support system. Note that in our current sport system, where so many athletes have problems related to arousal, the psychologist treating those problems becomes part of the support system.

In fact, for most affective impairments, it would be best to change the demands made on the individual, rather than trying to change the individual. This would involve a massive overhaul of many sport organizations as well as of the social values underlying them in order to reduce the competitive pressures, stress, and conflict imposed upon the participants. Since changes in organizations are usually very slow and often rely upon generational change, practitioners are usually expected to try and make the individual adjust. Martens (1971, 1977) has addressed himself to the study and treatment of anxiety in sport and offers several insights on the treatment of anxiety in athletes.

6. Cognitive Behavioral Techniques. Most applied psychologists in sport currently practice what are known as cognitive behavioral techniques. Very frequently some form of relaxation precedes the cognitive training, which is essentially another form of mental practice. Growing out of the older behavioral techniques, which were clearly inadequate in dealing with most human problems, the cognitive techniques are backed by the assumption that the human animal has a mind which guides and regulates behavior. The older techniques which grew out of work of Watson (1913, 1919) and Skinner (1953) still have some application in sport. Rushall and Siedentop (1972) have done much writing and practice of the orthodox transplantation of behavioral principles to sport. In fact, although theory and experimentation can be kept pure (true to scientific criteria), practice cannot. It is clear that Rushall's applied work has been attentive not only to the behavioral rehearsal of athletes, but also to their cognitions and affects. Thus it is to Wolpe and Lazarus (*Behavioral Therapy Techniques*, 1976), Craighead, Kazdin, and Mahoney (*Behavior Modification*, 1981); Mahoney (*Cognitive and Behavior Modification*, 1974); and Meichenbaum (*Cognitive Behavior Modification*, 1977) that one looks for the theoretical background and techniques for the application of clinical treatments to sport. At present, clinical psychology focuses on these techniques and their applications. They have been widely used for educational purposes in terms of encouraging positive mental approaches toward learning and for the treatment of pathology, for example in attempts to alleviate smoking, anxiety, obesity, and insecurity. Some of the well-known techniques are *desensitization*, in which positive reinforcement and cognitions are associated with a regulated approach toward functional responses, and *aversive conditioning* where negative reinforcement and cognitions are linked to undesired responses. These techniques and others provide guidelines for the reinforcement of functional behavior and thoughts and the negative reinforcement of dysfunctional behavior and thoughts. For a full description of the cognitive techniques now applicable to sport see Staub and Williams (1984). The behavioristic tradition continues as an adjunct to cognitive psychology.

Few practice radical behaviorism today in sport. It tends to neglect important aspects of human functioning, namely the individuality or the personality of the client. Behavioral theory misses any specification of the "core" or basic assumptions surrounding individual differences and also fails to develop any "peripheral" hypotheses of personality. It is therefore very difficult to apply it effectively when treating individuals, who are reacting, thinking, and assessing during the course of treatment. However, cognitive psychology, along with the skillful use of reinforcement, has provided an array of clinical training techniques, which sometimes have innovative or direct application to sport. Again, what psychology yields to sport is terminology, precision, and goal specification for practices which some people in sport have been using for many years. Many athletes and coaches have used mental practice and goal setting techniques in their training regimens long before psychologists formalized the procedures.

7. Autogenic Training (and Biofeedback). A forerunner of biofeedback, autogenic training was popularized by Schultz and Luthe (1959) in Switzerland. Termed a physiological approach to psychotherapy, this training can be carried out with individuals or in groups. The aim is to gain control over the involuntary nervous system by homeostatic self-regulation. For example, in archery, where involuntary release of the arrow is common, the instructor assists the client to concentrate on various regions of the body in order to gain control over each in turn. The heart and respiratory system may be the focus of concentration, or the warmth of the extremities or the tension within neck muscles.

There is some indication that the practice of the technique can lead to reduced respiration rate, blood pressure, and tension and that self-confidence and concentration may improve as byproducts. The technique is much applied in the European sport world; there is, however, no hard evidence of improved performance.

In the late twentieth century biofeedback has become a popular variation on the principles of autogenic training. It fits neatly into the *zeitgeist* (spirit of the times) due to its emphasis upon and use of instrumentation to monitor and inform the client of various bodily processes and functions which he or she is then trained to control. For example, one might be trained to control heart rate by watching it on a monitor, tension by carrying an instrument to measure galvanic skin response, and so on. There is no doubt, due to its appeal and the rampant commercialization of equipment, that we will continue to witness its development in both clinical and sport psychology. Some advocate the use of biofeedback machines in sport for everything from strength training to early injury detection. As Nideffer (1981, pp. 169–170) points out, the expense of the equipment involved and the equivocal results make biofeedback an impractical but promising addition to the practice of sport psychology.

8. Visual Motor Behavioral Rehearsal. The method developed by Suinn (1980b) in his work with skiers in Colorado includes a relaxation phase followed by special cognitive training. Suinn believes the quality and intensity of imagery rehearsal to be higher and more intense after relaxation. He writes that the imagery created must be more than visual. It is also tactile, auditory, emotional, and muscular. That is, the athlete training mentally can experience all of the sensations that are felt when he or she actually is performing. They can then practice specific skills when in the state. The skiers, for example, practiced specific racing techniques, course concenration, and memorization of the course. If an athlete were having trouble with a specific turn, one might show him or her a video of it being successfully executed. The athlete can then imagine him or herself over and over again, executing the actions successfully and actually experiencing the feel of doing it. This is a variation on the theme of mental practice, which has been in the literature for many years. In this case, note that there is a highly trained and concerned psychologist, Suinn, who is assisting in the training, techniques, and goal setting. In assisting with these decisions and problems on a daily basis, the psychologist becomes an important part of the social support structure for both coach and athletes; that is, he and his assistants may be seen as part of the team.

9.   Attentional Control Training. The underlying assumption of the technique (Nideffer, 1978b; Nideffer and Sharpe, 1978) is that concentration is facilitated or blocked by one's attentional style (see p. 230). Thus an athlete with a narrow attentional focus might have a tendency to choke because he or she fails to react flexibly or quickly in sport situations. For example, when in a tight corner in basketball, a player might fail to see openings and alternatives in play because of tension and self-absorption. The athlete needs to react to important cues and ignore interfering cues. This might be accomplished through relaxation training, mental rehearsal, and general discussions on what the problem is and what can be done about it. Nideffer has developed an assessment technique for clinical and/or computerized feedback for the sport community, and in so doing has commercialized a highly specialized psychological consulting service. Its strengths lie in the assessment of individual style, consideration of the unique demands of the sport, and suggestions on how the individual might adjust or alter deficits.

10. Religion and Spiritual Exploration. In spite of the elaborate psychological techniques now available to athletes, many athletes, particularly at the professional level, still suffer from severe emotional crises, as well as motivational and behavioral problems. Some claim to have found relief from their anxiety, value crises, and personal problems not in training techniques or in psychological practitioners, but in the security and renewal accompanying religious conversion. They claim that their religious belief and recognition of a greater power outside themselves has allowed them to continue successfully in sport from what were originally positions of extreme setback and personal and psychological crises.

We do not mean here that religion may be used as a quick patch up for athletes such as in the use of the pre-game prayer so that they play better (see pp. 176). We are referring to genuine and total conversions in which the individual feels renewed, "born again," a different person. Although not a psychological technique, it would be remiss not to include religion since many athletes have found it helpful. Note that there is overlap between some religious training and the techniques of both meditation and relaxation. Note also that religion can be an important source of social support and can also give value support or increase the breadth of value commitment. The individuality in commitment fostered by competitive and commercial sport can be broadened to a more communal and widespread commitment through religious perspective and belief. We can expect to see increasing numbers of athletes taking to religion as an important step in their search for cohesion with others. Religion then in all its forms of faith, rebirth, and life satisfaction is an ally of clinical and psychiatric treatments for the alarming number of problems found in the sport world. Religion can be an important source of cure and support and it deserves more attention from serious sport scientists.

16
Stress

DEFINITION OF STRESS AND
RESILIENCE TO STRESS

Two themes have been unfolding in this examination of the psychology of sport. The first is the theme of competence in which the organism interacts successfully with the environment, to produce individual growth, adjustment and constructive relationships with peers and the social environment. The challenge of the athletic life is a positive one. The second theme is one of competitive stress, which is often accompanied by psychological conflict and anger (aggression), producing unhappy adjustment and usually poor relationships with others. Selye (1981, p. 6), the pioneer stress researcher and theorist, has stated:

> Each period of stress, especially if it results from frustrating, unsuccessful struggles, leaves some irreversible chemical scars (think of them as insoluable precipitates of living matter) which accumulate to constitute the signs of tissue aging. But successful activity, no matter how intense, leaves virtually no such scars. On the contrary, it engenders the exhilarating feeling of youthful strength, even at a very advanced age. Work wears people out mainly through the frustration of failure.

Selye also notes that: "The most eminent figures in any field of activity can continue to work creatively in old age." While this obviously does not cover aging in sport, it is important to note that we have predicted that the competence-oriented athlete will often continue to be involved in sport at either the organizational or educational level. If the athlete continues with active participation there will be scaled down expectations with age but not necessarily any diminishment in enjoyment.

The process of aging itself in sport will produce stress when youthful opponents inevitably overtake the older ones. In order for competitions to be fair, many "master's" leagues have been organized for persons over 35, 55, 75, and so on, with many variations on the theme. To avoid the inevitable stress of the aged athlete playing in top-notch competition, it makes good sense that the athlete adjust his or her goals in order to test competence against challenging but not impossible opposition.

When applying Selye's comments to sport, one must consider the implications of the hazards and hardships that go beyond a challenge to competence and enter the sphere of psychological and physical trauma. Because the stress of competitive failure is an inevitable part of sport, it is logical that persons who cannot stand athletic stress tend to get weeded out at early stages. Thus in Chapter 9 on personality we discussed the process by which this occurs and becomes manifested in the extraversion, stability, and resilience of many athletes. In examining the bomb disposal crews working for Britain in Northern Ireland, Rachman (1984) has studied persons able to resist highly stressful situations. He found the top members of the crews to be physiologically unresponsive to stress. Astronauts have been found to possess the same calmness, now known as the "Right Stuff," as have certain athletes such as Henry Cooper (boxer).

THEORY OF STRESS

Selye first introduced the concept of the *General Adaptation Syndrome* (G.A.S.) in *Nature* (1936) and the study of stress became his lifelong career. In that introduction he described three stages to the stress response: the alarm reaction, the stage of resistance, and the stage of exhaustion. The alarm reaction refers to the mustering of the body's defense mechanisms. This is the common fright and flight reaction with the flow of adrenalin and readiness for action and defense. The stage of resistance reverses the excitatory activity of the cells of the adrenal cortex that characterize stage one. Instead of the breakdown of tissue, due to increases in concentrations of cellular elements in the blood, along with abnormally small amounts of chloride, there is a buildup of tissue in the resistance stage and a dilution of cellular elements with abnormally large concentrations of chlorides. After a period of time the adaptation breaks down, followed by the stage of exhaustion. It seems that the adaptation phase cannot be maintained by the organism, which begins to succumb to wear and tear. The body loses its resistance and will begin to be vulnerable to tissue breakdown – the diseases of stress may appear, disorders such as gastric and duodenal ulcers, high blood pressure, allergies, mental breakdown, and heart attack.

Selye's (1976, 1983) original theory has become a backbone of modern medicine and clinical psychology. Increasing physical stress is placed upon individuals in the modern world due to pollution, noise, travel, drugs and alcohol consumption, radiation exposure, diet, and the competitive ethic, to name but a few examples. Increasing psychological stress has been placed upon individuals due to isolation and mobility, the achievement ethic, the ethic of sexual freedom, and the notion that happiness is possible if sufficient external reinforcement is gained from the culture at large. For many the concept of stress has become relevant to understanding both physical and psychological processes.

SPORT MEDICINE

Sport or sports medicine is a field that has emerged because of the stress athletes place on their bodies. Some put so much stress on their bodies that the term "trauma" is more accurate. Consider the cases of Darryl Stingley and Jocelyn Lovell, two of many athletes rendered quadriplegic by their sport careers. Stingley was injured when he was tackled in an exhibition game by Jim Tatum and Lovell when he was hit by a truck in Toronto while training for cycling. Some will attribute such injuries to accident. But it is perhaps more accurate to see them as examples of athletes who have placed themselves in a very high risk situation courting physical danger, hardship, and stress. They may be seen as tests of competence which were too dangerous. Similarly, one can view the brain damage suffered by many boxers as a willingness to undergo a very dangerous form of punishment in the name of sport, individual achievement, and profit. Stress is central to modern life and it seems to be increasing. For example the large number of young people who die or are seriously injured in car accidents, from suicide, and from alcohol and drug abuse can be seen as persons who have not been able to cope with the speed, hazards, and social traps of the society in which they are living. Their unfortunate plight, then, can be seen as a failure to adapt and a failure to make self-protective decisions in dangerous and stressful situations.

The field of sport medicine has grown up as a largely interventionist branch of medicine and many journals are devoted to the subject. Among these are: *The British Journal of Sports Medicine, Exercise and Sports Sciences Review, The Journal of Sports Medicine, Medicine and Science in Sports,* and *The Physician and Sports Medicine.* There is some debate about whether sport medicine should be more a preventive field than an interventive field as illustrated by the physicians working with youth groups and doing longitudinal studies on the benefits of exercise and healthful life styles over time. The preventive focus of sport medicine is of crucial importance and opens up new horizons not only for that field but more importantly for sport psychology. Much of the stress that results in sport injuries is caused by the cultural, social, and psychological values which overemphasize mastery, competition, and achievement. When these are imposed on children and developing athletes the result is often physical and psychological injury. There is little doubt that many avid athletes would have longer and happier sport careers if sport consultants counselled parents, schools, and athletes on stress levels, management, and prevention.

The role of sport medicine practitioners, such as orthopedists, becomes increasingly subject to ethical and legal scrutiny. For example, many accept the premise that the most important goal in dealing with skiers and other professional athletes is that they be patched up and sent back into competition. The role of the physician in boxing comes under the same scrutiny. The question is: what role and responsibility should the physician take in the assessment and control of stress levels? It is time that the values supporting sport and the risks of injury be critically assessed on a long-term basis. This will necessitate people in sport, as well as the experts who consult with them, taking a new and ethical look at the burden of stress in sport, not in terms of the commercial needs of the sport, but in terms of the long-term welfare of the participants.

EFFECTS OF SPORT STRESS

The world of sport offers hazards to many young people who often are not equipped to assess the degree of risk to which they are being subjected. For example, Sarno (as quoted by Palango, 1982) has noted that young football players should be forewarned that there is a one in 54,000 chance of their making the professional leagues. If they do make the professional leagues the average player lasts a mere four and one-half years. Thus football should be kept in perspective and the benefits derived from it in terms of training and education must be balanced against the risks. Those risks entail the possibilities of neurological damage and permanent injury against a very small chance of success. Note also the broken bones and skeletal damage thought to be inevitable in downhill racing. Orthopedists seem willing, for the most part, to fix the structural damage without considering the possibility of making the sport less hazardous. Yet some orthopedists have spoken out (as well they should) over the steroid controversy.

The culture of sport has recently been exposed for having alarming numbers of drug and alcohol abusers among its ranks, even among young players. Drugs are readily available in and around the locker rooms and it seems that once a player becomes dependent upon them other hazards follow. For example, the player begins to push drugs, is more easily prey to gambling interests, becomes poorly coordinated, shows motivational failure, or sometimes may fail to show up for competitions. Good studies are desperately needed on incidences of self-destructive and criminal behavior across time and sports. It will also be important when statistics become available in another 10 or 20 years on the longevity of the current crop of professional sport participants.

Stress in sport is both physical and psychological. It is easier, however, to chart the physical injuries that cause young athletes to leave the arena than it is to chart psychological injuries which may also be disabling. Psychological stress often accompanies physical injury or precedes it. One example is provided in the lawsuit (New York Times, December 6, 1981) of Vorhies versus the Virginia Polytechnic Institute over the death of Bob Vorhies after he had completed punishment drills following a football practice. Many coaches sanction and enforce training regimens involving rites of passage which are both humiliating and sadistic to players. We have already cited the case of the father of 16-year-old Claudia Casabianco of the United States who slapped his daughter in the face for hitting a poor shot when she was playing in Argentina in front of 3,000 spectators.

These sorts of abusive behaviors on the part of the powerful are often accepted by the less powerful. Because of this they show some similarity to the well-documented cases of wife and child abuse. Until social agents and others within the sport culture are willing to deal with the perpetrators and act against their damaging styles such abuse will continue to mar the world of sport.

Psychological stress also occurs in sport when the athlete must struggle to maintain a competitive position. This occurs at all levels of sport. On the elite level one finds a Borg retiring from active tennis competition due to the pressures and constrictions competitive tennis placed upon him and his life style. On the developmental level, it is very common for young athletes entering puberty to find it increasingly difficult to maintain the level of excellence and status which they previously held. Puberty results in new social interests, emergence into a new role (pre-adulthood), and changing physiology. The latter involves new challenges to control and coordination due to added weight, height, and muscular strength. This results in additional and often unpredicted stress on a social level. Popularity with peers may change, coaches may become increasingly demanding, parents may be upset at the threatened loss of social and financial interests they have invested in swimming, figure skating, basketball, etc.

A significant number of teenaged athletes become disgruntled and seek to change their directions in search of new competence feedback. We suggest that this is due not only to physical and psychological stressors but also to specific competitive pressure compounded by social and peer pressure. Since many adolescents will not be able to take the decision to diminish or drop their previous investment in sport, bizarre reactions to the stress may occur in the forms of symptoms or behaviors. To name but a few, drug taking, being abusive to parents, refusing to show up for practices, poor school work, and extreme swings in emotion, weight, or eating and drinking habits. An older individual may become abusive or withdraw from a marital situation.

Stress, both physiological and psychological, can be self-generating once it gains the upper hand and is ignored. This has resulted in some well-known lawsuits in sport. One example is that of Mike Robitaille versus the Vancouver Canucks' Hockey Club (1981). Gaining the reputation of a quitter, a psycho, and a malingerer, Robitaille was forced to play in games which resulted in severe aggravation of a long-standing back problem. He was awarded 348,000 dollars in compensation for career damage and loss of reputation and self-respect. He could no longer continue his career. Robitaille suffered from Valium addiction, anxiety, and depression. He was ostracized by team members. Thus a combination of factors, including severe stress mismanagement, led to his career decline.

It is a widespread North American belief that sport involves the athlete's ability and willingness to withstand pain and overcome pain. This belief is by no means universally accepted. Bell (1983, p. 150) quotes Lothar Kipke, head of the Institute of Sports Medicine at Leipzig, as saying: "There is no pain in sport. Pain is when they (the athletes) are sick or injured. Pain is bad. Sports are fun. They never go together." Most top athletes as well as most promising young athletes will enjoy their sport participation without the regular experience of pain. If they do not enjoy their sport participation and do experience pain, one must start to look for stress and the causes of that stress. Some of the more common sources of stress are: competitive stress, unrealistic goals, overly demanding training schedules, parents, coaches, sport associations, unrealistic self-perceptions, conflicting social values surrounding sport, and inadequate social support.

DYNAMICS OF STRESS

A model can be used to explain both physical and psychological stress. The model described by Maddi (1967) in his well-known theoretical paper on the existential neuroses, involves the concepts of premorbidity, type of stress, and resulting symptoms. It is rather similar to Adler's (1917) proposal of organ inferiority causing the individual to compensate or cover up such morbidity. Goldstein (1939) had a similar theory of personal adjustment in that he noted symptoms and breakdowns were always indicative of the organism's striving to overcome some deficit, some inability to cope with environmental demands. Maddi proposes that a person becomes dysfunctional under stress when that stress acts on a part of the person which is vulnerable to breakdown. Thus the stresses of life will play on that part of the body or mind which is weakest under that particular stress.

In the stress model, one first considers the premorbid state of the personality or physiology. This again refers to a vulnerability. An unhappy relationship with a father in childhood may yield an individual who has difficulty with men in roles of authority. An unresolved Oedipal situation threatens the formation of emotional attachments in adulthood. Or structural inferiority makes a knee or an organ system vulnerable to emotional and/or physical breakdown with the passage of years. Constant travel, social pressures, and fleeting relationships as well as constant physical strain can grind at the athlete until a form of breakdown occurs. For example, among hockey players, Robitaille became increasingly emotional and subject to weeping; Larry Mickey became increasingly depressed and eventually committed suicide; Jim McKenny became increasingly alcoholic until taking himself in hand. On the physical side, Larry Gordon of the Miami Dolphins and Karen Krantzcke of tennis both died of heart failures when jogging at ages 28 and 30 as have many more including Jim Fixx, well-known advocate of running and fitness, who was found dead at roadside of heart failure at age 52. The question we ask is: would these individuals have had the same psychological or physical breakdown without the world of sport to provoke them? They may have. On the other hand it is clear that regulation of life style and degree of stress can prevent both the development of disease and increase life expectancy. Simply put, we are hypothesizing that a certain type of premorbidity and a certain type of stress lead to breakdown. Most athletes are well aware of stress will usually develop specific techniques to try to overcome it. They may spend their time in hotel rooms relaxing or engaging in various acting out behaviors (gambling, drinking, sex), or read poetry or pursue family and emotional outlets in order to break away from the pressures and stresses of competition. It is when these outlets are self-destructive and too severe that the results of stress are most noticeable. Thus physical injury, alcohol and drug addiction, and breaking the law are commonly observed in athletes.

The personality structure of the average professional athlete is a type that will be able to resist pain as well as physical and mental hardship. Thus the forms of abuse that they are likely to develop as outlets for stress become long-term habits and deeply ingrained. In addition a good deal of damage may be done before they seek help or are identified through their clubs and leagues as needing help. One long-term adjustment is, therefore, to accept psychological and physical damage as part of sport. For example, *pugilistic dementia,* or brain damage resulting from boxing, has been known for years in the psychiatric literature and to the boxing community. Yet little has been done in North America by athletes, sport associations, or professional mental health workers to prevent the permanent brain damage of many boxers because of the nonregulation of the sport. The publicity surrounding the case of Muhammed Ali and his apparent brain damage (*N.Y. Times,* Sept. 23, 1984) has brought public attention in North America to the seriousness of the stress to which professional boxing exposes its athletes. The damage done by boxing to the brain has long been known in medical circles. Several nations such as Iceland, have banned boxing. Increasing numbers of authors are suggesting that boxing has no place in a civilized society. The British Medical Association's policy board voted in 1982 to abolish it while George D. Lundberg, editor of the *Journal of the American Medical Association* has done likewise. In spite of mounting evidence against it, boxing continues due to its profitability for some, its crowd appeal, and the fact that there are lower class young men who seem willing to risk all for financial reward in the ring.*

---

*Note that apart from the medical aspects of boxing safety, several governmental bodies have moved for its abolition due to its connections to organized crime.

The most important time to tackle problems of stress in sport is at the earliest level, that is, with children in sport. As one example, a winning five- and six-year-old boys' ice hockey team was being forced by parents and some officials into the competitive ethic by strong pressure to win. Tears and trauma were observable in at least half of the boys. The coach, in this particular situation, sought support for the view that the adults' behavior was damaging to the children and went against the philosophy of the league and rules of the board of directors. It is very important that thoughtful and concerned adults intervene in such situations, and that both the adults and the children learn how to educate themselves to avoid unpleasant stress.

It is often the coach who perpetrates the stress and its consequent damage on young athletes. Coaches will sometimes goad children on to destructive behavior against their peers in the name of competition. Lloyd Percival (1974), one of the first fitness experts in Canada, has said that all of the psychological problems he had seen in sport resulted from competitive pressure and stress. Stress is the psychological villain of the sports world. It can take away the joy of sport and leave sad and defeated athletes of all ages at all levels.

PART V

CONSULTING PRACTICES AND ISSUES

17
Conducting the Interview

INTRODUCTION

Conducting an efficient interview within a limited period of time is an art that requires training and experience. It also requires intelligence, concentration, and empathy, or the ability to appreciate the goals, concerns, and problems of the client or clients. It is rare that the psychologist will have unlimited time to sit on the sidelines and become "involved" in the sport and there is no need for the psychologist to constantly accompany the athlete. On occasion the psychologist may watch or participate in practices on a voluntary basis, or when he or she is being paid as part of a team support structure, or is working on a specific behavioral analysis of a training or practice sequence. However, usually these functions are quickly passed to other sport personnel such as team members, coaches, managers, or captains. There is no need for sport organizations to pay a psychologist's fee to perform on-site functions unless clinical services are required.

In this section, focus is on the first interview in which the consultant explores what the major referral questions are and what the best avenues of action, treatment, or training techniques are in the future. It should be noted that most often the client will be an athlete but at other times the client will be a coach, a parent, or a representative of a sport association. On occasion the client will be a lawyer or another professional. Sometimes a whole team will be a client and the psychologist will work with the team as a whole or with a team representative. For the most part, the suggestions made in the present chapter apply to both individual and group interviews.

Before any interviews or sessions are held the question of payment should be dealt with. If a client is worrying about costs and payment, it might detract from the flow of information and rapport. It may be that a governmental organization, school, or other organization is paying for the interview, and if this is so then both the cost and the number of possible sessions should be discussed with the proper representatives. The consultant should then make clear to the client what the time allotment is, or how many sessions are covered, for example, in an extended services medical plan. Secondly, it is excellent policy all around if the consultant is able to give an initial free interview to the client, particularly to those who do not know much about the type of services offered. The consultant then volunteers the interview time in order to guide the client into the right type of treatment program, if indeed, the client decides this is what he or she wants. There are cases in which the consultant may guide the individual away from any kind of treatment program. This would occur when the individual is capable of solving his or her own problems or developing his or her own psychological training program or does not need psychological services at all.

NINE ELEMENTARY RULES IN PROFESSIONAL INTERVIEWING

As in all counseling and interviewing there are a few simple and elementary rules to be followed that will facilitate the interview and make it considerably more productive.

1. *Interview in a quiet, neat, and comfortable room.* The atmosphere of the interview space can serve to facilitate or damage productivity during the hour. A neat office with furniture and equipment well spaced will do much to facilitate interaction. A windowless room little bigger than a cupboard, stacked with boxes and just above a children's playground, will create an interview situation which both client and psychologist may be delighted to see finish.

2. *All phone calls should be re-routed during the interview.* No incoming phone calls should be taken when an interview is in progress. They should be re-routed to a secretary or handled by an answering machine. If this is not practical, unplug the phone, as the client should have full attention during the allotted time.

3. *Place a sign on the door to handle office visitors if a receptionist is not available.* Knocks at the door and other interruptions have the same effect as an invasive telephone. They will break the train of thought and the delicate balance that is created as rapport, empathy, and trust develop.

4. *There should be no desk or barrier between the client and the consultant.* The most comfortable consultative space is between four to seven feet (Hall, 1969, p. 121). Planting a desk between the client and the professional creates a physical barrier between them which may well be reflected in a distancing in the communication and a slackening of the flow of information passed between the two.

5. *Be on time.* Once an appointment is given it should be kept and kept on time. Clients from all walks of life, including athletes, have family commitments to juggle, work schedules to adhere to, and often busy and complicated lives. Most athletes, coaches, and sports personnel are even more punctual than the usual clientele, having been disciplined within sport schedules and game

times. They are used to appearing on time and the psychologist should do likewise.

6. *Always have the client's phone contact number and see that the client has your card and phone number.* If unforeseen circumstances occur in which either party cannot make an appointment, it is important that it be cancelled with the least amount of disruption to both parties. Although such a small item may seem obvious, the failure to keep an appointment, at the cost of time to the other party, can damage the consulting process.

7. *End the interview at the set time.* Working hard for an hour or an hour and a half should accomplish as much as working for three hours with concentration lapses and time out for coffee. It is important that the client consider the information from the interview. It is therefore most profitable to set a given time for the interview and to end it as close to that time as possible.

8. *Summarize the content of the interview five minutes before it is to end.* This detail allows the client to prepare for the end of the hour and to add any important comments or concerns. It allows the consultant to give an overview of the interview and to reinforce important points that have been made. The summary can cover the content of the preceding discussion, what has been accomplished, what solutions or possibilities for solutions have been discussed, what actions the client might take from the material covered, and what is yet to be accomplished.

9. *Does the client come again?* Continuation in a program of treatment, psychotherapy, or consultation is entirely up to the client. The psychologist will comment and advise. By the end of the first interview the client and psychologist will have covered and specified what the client hopes to obtain by seeking the help of a sport consultant or psychologist. The psychologist will have outlined the possible techniques and programs for accomplishing those goals.

The consultant may wish to refer the client to another practitioner who focuses on a certain technique appropriate to the needs of the client. Or, the psychologist may refer the client for group educational lessons in order that he or she answer the general question of what techniques are available for self-help training in sport. The information can be gained in detail and at lesser cost than in individual sessions. Another outcome: the client and consultant may decide on a series of five interviews in order to build knowledge and confidence as well as to explore personal motivations and goals. This is extremely time-limited therapy but also extremely practical in sport in that the cost will be low and motivation high when the sessions are time limited. If extended sessions are needed at the conclusion, they can be worked out within the perspective of what has been learned during the initial five sessions. Finally, many individuals who have an initial interview end up with no further contact. The psychologist can refer them to various sources for reading in order that they follow up on their questions. Or, it becomes clear that the individual is handling all of the training and supervision that he or she can and to introduce another expert into the training program would be redundant. Cratty and Davis (1984, p. 328) have noted that many athletes are "over coached" and the psychologist will do them most good by not adding to the burden. The client can often work with the support groups and educational system that is already offered through his or her sport.

CONTENT OF THE INTERVIEW

During the initial interview, several topics should be covered after a brief intro-duction. It is quite possible that both the client and the psychologist will know something about one another before the first interview. However, somewhere after the initial interchanges the psychologist will make the purpose of the hour clear with a statement such as: "The next hour is completely yours so we can talk about what brings you here, where you are, where you would like to go, and what we can do to help."

Some sample replies are:

"My mother sent me."

"My coach says I should see a psychologist. We don't get along."

"I know a lot of tennis players seeing psychologists and I don't want to miss anything."

"Well, seeing the association is paying for us to see you I thought I might as well come and see what is going on."

"I want to quit swimming and my parents won't let me."

"I want to launch a legal suit against my sport association for national team selections and I want to know what you think about it."

"I'm not doing as well as I know I can so I want to work on mental practice, key words, and relaxation because I've heard they've worked with some of the people I know."

"Everyone in my club [figure skating] hates me. They're jealous of me. And I'm not doing as well as I used to."

"I have some real problems in my personal life and they're interfering with my hockey."

Sometimes there is no clear statement because the problems are serious and involve identity and self-confidence. The athlete will then usually begin with concerns about diminished and conflicting feelings about his or her sport and other people involved in it.

During the interview the following points should be covered:

1. What are the client's goals? Are they realistic? A 14-year-old figure skater who yearns to be world champion under parental pressure may be con-trasted with the 38-year-old depressed ex-professional ice hockey player now doing volunteer coaching in order to salvage some identity with his sport.

2. What life history information is relevant? Sample information includes: age, sex, family constellation, significant figures in development, current support and friendship network.

3. What is the client's level of achievement in sport and current situation in sport? This might include team affiliation, level of financial support, depth of exposure, and experience.

4. How was the current level of performance achieved? Discussion might cover the client's developmental background specific to sport, experiences with coaches, fellow athletes, the circumstances surrounding periods of growth in sport and periods of difficulty or decline.

5. Is referral for a problem in sport (or sport specific) or is it for a more deeply seated psychological problem or social concern? If this distinction is not readily apparent from questioning and an ingrained problem is suspected which the client cannot verbalize, then a full clinical assessment may be advised.

6. What are the athlete's attitudes toward the current coach and toward past coaches and authority? Unworkable relationships between athletes and coaches, when the coach has almost complete authority, can be devastating to an athlete and are a common occurrence in sport. Conflicts surrounding the coaching relationship have caused many athletes to drop out of sport. A good relationship, on the other hand, can provide an important resource in helping the athlete both to solve problems and to maximize his or her potential.

7. What are the athlete's motivations in sport? The key to understanding the athlete from his or her perspective is motivational style. This may be simple or complex, constructive or destructive, offer infinite promise or be almost entirely delimiting. The entire first section of this book is given over to the discussion of motivational theory in sport and its complexities.

8. What are the attitudes and support levels of parents, friends, spouse, children, and other intimates at the present time? An understanding of the emotional and social support network of the athlete is often essential information. This can be the missing factor in an athlete's promising yet faltering development. It can also be related to the failing performance of professional athletes.

9. Has the client already seen sport psychologists or been in previous psychological treatment programs? Often, relatively young athletes will previously have been sent to psychologists. Almost all elite athletes will have had some exposure in group lessons or individual sessions in the psychology of sport. Sometimes the exposure has been so brief at times that the athlete has carried away some very false ideas about the application of psychology to sport. At other times the athlete has benefited from previous training and is quite sophisticated about techniques. At still other times the athlete's major experience in sport psychology is having acted as a participant for a research thesis or for other studies.

10. What can psychology as a field offer to the client in terms of education and development, special techniques, psychotherapy, treatment, or referral

elsewhere? Some summary of the alternatives available to the client in order to meet his or her needs wll be valuable. Often there is an array of possibilities the client will go away to think over before deciding on the appropriate course of action.

THE PSYCHOLOGIST OR CONSULTANT
DURING THE INTERVIEW

The master of the self-management of the counsellor is Carl Rogers. In a series of books and papers he (1951, 1961, 1970) laid the foundations for counselling techniques which he followed up with research on the process of psychotherapy and the measurement of that process. The classic paper on how to establish a helping relationship during the interview is "The Characteristics of the Helping Relationship," first published in 1958 and reprinted on many occasions (for example, in Rogers, 1961). It is required reading for the serious student. In this paper Rogers describes the emotional atmosphere necessary for "movement" and growth in therapy. Although the psychologist is much less likely to be carrying an athlete over time in a therapeutic sense, the principles laid down by Rogers and the concepts used are very important in establishing rapport and trust. And these are necessary so that the client can feel free enough to describe his or her total situation and to consider all possible alternatives. The interviewer should pay attention to such concepts as *unconditional positive regard* in which an uncritical attitude will be struck toward the client. He or she listens and does not attempt to structure the material until the client has had the opportunity to fully state their situation and needs. The interviewer must genuinely like the client and want to help them. Finally, the interviewer must show trust in the client to be able to choose his or her own solutions to the problems posed and the goals desired. The consultant is wise not to launch on a pattern of treatment until the client has made the decision that it is indeed the treatment that he or she feels is compatible.

In contrast to Rogerian technique, the interviewer in sport psychology may be somewhat more directive. This is because most athletes will be primarily interested in increasing their performance level. In this situation the psychologist usually suggests a series of techniques which might be experimented with and subsequently may give a series of training sessions with concentration on those techniques. During the first session, a guideline would be to spend the first half hour on Rogerian-type client-centered interviewing. The second half of the hour could be spent more directly on specific techniques and treatments.

If a major thesis of this book is correct, that personal development is more important than an immediate assault upon performance increase and, in fact, that the former facilitates performance, then personal counselling would be indicated for many clients from sport. By exploring attitudes, decisions, and frustrations in sport and their concrete bases (relationship to coach, time needed to train, problems with peers, problems related to travel, stress, money problems or declining status), genuine movement toward maturation and self-confidence can be made. It is when such self-explorations are carried out freely and in an atmosphere of complete trust that insight can occur in a short period of time to the benefit of the client's personal growth and to the benefit of his or her sport performance.

When the interview changes in emphasis from the facilitation of personal growth to the discussion of techniques for improving performance we pass from the area of what one would call psychotherapy into the realm of behavior therapy or technique training: mental rehearsal, whole versus part learning, anxiety reducing techniques, behavioral techniques, and biofeedback. The counsellor uses these techniques as suggestions and vehicles through which the athlete might improve performance by tackling specific problems or specific areas that need improvement.

A third situation arises when the client has severe psychological problems but happens to be an athlete. Such would be the case with a troubled adolescent, a professional athlete suffering from alcoholism, or an older athlete facing the depression of lowered status. Such athletes are likely candidates for varying numbers of psychotherapeutic interviews until the best assessments and treatment plans are considered. Many cases will require specialized clinical training and knowledge plus follow up with specialized treatment programs.

INTERVIEWING IN THE SPORT ARENA OR SETTING

When the psychologist is engaged by a sport organization it is very common for him or her to interview and conduct sessions in the athletic arena. Such appointments often involve time spent at training camps, coaching sessions, and even travelling with teams. This, of course, raises all sorts of problems for the busy psychologist, who will usually be unable to take weeks or months off to travel with a team. Thus one is likely to find advocates of the sport, who are also sport psychologists, in such roles.

When sport consultants fill such roles, they can be an important part of the team support structure and facilitate communication, education, and team morale or stability. However, other than boosting morale and offering emotional support and ongoing education, one must still question whether adequate mental preparation has been done prior to the tour or competition. A mature, competent athlete with sufficient background experience and adequate training will not need psychological services at rink, field, court, or bedside. These comments do not negate the extreme importance of maintaining morale during major competitions. However, if adequate preparation is done at home, team morale will be attended to on an ongoing basis. In the heat of competition, it is the athlete who performs. It is not the time for new techniques, interference, pep talks, innovations or pushing from the sidelines. There are, unfortunately, numerous incidents of sport consultants who have become a burdensome interference rather than help to a team or to athletes. The psychologist must remember that the use of any technique and of any psychological service is always the choice of the athlete and the coach.

18
Clinical Screening

INTRODUCTION

In Chapter 8 we examined the Sport Protocol as used in theory development as a test of the descriptive model of motivation that has been employed in this book. The Sport Protocol was constructed both for research purposes and to assist coaches and athletes in thinking about sport, their involvement and background in sport, and their sport motivations. The instrument is set out so that it can be used as an initial screening instrument in a very short period of time both with groups and with individuals. The Sport Protocol can be answered in 20 minutes, scored and perused in 15 minutes, and discussed in the last 25 minutes of an hour-long interview. Thus its proper position in individual client contact would be in the second interview. In some cases the client may have completed it before coming to the first session so it can become part of the discussion during the first hour. In assessing and discussing groups, the Sport Protocol is valuable in obtaining a great amount of relevant information in a short period of time which can be computer scored and profiled for quick and efficient feedback. The Sport Protocol, is not seen or introduced to clients or research participants as a powerful or all-encompassing instrument that will result in a complete assessment. It merely organizes knowledge that one has about oneself for study and discussion purposes. There are no surprises in the instrument and any discussion with a clinician will explore and follow up on certain areas of content or answers to questions. Complete accuracy is never assumed and consensual validation of answers with discussion is always called for. A discussion of the use of each section of the Sport Protocol for screening purposes follows.

BACKGROUND INFORMATION

In the background information section, one notes the sport in which the client is involved, the length of time of participation in the sport, the highest level of participation, whether the athlete has ever thought of giving up the sport, and his or her ambition and the perceived ambition of the coach. One notes attitudes toward the coach, whether the sport is placed at the top of the value list, occupational goal, family constellation, and attitudes of and relationships with parents. From this section one is alerted to problem areas within sport and obtains a very general description of the athlere's position in sport. Parental status can usually be gauged from the occupational fields of the father and mother.

Sometimes key issues will be revealed very rapidly. This was the case when a young gymnast, whose problem was frustration and temper tantrums surrounding competitions, showed an extremely close rating to her mother and an extreme emotional distance from her father. The mother was completely absorbed in her daughter's career, for which she (the mother) paid with her job earnings. She travelled with her daughter and always referred to her daughter as "we." For example, "We didn't win that one, but we are really going to concentrate on that routine for the nationals." The father was affluent and spent his own leisure deeply absorbed in golf. There was little overlap in the lives of the mother-daughter team and that of the father. In fact, there was a symbiotic relationship between the mother and daughter against which the girl was starting to rebel at age 12.

Significant comments may be made on the coach, the parents, sport injuries, ambitions, and so on. For example a 20-year-old competitive golfer who was very ambitious but making a poor living at the game described himself as very close to his father and very frustrated at his limitations in golf. He also commented that it was hard for him to pursue his sport because his father placed continual pressure on him (the son) to give up his golf and return home to take over the family business.

AFFECT SCALES

The first indexes to examine in the personality profile are the Affect Scales, and the number of happy or unhappy feelings endorsed by the athlete. The affect scales were developed and used by Bradburn and Caplovitz (1965). They gauge a person's affective or emotional state. Is the individual generally positively disposed to life? Is the person tending toward discontentment and depressive feelings?

SPORT MOTIVATION SCALES

Second, one examines the sport motivation scale responses and compares them with the affect scale profiles. General happy feelings will tend to be reflected in competence and cooperation endorsements, while general unhappy feelings tend to be reflected in conflict and competition endorsements. This does not hold constantly for elite athletes. In elite athletes competitive feelings are sometimes associated with happiness, for two major reasons: first, social expectations are being fulfilled when the athlete is competitive in motivation, and second, considerable reinforcement may have come from competitive success. The athlete may therefore come to associate high levels of positive reinforcement with competitive motivations.

If the client has endorsed many general unhappy feelings on the affect scale, then it is of particular interest to see if it is reflected in the conflict scale. In some generally unhappy people, sport is free of conflict. Thus sport provides an important outlet or escape from the unhappiness of everyday life. Conversely, some will endorse several (three or more) conflict items with regard to sport but will be relatively happy in their everyday life. One then needs to explore why sport causes them unhappiness and conflict. Usually they are being pushed too much by themselves or others, or they are psychologically unsuited to the sport, or they may have outgrown the sport. Or, as is the case with many teenage athletes, growth spurts and the consequent changes in physical functioning interfere with coordination and the execution of the sport.

One next examines the entire motivational profile; high scores on competence and cooperation should indicate a good adjustment in sport while high scores on aggression, conflict, and competition may indicate a more problematic adjustment. However, the latter may not be always the case for certain sports, levels of competition, or within certain subcultures of sport. We have found that some field hockey players have a high level of aggression, competition, and cooperation (Butt, 1980), while Japanese karate students had a very high level of conflict (Butt, 1979b). Thus one must be flexible in assessing any client in terms of a theory. It is always necessary to ask the client what he or she thinks of the profile in terms of the demands of the sport in which he or she is invested.

THE ACTIVITY SCALES

The activity scales, as noted in Chapter 8, due to frequent low reliability indexes, give only a rough indication of the client's degree of expressiveness versus their instrumentality, that is, passivity versus assertiveness. In some studies we have included Bem's Sex Role Inventory (1974) as an adjunct to the activity score measures, with considerable success. For example, it was found (Butt, 1980b) that a national women's field hockey team rated themselves, on the average, as relatively high on expressiveness. However they rated an ideal member of the national field hockey team as very high on instrumentality. Clearly some resolution was needed between such a widespread cognitive discrepancy.

GOUGH'S SOCIALIZATION SCALE

Gough's socialization scale (Gough and Pederson, 1951; Gough, 1964) reflects "the degree to which the individual has internalized common social mores and

SPORTS PROFILE SHEET – FORM B

ID:
Sport:

Age:
Sex:
Accuracy:

Sports Motivation Scales

Rating scale for each item: 5 4 3 2 1 0

Aggression	Conflict	Competence	Competition	Cooperation
5. full of energy	1. listless and tired	3. thrilled	2. determined to come in first	4. helping someone else to improve
9. impulse	6. moody for no real reason	11. happier than you have ever been	7. winning is very important	8. like part of the group (pair, team)
13. powerful	12. guilty for not doing better	16. like you performed your best yet	10. irritated someone else did better	15. pleased someone else did well
18. telling someone off	14. very nervous	19. more interested than in anything else	20. annoyed you did not win	21. doing something to help team or group
22. let some have it if in your way	17. like crying	23. you had accomplished something	24. others getting more than deserve	25. congratulating someone who did well

Activity Scales

Rating scale for each item: 5 4 3 2 1 0

Force	Lack of fear	Insensitivity
1. mechanics mag. (+)	2. strange place (–)	6. boast (+)
3. outdoors (+)	5. dark (–)	10. adventure st. (+)
4. building con. (+)	9. hurt (feelings) (–)	13. spitting (–)
7. racing car (+)	11. windstorm (–)	14. dress designing (–)
8. fist fight (+)	12. excited (–)	15. empathy (–)

Affect Scales

Rating scale for each item: 5 4 3 2 1 0

Positive	Negative
1. accomplished	2. restless
3. going my way	4. bored
5. proud	6. depressed
7. excited	8. lonely
9. on top of world	10. criticized

Socialization Scales

Family Stability	Control	Security	Confidence	Social Concern
5 4 3 2 1 0	5 4 3 2 1 0	5 4 3 2 1 0	5 4 3 2 1 0	5 4 3 2 1 0
3. leave home (–)	4. trouble (teachers (–)	2. no fair chance (–)	1. wrong choice oc. (–)	7. no worry looks (–)
5. home less peace (–)	11. spur moment (–)	9. strong likes (–)	6. not getting anyw. (–)	8. never excited (–)
10. home happy (+)	15. showing off (–)	12. more share worr. (–)	14. no win arg. (–)	13. seek trouble (–)
22. family close (+)	18. no heavy dr. (+)	19. talk behind bac. (–)	21. not happy as oth. (–)	16. impress oth. (+)
24. home pleasant (+)	25. alcohol exc. (–)	20. feel wicked (–)	23. hard to hope (–)	17. easy drop fr. (–)

Murray's Constructs

Succorance	Autonomy	Affiliation	Endurance	Leadership
6 5 4 3 2 1 0	6 5 4 3 2 1 0	6 5 4 3 2 1 0	6 5 4 3 2 1 0	6 5 4 3 2 1 0
2. friends enc. (+)	3. come & go (+)	4. new friends (+)	5. work hard (+)	6. act lea. (+)
8. both. attent. (–)	9. bother-uncon. (–)	10. obj. imp. (–)	11. hate stay up (–)	12. avoid resp. (–)
14. friends-kind (+)	15. feel free (+)	16. strong att. (+)	17. stick job (+)	18. enjoy auth. (+)
20. tr. no help (–)	21. thoughts-self (–)	22. not out of w. (–)	23. dt. mind int. (–)	24. avoid p. sp. (–)
26. friends-sick (+)	27. independent (+)	28. warm grps. (+)	29. long hrs. (+)	30. usu. lea. (+)
32. fuss-sick (–)	33. crit.-auth. (–)	34. both share (–)	35. new jobs (–)	36. both to sup. (–)

Achievement

6 5 4 3 2 1 0

1. do best (+)
7. bother do bet. (–)
13. accomplish (+)
19. don't mind fail. (–)
25. recog. authority (+)
31. give up (–)

COMMENTS:

Figure 10. Sport Protocol Screening and Discussion Sheet.

values." The scale generally reflects how well the individual is adjusted socially or how well he or she is integrated into and is responsible to him or herself and to others. Butt (1973) carried out a factor analysis of the scale and we have subsequently used the shortened scale with five subscales: *family stability, control, security, self-confidence,* and *social concern.* Each of these subsets of items have import in describing a person's social adjustment.

Family stability is usually associated with happiness and cooperation with others. Interestingly, we have found cases in which family stability is low (no items endorsed) and yet the person seems to have compensated for this in identifying with other groups. We have found successful coaches of teams with low scores and some team players who are very closely identified with their teams, it seems as a substitute family. *Control* reflects the individual's ability to keep out of trouble and not to act out impulsively. Although many athletes score highly on control, many others do not. Note the heavy drinking items on this scale. If four or five items are endorsed on this scale the client should be asked about problems with acting out behavior. *Security* explores whether the individual is free from worries and being done in by others, while *self-confidence* reflects the optimism stemming from feelings of self-worth both in the present and for the future. These two scales reflect a general contentment with the self and the life situation versus ingrown concerns about failure and the inability to cope. The client low on these scales may want to consider ways to overcome this negative orientation in order to become more optimistic about life. Finally, *social concern* reflects the degree to which the person cares about his or her effect on others. The person scoring high on social concern is involved and vulnerable while the person scoring low is relatively unaffected by the input and/or evaluation from others. The client scoring low on the socialization scale (low profiles across the scales) may have problems in sport from impulsive and acting out behavior, low motivation, or difficulty getting on with the group. The athlete scoring high (high profile across the scales), if he or she has problems in sport, is more likely to have problems of a neurotic type. That is, he or she may tend to be overly concerned about conforming, feel overly guilty when things go wrong, and be overly expectant of his or her own performance.

MURRAY'S CONSTRUCTS

Murray's constructs are based on Murray's (1938) theory of needs. Several of the six scales included have been found in previous studies related to sport performance and thus are of interest when discussing the athlete's motivations and feelings about sport. Achievement, autonomy, and endurance might be called the "big three" when describing the needs of well-motivated athletes. They want to do well, they will pursue this desire independently, and they have the will to withstand long and rigorous training. Although this pattern of needs may be promising, it is by no means the only road to sport adjustment, enjoyment, and success. Some team players are low on autonomy, and competence motivation may replace achievement motivation. Endurance, in these cases, may be developed over time as an individual receives reinforcement from their efforts in sport. However the athlete having a high profile on these constructs is usually assertive, motivated, and untroubling to the coach.

Athletes who are high on succorance and affiliation will in general need more "attention" from coaching staff, team members, and support group members. If a coach cannot handle the nurturing and caring for the team or special individuals on the team, then this job should be assigned to someone else. A team manager, the captain, one of the players or team members, or a support group member (such as a physician or sport psychologist) may fill this role. In consulting clients who have high needs on succorance and affiliation, the counsellor can check with the client to see how these needs are being met and if not, how they might be met. Such individuals are often warm, supportive, and capable of supplying cohesion for other athletes with whom they train and/or travel.

Finally, the leadership items are important in screening clients who may have some leadership potential. If the client has a low score, one may question him or her in order to explore whether he or she should like to develop leadership skill. Athletes endorsing most of the leadership items may fit easily into assigned roles such as captain, morale leader, training assistant, and so on.

THE SPORT PROTOCOL AS AN OPTIONAL TOOL

When a client chooses to respond to the Sport Protocol, many avenues for discussion are opened up. In addition, by running over the client's responses, the psychologist has at a glance a portrait of some important features of the client in sport. These observations should always be checked out against the client's opinions and interpretations. Further, the information from the Sport Protocol should not preclude other areas of discussion that the client wishes to bring up. The author has had clients who have responded to the protocol for research purposes or team purposes (that is, it has been given to an entire team), but who prefer to discuss other features of their sport career than the questionnaire results. A first rule in counselling is to function from the point of view of the client and not to move too fast for the client. It is always important to proceed in small increments from the client's point of view. Steps taken must relate to the client's concerns and goals.

OTHER USES OF THE SPORT PROTOCOL

In addition to its use for discussion and screening of individuals, the Sport Protocol can be used for at least two other purposes. First, it can be used when a pair of individuals are being counselled. Second, it can be used in group counselling. In the first case, the most common situation is to have the profiles of two persons who have some sort of a partnership in sport: a parent and child, a coach and an athlete, or a team such as a doubles team in tennis or a pairs team in figure skating. Since all of these individuals must work together, the interactions of the profiles are often of great interest. In the second situation, one assesses a group or club with the Sport Protocol in order to isolate the important concerns among athletes and coaches that could be worked upon, developed, or changed. An immense amount of information on the group can be gathered within a short period of time by using the method of group "interviewing" via a standard questionnaire. For example, the athletes' ratings and comments on what they would like their coach to do differently and what they think about their coach can be very worthwhile information and can result in immediate recommendations to the coach and immediate benefits for the team — should the coach decide to act on them. In one team of 12-year-old ice hockey players from the British Columbia interior that travelled every weekend during the season with a dedicated group of adult volunteers, the centrality of the boys' hockey involvement to family life in an economically hard-pressed mining town was immediately evident. This resulted in pressure being put on the boys through their families, who sacrificed finances, time, and energy in order to participate in what was the families' major leisure activity. It was suggested that more attention be given to the boys' development, growth, and enjoyment of the game instead of to hockey victories as an escape. Several of the team members were showing discontent and conflict with their participation because of the stress being put on them by their families. In this situation, some members of the coaching staff were already well aware of the problem, but left counselling with confirmation of their concerns and plans for better communication with parents and ideas on how to create a more supportive group atmosphere for the players.

CLINICAL ILLUSTRATIONS

In order to illustrate how the Sport Protocol can be used to engender ideas and possibilities for the athlete and coach, four cases are discussed which represent two high performers and two low performers in figure skating. Two of these have a positive adjustment in sport and two have a more problematic adjustment. *Each case discussed has been disguised in order to make recognition of the individual impossible.* Many of the points illustrated in the cases come up frequently when one is dealing with young athletes.

Case 1. A Positive Adjustment in a High Performing Female. A 15-year-old girl, the coach gives her a rating of 6 out of 7 on potential and she is competing at the national level. The coach describes her as a good worker, as cooperative, and as quickly improving with good athletic and artistic ability. The coach would like to see more thought and intelligence in her approach to her skating. The highest scores on sport motivations are competence and cooperation. In keeping with this the skater says she has never thought of giving up and will be competing in five years time. She has high achievement values and repeatedly writes that she wants to excel in her skating. She describes both her parents as pushing her and interfering. This may reflect or be reflected in her being slightly critical of her family situation and being slightly insecure, although such features are not at all unusual in teenagers. She likes her coach and checks off four categories for what he or she does best. She is a generally happy person and except for the slight family tension seems to be maturing in a very positive manner. Skating is an important part of that process of maturation for her. She describes herself as liking to depend on others. Her abillity to follow through on her strong ambitions will be suitabily tested in the future. With such an athlete the coach has few problems. The coach will most likely continue to find the girl easy to work with. Through increased competence in skating and through the support of the coach, she will be encouraged to develop in self-confidence and security through her pursuit of sport.

Case 2. A Difficult Adjustment in a Low Performing Female. This is an example of a case where a coach, with a little extra care, may contribute greatly to the quality of a life and to the growth of an individual. This is also a 15-year-old girl, who is given a potential rating of 3 out of 7 by her coach. She is not cooperative and lacks trust. She has recently levelled out in her skating after a late start and what was originally a very fast development. This girl says she will not be active in her sport in five years, has thought of giving up because she is not doing well, and describes herself as mildly ambitious. She sees her coach's ambition for her as lower than her own. She is close to her father and neutral toward her mother. Neither parent pushes her in sport.

Psychologically this girl is high on conflict and cooperation (the latter is a positive feature). She has endorsed three competition items, so she wants to win. But the feature of her profile is that she has endorsed no competence items at all. At the time of her testing she saw herself as getting little or no internal feedback or joy from her sport. She describes herself as unhappy in general life. She is high on socialization but again (common to teenagers) has slight deflations on security and self-confidence. She does not see herself as having strong general needs for achievement and support from others.

Although this girl does not seem destined to become a champion in any sense (but one never knows), the coach can become a very positive influence in her life. She is unhappy and is not experiencing joy in sport. If the coach is able to awaken feelings of efficacy and reward from skill and mastery, and she begins to enjoy her sport, her whole life and mood may well be influenced. This kind of change may be initiated by relating personally to the girl, by giving her praise when she does well, by removing pressures to compete and to produce, while at the same time showing her that the coach has interest in and expectations of what she can do. The coach must also, of course, teach her how to progress technically. In many such cases the coach is the only person who has both a personal relationship with the individual and a medium (sport) through which to initiate positive growth in the youngster's life.

Case 3. A Difficult Adjustment in a High Performing Male. This interesting 14-year-old skater is given a 6 out of 7 on potential from his coach, who describes him as very independent and difficult to coach. The coach wonders if he is demanding too much because the boy does not respond well. The skater describes both himself and his coach as oustandingly ambitious for him. He likes his coach but would also like more encouragement from him when he does something well. The boy has considered giving up his sport due to disappointment and dislike of it but still expects to be involved in five years at the national level. Skating is very important to this boy, who sees himself as closest to his mother. He is distant from his father who he describes as pushy, interfering, and disrupting. Psychologically the boy should be encouraged, again, to get more competence feedback from his sport. This will have to be directed overtly and obviously by the coach. The relationship with the father is crucial in this case and the coach will have to inspire an entirely new sort of relationship in order to stabilize this very ambitious boy. The coach does not have to push him. He will push himself. The boy needs support, reward, and an appreciative tutor in his skating. He has said exactly what he wants: personal understanding, recognition, and support.

Case 4. A Positive Adjustment in a Low Performing Male. This 13-year-old boy is given a low rating on potential and is described by his coach as lazy and unmotivated. He is seen as someone who should be doing much better even though he will not be outstanding. The boy says he does not intend to give up his sport and that he wants to become outstanding. He (accurately) rates the coach's ambition for him as much lower. He likes the coach for the support and understanding given. He is close to both his parents. Psychologically the athlete has an excellent profile. He is getting just what he wants from sport: the attention of a coach, feelings of efficacy, and a shared activity with others. He is generally happy and his only flaw (if one may call it that) is his rather low overall achievement motivation and his lowness on traits which would work in support of achievement (such as autonomy and endurance). Such an individual may not grow into an outstanding athlete. (He is, incidentally, already outstanding scholastically.) It appears he will use his sport as a vehicle for personal growth rather than for competitive accomplishment. Sometimes such types provide a surprise with their persistence and eventual accomplishment. As their feelings of competence grow in sport, it sometimes surpasses the competence experienced in other areas of life. Thus the person may blossom late.

CONCLUSION

In this chapter the use of the Sport Protocol as a screening instrument has been demonstrated. It is used in order to counsel the athlete on some of his or her major thoughts, feelings, and motivations with regard to participation in sport. The profiles may also be used, with the athletes' permissions, to consult with other coaches in order to increase the coaches' skills in dealing with their athletes.

The basic clinical assumption in the chapter has been that an understanding of the athlete's psychology, goals, and concerns is necessary to assist maximum personal growth in sport and consequently with the achievement of maximum potential in athletic performance. The ideas and techniques offered for discussion by the psychologist are given with the premise that (1) the consultant psychologist will complement and never interefere with the roles of the athlete or the coach, and (2) all ideas and possibilities offered to the athlete, coach, parent, or other consultee are given with the understanding that their application is entirely the choice of the client.

19
Assessment Procedures

INTRODUCTION

Assessments of the client's status and needs may be made through interview questions or through the administration of some standardized instruments developed for specific assessment needs. The purpose of using any such instruments is to specify problems, questions, or directions and goals that can be pursued in the subsequent sessions. There is an array of assessment techniques and procedures available for clinical and consulting work. The following will describe some representative instruments which are frequently used. They are discussed and described under three headings: the tools of classic clinical psychology, personality inventories, and sport-specific measures.

There are some in society who criticize the use of tests with athletes. The misuse of information, procedures, and ethical guidelines are cited as evidence that tests and assessments should be used minimally or not at all. In one case, the American Football League banned the use of test data for selection purposes. Generally, however, it is not the assessments per se that are invalid and unwanted but the way in which they are used by certain people. In the hands of well-trained and competent professionals, assessment procedures can be an aid to understanding, planning, and goal setting.

TOOLS OF CLASSIC CLINICAL PSYCHOLOGY

On some occasions, the client may need a clinical assessment in which abilities, personality, cognitive functioning, and psychopathology are explored. Sometimes all of these may be relevant and at other times only one or more may be of interest. When such assessments are needed they must be carried out by a trained clinical psychologist with the requisite experience. The clinician will use skill and experience to draw conclusions and make recommendations on the best possible courses of treatment, diagnosis, and/or life planning, in consultation with the client. Selections of tests to be administered will vary with the presenting problems. For example, if the referral is for a 45-year-old hospitalized ex-boxer who is depressed and suffers from brain damage, the battery of tests might include the Wechsler Adult Intelligence Scale, the Rorschach, the Thematic Apperception Test, the Minnesota Multiphasic Personality Inventory, and the Bender-Gestalt Test. Other tests will be used according to the presenting problems of the client. All of the instruments require training and experience if they are to be used accurately, and the skill and clinical abilities of the clinician doing the assessment far outweigh the importance of the tests used. From clinical testing the psychologist will gather information on how the client copes, what pathologies or difficulties are evident, what strengths and competencies the individual uses to deal with problems, and what cognitive styles and strategies the client tends to use in various situations. Full clinical assessments are generally done only when an athlete is disturbed and entering clinical treatment. Since the student and the prospective clinician will want to be familiar with some major clinical instruments, they are discussed under three headings: tests of intellectual competence, projective tests, and tests for psychopathology.

1. Tests of Intellectual Competence. The three major tests of intelligence are: the Stanford-Binet test, the Wechsler Intelligence Scale for Children Revised (WISC-R), and the Wechsler Adult Intelligence Scale (WAIS).

The Stanford-Binet Intelligence Scale, Third Revision (1973) can be used for children aged two and up and for all adults. It yields an intelligence quotient based on the individual's overall performance on a wide variety of subtests. The subtests are heavily weighted toward verbal ability in the age ranges of six and over and this weighting increases in the adult sections of the test. For this reason the Stanford-Binet, although of great historical importance, is not in as widespread general use as the WISC-R and the WAIS. The test was originally developed by two French psychologists, Alfred Binet and Theodore Simon, who were asked by the French government to develop measures to identify children in the school system who would have difficulty with the academic curriculum and would be better streamed into trade programs. Thus was the first intelligence test, developed in Paris in 1908. It was later adapted for American use by Lewis Terman at Stanford, yielding the Stanford-Binet in 1916.

The WAIS, developed by David Wechsler (1949–1981), provided the next major innovation in intellectual assessment. Applicable for those aged 16 and over, the WAIS yields 14 scores: a verbal score comprised of subtests entitled information, comprehension, arithmetic, similarities, digit span, and vocabulary; and a performance score comprised of subtests entitled digit symbol, picture completion, block design, picture arrangement, and object assembly. Finally a total score combines the verbal and performance indexes. The tests yield important clinical information in terms of score discrepancies, score patterning, and different styles and problems the client may have in approaching the subtests. The WISC-R (Wechsler, 1974) is the downward extension of the WAIS for children aged five to 16. It yields from 13 to 15 scores which are: the overall *verbal score,* which is made up of information, comprehension, arithmetic, similarities, vocabulary, and digit span (optional), and the overall *performance score,* which is made up of picture completion, picture arrangement, block design, object assembly, coding, and mazes (optional).

2. Projective Tests. The two most widely used projective methods, the Rorschach and Thematic Apperception Test will be noted. These tests, particularly the Rorschach, have been the subject of heated debate over their psychometric inadequacies. But they remain firmly in use for both clinical and research purposes. For the issues engendered the reader is referred to the general texts of Anastasi (1982) and Cronbach (1984) and to the many critical and specific reviews of the tests in Buros *Mental Measurements Yearbooks.* The Rorschach Ink Blot Test, developed by Hermann Rorschach in Switzerland between 1921 and 1951, can be used for those aged three and over. It consists of ten cards featuring multifaceted ink blots about which the client freely associates. These are followed up with various lines of questioning and clarification. Although controversial, the Rorschach is still widely used and researched. It is particularly used for the evaluation of personality and emotional disturbance and provides the basis, in a standardized interview format, for theory-based opinion by experts. The training, skill, and perspective of the psychologist thus become paramount in the use of the Rorschach Test. The Thematic Apperception Test, developed by Henry A. Murray and C.D. Morgan between 1935 and 1943, may be used for ages four and over. It consists of 20 cards. The client is asked to tell a story with a beginning, middle and end about the somewhat ambiguous pictures. To a trained interpreter the output purportedly yields a summary of the conflicts, needs, complexes, and emotions of the client. The TAT has been subject to an immense amount of research over the years and remains a firmly entrenched clinical instrument. Again, the experience and ability of the test user are crucial factors in its viability.

3. Testing for Psychopathology. Two divergent tests will be noted: the Minnesota Multiphasic Personality Inventory (Hathaway and McKinley, 1943–67) and the Bender-Gestalt (Bender, 1938–46) test. The Minnesota Multiphasic Personality Inventory (the MMPI) for those aged 16 and over yields 14 scores: four validity scores (question, a lie score, a validity score, and a test-taking attitude score) and ten clinical scores (hypochondriasis, depression, hysteria, psychopathic deviate, masculinity and femininity, paranoia, psychasthenia, schizophrenia, hypomania, and social introversion). It was published between 1943 and 1967 and was largely the work of J. C. McKinley, a neuropsychiatrist, and S. R. Hathaway, a clinical psychologist. The MMPI is the most widely used and researched instrument for personality assessment. It has been used and misused for many purposes and many consider its major strength to be its convenient pool of 550 personality items. Used frequently in sport research, the most interesting use has no doubt been in the research program of Morgan (1978) at the University of Minnesota. The MMPI was administered to all U of M freshman, allowing for a follow-up study over the next several years and a detailed study of those athletes who were successful participants in sport and those who were not.

A second test which can indicate pathology of a very different sort is the Bender-Gestalt Memory for Designs Test (Bender, 1938–1977). This test consists of 15 designs, successively increasing in complexity, which the client is asked to reproduce by memory after a restricted period of time in which to examine them. The test can be indicative of disturbances in psychomotor coordination as well as indicative of brain damage in severe cases. More detailed assessments of brain functioning require the administration of test batteries such as the Halstead-Reitan Neurological Test Battery (Reitan, 1981). Again, all of these tests require skilled clinicians for their interpretation and use.

PERSONALITY INVENTORIES

In early work in sport psychology most researchers used a general personality inventory for the assessment of individuals and/or groups. As described in Chapter 9 there was much controversy over whether differences could be detected in the personality of athletes versus nonathletes, team versus individual athletes, athletes in various sports, athletes showing different levels of skill development, and athletes playing different team positions. Basically differences have been shown between all of these divisions and yet controversy has continued to rage, much as it has in general psychology, over whether personality differences are due to trait differences or merely reflect situational demands. The conclusion, as noted in Chapter 9, is that personality traits account for a small but significant proportion of the variance in many criterion behaviors, and this is also true of sport. Thus we list some of the major personality inventories that have been used in sport research.

1. California Psychological Inventory. Developed by Harrison G. Gough, the scale is applicable to ages 13 and over. It was published and revised between 1956 and 1975 and yields 18 scores. These are dominance, capacity for status, sociability, social presence, self-acceptance, sense of well-being, responsibility, socialization, self-control, tolerance, good impression, communality, achievement via conformance, achievement via independence, intellectual efficiency, psychological mindedness, flexibility, and femininity. The scales were developed on the basis of criterion or empirical item selection (the item's capacity to differentiate between preselected groups). It provides a profile of socially relevant personality traits and has been much used in studies on sport.

2. Eysenck Personality Inventory. Developed by H. J. Eysenck and S. B. G. Eysenck, and formerly known as the Maudsley Personality Inventory, the scale is applicable to ages seven and over. The current scales were published in 1975 and 1976 and the forerunners between 1963 and 1969. Four scores are yielded by the test: psychoticism, extraversion, neuroticism, and a lie score. Scales range in length from 18 to 25 items and scale content is based on Eysenck's personality theory. Reviewers on the one hand compliment the scale for tackling the measurement of the two much replicated personality dimensions which were originally developed from factor analyses and proposed for measurement by Eysenck. On the other hand they note the experimental nature of the psychoticism scale. In view of Eysenck's general personality theory on sport and the brevity of this instrument, it should be well used in future sport studies.

3. Hostility Scales. In 1957 A. H. Buss and A. Durkee published a scale for measuring eight types of hostility. Because aggression is central to sport and there is much concern with negative aggression, the items developed by Buss and Durkee have considerable interest to sport researchers and practitioners. Eight types of hostility are measured by scales from 8 to 14 items in length. The scales purport to measure assault, indirect hostility, irritability, negativism, resentment, suspicion, verbal hostility, and guilt.

4. Locus of Control. In 1966 J. B. Rotter proposed that an important motivating feature of an individual was that person's expectancy of his or her belief with regard to perceived locus of control. That is, does the person attribute success of failure to internal and external factors? Rotter's original scale is available in the above publication. In addition E. J. Phares in 1976 developed a scale measuring internality versus externality of attitude, consisting of forced choice items. Because of the immense amount of use of these scales in the general psychological literature and their equal relevance to the psychology of sport, they are listed here for possible use.

5. Personality Research Form. Currently one of the most widely used general tests of personality, the Personality Research Form was developed by D. N. Jackson during 1965 to 1974. The standard edition takes approximately 30 to 45 minutes to complete and yields 15 scores: achievement, affiliation, aggression, autonomy, dominance, endurance, exhibition, harm avoidance, impulsivity, nurturance, order, play, social recognition, understanding, and infrequency. The scales are very well constructed, employing a combination of statistical techniques for scale construction. This and the continued relevance of Murray's need theory, upon which the scales are based, have made this a highly acclaimed instrument for the measurement of personality.

6. Sixteen Personality Factor Questionnaire. The 16 Personality Factor Test was developed between 1949 and 1980 by R. B. Cattell. Twenty-two scores are yielded by the test, 16 of which are described as primary factor scores and 6 of which are described as second-order factors (higher order combinations of the first 16). The first-order factors are reserved vs. outgoing, less intelligent vs. more intelligent, affected by feelings vs. emotionally stable, humble vs. assertive, sober vs. happy-go-lucky, expedient vs. conscientious, shy vs. venturesome, tough-minded vs. tender-minded, trusting vs. suspicious, practical vs. imaginative, forthright vs. shrewd, self-assured vs. apprehensive, conservative vs. experimenting, group-dependent vs. self-sufficient, undisciplined self-confident vs. controlled, and relaxed vs. tense. The six second-order factors are: introversion vs. extraversion, low anxiety vs. high anxiety, tender-minded emotionality vs. tough poise, subduedness vs. independence, naturalness vs. discreetness, and cool realism vs. prodigal subjectivity. Although the 16 P. F. Test is much used in sport research, recent opinion and criticism does not recommend its use. For critical reviews of the 16 P. F. Test and most of the tests discussed thus far the reader is referred to Buros' series of *Mental Measurements Yearbooks* (Buros, 1978; Mitchell, 1985) before selecting the scales for either study or practical purposes.

SPORT-SPECIFIC MEASURES

A trend in recent years has been toward the development of specific sport-related scales for use in physical education and sport psychology. These scales, which are sometimes but not always simpler than the general scales just described, focus upon sport. Some examples follow.

1. Athletic Motivation Inventory. Developed by T. A. Tutko, L. P. Lyon, and B. C. Ogilvie, this scale measures 11 trait scores (drive, aggressiveness, determination, responsibility, leadership, self-confidence, emotional control, mental toughness, coachability, conscientiousness, and trust) plus two validity scales (accuracy and desirability). The scales were developed between 1969 and 1977 and have been extremely controversial because they have been used as a selection instrument in the face of scanty validation data (Martens, 1975; Buros, 1978, p. 547–8).

The psychologists who developed this scale pioneered the area of sport-specific assessments in psychology. They have been soundly criticized for not publishing reliability and validity statistics and yet they have highlighted personality factors which have consistently emerged in sport studies: dominance, endurance, extraversion, and aggression.

2. Sport Competition Anxiety Test. The measurement of anxiety has always been a central topic in psychology. Taylor (1953) published a much-used scale to measure manifest anxiety. Another major step was taken in the assessment of anxiety by D. C. Spielberger, R. L. Gorsuch, and R. Lushene (1968–70), who published the State-Trait Anxiety Inventory. This test takes about 20 minutes to complete and measures both the state of anxiety which is situationally produced and trait anxiety, which is the intrinsic disposition of the individual to manifest anxiety. Later, Martens (1971, 1977) extrapolated this research to sport and developed the *Sport Competition Anxiety Test,* a simple measurement of anxiety specific to sport situations. This test has subsequently been used widely in sport studies.

3. Test of Attentional and Interpersonal Style. Nideffer (1976a, 1976b, 1978) has done considerable work in developing a test central to sport performance. It focuses upon the individual's style of concentration as well as his or her style of interaction with others (such as introversion-extraversion). Because the interpersonal style descriptions are for the most part common to other tests (they are, for example, self-esteem, obsessiveness, introversion, extraversion, positive affect, and negative affect) we will focus for the most part on Nideffer's descriptions of attentional style. Six scores are obtained, as follows: *Broad-external* indicates that an individual can deal with and react to a breadth of external stimuli in an effective manner. *External overload* indicates that the individual will tend to become overloaded by external stimuli and hence may make errors and have trouble concentrating. *Broad-internal* indicates an individual who is able to concentrate and integrate input when many things happen at once or when there is much information to integrate and draw conclusions from. *Internal overload* indicates a person who becomes confused by his or her own thoughts and/or feelings and therefore is prone to error. *Narrow effective focus* indicates a person who is able to concentrate effectively when the situation demands it and block out interfering information. Finally, *errors of underinclusion* show an individual who is unable to get rid of interfering thoughts and ideas. This person may be obsessed with a single event such as an error which he or she has made and be unable to erase it and get on with things at hand. The ability or inability to concentrate is very relevant in the sport situation, which accounts for the readiness of many people in sport to use this assessment procedure.

4. Behavioral Assessment. Some sport practitioners would de-emphasize the personality assessment within sport and emphasize behavioral assessment. Rushall (1978) has been a major proponent of "environment specific behavior assessment" as applied in sport. These are for the most part checklists of behaviors that are applicable to the sport under study. Rushall would follow up such assessments with incentives for increasing desired behaviors and disincentives in order to decrease undesired behaviors in both training and competition situations.

5. Analysis of Incentive Motivation. Alderman and Wood (1976) developed a scale to measure the motivations of athletes. Their working version consisted of 70 items, with ten items representing each end of the seven subscales of the test. Both subscales and items were rationally developed. The subscales are: independence, power, affiliation, arousal, esteem, excellence, and aggression. The scale offers a quick and easy assessment of motivation for research and discussion purposes.

CONCLUSION

The foregoing sports scales are examples of available measures which are specific to sport. The list is representative, not all-inclusive, of the work that practitioners in sport have done on problems of measurement. Thus, there are a number of inventories available for both general and specific use in the psychology of sport. These range from those which are impossible for the layman to use (e.g., the TAT) to those which are dangerous for the layman to use because of the possibility of misinterpretation (e.g., the MMPI), to those that the layman can use if he or she develops sufficient motivation to do so (e.g., Butt's sport motivation scales, Marten's sport competition anxiety test, and Alderman and Wood's incentive motivation test). Other sport tests are quite advanced in terms of psychometric theory and have been made commercially available (e.g., Tutko et al.'s Athletic Motivation Inventory and Nideffer's Test of Attentional and Interpersonal Style.

Considerable work has been put into both the development of norms and the marketing of the latter two relatively extensive instruments. It is important to note that even the simpler devices are more meaningful if used by someone who knows the theory and the limitations of psychological measurement. Recent test theory has suggested (Burisch, 1984) that the simpler a personality inventory, the better. Burisch suggests that the sophistication and elaborate methods of the psychometricians may offer little in accuracy over very direct and well put questions. If such a statement holds true, much psychometric literature will have to be rewritten. At present it seems that there is a place for personality as well as performance assessment. These summaries can save time, allow clients to explore their own answers, and save money when compared to the same amount of self-exploration through counselling or psychotherapy. The disadvantages are that the summaries are sometimes too complicated for the layman to understand and use (Klavora and Daniel, 1979, pp. xvii–xix) and that they can be controversial and even dangerous if they are misinterpreted or misused.

Test results, whether psychological, physical, or performance, must be used with flexibility to gauge the special circumstances in which they are given and the special needs of the client. There are many cases on record of misdiagnoses in the psychological and medical literature, and the field of sport is adding its own list to these errors. Caution, sensitivity, and understanding are always essential for users of psychological measures.

20
Ethics in Clinical and Consulting Work

THE CLINICAL AND THE DEVELOPMENTAL
MODEL IN SPORT PSYCHOLOGY

Conflicts exist within the field of sport psychology over who should practice it and what training is needed to practice it. The question is how to identify those capable of helping clients to develop and to enhance performance in a constructive manner. Since the psychologist does not want to support the unhealthful stresses of sport, he or she must be able to assess the risks an athlete takes, for example, in trying to perform when injured, in pushing him or herself too hard, in taking steroids or in training in a manner which is injurious to physical and/or psychological well being. If an athlete is suffering real or potential breakdown, the psychologist has the responsibility and training to make a proper assessment and put the welfare of the client first and foremost. And yet there are often conflicts of interest when the psychological consultant is hired by management which sees the psychologist's function as one of keeping an individual or a team performing at a high level.

In clinical work the psychologist has traditionally been a mediator between the needs of the individual and the demands of society. The psychologist will attempt to operate in an unambiguous way that will ensure the client's trust. This is the essence of the therapeutic relationship. The clinician will understand the social criticism contained within the client's symptoms be they of stress, anxiety, or depression. The preservation of the client's marriage, job status, or need to achieve are not seen as central to the therapy unless the client makes them so. Similarly, when the psychologist works in sport, he or she must understand and work with the client in order to understand the social criticism inherent in the problems which develop as the result of the sport activity. The client will then work toward solving the problems in a manner that is uniquely suited to the client. The clinician's major responsibility is to the welfare of the client.

There are many persons working in sport consulting who are not psychologists and who do not put client welfare first. Their first responsibility may be to the sport or to performance enhancement. Many trained psychologists will work in this way when their function is to assist a team, organization, or individual to increase performance level. However, many other people who do this kind of work also are not trained psychologists. They may be physical educators who are trained in health, education, or kinesiology. Such training may have involved many courses in coaching, developmental psychology, and educational psychology but few or no courses in psychopathology, the assessment of personality, or psychotherapy. Thus the major difference between the psychologist and the physical educator in sport is that the former is trained as a clinician (and usually as a researcher) while the latter is trained as a developmentalist, (that is, an educator).

These two major preparatory schools for people working as sport consultants have resulted in much confusion. Many educators may call themselves sport psychologists but are really more like educator-coaches than psychologists. The educator has as his or her major aim the encouragement of maximum performance through the use of a variety of techniques. Unless the educator-consultant treads carefully this can result in ethical and role problems when people acting as "psychologists" impose their views on athletes and the coaches. The psychologist (clinician) is less likely to trespass on the roles of the coaching staff or athletes than is the educator. This is because, *first,* psychologists operating according to the code of ethics of their psychology associations, always put the client welfare, meaning his or her psychological and physical health, over and above sport performance. *Second,* the psychologists, due to their professional orientation, should be secure in their clinical role and therefore be less likely to assume the roles of other sport positions (management, athlete, and coach). *Third,* the psychologist should not long to be part of a winning team, nor should he or she be looking for glory in sport or a team blazer. Rather the psychologist will help the individual or team to prepare mentally for contests, to decide upon goals, and to grow personally from the experiences of both wins and defeats. *Fourth,* the psychologist will feed ideas, techniques, and opinions to athletes, coaches, and organizations. The decision of whether to use those ideas and how far to pursue them, or whether to adopt alternative routes or goals, is always up to the coach and the athlete.

The educational (developmental) approach is somewhat different from the psychological (clinical) approach. The same objectivity and humanism may not always be present. Although the best educators seem to have been humanists, they also have been functionalists. That is, the educator assumes that in at least some areas he or she knows better than the client what is good for the client. An educator is sought in order to teach something, to train and to outline, to mold and to impart knowledge, skill, or technique. Individual growth is considered very important but only to the extent that the person becomes maximally functional to and in society. Creativity cannot be taught, talent cannot be taught, and inspiration cannot be taught. Facts can be imparted, skills can be communicated, and technique can be trained.

The distinction between the clinical or psychological approach to sport psychology and the developmental or educational approach to sport consulting is somewhat arbitrary. However, the distinctions provide some understanding of the confusion that exists over the role of the sport psychologist. First, the client is often puzzled about what to expect from the "sport psychologist" because many clients have not distinguished between psychologists and developmentalists. Second, there is conflict among the professions over who is allowed to practice sport psychology. It is common to hear psychologists complain that persons calling themselves sport psychologists are not psychologists. The physical educators frequently complain that most psychologists know too little about sport to be credible when consulting in sport.

Harrison and Feltz (1979) forecast that potential legal conflict could arise between unlicensed sport psychologists and the state and provincial psychology licensing boards that exist throughout Canada and the United States. They note that although the term "sport psychology" implies a specialty within psychology, many sport psychologists identify with other fields and are not even eligible for a license to practice psychology. They also note the detailed curriculum a sport psychology program should cover if sport psychologists were to be eligible for licensing (Harrison and Feltz, 1979, p. 189):

> Perhaps the most controversial item of all is the requirement that the curriculum should encompass a minimum of 3 years and include instruction in scientific and professional ethics, research design, statistics, and psychometrics. In addition, the core program should require each student to demonstrate competence in each of the following areas:
> a. Biological bases of behavior (physiological or comparative psychology, neuropsychology, sensation, psychopharmacology).
> b. Cognitive-affective bases of behavior (learning, thinking, motivation, emotion).
> c. Social bases of behavior (social psychology, group processes, organizational and systems theory).
> d. Individual differences (personality theory, human development, abnormal psychology).

Many have suggested that guidelines and ethics should be developed for sport psychologists (Martens, Singer, and Harris, 1977; Butt, 1979d). This challenge was met when a code of ethics was adopted by both the Canadian and U.S. sport psychology associations. First sponsored by Sport Canada, the Canadian Society for Psychomotor Learning and Sport Psychology organized a committee under the directorship of Dr. Peter Klavora of the University of Toronto. The committee proposals were later adopted by its American counterpart. The principles, largely modelled after the American Psychological Association Code of Ethics, offer to guide the practice of sport consultants, whatever their primary professional identifications. This is necessary when people are operating in a relatively unstructured area with maximum personal freedom. The temptations to break common ethical values seem to be great in an achievement-oriented society where the value of achievement may be placed above and beyond the value of individuals.

Danish and Hale (1981, 1982) aruged for an educational-developmental framework in the practice of sport psychology. They contend that imposing a psychological-remedial-intervention model would be dysfunctional to this growing branch of knowledge and applied work. If licensing rules were applied, then athletes would have to be diagnosed psychiatrically for health scheme programs (payment) and this would immediately be dysfunctional. They note that most athletes wish to grow, to develop, and to enhance performance. Their referral problems are better treated as states of imbalance which make subsequent growth possible (Riegel, 1975).

At the present time it seems reasonable not to restrict the practice of consulting in sport to any one group of professionals. Physical educators and coaches have applied their special knowledge of psychology throughout the years and, although some practitioners show much need of improvement themselves, others have been outstandingly successful. Thus there are many dedicated coaches who have been praised by athletes not only for their excellence as coaches but also for overseeing the total development of their athletes.

The legal conflicts that are developing between psychologists and sport consultants center mainly on who can call him or herself a psychologist. In most states and provinces there is a fine for breaking the equivalent of the "psychologist's act." In the province of British Columbia the fine is $500 per day. There are many "sport psychologists" breaking this law because they are not trained psychologists. One simple way around the problem is that these people call themselves what, indeed, they are: "sport consultants" and not "psychologists".

In conclusion, many professionals are involved in the field of specialized sport consulting: physical educators, clinical psychologists, social psychologists, general psychologists, psychomotor learning specialists, general practitioners, psychiatrists, coaches, and various other sport specialists. Increasing numbers of students are training in psychology as the specialized route to sport consulting. These individuals will meet the educational requirements needed to become qualified psychologists while at the same time mastering their specialty area of sport psychology. It is quite clear that professionals trained as sport consultants fall into different professional categories which are often defined by law. These professionals should represent themselves according to their professional training — as physical educators, medical doctors, psychiatrists, psychologists, etc., working in sport.

CODES OF ETHICS

Most professional associations have codes of ethics to which the members subscribe as a prerequisite to membership. The reader is referred to the Ethical Standards of Psychologists adopted by the American, Canadian, and most state and provincial psychological associations. The ethical guidelines can be grouped under nine areas: responsibility, competence, moral and legal standards, public statements, confidentiality, welfare of the consumer, professional relationships, use of assessment techniques, and the pursuit of research activities. These principles are centrally concerned with trust and honesty between the provider of psychological services and the consumer. For most people in the field the ethical guidelines may not be necessary. However, there are circumstances, sometimes outside the psychologist's control, which may place him or her in a compromising ethical position.

The basic premise of professional ethics is that the professional, due to his or her privileged status, must put the welfare of the client and others ahead of his or her own within the confines of the professional relationship. In sport psychology this means that a client will not be subjected to a win-at-all-cost philosophy on the part of the psychologist. The individual will not be sacrificed to the goals of others or to dangerous or harmful treatment techniques or training regimens. The psychologist is devoted to the welfare and healthful development of the client and will point out in a considered manner situations which work against the client's needs.

UNIQUE SITUATIONS AND QUESTIONS
OF CONFIDENTIALITY

Even experienced and highly qualified practitioners have found themselves in ethical dilemmas due to the newness of the field, the changing values of society, and the divided loyalties that can arise when the psychologist-consultant works in sport. In an interesting and informative paper Ogilvie (1978) has discussed the importance of trust in consulting work and the problems of divided loyalties within sport. A pioneer in the field, Ogilvie has done much counselling and clinical work in professional sport. He notes how quickly the psychologist can fall out of favor with management, who are usually paying the bills, and be sidelined from the team. The psychologist paid by management to consult professional athletes can be placed in a difficult situation if management thinks it has the right to psychological information resulting from the treatment. This problem must be dealt with diplomatically and definitively at the beginning of the consultation by the clear definition of roles and consequent confidentiality. The psychologist's participation and responsibilities are clear to all before the consultation work begins. The sport psychologist-consultant must chart out the type of information he or she will be giving, or not giving, to management and to the athlete. For example if the psychologist is consulting for management as an organizational psychologist, this must be specified to players or athletes and their options in giving personal information described fully. The same problems can arise consulting for coaches. Again the role of the psychologist and the options open to the athletes need to be spelled out. When the psychologist is consulting for managers of national teams, the writer is of the opinion that more can be asked from athletes in the way of psychological information than in some other situations. There is a privilege and responsibility which accompanies national team placements which is paid for by taxpayers. Therefore athletes, and others should contribute whatever they can to team and program development in the way of studies and program assessment. When consulting for coaches and managers the psychologist should realize that his or her participation will probably be no longer than the term of the manager who hired him or her. A different situation exists when the psychologist acts as a team psychologist. Then the primary responsibility is to look after team building, morale, and group cohesiveness, and to counsel athletes on group issues. Such psychologists usually meet with the team or group on specified dates for training sessions and may sometimes even travel with the team. The responsibility is to the overall welfare of the team, although the psychologist could carry team members in individual therapy. In most cases however, the team psychologist would be advised to refer the player needing extensive individual attention to another counselor. This is so the psychologist's responsibilities to the team as a whole will remain uncompromised. If the psychologist is hired to treat athletes on an individual basis then the lines of loyalty are very clear. He or she is the confidante and educator of an athlete with no responsibilities to the team or to management.

Because many people in sport are public figures, it is sometimes difficult to draw the line between what should and should not be made public about them. When their stories are published, what kind of discussion or writing is ethical as public education? As public figures, the lives and problems of athletes are often examined in the press. It is becoming increasingly common for athletes who have had major problems to write about them in books for commercial sale. Psychologists who have treated lesser known athletes commonly disguise case histories or identifications when they reported them in journals, books, or other forms of writing. There are exceptions: when the athlete has given the consultant permission to use his or her case for purposes of illustration.

Sometimes the consultant is held up to public scrutiny. In a well-publicized case, Arnold Mandell, formerly co-chairman of psychiatry at the University of California at San Diego, was at the apparent height of his career when he became psychiatrist for the San Diego Chargers and wrote a book in that position, *The Nightmare Season* (1976). By pioneering an area and writing a very critical book, Mandell triggered an avalanche of criticism of his own ethical practices.

This led to his being cited by the medical board for gross negligence and gross incompetence. He was also accused of betraying confidences and reaped little but disaster as reward for venturing into a new area and writing about it. Mandell found serious drug problems among the players and felt the best way to wean them was to prescribe the drugs they wanted. Presumably, the players would have obtained them elsewhere if they had to. Mandell was charged with prescribing 400 amphetamines to one player and from 50 to 300 pills to other team members. He wrote about his disastrous involvement with the team and concluded that football and psychiatry did not mesh. Whatever the quality of his own behavior, Mandell brought many important ethical issues to the attention of both students and practitioners in sport consulting work. He made significant contributions to the field at important costs to himself.

We have already mentioned (p. 229) the ethical problems the pioneers Tutko, Lyon, and Ogilvie ran into in the publication and use of the Athletic Motivation Inventory. The problems here: the mail order use of the test and its use for selection purposes. This inventory, founded on good psychometric theory, was developed at a time when it no doubt seemed quite appropriate to provide coaches with a questionnaire to help them in their selection decisions. With changing times and values, however, the use of tests quickly fell into disrepute. The possible misuses of scores, the inaccuracies in measurement, the individual variations that can culminate in strong athletic performances, all combined with other factors to question this and other tests on ethical grounds.

Although most practitioners today can take guidance from these cases, much consultation work in sport today could equally be criticized. The sport psychologist-consultant's role is almost inevitably controversial because many people assume a superior knowledge from the consultant, because people in sport are easily threatened by the consultant, and because, unless the consultant is continually alert, feelings and animosities which always run high in sport may be vented against him or her. The psychologist needs to be alert to possible misperception of his or her role. Such misperceptions need to be dealt with immediately and openly so that they can be corrected and that participants can remain cooperative.

WHEN CODES OF ETHICS FAIL

It is very difficult to prescribe codes of ethics for professional groups because every situation is unique. Probably every professional has at some time had good reasons for crossing the line prescribed by an ethical code. Such actions rarely result in accusations of ethical lassitude. The psychologist, trying to be fair, responsible, and considerate of the welfare of others, may decide on occasion to stretch common ethical rules and even to break them.

Let us consider three examples of ethical dilemma. (1) A client may expect too much from the psychologist. Does the psychologist correct this error in perception, and if so when? (2) A coach or a manager may ask the psychologist for information on an athlete which the psychologist has obtained from a confidential relationship. Does the psychologist pass on the information? (3) A governmental body offers to hire the psychologist in order to have him or her develop tests for the selection of the next Olympic team. Does the psychologist accept the challenge?

In situation (1), the psychologist, generally, would correct the client's expectations to be more realistic. However, in unusual circumstances, because of the condition of the client or because the correction of the perception might be the substance of the therapy itself, the psychologist may not take immediate steps to correct the misperceptions.

In situation (2), the general edict would be that it is a violation of ethics in all circumstances to pass on confidential information to a third party. This usually applies even when the third party is paying the bill — which might happen, for example, if a sport organization or a parent has sought the psychologist's services for an athlete. However, in some circumstances, the psychologist might pass on information to a third party even without the knowledge of the client. This would occur in emergency situations in which the client might be considered a danger to himself or herself or to others. Whenever there is the possibility of transmitting information about a client elsewhere, the probability should be discussed with the client. In very rare circumstances a client may not give permission to pass on information and the psychologist may do it. Consider the example of a 14-year-old figure skater, unable to perform because she is in love with her male coach who is 40. In very unusual circumstances this information might be transmitted to the coach for the welfare of all. If the psychologist does ever deem it necessary to break a confidence, he or she risks losing the trust of the client and very likely the therapeutic relationship will end.

In situation (3), the psychologist must decide whether to develop tests for Olympic team selection which will inevitably be imperfect. The psychologist may rephrase the assignment in order to make it a possible instead of an impossible task and thereafter follow closely the ethical guidelines for the use of psychological tests and their development. The psychologist may, for example, make the assessments experimental and use them for development and growth rather than for team selections, introducing a multifaceted assessment procedure involving performance testing as well as athlete, coach, and committee input. However, in different cultures — let us say the psychologist is on assignment abroad — it might be very reasonable to develop and apply such assessment procedures. If there is a very large population from which to select for the team and not everyone knows all the athletes, then such an assignment could conceivably be taken on with enthusiasm and with the support of athletes, coaches, management, and government. That is, the application of assessment procedures may be seen as quite legitimate in countries with different philosophies of sport. Although ethical guidelines are helpful and necessary for both professionals and students training in many fields, the ultimate ethical decisions must be made by the individual practitioner. In making such decisions the practitioner must take into account the special circumstances in each situation. He or she must also take the responsibility for the decisions.

One of the most important responsibilities the psychologist or sport consultant should have is that of the assessment of programs. The psychologist is trained to objectively evaluate programs for their success or lack of it. Simple evaluation procedures could be carried out by surveys on consumer response, athlete response, sponsor response, and management response which would give important information on morale, innovations, growth, or decline within the programs. Clearly this information could have ethical implications in that some programs and coaching styles, upon which much funding and energies are spent, might turn out to be damaging athletes. Clearly, people in sport are not always accountable for their actions and programs. Many assume that sport programs must be good programs. If psychologists could work with people in sport to evaluate and improve programs, it is clear that a major service would be performed for the general good.

PART VI

SOCIAL VALUES
AND SPORT

21
Subcultures of Sport

INTRODUCTION

The world of sport presents a highly organized social structure that may be divided into individual sports, each with its own subcultures. These subcultures include: *the audience*—the spectators, and fans; *the officials*—the referees, the judges, and the hierarchies of the sport associations; *the athletes*—those who play in the contest or perform; *the owners or sponsors*—those individuals or groups who own or sponsor sports enterprises for corporate, personal, or financial gain; and *the promoters and their agents*—individuals and corporations who promote sport for secondary gain, and the various forms of media. Other subcultures might include coaches, managers, the press, and the sport psychologists. This chapter deals with the first five subcultures. The psychology of coaching and managing has been discussed in Chapter 14; the press is discussed in Chapter 22; and sport psychologists have been discussed in Chapter 20.

Each group, as a subculture, has its own unique function within the sports culture. It has its code of conduct, its status hierarchy, its own language, style of dress, and behavior, and its assigned area of space within the athletic arena upon which the members of other subcultures usually do not trespass. Individuals within the sport world are rigidly typed as belonging to a given subculture. A book in which this insular psychology is well illustrated is Parrish's (1972) *They Call It a Game.* Here are several examples drawn from that work.*

On owners:

Art was excluded from our company. Owners may pay us, they may trade us and fire us and blackball us and subjugate us and try to break our spirits for the sake of their power complexes and a few dollars, but they can never be one of us, and without us they would be anonymous.

On coaches:

Coaches are more a part of a society of coaches than they are members of their own teams. Under the system, a coach cannot afford to embarrass or be

---

*Copyright c 1971 by Bernard P. Parrish. Used with permission of Dial Press.

uncharitable towards opposing coaches because some day he may need a job from one of them. The often-repeated assertions that a coach would sign any player or trade his own mother to win are for public consumption only.

On the press:

In general, however, players look down on sportswriters behind their backs and smile to their faces. Players feel superior to them. Joe Namath once told a nettling writer, "I don't need any of you $100-a-week creeps to go around writing about me." Joe had another line for whenever a sports writer said to him, "I'm only doing my job." Joe would say, "Do it some place else." I can almost hear every football player cheering quietly in the background for Joe Willie.

On everyone:

But few players would deny, if you could get them to set aside their personal ambitions for a moment, that they don't really care much for the company of jocksniffers, whether they be sportswriters, owners, or front-office people.

Derision is common between the subgroups, though not widely publicized, perhaps because there is no love lost between the athletes and the press. (For example, Terry Bradshaw has been quoted: "I absolutely do not trust sports writers or broadcasters.") Real experiences separate the subgroups, as well as the fact that identities are sustained by holding negative attitudes toward the members of the other groups. Group cohesion and identity is attained partly by scapegoating out-groups or groups that are different in race, purpose, or membership. Thus the polarized groups become more tightly knit and punitive, rejecting other groups.

The subcultures of sport have vastly different entry requirements. Positions as fans and spectators are open to all. The fan usually pays a fee, but he or she may sit at home and watch television. Though in essence, spectators fill the weakest position in sport subcultures, their sheer numbers make them an important factor particularly because of mass marketing tactics. Sport fans are regularly bombarded by messages to buy otherwise indistinguishable brands of cigarettes, liquors, sports products, and so on. Thus, fans, are much courted, despite occupying the lowest status within the sport hierarchy. Entry into the subculture of the athletes requires ability. Entry into the role of owner requires social status, usually defined by money and business position. Officials and promoters enter their subgroups because of required skills that often include some previous background in the sport. Owners, officials, and fans are often frustrated players themselves. They "love" the sport, and aspire to a closer link with the athletes. Promoters are usually a different breed. For them money is the paramount objective. Durso (1971) observes that the emergence of sport promotion was largely attributable to commercial sponsorship in television. Having invested huge amounts of money, the sponsors of sporting events insured their investments by elaborate promotion schemes.

The fact that each of the subcultures can satisfy its unique needs simultaneously has allowed them, in the past, to subsist side by side without conflict. When the needs of two subcultures are in conflict, however, so that both struggle for mutually exclusive goals, the results are sometimes debilitating. One increasing conflict between sport subgroups is over the rights to the spoils of sport. Strikes of the National Basketball Association referees and National Baseball League umpires have both resulted in officials getting a piece of the money action in their respective sports. The 1982 strike by the National Football League players was hailed by business analysts as an example of labor strikes to come. Management is being forced to open its books in order that gate money and advertising dollars be distributed by the process of negotiation rather than by edict. Conflicts are increasing in sport because the subgroups have begun to intrude upon each other's domains.

Within the subcultures the value of money is usually greater than the value of the sport. Briner (1973) wrote about the monetary values of many players in the National Basketball Association which he felt would shock fans raised on the old ideals of team spirit, loyalty, and selflessness. In many ways, these ideals are archaic in the sports world and are "left to the suckers, to the fans." The athlete's perception of the fan is almost universally low. Ogilvie's (1971) study of this attitude concludes by asserting that the most general statement that can be made about the personal disposition of athletes is their low estimation of the sport fan.

Ironically, the members of each subgroup in sport perceive themselves as being held in high esteem by others. The promoter, official, player, and fan each sees himself or herself as central. But the athletes are the pivot of attention for all the other subgroups. Established athletes hold centerstage and often wield a weight that is perhaps far beyond their actual contribution. The newly arrived athlete, in contrast, wields little influence, because the public does not know him or her. Mewshaw (1983) has illustrated several of these points in his book *Short Circuit,* which describes the men's professional tennis tour. The officials, schedules, draws, and off-court privileges all favor established players in whom the promoter has often invested vast sums in appearance money. The promoter then protects his investment by insuring as far as possible that the main drawing cards persist longest in the tournament. Political weight and social pressures therefore converge to support the stars. Golf tournaments are subject to the same pressures and so is yachting (Levitt and Lloyd, 1983; Blackaller, 1984).

The contest which is staged by the promoters and swallowed by the fans is often approached in a different way by the athletes who "appear" as entertainers rather than as competitive players. In the athlete's mind, winning and losing usually take on a broader perspective the longer he or she is in a sport. Being the best means winning the big events, superceding other athletes on statistics and money, and maintaining position and status in the hierarchy of players.

Officials in sport have their own status system and rewards. Although of varied status, officials generally enjoy the experiences of the inner workings of the sport world. There are some very competent officials who are admired both by athletes and owners (some are even employed by sport promoters as lobbyists), but generally officials are not admired. They are looked upon as pretenders to authority and as "officious" men and women who want to feel important by exerting authority. The erosion of the officials' role is best illustrated in incidents where athletes use various tactics to downgrade referees. Hopcraft (1971) describing British football arguments between referees and players, writes that it is often difficult to determine who is reprimanding whom and "it quite often appears as if the official is about to be ordered off the field." Sometimes, the sponsor is also denigrated. Boorish behavior in Davis Cup competition by American players in 1984 led to sponsors and associations demanding that all players sign a code of conduct before being named to the team. John McEnroe is quoted as saying: "I don't see why I should have to sign it ... simply because they were backed into a corner by some sponsor who wasn't even involved the first six years I played."

Recently there have been incidents in which referees have been injured by athletes, players, and fans. Sometimes this hostility is inspired by the media. For example, Jimmy Piersall, in his new role as broadcaster, has been reported as blatantly inciting fans against umpires. The indignity that players and others inflict on referees can be caused by several factors. Many referees are volunteers and lack professional skill in their task. They make errors in judgment which are quickly perceived by athletes. Many athletes argue with referees' decisions so that next time around the referee will see things their way. This tactic is common in sport and often shows the arrogance of athletes who are so deeply involved in the play that they actually perceive lines, fouls, and play in their own favor. There is nothing more annoying to a hard-driven player, than to be adversely affected by a questionable referee decision. The player is quite likely to retaliate with rudeness, aggression, and insult, and he or she knows the crowd is usually quite willing to join the assault. The athlete knows that the referee probably wants to maintain his or her reputation for fair play in the critical gaze of players. The referee or umpire therefore is a perfect target for the frustrations and egocentricity of some athletes.

The athlete often correctly assumes that the referee wants to be part of the game, even though the referee sometimes may get minimal or no external reward.

The officials desire to closely identify with the athletes is in sharp contrast to the disdain in which he or she is held by the athletes. With increased professionalism in sport, there will also be increased pay and training for officials and a strengthening of the subculture. This is indicated by Peter Ueberroth's recent decision to create a post-season compensation pool for all major league baseball umpires and the publication of Ron Luciano's (with Fisher, 1983) best seller, *The Umpire Strikes Back.* In spite of referees' improved status, it remains that spectators are usually unaware of them unless they make a questionable call. Athletes merely tolerate them. Even so, referees will continue to think that they are more important and central to the game than they actually are in the eyes of others.

The promoters and owners in sport are two more subgroups within the system. Today, more and more, the old, wealthy sport barons are giving way to corporate sponsorships. Corporate sponsors are becoming high profile in naming events, identifying themselves with teams, and seeking endorsements from athletes who have been described as "walking billboards." Even national teams can become placards for commercial sponsors, and it has been predicted that Olympic athletes, if the Olympics persist, may some day end up representing corporations and not nations.

The rewards from being involved in sport for both the old owner–sport barons and the new corporate investors fall under the categories of financial return and public relations, personal interest, amusement, and status. Promoters and fund raisers offer corporations direct ego enhancements for giving money to sport. For example, recently, a national tennis association paid a fundraiser $50,000 to raise money from corporate sponsors. In return for large contributions, corporations would receive perks ranging from life membership in an exclusive club during competitions to weekend tennis camps for themselves and their spouses. The plan failed for all but the fundraiser, who raised only a small sum, but took the $50,000.

The desire for involvement in sport is a strong motivation, and owners and officials will sometimes travel the world for their love of sport. They may obtain a few important privileges as part of the elite subculture of owners and management—expenses, the best seats, the possibility of speech-making or being on television, the admiration of others as the "inner class." Thus image making and ego enhancement remain major motivations for the sponsors and the guardians of sport.

THE SHIFTING SUBCULTURES

Until recently the owners, directors, and organizers in sport had almost total control over decision-making compared to athletes, fans, or arbitrating officials. In years past, the athlete who was socially aware, who had superior intelligence, and whose values conformed to the status quo and its public ideals of sport tended to re-enter sport in an organizational capacity when they finished competing. In most cases, these ex-athletes had other professions and were attempting to put back into sport some of the benefits they had derived from it. Classic examples of this are: Roger Bannister, Chris Chataway, and Avery Brundage*. The modern athlete does not follow this pattern from athlete to profession and back into sport. Athletes today do so well financially that they stay in it for a much longer time. If they invest wisely they can often go on to become sport entrepreneurs.

Some of the early sport entrepreneurs were from golf, such as Sam Snead, or from tennis, such as Jack Kramer. Later examples include: Wilt Chamberlain in basketball, Reggie Jackson in baseball, Nancy Greene in skiing, and Karen Magnussen in skating. Currently outstanding athletes in North America can command 500,000 dollars a year and some are paid several million dollars a year. Today's athlete may own or endorse companies, products, and even teams. Because making money was a major goal in their competitive career, the successful athlete will continue this pursuit when his or her playing days are over. Players' associations are aimed at wresting a larger piece of the pie from the promoters and management in sport. They are also concerned with the expansion of sport for the purpose of money-making, and essentially they have set out to regulate and govern a flourishing new enterprise. Players associations tend to do little for those who are not players, however, causing the isolation among the subgroups of sport to become even more acute. However, some sportswriters have noted that the emergence of players associations have had positive developments. For example, formerly immature athletes have had to take on roles involving responsibility, leadership, and concerns for others.

Until recently athletes have been high in participation and low in influence in sport. This has been changing rapidly. In fact, the subgroups of sport can be represented as falling into a two-dimensional structure representing the degree of power in decision-making and the degree of participation. These relationships are represented in Figure 11.

This movement has increased insularity among the low status subcultures because each has converged on the spoils of sport, only looking out for its own interests. At the same time a working coalition of very high status members representing the various subcultures has emerged to dominate most sports. Thus a coalition of high status players, promoters, media personnel, and sponsors seeks dominance, and does dominate, in many sports. At the lower levels, the insularity of the homogeneous subcultures acts to foster rigid standards of

---

*A recent analysis of Brundage (Guttmann, 1983) has shown a split between private life and public persona. In private life Brundage is described in detail as a bigot, womanizer and hypocrite.

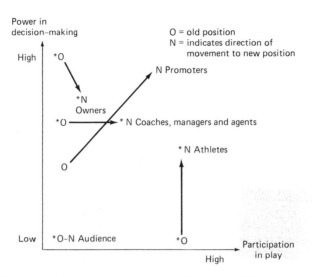

Figure 11. Movement of Sports Subcultures on Two-Dimensional Framework of Power and Participation in Play. Current movements of the subcultures in sport in terms of their power in decision-making and their degree of participation in the sporting contest are represented above. The owners have declined slightly in power. The athletes, always highest in participation, remain so, but with a sharp rise in decision-making power as they increase their autonomy through players associations. Coaches, managers and agents have increased their participation, largely operating as buttresses or mediators between athletes and owners. The audience continues to remain on the outside, looking in. Promoters show the greatest change due to their centrality in the commercialization of sport.

behavior to ensure conformity. Bouton's early books (1970, 1971) make reference to the conformity induced among baseball players. Bouton, always somewhat different from his fellows, with strong opinions and a healthy disdain for the average "jocko," decided at one point in his faltering career to play down his differences. He became convinced that to be "marginal" affected one's chances of success.

THE LOSERS

The function of losing in sport is often missed in North American society. In fact, most psychological problems in sport are precipitated when an athlete fails to execute actions at the desired level or loses to another individual or team. The experience of losing has been well analyzed by some sociologists (Ball, 1976; Harris and Eitzen, 1978). They note the gradual easing out of the professional player who is not making the team. For children, the significance of loss is also important. The child in school who tries but does not make a desired team may suffer a loss of self-worth. Still, losing can have an important function at times. For example, a squash player playing his or her boss might lose intentionally in order to directly enhance the opponent's ego. In professional wrestling, a wrestler might lose a bout to keep the audience interested in the rematch. Sometimes however, loss is real. The athlete has been going all out and is defeated. A series of such losses can often be the final stages of decline by which an athlete is eased out of the sport. This process can be extrapolated to other walks of life in which an individual occupies low status or is excluded from a group.

Losing has a positive side, in that it is an important avenue of feedback for an athlete. If an athlete fails to execute a desired skill losing can serve to remotivate, to enlarge horizons, and to make correction. Loss against superior opponents can also mark the athlete's introduction to high levels of competitive excellence. However, when accumulated losses send a message of decline from which there is no recovery, the athlete is faced with a dilemma. When he or she can no longer perform up to standard, other dimensions of life should take over from the athletic career. In fact what often happens is that the athlete depends upon the sport career for much of his or her identity, and he or she is unable to accept the inevitable decline. Depression and disintegration of personality and character may occur until the athlete is able to build up his or her life in other areas. Several observers (Edwards, 1983; Ashe, 1981) have written of the very small number of professional athletes who, in fact, do well. Black athletes in particular have a difficult readjustment to make if they fail in a sport at which they were once outstanding. For example, the number of black students in the United States who must readjust after having failed at college sport is large. Both Edwards and Ashe advocate that a good education is important for any athlete. It will increase breadth of knowledge, give the athlete additional interests that he or she may carry into later life, and open up more career opportunities should a career in sport fail to materialize. Even if the male athlete makes the major leagues, his life span in the sport will average around four years. Clearly the best defense against loss of any sort is personal breadth.

FAN DILEMMAS

Sport fans have a choice. They do not have to turn on the television set on the weekends. They do not have to read the sport pages or buy sport magazines. The needs of the fan are, however, very strong. There are few outlets for emotional expression and frustration in society. Underneath the entertainment value of sports events lie deeper and symbolic meanings and values. We will argue here that sport, unless it inspires people with excellence, draws them together in an unnatural communion that is not as harmless as may first appear. Sport draws people together to witness, identify with, and participate in a contest where the predominant perception is of people struggling against one another. The focus of communal attention in sport is on a struggle for superiority in which there is a victor and a vanquished. One must ask whether this struggle has some intrinsic merit, or whether the media, corporate sponsors, and promoters are exploiting a relative lack of fulfillment in the public who are also struggling for material gain, status, and position. In their book, *War Without Weapons*, Goodhart and Chataway (1968) question the function of sport spectatorship and attribute the huge increases of spectators over the years to their lack of involvement and satisfaction in their everyday work and lives. Passions that should be directed elsewhere are spent on the athletes performing. The authors correctly predicted that sport's power to involve audiences would become an increasing concern of governments and politicians. They did not predict that in many countries, corporate economics would be the strongest force to emerge in the organization of sport. Paul (1974) expanded on the above opinion by acknowledging the relationship of sport spectatorship to a lack of satisfaction in everyday life. He says, in addition, that spectator sport preserves that status quo by taking peoples' minds and energies away from important issues that concern their own lives and society. Because of this, mass spectator sport is detrimental because it prevents constructive social change. McMurtry (1971) analyzed North American football, one of the greatest consumers of public energy, as being socially destructive because it idealizes some of the most inhumane values of our society: "violent aggression ... corporate obedience ... greed ... obsession with personal success ... fakery ... and mechanical efficiency." He says football has the tendency to reinforce these values in both the athlete and the spectator, but he sees as most serious the draining of the energies of some of the ablest youth in the service of an unexamined "discipleship" (More recently the journalist, Underwood (1979) has likewise documented the decline of American football.)

Note that these ideas are those of outstanding athletes. Each author above has shown considerable success in other endeavors as well as athletics. From all perspectives they are among the most qualified to judge. What is the spectator missing? Sport could be a vehicle for the development of competence and the experience of self-fulfillment by the participants, yet this is often not the case. Instead, potential actors stream into sport arenas where their emotions are aroused without purpose and sometimes without satisfaction. The sporting event becomes a fix that the audience is too ignorant to question and too passive to correct. Fans substitute their presence at athletic events for their rightful position in society. But their thrills should be much deeper than those which come from observing a struggle to win or lose. Their appreciation of competence should be greater than what they get from watching a faked wrestling match, a fixed horse race, or a final apathetic struggle between injured giants at a Super Bowl. The thrills that could come to people through interpersonal experiences have often become minimized for the sport fan. Because there are no external rewards resulting from these other activities, they are often less appreciated. It should be of concern that so many are unable to experience or value the psychological rewards of human growth. It is not at all reassuring to see that on both individual and social levels, people will invest themselves in the pursuit of meaning by proxy.

There are some signs of change, however. Attendance at English First Division soccer games, for example, has dropped 30% in 15 years. One absentee is Michael Hancox of West Bromwich who supported his local team for 20 years before taking up playing rugby himself. The 38-year-old factory worker said: "Watching professional soccer didn't interest me anymore. I was watching vastly overpaid prima donnas serving up rubbish for fans who had to put up with lousy facilities." (Globe and Mail, December 21, 1985).

Yet the sporting event remains a social and communal event for many. It is a place one goes to see others, to share the spirit of the day, and to have status confirmed. It is a place of enjoyment and celebration, an escape that demands little personal investment from the fan. The athletes are performing for fans, who can shout derision or approval, or criticize, swear, and cheer, as if their being and skill and effort were at stake. But it costs nothing. What the fan does has no effect. What the fan says does not matter. The sport fan is the mark in a fraudulent event: he or she is led to believe that their presence is meaning-ful, when it is not, just as the fan is led to believe that what he or she sees has a certain meaning when it has not. The sport event does not often lead to the psychological growth of the fan—it only stagnates him or her further.

The expansion of commercial sporting events over the years to include the middle and lower classes is a further tragedy for the fan, particularly since much sport participation now involves only spectatorship. In 1899 Thorstein Veblen first published his well-known *Theory of the Leisure Class.* In it he writes of the sporting event as a manifestation of man's predatory instinct, and of its relation-ship to social class, economics, and social development. He assumes that sporting contests represent a biological inheritance from man's predatory past, which is expressed in "civilized" life through competition and aggressiveness. Although he notes that such motives may serve the individual, they are of absolutely no service in civilized community living, if the community is to develop and pros-per, and relationships between people are to remain peaceful. If the social environment is predatory, however, the individual with parallel traits will pros-per. What traits does sport foster? "Ferocity and cunning ... chicanery, false-hood and browbeating" are some, as is deceit, an observation supported by the presence of referees and umpires to assure that the competitors will not gain unfair advantage. Their presence assumes that athletes show a lack of concern for the rights of others and are entirely involved with their own welfare. Veblen cites how these characteristics further many economic enterprises. He also notes that the predatory instinct tends to be concentrated in the leisure class, the members of which have done well for themselves, and tend to be those most involved (in Veblen's time) in sport. Delinquent individuals are also said to have a highly developed predatory instinct, and Veblen describes the overlap between the swaggering, craftiness, self-interest, and lack of spiritual development of the sportsman and the delinquent.

Veblen's view of sport neglects the theory of competence development, which in 1899, had not yet been developed. Sport today in keeping the spectator passive is reinforcing a value system that the spectator is led to accept. This occurs even though the spectator may show cardiovascular arousal before, during and after an event. At the same time the spectator is unwittingly giving away his or her rights to participate and have an effect — giving these, by proxy, to others. His or her increased leisure has not been claimed in the public interest, but in the private interest. The promoters, media, advertisers, and owners of commercial sport have an interest in preserving materialistic, win or lose-type values, and the members of the crowd are skillfully conditioned to value what they see passing before them. The number of sporting events staged has mushroomed during the past few years. Leagues are proliferating and increased amounts of money are poured into sport by owners, advertisers, fans, and taxpayers. Sport has become aligned with big business. Large proportions of the cost can be written off as expenses as sport undergoes its own business boom. Commercial sport has offered a new territory to entrepreneurs and advertisers. Because it is an enterprise that feeds on the strong needs of the spectator, products can be effectively peddled by it. Sport is a medium for many messages to the spectator, concerning products and the prospective status of those who use them. It is also a medium for the competitive ethic. These messages do not benefit the spectator; they merely preserve a system that may not be serving the people as well as they think. The system they preserve is purely economic — it is not a system either applicable or helpful to family, community, the spiritual development of human nature, or the the future of humankind.

Some of the purest exploitation and satire of this attitude is found in the staging of professional wrestling. Consider "Macho Man," Randy Savage's diatribe at a press conference: "You get started on that issue and I'll bust your head.... You wanna come up here and discipline me? I'll slap you just like I would George Steele or Hulk Hogan. You'll feel the pain and truly understand Macho Madness....The world is Macho Man Territory—and you're trespassing." (NWF Magazine, 4, 1986, p. 19).

The ugly spectator is exposed when emotion that cannot comfortably be expressed in the rigid role he or she occupies erupts during the sport spectacle. The spectator learns little about him or herself from the emotion displayed. As the fan becomes increasingly alienated, however, increased violence can be expected. Perhaps the best example of fan violence comes from the much publicized pre- and post-game rampages among British soccer fans. The fan can for a brief time, reign supreme in an exciting battle, until it runs its destructive course or until the police intervene and jail an unfortunate few.

ATHLETE DILEMMAS

Athletes are a diverse group, although they have in common the development of superior physical qualities and skills which are in high demand. The star athlete is sought after in the way film stars are sought after. The athlete is trained, groomed, cultured, and nursed along the path to higher and higher sporting positions and increasing public exposure. During development, there are many influences and pressures on the athlete. Depending upon the sport, the athlete must learn, in varying degrees, to be competitive, tricky, and shrewd. He or she must learn to protect his person and position from other players and from challengers. He or she must learn to insulate himself from those who might draw him off course, and to present a suitable public image in keeping with the sport.

The athlete is, therefore, molded into his or her position more than is generally realized. The athlete's niche is waiting, should he or she have the ability and the willingness to fill it. As the athlete becomes valuable to the sport system, increasing demands can be made by the athlete. In spite of these rewards many athletes question what is happening to them along the professional development path. They are called upon to conform to the team norms of behavior, attitudes, and dress. They may also be encouraged to execute questionable acts such as taking drugs, performing when injured, or ignoring the rights and needs of other athletes. It is this psychological exploitation, which prevents growth in character and provides the greatest dilemma for the athlete. He or she is usually not exploited materially, although some would claim so and certainly athletes have been materially exploited in the past. Some still are, as in the case of many boxers. Because athletes have usually had some experience with being exploited, many have developed a widespread distrust of officials, organizers, and managers. The athlete's perceptions of the judges of his or her performance are almost always negative. The athlete often perceives others as out to get him and take from him what is rightfully his. Until the athlete arrives at a senior position in his or her sport, the athlete may always carry within the seeds of suspicion. The usual athlete's dislike of the fan has already been considered. Although the athlete needs the fan to watch him perform, he or she does not want a personal relationship with the spectator. All top athletes are well aware of the fawning fan who loves him or his image and longs to walk in the glory reflected by that image. Two people can be no farther isolated from each other than the athlete and the "jocksniffer." Today, top athletes are paid to spend time with fans, usually corporate, political, and/or entertainment people. Thus the jocksniffers are integrated into the sport structure in a manner which is acceptable to the athletes. They are willing to do a certain amount of pro-celebrity activity when paid or required to do so. Charity work is also encouraged. Sometimes the athlete is paid for charity appearances.

The typical athlete, who has emerged through competitive sport, exploits his or her position with little regard for others or for the consequences of his actions. The athlete also typically knows how to coast, play for his own statistics, or "fix" a performance if it is to his advantage. The question of fixing sport events for monetary gain surfaces again and again in the history of most sports. It has occurred in British football and basketball, and in American football and baseball. Few sports are without notorious scandals. Even other athletes can rarely be certain that fixing has occurred, and it is likely that only a small proportion of fixes ever become public. Examples of athletes who were willing to exploit their positions for financial gain are easy to find. It is just a little farther along the continuum of pretense than such entertainments as television wrestling and roller derby which are completely fraudulent and even farcical. The audience and performers are all willing to ignore the unreality of the event and let the action and the acting rule. The motives behind them seem to be of no concern.

The quandary of the athlete, then, as he becomes increasingly involved in the sporting enterprise, is how to keep his or her interests and motivations upon the internal discipline necessary for excellence at sport, as opposed to the external rewards that call forth the qualities necessary for showmanship, salesmanship, and one-upmanship. The kind of distortions that take place in sport do not usually stem from premeditated plans to exploit others or from dishonesty. Rather, the exploitation and dishonesty grow from the athlete's overvaluation of him or herself and his unconcern about others, and from movement within a culture in which the norms of deception, the breaking of rules, and trickery are all accepted. Examples of the sport environment in which youth develops are portrayed by Ralbovsky (1974) in his description of the 1954 Little League baseball champions, by Woodley (1974) in his analysis of the case history of a cheat at the Soap Box Derby, and by Kennedy (1974a, 1974b) when he writes about the violations of college sports policies at the Long Beach, California State College. More recently Bruce (1984) and Wulf (1981) have described the widespread expectation of cheating in sport, and others (Todd, 1983, 1984; Johnson, 1985) have described the widespread attempts to gain unfair advantage through drug use.

It is not surprising, in view of their development, that many athletes are encouraged to use a situation to their own advantage with little consideration of the moral implications, the effects of their actions upon others, or even their own welfare. The athletic subculture is so insulated by its training structure that the athlete has little chance to experience cooperative values or to develop the reflective, empathic side of his or her character. Spectators are held in low esteem — and kept ignorant of the real culture of sport. Brosnan (1964) accepted the sharp division between the subcultures of the baseball fan and the baseball player when he stated that as long as the baseball player portrays what the fans want him to be, the magic of the baseball ritual will be maintained. The truth about players must not interfere with the fantasy of the fan, who considers himself an expert even though he attends, on the average, only two or three games a season. In spite of that, he talks baseball, thinks baseball, and lives baseball the way he chooses in his own fantasy, while being barraged daily with scores and other statistical tidbits from promoters. In few activities are people so obsessed with so little actual involvement. The fan asks little else from the player than that he appear, perform, and preserve his image. The fan invites the players to exploit him.

THE ATHLETE'S CONTRIBUTION TO THE CROWD

Concentration thus far has been upon the mutual negative influences of the subcultures upon one another, although together they sustain the enterprise of sport. There are positive forces at work as well. For example, public needs are served, even if vicariously, by the sporting events to which fans flock to in great numbers. Probably an even more fundamental attraction for the spectators than the competition or the competence of sport is the heroic quality of the athlete. The athlete, as hero, symbolizes for the spectator his team, his country, and his fantasized fulfillment in sport achievement. The athlete's hobbies, life style, dress, and personality become a banner to follow. To young people, often deprived in the modern world of intimate relationships with their elders, the athlete serves as a cultural hero. To the extent the athlete serves as a constructive cultural force, combining competence at sport with strong character, he contributes a healthy model to the young. Hopcraft (1971) in his description of Nat Lofthouse, a major figure in British football after World War II, describes this. Lofthouse retired comfortably on his football earnings before the overwhelming prosperity of the 1960s. He was as close to his fans as to his neighbors. He felt fortunate in his career and frequently said so. The fans liked him for what he was and he was what he seemed to be. The Lofthouse image in the minds of fans was not made by promoters, publicity, or public fantasy. The image was true to the man. He was a hero to the people as a person and as a player.

An athlete can also make a negative contribution to the crowd by proving to be a destructive figure of identification. He can captivate people by his skill and then lead them astray by his unethical or unfair behavior. Tennis has provided a notorious string of such destructive characters. A statement on the development of a society is how it handles the effrontery from its privileged members. Hopcraft (1971) interviewed Tony Kay, who was banished from soccer for "fixing." Although a highly-skilled player, Kay's influence upon British football was eventually found to be destructive. He despised referees as "weak nobodies" trying to exert their authority over "the big men" on the field. During his playing days Kay was not popular with the referees and was disruptive in his play. He was well versed in the dirty work of the game and used those skills, but did not know how to conceal his illegal conduct, so eventually the sport disowned him.

An athlete's image can lead youngsters into a life of denial or compulsive fun-seeking as might be seen in the cases of George Best and Joe Namath. The image of George Best changed from one of charm and glamor in 1968 as hero of the British people, to one which was increasingly egocentric, disruptive, and intolerable in 1971. Best left football in a state of conflict and indecision only to reappear on the American scene where the public briefly applauded his old weaknesses. Finally, the alcoholic Best deteriorated further into self-destructive behaviors. The impact of Joe Namath can be similarly evaluated, although the Namath image was taken up by promoters and pruned and polished accordingly. In addition, Namath was not subject to the same outbursts of immaturity under stress as are so many athletes. But should the effect of his image be positively or negatively assessed? The athlete contributes more to the audience than an enactment of competence and competition. He also contributes his way of life. Whatever the admired athlete does, the crowd, particularly the young, tend to emulate.

In the 1980s it has often been noted that there are few sport heroes. Although some lament the passing of the superstars, the overall trend away from heroes is good for sport. As long as there is a crop of good athletes, fair treatment for the athletes, and responsibility and social interest from the fans, then the athlete can make a continued contribution to the spectator, to youth, and to the quality of life in the community. It is far better that fans be nourished with a steady stream of competent athletes than that they be fed a continued fantasy of false images surrounding the so-called superstars.

THE POWER OF THE PROMOTER

"Money is the name of the game," has become a popular slogan in sport organizations as in other sections of Western culture. Note that in spite of all of the problems with the staging of the 1984 Olympic Games — for example, the Soviet boycott — the ultimate success was that the Games made a multimillion dollar profit. The current power and decision-making of sport rests with the promoter. He or she decides whether the game will be played and often how it will be played. The promoter must contend with national associations, players' associations, and the local personnel who stage the contests. However, the promoter controls all of these factions because it is his efforts that largely determine the profits to be made. The interests and the motivations of the promoter are varied and may range from a pure desire to make money, to advertising conquests, to personal drives for power or personal enjoyment in a job well done. The promoter may be looking for status himself, may genuinely want to encourage the sport for sport's sake, or may simply want to "belong" in the sports world. He will usually occupy a very central position within the sports matrix: he holds the reins of power.

The large promotional-management firms such as the International Management Group and ProServ have made increasing inroads into controlling sport, as have some of the smaller private promoters. However, their road is not always smooth. If the athletes or fans feel they are not being treated fairly, the promoters may become the targets for retaliation. Second, by stressing commercialism and money in sport, often in exhibitionlike displays which have little sport merit, the promoters sometimes inadvertently kill off some of the spontaneity and enjoyment within sport upon which the continuation of the sport relies. Last, many corporate sponsors are taking a close look at the money they are spending on sport and are tempted by the grass roots sport movements as opposed to the professional events which they now tend to sponsor. Grass roots and developmental sport programs are surrounded with more defendable values, more fun, less greed, and fewer staging costs.

This gradual turning toward grass roots sport is not expected to have great effect until well into the 1990s, when leisure activities will surpass entertainment activities in importance. Until then there are some within the sport world who will struggle for the basic integrity of sport without emphasizing its monetary side. No doubt,it will be difficult for these people to preserve their position in that athletes in almost all nations are paid well for their outstanding efforts. Money attracts youth as it does adults. The control of sport is very much a new frontier that is being battled for by regional associations, governments, entrepreneurs and others. Sport has changed from the preserve of the elite into an instrument of corporate expansion and image making. The executor of the sport legacy is the promoter.

22
Social Institutions and Sport

MONEY

The power of the promoter in sport was noted at the end of the preceding chapter. This power is due to control over money. John Hudson, director of media for Labatt Brewing Company, has said (Financial Post, Oct. 1, 1983): "The easiest way to reach our marketplace is through sports according to all the available statistics." The target group for the company is males between the ages of 19 and 34 years. Cigarette and brewing companies are prominent sponsors of golf, tennis, and skiing. Other companies control and own teams. Even the Alberta Gas Line Company, a consortium involved in constructing the northern natural gas pipeline in Canada, has provided $175,000 over a five-year period to Skate Canada for figure skating. Not only do sponsors put down large sums of money to have their name associated with staging sport events, but the promoters and organizers have another major source of funds. This is in the bonanza reaped from the television rights. As Barnouw (1978) writes in his book, *The Sponsor*, "Of the 100 top network sponsors of 1975, 81 were multinational corporations." Commercial time worth up to $500,000 per minute in the United States is possible if the promoter convinces the sponsor that a maximum number of television viewers with the desired demographic characteristics will tune in at the time specified. Sport is relatively cheap to stage, it capitalizes on the drawing power of both leisure and social status, and the sponsor can manipulate the presentation of the event in order to satisfy the television needs. Recently there have been ominous signs for the future of TV sports (Taafe, 1986). Huge losses have been reported by the TV networks as sponsors have found other advertising outlets and the glut of sports on cable TV has resulted in less efficiency and less money for the athletes.

However, the promoter flourishes at time of writing. He handles most of the money in sport. He represents athletes, sport associations, organizers, and corporations. Sometimes the promoter represents one interest and sometimes several. Alan Eagleson is a good example of a promoter with many conflicting interests (Papanek and Brubaker, 1984). Donald Dell is another. The promoter can handle schedules, endorsements, sponsors, contracts, investments, and taxes for athletes.   Mark McCormack, the founder and president of International Management Group (IMG) runs a set of lucrative businesses.   The group has offices in Los Angeles, New York, and Cleveland and it manages sports, athletes, markets, and merchandising with a cut in the profits that reportedly ranges from 10 to 25 percent.   Schneider (1983) notes that IMG has 400 to 500 top clients and grosses yearly revenues of from 100 to 200 million. It boasts John Newcombe (endorsing Prince tennis racquets and Canon cameras), Bjorn Borg (Fila sportswear, Donnay tennis racquets, Diadora shoes), Chris Evert Lloyd (Lipton tea, Rolex watches, Ellesse clothing), and Arnold Palmer (Pennzoil, United Airlines, Sears Licensing agreement, Hertz, Lanier business products), as well as Nancy Lopez, Jan Stephenson, Jean-Claude Killy, Jackie Stewart, and even Captain Mark Phillips, who endorses Land Rovers.

Meanwhile corporations are using sport as a lucrative promotional vehicle. It is lucrative because the public pays for it. The public pays for it through their tax contributions to the building of big league stadiums, through their ticket purchases, through their purchasing of the products pushed, and through their taxes: the corporations' contributions to sport are tax writeoffs. But trouble has been brewing in the world of corporate sport advertising. Athletes have access both to the public and to the media. Thus in Canada there has been an active movement to ban cigarette advertisers from riding on the backs of sportsmen and sportswomen. At the center of the controversy has been the National Skiing Association, which has been sponsored over the years, as have been the athletes, by the RJR Macdonald Tobacco Company. Although the Association had accepted money from the company for the staging of a national competition, the men's winner of the event, Steve Podborski refused to accept the Macdonald Export "A" Cup. Shortly thereafter, Ken Read, followed suit in a subsequent competition. The company advocates point out that the funds they have contributed have done much to develop the very athletes who now protest against them.   And they note that the Canadian government has profited immensely from its share of tobacco taxes. Still, there is now a plan to phase out cigarette company sponsorship of all national sports over a five-year period.

Although the last example indicates a growing tension between the athletes and companies exploiting them for market shares, such sponsorship pales in comparison with the implications of a subterranean culture upon which much sport is founded – gambling. In the United States the gambling revenues from football are estimated to be $50 billion a year, a tax-free subculture which has much to do with fan enthusiasm, press coverage, and the nature of the sport. Gambling and racketeering can lead to many illegal activities including the fixing of sport events. Professional gamblers, fans, athletes, and members of management may all do what they can to reap profit. This is by no means solely an American activity.   The Hungarian Supreme Court recently upheld sentences against 30 people convicted of running a major soccer pool fraud. In one fraud, the estimated take was $500,000. It occurred in 1982 when 66 matches during nine weeks were fixed by bribing coaches, players, and referees.

TELEVISION, RADIO, AND THE PRESS

The media exert another crucial influence on commercial sport. Access to the sports pages of daily newspapers is invaluable to the commercial enterprise, as is television exposure. For these reasons corporations or promoters of products will pay huge sums of money to be linked with the presentation of sport. To be aligned with the leisure, aggression, and affluence in the image of the athlete and athletics is sometimes the only thing needed to sell a product. Otherwise, the product would remain little more than just another bland new cereal or drab and dangerous cigarette. The product need do nothing as long as it achieves "exposure" through the media in the ways developed through the psychology of advertising. The announcers and sports writers know who is paying their way. Although a few media personnel pass on the intrinsic pleasures of sport and are uncorrupted by the courting of sponsors, most concentrate almost entirely upon the competition in sport. The announcer's voice usually reflects the excitement of the goal, the score, the prize, and the violence. Too seldom are the skill and competence of sport even acknowledged. Too frequently is the camera focused on fights and bloodshed.

There have been some attempts to correct the media's simplistic and uncritical portrayal of sport. Knowledgeable athletes have been hired as broadcasters, sport telecasts are interrupted with lessons on skill and technique for those who would improve their golf, and some history or background to the sport is included. This does not excuse sport contests being presented as battles in which the competitive urge is highlighted on every play. The hype and lack of understanding of the athlete's world represented in the work of most sport media personnel is a major problem. But the press and the media have other problems as well. One is being bought off by corporations. A working relationship has been established between the media and sport sponsors in which the media are not only highly paid for the most part but also showered with free entertainment, gifts, and travel, leading to a suspension of critical powers and at times inaccurate reporting. If there is accurate reporting and a sport is criticized by a writer, a reporter or even a whole newspaper staff may be banned from the clubhouse so that the reporters cannot function easily. Thus the editor is blackmailed into censuring reporters.

It is interesting to note that if the sport media had been free to report accurately on sport facts instead of fantasy, it is likely that the sport psychology movement would have emerged much more slowly or not at all. But, by failing to analyze the foundations of sport and failing to write accurately about sport the press left a huge vacuum. Thus there was an extreme need for external criticism. This took place in a wide and disparate group of publications in the 1960s and 1970s, of which the first edition of this book was one.

THE LANGUAGE OF SPORT

Sport writers and promoters seem obsessed with the competition and the conflict in sport. To remind the public of these themes, teams are often named after symbols of combat or warfare: Bombers, Roughriders, Lions, Rams, and Chargers are typical. The press accounts of contests often feature verbs such as whipped, annihilated, crushed, and defeated. Massacres occur and post-mortems are conducted. One often has to search deeply within press accounts before reference is made to the competence of the athletes. The spotlight is usually focused on the fouls, the fights, the combat, and the brutality of the game, or on the lawsuits, even when the game is golf. In general a "good" newspaper reporter understands the sport and focuses more upon skill and competence than does the "good" television announcer. But television announcers and inexperienced writers usually highlight the combat because they do not understand the subtleties of the sport they are reporting on. Without attention to the intrinsic psychological meanings and the social implications of a sport to its participants, sports writing has little value. When an enterprising social scientist gets around to doing a content analysis of major sports pages and sports writers in various countries, some interesting conclusions may be drawn. For in the writing of many papers there exists a harsh, combative, and brutal representation of sport in which the strengths are ironically by passed. In addition, the language of the athletes themselves is one of defiance. It refers often to sex, aggression, and the stupidity of authority. Locker room language is not a fiction, it is a fact for both male and female athletes. The language of sport is disparaging, disdainful, and bitter. It is one mechanism by which the athletic subculture attempts to maintain the isolation and independence of ego structure that are necessary to operate in the competitive atmosphere of sport.

SOCIAL STATUS AND ATHLETIC GOALS

Sport is an avenue through which status in the general social system can be quickly obtained, though sometimes the possession of it is only temporary. It is much like the entertainment field used to be, in that a lower class boy, even "a black boy," could make it by achieving an international reputation and money to match. In sports, as in entertainment, some athletes lose their status at the end of their playing days more quickly than they gained it. Lever (1969) has observed that this is typical of soccer players in Brazil, where the norm is for the player to gain only temporary status while he is playing. Weinberg and Arond (1952) made the same observation of the North American boxing subculture.

In general the fees and prize money in sports are dependent upon the spectator demand, television exposure, and advertising potential. It is the large payoffs in sports that allow the successful performer to achieve high socio-economic status. In almost all cultures, income and the amount of capital one accumulates determine, at least in part, the individual's position in society. The successful athlete, therefore, has a unique and fast moving escalator before him if he is able to handle his finances sensibly.

From what parts of society do athletes emerge? Is there a particular segment that tends to produce individuals who will join the unique culture of sports and form the athletic subgroup? This becomes a question of values. The individual must have the talent and the time to develop skill in sport, and, what is most important, he must have a value system that parallels or complements the values of the sports world. The individual must be competitive, eager, ambitious, talented, highly motivated, fond of money, and sympathetic to the demands of the sports life. Individuals already of a high status in a society are rarely equipped with these essentials. They do not perceive in sport the potential to improve their lot in life. Rather, athletes tend to be drawn from the middle and, especially, the lower classes. In a few nations, the upper classes are still the only source of athletes because the poor have little time for sports or access to facilities. Women also present a different picture in that in many countries the upper-middle and upper class females are the only ones likely to have the freedom and the unusual family circumstances that could provide the necessary stepping stones for a woman to become interested in sport.

Different sports have become the folk vehicles of different classes within a society. For example, although British football has its upper class followers, it largely belongs to the working class. On the other hand, equestrian competitions are still the possession of the upper classes, and it is much less surprising to find Princess Anne and her husband deeply involved than it is to find a Harvey Smith, ex-stable boy. Yachting and polo also belong to the upper class. In the United States, a more egalitarian society (at least to the middle class), football and baseball are the vehicles of all. Tennis has recently migrated from the country clubs to the middle class in North America. Golf, because of the space it monopolizes and the time it takes, will always remain in the hands of those who have both. It is well to note, however, that the commercial performers of all these sports increasingly tend to be of middle and lower class origins, because if an athlete shows sufficient promise and talent, commercial interests will make the facilities available to him. In the past the athlete needed either the good graces of the rich or a military position to achieve these privileges.

STATUS AND PERFORMANCE

Within the subculture of athletes in each sport, there is a status structure that affects the performance of its members. This makes the subculture less egalitarian and democratic than it is often said to be. Many years ago, Whyte (1943) wrote about this social phenomenon in his intensive study of a Chicago gang. Bowling scores seemed to be dictated not by bowling ability but by the players' status within the group. Whyte attributed success in making a shot largely to self-confidence. What experiences of success did the bowler have in the past? Still there were other crucial influences: Did his fellow players have confidence in him? Did they believe he could make the shot? A bowler's score can be raised when the opinions of those who are important to him support him, just as it can be lowered when opinion is against him. Alec, one of the gang members having little status, illustrated this clearly. When bowling with a few other members of the gang he frequently produced high scores, including the highest individual score of the season. But on the nights when the team bowled together he was never able to bowl as well and always had "an off night." Verbal barbs and heckling would be slung among the members, and sides would be chosen, so that at season's end there was a close relationship between the social status of the team members and their bowling standings.

The observation that status within a group influences performance has been demonstrated many times both in experimental studies and in field research. In one study, Harvey (1953) concluded that the higher a subject's status in the group, the more that subject and the other group members tend to overestimate his performance. The lower a subject's group status, the less the tendency to overestimate his performance. Sherif, White, and Harvey (1955) confirmed these findings in a study done at a summer camp for boys. Social perceptions influenced performance, sometimes to ridiculous extremes. Illustrative of this is journalist Wright's entertaining account (as reported by Goodhart and Chataway, 1968, pp. 105–106) of the sports performance of ex-Prince Sihanouk of Cambodia. It seems that the Prince claimed to be an outstanding basketball and volleyball player. At the age of 40 he had set a new Cambodian basketball record by scoring 92 points in a game. How was this extraordinary feat achieved? The cooperation fo the Prince's lessers had much to do with his performance.

This type of voluntary or involuntary "fixing" occurs very frequently in sports. A boss playing tennis with his employees can be expected to come out on top more frequently than his skill alone would dictate. Such determination of athletic outcome is not confined to amateur performances. After studying the sociometric choices and passing patterns in the first division Hungarian football teams, the British psychologist Yaffe, (1975) was able to conclude that the major factor determining passing patterns and ball distribution during matches was the sociometric friendship ties on teams. Furthermore, when matches were tight and players were under pressure, this trend increased so that there was a tendency "to pass only" to those players who were well liked. Thus, psychological relationships played a major part in determining not only the ball distribution patterns but very likely the outcome of play. Most ball players are well aware of the subjectivity involved in passing. In his story of Connie Hawkins, *Foul!,* Wolf (1972) describes one basketball player's attempts to be in the action of the game: He first approached Connie Hawkins and suggested they "work together," as the rest of the team was not producing. Hawkins agreed. He then repeated his confidential arrangement with four other players.

Performance on a team, then, reflects the social and psychological structure of that team. Similarly, in individual sports, the performance of athletes tends to reflect a status structure. It is essential, of course, for individual advancement in the sports structure, that heroes and champions be upset by younger athletes and replaced by them. Thus, successful athletes must make themselves as immune as possible from their own consideration of the quality of the player they are facing. They are best off identifying with a small group of supporters and isolating themselves from the status structure within the sport. Alternatively, if a developing athlete can identify and align himself with a high status athlete, it will likely help the young athlete's performance. It helps an athlete to think he is "ahead" of an individual he is facing on the playing field even if this is not true. If he is mentally aware of the superior status of his opponent, however, his job will be made more difficult for him. The athlete of recognized superior standing will perform better than the athlete of inferior standing. This makes sports difficult for newcomers to break into. The "old pros" will have a psychological advantage over the newcomers. Furthermore, should an "old pro" perform poorly on a given day and lose, his superior status will protect him. If the newcomer performs poorly he will be perceived as "not so good," and he may find himself locked into a status that will be difficult to overcome. To overcome this psychological barrier in sport, the athlete must be either outstandingly competent or intolerably egocentric. Very often he or she is both.

Some sports carry within them a challenge for underprivileged groups. For example, black participation in professional sport in the United States is out of all proportion to the representation of blacks in the general population (about 20 percent). Edwards (1983) notes a participation rate of 70% in basketball, 55% in football, and 19% in baseball. Yet, writes Edwards, only about 1,400 black people make their living as professional athletes. In fact, estimates are that 25 to 35 percent of black males who qualify for college athletics *cannot* accept their scholarships because of their poor academic records. Of the blacks who enter college on scholarships, an estimated 65 to 75 percent never graduate.

The social struggle of the black in the United States was apparent in team structures and team selections throughout the country before it became a major issue in the minds and souls of ordinary citizens. The indignities suffered by blacks as they attempted to enter sport are well documented. Even when blacks achieved team status, they suffered abuse, ostracism, and unequal treatment. Not only did they occupy inferior positions on teams, they also received fewer opportunities to advance. Blacks found themselves in key positions as players, coaches, and managers far less frequently than whites. The rewards for those who strive to upset the social status of a system are not always positive, particularly for blacks in sport. Blacks may be met with bitterness and indifference, or even with tolerance or favoritism and positive discrimination, but they are not rewarded with equality in the minds of those who use racial differentiation to justify their own psychological identity and feelings of worth. We are referring here to psychological dimensions other than salaries. Note that Rae (1981) found that in 1970 black major league ball players had an average salary greater than for whites — and they also performed better.

It is the competence-oriented athlete who most readily uses sporting events for political purposes because he or she is not so dependent upon the external rewards offered. Such blacks raise many possibilities for black youth both within and outside of sport. If they are appealing to the public and publicized through the media, they can continue to exert a very positive influence on both black and white Americans as well as make leadership roles easier for those who follow them. Athletes such as Chamberlain, Robinson, Sugar Ray Leonard, Simpson, Ali, Daley Thompson and Debbie Thomas* form a high profile sub-group whose presence has or can boost the status of other blacks whether they are politicians, performers, or other athletes. The widespread use of publicity surrounding the abuse of drugs and alcohol by the current crop of black athletes has caused major image problems. As well it has raised questions about how sport affects lower class black men moving up the sport ladder who quickly come into a lot of money. Such questions require extensive study and analysis.

PSYCHOLOGISTS, SOCIOLOGISTS, AND MEDICAL PERSONNEL IN SPORT

The serious criticism of sport that sprang up in the 1960s was much needed. A dilemma was created by the movement of money into sport from commercial interests and by the payoff to sport organizations from the media and vice versa. When advertisers and consumers became more influential in sport than the old sponsors and fans, great importance was placed on preserving the form and the image of sport while little emphasis was placed upon protecting the substance or core values of sport. This rapid change brought forth first a trickle of analyses and later a flood from social scientists who were for the most part both ex-athletes and academics. They had information and theory at their fingertips in order to both question and to reinterpret the commonly held perceptions of sport. Examples of such interpretations are Singer (1972), Edwards (1969, 1973), Hoch (1972), Goodhart and Chataway (1968), Scott (1974), and Butt (1976). This trickle of critics, each with his or her own theoretical orientation, became a flood in the 1970s and 1980s. At the same time there emerged a more structural analysis of the sports world from sociologists interested in sport. They tended to analyze the variables that made sport a reflection of the society at large (Loy, Kenyon, and McPherson, 1981; Gruneau, 1983; Whannel, 1983; Cantelon and Gruneau, 1982). Recently, a third force or trend has emerged in academic sport study and application. This is in the introduction of technology for the purpose of improving athletic performance. These researchers

---

*Note the Californian, Thomas, says she has never been subjected to racial discrimination.

and practitioners tend less to offer a critical appraisal of sport than to use their expertise to measure the variables and techniques that might increase psychomotor performance. At the same time, increasing numbers of persons with training in psychological techniques and clinical practice entered the world of sport in order to provide corrective psychological treatments. In a short period of time athletes saw the need for the institution of psychotherapy just as a few years before sports medicine was created by the need for special physical therapy and treatment. It was quite obvious then, as it is now, that the physical stress placed on many athletes was abnormal and too great for their level of physical endowment and resistance. Thus the orthopedic surgeon became a crucial member of the downhill skiers' world. The medical practitioner became a standard on the sidelines of the football field. The exercise physiologist became part of the training program of every national team. These specialists have as their goals either the maximizing of training programs or the patching up of the consequences of that maximization − or both. Similarly, the psychological stress suffered by athletes and reflected in the pathologies discussed in this book has added and will continue to add the institution of psychological therapy to the athlete's life. The drug and alcohol addictions, the burnout, the chronic symptoms of nervousness and anxiety, the phobias, the refusals to continue, and the failures to improve performance are all subjects of attention. Psychological treatment will remain a major avenue in the search for solutions because our society promotes individual solutions instead of social solutions to such problems. It is a fact that society causes much illness and nonadjustment. In sport we see clear examples of individuals being pushed by social values and their own ambitions beyond their capabilities. What should be sought is an amelioration of the social pressures upon the individual so that he or she can advance in sport in keeping with internal rhythms and the level of competence attained.

In the business of analyzing society and its pressures, the sport sociologists could be considerably more prominent and more active than, in fact, they are. Other than a few outspoken critics (Edwards, 1973; Hall, 1978; Hoch, 1972) most write in the most esoteric tradition. That is, much of the writing is incomprehensible to the layperson. There is much potential within the field of sport sociology and the sport world is waiting for meaningful and applied analyses.

COMPUTERS

The computer has entered the world of sport, and as in most aspects of life it has provided much form and little substance. Computers have enabled the equalization of rankings and the more accurate keeping of statistical records. They have enabled improved international communication, and they have revolutionized gambling in facilitating the amount of betting and the number of transactions that can be handled within a short period of time.

Computer games, with their superficial attraction and repetitiveness, have captured the attention, time, and money of countless youths and adults throughout the world. In return users receive some stimulation and a sense of security from the limited structure of the games, but they receive little of substance. The development of substance and self must be held in abeyance while games are in progress. Clearly the amount of money, time, and space wrapped up in computer and arcade games suggests an enterprise which is dehumanizing and uncreative, in that it serves to prevent the human being from growing and contributing to the surrounding environment.

In contrast to this dreary picture, computer companies are now suggesting that creative games be introduced in which players can program their own games and outcomes. Thus the computer will work for the individual and not impose structure. Although this is a step forward from the earlier game concept, the computer can provide nothing of substance unless the human being wills it. Thus space arms and space probes can execute and transcribe or transmit information but both input directions and interpretations must ultimately come from the human being who must anticipate, appreciate consequences, and understand causal relationships. These are quite separate from computerized instructions and executions. Computers have an important function in recording data and in helping to outline academic models which may attempt to predict the future of our resources, or to plan for peace and prosperity on a statistical basis. The work of Meadows and Meadows et al., (1972) described on page 289 ff. provides an example. So does the work of Axelrod (1984), who in his recent book sketches out the possible achievement of peace, in accordance with von Neumann and Morgenstern (1953), who first devised the zero-sum game phenomenon and applied mathematical models and games to the understanding of economic and other conflict situations. Decisions on whether to apply results from such work remains value based. In summary, computer technology can monitor, record, execute, count, store, watch, and destroy but it cannot know good from evil. That is a value decision to be made by people. If people of good will and substance dominate technology then it can and will be an important way of stabilizing the world scene.

GOVERNMENTS AND THE OLYMPICS

Governments are becoming increasingly involved in sport. In some countries strong grass roots participation is encouraged and sport is an integral part of physical training in the schools for both health and military purposes. More prominent is the role of government in the training and management of national teams and in the staging of world sport competitions. A staging of Soviet against American athletes in almost any event can, through the power of the promoter, put the prestige of the two nations in the balance. For many athletes the Olympics are the premier event because of the tradition of the games and the fact that they are the most widely promoted sport event in the world. If the Olympics represented only tests of competence for the athletes, then they could be staged in small countries in any part of the world. However, in the current staging of the Olympic games, great sums of money are spent by governments and other sponsors in preparation for the games as a promotional vehicle. It is a bonanza marketplace for sponsors and for athletes to meet and make connections. The eyes of the world are on the games because of their worldwide television audience. If it were not for the Olympics, governments would likely put less money into the development of elite teams. For example, it is doubtful that the Canadian government, with a country of 25 million people, would feed over $45 million a year in order to run subsidized sport programs. Although the United States does not have such subsidized programs, its athletes are, in fact, subsidized in a different way. They are sponsored through the university and college system, which paves the way for the commercialism and nationalism that will come into full flower should the athlete advance to professional and/or Olympic sport.

There are some purists who claim that politics and sport do not mix. This may have been true in days when sport was the domain of the upper classes who had no status to gain and only enjoyment, exercise, and excellence to pursue. Almost any aspiring athlete today will claim that their sport is highly political. They are correct. Politics comes into play as athletes vie for status in a sport subculture. Training programs, location of participation, coaching, sponsorship, judging, and umpires all can carry weight in determining how good the athlete can become. If a privileged athlete is motivated to participate in competitive sport, he or she will probably participate at a higher level than a lower class athlete of equal ability because of backing and social position. Contrast for example the equestrian participation of Princess Anne of England with the position of a black rider of equal potential. The advantage for the privileged is apparent in their superior training, over a longer period of time, their dress, their demeanor and manners, their speaking ability, and their training in the skills valued by the society. They also have courses of action available, such as access to support staff and educational facilities, which the lower class individual does not.

Similarly, nations of high status and power can readily muster the people and materials needed for status displays and they can do this best when on the Olympic stage before a world audience. It is therefore no surprise that the Olympics is a showcase for politicians and political values, paid for by governments. Although the 1984 Los Angeles Olympics was said to be run on funds from private enterprise, this was only partially true. Hundreds of thousands of hidden dollars were borne by the community in payment for security, public works, and in volunteer work. Direct payments from government are allotted for travel, team, and site promotion. Again, the people, the community, and the government pay for the Olympics in tax allotments either directly or indirectly. Although the Los Angeles Olympics were promoted as a feat of private enterprise, this is in itself a direct political statement in support of capitalist America. The Los Angeles Olympics were perhaps among the most biased political games to date. The bias toward American athletes shown in the organization and television coverage was at best vulgar and at worst misrepresentation. Even Americans became enraged at the lack of fair play and appreciation of excellence.

There is a disturbing fallout from the politics of Olympic competitions. By riding on the backs of competence-oriented athletes, by casting the show in a competitive instead of a competence framework, by putting pressures on services, construction firms, police, and volunteers — the whole process depends upon the management of funds and of people. An immense opportunity is opened for graft, corruption, and waste, and for the worst and most exploitative to prosper while the genuine withdraw. Olympic corruption starts early with the feting and bribing of the Olympic Committee, which decides upon sites with free gifts, travel, and ego stroking (Johnson, 1984, p. 8). The city of Montreal ran up an accumulated deficit of $3.5 billion (Canadian) for which charlatans are still being tracked and prosecuted. In 1983 Gerard Niding, former chairman of the city's executive committee, was fined $75,000 and put in jail for one day for breach of trust and accepting unwarranted "benefits." Prior to the Olympics his committee had awarded contracts without public tenders and he had accepted a luxury house from Regis Trudeau, an engineer whose firm was given $7.2 million in contracts. Niding returned the house in 1978 when a public commission began investigating the irregularities. Such corruption is not the only type that takes place in the Olympic system. When President Carter led the boycott of the 1980 Moscow Olympics following the Afghanistan takeover, at least some athletes were paid off by their governments for the boycott. Raelene Boyle, former Olympic sprinter from Australia, said she was paid $6,000 by her association four months after the games. Other athletes confirm such payments but said they were to compensate them for the funds that would have been spent in sending them to Moscow.

The ultimate question is: should the Olympics continue in their present form? The answer is no. There are thousands of problems more immediate to taxpayers and sponsors and even to the international corporations that promote the events than the ego massaging of a few governments, athletes, and conveniently placed opportunists. There are grass roots problems of poverty, facilities, peace, education, inner city renewal, and community structure, the solutions to which would affect the lives of many instead of few. The overall problem in society which leads to such madness as the staging of the Olympic games is one of leadership and the fact that the subgroups of sport are allowed to exploit the public purse in their own interests with little concern for the public good.

When the Olympic torch is lit and the emotions of fans and a few athletes are fired up, it is the signal for large numbers of entrepreneurs and opportunists from all walks of life to prepare for major onslaughts on public funds, private funds, tourist dollars, and future marketing and promotional profits. Greed is unleashed and officially sanctioned along with the competitive struggle for gold medals.

The two major themes of the Olympics are money and propaganda. That the games have been used for government propaganda has been more than obvious since the 1936 Olympics, when Hitler ostentatiously used the games for the magnification of Germany and the Nazi ideal. Although Americans like to suggest that the plan backfired through the performance of Jesse Owens, a black man, in fact the games were an outstanding success for Nazi Germany. Participation was high, Hitler's outstanding gifts for moving a mob with his speeches were given prominent display, the staging and organization was precise, and all was recorded for posterity by the brilliant filmmaker Leni Riefenstahl. The films have lived on and allowed the 1936 Olympics to provide a very current lesson in history on the political use of the games, even as it continues today.

In spite of the argument of Lenk (1979) and others that the Olympic movement does achieve most of its aims for the athletes, officials, or even the fans — that is, that it provides a fair opportunity to test performance under enforced rules with relative equality — the Olympic movement cannot be seen as only existing for the service of sport and as independent of world trends. The point is that the billions of dollars being spent to stage the Olympics every four years for propaganda purposes would be better spent elsewhere. The lubrication of a few egos and the eulogizing of athletes commonly raised on drugs and nurtured on publicity and money is not the best use of financial resources to the benefit of humanity.

23
Crosscultural Perspectives

INTRODUCTION

Sport cannot remain apolitical as long as the athletes' identities act as symbols to their fellow athletes and to the peoples of the world. Nor can it remain apolitical as far as governments are concerned. The question is: how will the power and status of sport be used? It is often disconcerting to find that in the wake of political stalemates and sometimes disaster athletic contests continue as though nothing had happened. The deaths of the student rioters in Mexico; the massacre at the Munich Olympics; and the boycotts of the African countries, the United States, and the Communist nations at various Olympics all carried powerful messages. The Munich massacre, for example, taught much about the psychology of sport. The games resumed after a day's ceremony and eulogies for the dead Israeli athletes, showing that collective responsibility was denied and ignored. People cannot suffer alone, and injustice cannot flourish unless the people of the world allow it. Munich offered an opportunity for the athletes of the world to unite and speak out about the act of desperation which had occurred through their medium, sport. The athletes, however, continued to play their games, and some expressed pleasure in getting a needed day of rest from competition as a result of the disruption. They felt it would improve their results.

The world still awaits a change in the consciousness of athletes and their direction. The isolation of sport from politics called for by Avery Brundage, Lord Killanin, and Juan Antonio Samaranch has led nowhere since sport is, by its very nature as a test of status, political. Nationalism in athletics has consistently led to disaster. Commercialism has led far away from the interests of public welfare. Internationalism and competence offer the hope of the future. International attitudes feature cooperative behavior, the endorsement of world organizations, trust in other nations, and belief in mediation and negotiation when there are conflicts and/or tensions. Competence features intrinsic pleasure in excellence and an identification with the skills of others who are also excellent. The latter motivations would allow sport to remain an activity that involves a contest, but a contest not characterized by psychological competition. These attitudes would allow sport people to contribute openly to the welfare of others, instead of contributing only to themselves. Athletes currently contribute only to themselves and the economic system through the pursuit of money. Athletes perform less and less out of a sense of nationalism, although national representation is still played up by governmental organizations and sometimes by professional promoters.

It is always a shock to North Americans when they have trouble winning team sports in the Olympics against teams comprising inferior individual players from Cuba, the USSR, and other Communist nations. This has occurred in various Soviet-Canadian hockey series over the past two decades. There were some who saw victory as a matter of national pride for Canada and defeat as a blow to the national ego. The egos of the Canadians who have felt buttressed by the eventual victories that some of the Canadian teams eked out all belong to individuals who would do well to consider Anatoli Tarasov's (1972) comment:

... after carefully studying the Canadian professionals for the past few years, I have come to the conclusion, excuse me for frankness, that you play only for the spectacle. Of course each Canadian team strives for victory, but your brand of hockey as a whole is directed only secondarily toward success and creative growth.

Both the North American and Soviet systems of training have no doubt benefited from the study of one another and both systems have suffered times of setback and times of extraordinary success.

The current direction of sport for outstanding athletes throughout the world is away from nationalism and toward individualism and commercialism. This is illustrated through defections and other arrangements by which Eastern bloc athletes enter North American or Western professional sport. The athlete who plays for himself or herself and easily crosses national and team boundaries has little in common with the fan. The more the fans are kept in the old ways of thinking about team allegiances and loyalties, the better for commercial enterprises. The commercial mind is better able to exploit the market financially when fans do not critically assess the quality of a sport presentation. National associations, by contrast, usually have been against the commercial expansion of sport because this tends to lessen the emphasis upon international events and national team development.

The Los Angeles Olympics represents the trend of private commercial sponsorship taking over from governmental sponsorship. The clash between the Soviet system and the American system was apparent in Soviet claims that Olympic ideals were broken with the commercial management of the games. The Olympics have not been the only shotgun marriage between governments and private enterprise. Increasingly, because of the high costs of training and sponsoring athletes, corporations have been welcomed as backers of local, national, and international teams. It is common to see commercial emblems pasted on Davis Cup blazers, national ski team equipment, and Olympic track stars' gear. Still more apparent is the entrepreneur's inroad into, for example, Communist China through sport. In Canada this has gone so far as businessmen planning to accompany and sponsor junior sport teams. Business connections can be made more readily through sport than through some of the normal channels.

Since Grecian times, governments have sponsored sport. During times of peace, sports flourish for entertainment and training purposes. During times of war, sports either subside or cease altogether, as the popular energies are involved elsewhere. Governments have made good use of sport as training grounds for military personnel. In some countries, entire sports programs, particularly for elite athletes, are intricately interwoven with military structures and programs. Riordan (1982, pp. 30) describes the military status of many Soviet athletes. The comic portrait of the involvement of generals and admirals in their soldiers' competitive sports is a frequent theme in writings about the American military. The examination of the values characteristic of a number of nations and regions should allow us to get an idea of the variations in value orientations toward sport. The following review is not intended to be exhaustive but merely to acquaint the reader with the diversity of cultural approaches to sport.

THE UNITED KINGDOM, THE UNITED STATES, AND CANADA

The annals of British colonialism contain numerous references to the practice of sport, particularly cricket, as a way of civilizing the natives, or more accurately, of making them amenable to the British way of life and command. However, even cricket did not always suffice, as the natives sometimes imposed their own rules upon the game. Grimble (1952), in *A Pattern of Islands,* describes how the 11-pound cricket bats improvised by the natives of Samoa became instruments of slaughter as a cricket match between villagers wore on, sometimes for weeks at a time. Cricket was finally banned by the missionaries in the name of Christianity.

In Britain, the sports training of the boys at Eton and Harrow has often been proclaimed as a reason for the success of the British military leadership. The boys perhaps learned the lessons behind the rules of the game better than the natives of Samoa. The values passed to the future leaders of England were the values of class privilege and territorial expansion, not of cooperation, equality, and good will toward the less developed territories they would eventually dominate.

In its more primitive forms, competitive struggle in sport is often symbolic of the rights of the strong to humiliate and destroy the weak. Thus the fox hunt still thrives in England and is enjoyed by members of the British royal family in spite of widespread opposition from the members of animal protection leagues. Hunting and gaming, and in fact any blood sport, similarly represent a direct replay of the annihilation rights of the powerful, with animals occupying the weakest echelon in status. Status and privilege are still much symbolized and preserved in British sport. There are different sport opportunities for the upper classes (yachting, equestrianism, polo, and tennis for example) than for the lower classes (darts, football spectatorship, and lotteries). In spite of these status preservations, the public and the private school systems in Great Britain have well-developed physical education programs in which the training of the body is seen as important as the training of the mind. However, these programs do not hold together well in the lower class regions of England, Wales, Northern Ireland, or Scotland.

In Great Britain, the Sport Council is charged with the development and management of elite athletes. In spite of a few successes over the years and some very fine athletes Britain has not been outstanding recently in international competition. In short, the declining influence of British sport reflects its overall decline as an influential world power. Indeed, the healthiest element in British sport is gambling, in which the general model is one where large numbers of lower class participants bet on the performances of a few privileged and highly paid professionals.

In the United States the Government faces a different kind of struggle with sport. Its struggle is in upholding the antitrust laws that must be levied against football, baseball, and other sporting monopolies in order to protect the rights of small businessmen to develop and conduct similar enterprises. The U. S. Government is in a bind in these cases because it is fighting against the forces that epitomize success in the American system. The United States has a sports regulating body called the U. S. Olympic Committee which has administrative and legislative control over Olympic and amateur sports. This is the equivalent of the Sports Council in Great Britain, although the latter encourages mass participation as well as elite sport. In Canada the function is carried out by Sports Canada, which administers both elite sport and encourages mass participation through Fitness Canada. There are no comparable programs for mass participation in the United States where Little League and Pop Warner football often seem to pass on to the young all of the problems of the adult commercial leagues. In few societies are the generations as isolated from each other as they are in North America, where the need of all children to develop competence clashes drastically with the adult world's value of externally rewarded achievement. Organized sports programs could do a great deal to correct this conflict. In fact, they do very little.

In Canada, the budget for sport unfairly favors elite sport over mass participation, still, there is an attempt at least to encourage mass participation. This resulted from various surveys which found the typical Canadian to be in poor physical shape. The government-sponsored "participation" program from the schools to adult level has induced important changes in the fitness-consciousness of Canadians to the extent that at present there are high levels of participation in general sport activities. The $56 million spent annually by Canada on 48 national teams and/or programs is a model which attempts to parallel the East German rather than the American system. Athletes are "carded" when they reach a criterion level of performance, meaning they receive government stipends while training. Most attend universities. Sport research, coaching, and sport psychology are all heavily sponsored in Canada and, although to date there has been little payoff in gold medals for international competition, grass roots development has been very successful. Although Canada did much better in terms of medals in the Los Angeles Olympics than in previous years, this cannot be considered improvement when the results are corrected for the absence of the Eastern Bloc nations. Athletes in Canada still struggle under the burden of the competitive ethic which produces individualism and precludes feelings of support that, in fact, form the backbone of the systems which follow.

THE SOCIALIST SPORT SYSTEMS: THE SOVIET UNION,
THE GERMAN DEMOCRATIC REPUBLIC,
CZECHOSLOVAKIA, AND CUBA

Riordan (1981) has given Western readers a welcome review of organized sport under the communist system. Sport in most of these countries is broadly encouraged in the school system and as part of military training. It is closely controlled by government programs at the elite level and is very supportive of athletes in both funding and sactioning the social role of athlete. A cooperative and nationalistic purpose is striven for in athlete socialization. This is easier to achieve under some systems. For example in the Soviet Union child rearing practices (Bronfenbrenner, 1970; Ziferstein, 1983) stress corporate or communal welfare. The individual under communism has been subjected to both the discipline and the order of the group. Thus the level of social as opposed to individual identification in the Soviet Union starts earlier and is theoretically stronger than in the Western world. Teams are selected on the basis of the athletes' abilities to cooperate with each other and to conduct themselves in a manner which will facilitate and not deter the development of other team members.

Although there is deserved praise for the Eastern system, it should be noted that it has its share of problems. That system too, pushes its individuals beyond their level of ability in the name of competition as does the Western system. Again, the case of the Soviet diver, Sergei Shalibashvili can be used as a tragic illustration. There are also, on occasion, athletes who, along with some Soviet ballet dancers and opera singers, defect to the West, claiming that they are creatively stifled and can no longer continue under the repressive Soviet system.

All athletes at the top of their field are under competitive pressure to preserve their position. No matter how hard they strive they must inevitably give way to younger athletes who overtake them. In many ways, the Soviet athlete is better cushioned against the aftermath of decline than is the Western athlete. Like his colleagues in East Germany or Czechoslovakia, the ex-athlete in the Soviet Union can expect a continuing involvement in sport upon the completion of his or her competitive career. In addition, many athletes are highly educated in other fields as the result of the system in which they develop. Riordan (1981, p. 53) cites examples of a few Soviet boxers which prove of great interest when compared to the plight of American ex-boxers (Murphy, 1985). Riordan mentions Konstantin Gradopol, former USSR champion, a university professor; Gennady Shatkov, former Olympic champion, rector of Leningrad University; Boris Lagutin, former Olympic champion, a practicing barrister; and Valery Popenchenko, Barker trophy winner as best boxer in the 1964 Olympic Games, Ph.D. researcher. The extreme contrast with American ex-boxers is astounding. American boxers are often lower class blacks, Orientals, Mexicans, or whites. They start out poor and most end up poor and brain damaged as well. In making the comparisons one must note that the Soviets box for a shorter time and under a different set of rules, and that they may be very highly selected before they enter the training system.

It is important to note that in the USSR sport is not conducted solely for individual glory. It is conducted for national pride and also as part of an educational system in which a major goal is to preserve selected values. These values are then continued, as policy, within the educational and sport system. Note a recent report on the outlawing of private karate schools in 1981 in the Soviet Union. Although karate had become somewhat of a fad in the Soviet Union and was being encouraged by Japanese adventure movies, the Soviet Sports Committee accused the 30,000-member state-run karate federation of encouraging activities that "lead to the application of alien rituals in our society by teaching individualism and cruelty."

In his many publications on the Soviet sports system Riordan (1977, 1980, 1981, 1982) has given Western readers a valuable survey of sport under communism. He concludes that whereas the Soviet system is dominated by *collectivism,* Western sport is dominated by *commercialism.* These are very fundamental distinctions between the purposes and principles of sport in the two regions (Riordan, 1982, pp. 266–279). Each can learn from the other. Although there is corruption in Soviet sport, specifically with regard to athlete smuggling and bartering on the black market and taking advantage of opportunities to hawk meal tickets and get cars and apartments, Riordan believes this is nothing compared to the million dollar payments to a few outstanding athletes in the West for commerical purposes. The latter must be weighed against the fact that the majority of Western athletes go without reward or eke out a meager living. The Soviet system itself has recently been under attack; Cantelon (1982) suggests that the system is losing status as seen by the current rise of the GDR and the potential rise of communist China; others have noted major shakeups in the hierarchy of Soviet sport and have cited inside corruption as the problem. Yet if one examines the Soviet Olympic record since 1952, it is by far the most outstanding of any nation. The key to success seems to have been that the Soviet system stresses the importance of working together as a group in training — for the collective good of its athletes. The first edition of this book, written in 1976, was devoted to this theme and to how such cooperative effort might be woven into the fabric of Western sport. Now writing in 1986, the author finds it even more important to emphasize the same theme.

Before leaving discussion of the Soviet sport system, one should note the extreme problems the Soviets have with the "wellness" or "fitness" of the general population. This is illustrated by the recently reported statistics documenting a decline in the life expectancy of the average male from 67 years in 1964 to 64 years in 1984. Such a decline is generally unheard of in the Western world.

Even more than the Soviet Union, the GDR provides an amazing success story in its development of elite athletes. For a nation of 17 million, the 40 gold medals won in the 1976 Olympics are phenomenal, especially when compared to the 40 firsts won by the first placed Soviet Union.* Both countries greatly outdistanced the United States, which placed third. Childs (1981, p. 69) claims that even the East German officials had a hard time explaining the 1976 Olympic success afterwards. The famous sport study center at Leipzig has become a testing ground for new studies in sport. The government has done its best to encourage mass participation in sport — although participation has fallen below expectation in that only 18% of the population partake in regular exercise (Childs, 1981, p. 96). In the GDR, sport is interwoven with military training, and the East Germans also have a long-time sporting tradition which they share with the West Germans. In spite of the state sponsorship of sport programs, most people participate with family and friends as opposed to engaging in state programs (49% versus 13% of regular participants). As in the Soviet Union, most athletes who are outstanding in their sports go on to assist others as coaches and in other high level positions in sport.

On the one hand, East German supremacy in athlete development has led to intense Western interest in their system and some emulation of it (for example in Canada). On the other hand it has led to an outburst of Western paranoia about East German training schemes, particularly in regard to the use of technology and drugs. Most evidence does support the Western belief that East Germans use anabolic steroids. However, Western accusations levelled against the East Germans can reach ridiculous heights. Leading up to the boycotted Los Angeles games were Western rumors that East German physicians planned to

---

*The Soviet Union won by accumulating more second and third place finishes than the GDR.

have their female athletes impregnated, since it had been found that hormonal changes in early pregnancy would lead to improved performances. Western lore had it that after the competitions the fetuses would be aborted. With no basis in fact, and less in logic, this item reached the pages of *Sports Illustrated,* where the myths were reported first and the facts second. The Western sport system has so many problems of its own that it would do better to study and learn from more successful systems than to attack them. At the same time, legitimate concerns such as drug control must be addressed through international regulation.

Cuba provides another example of outstanding athletic participation and development in a small nation. Rocked by revolution, depleted by the exodus of most technocrats and people of expertise, Cuba was left with a new set of social policies, a vacuum in many areas of expertise, and little funding to put new programs in place. With faith in rebuilding their country and some external support, innovations were made in the fields of education, medicine, and sport. The Cuban sport system, which is again based upon mass participation, has produced several outstanding teams and individual athletes. Training schools for sports abound and the most promising athletes are selected for special treatment, training, and privilege. As is central to the socialist bloc, the goal in training is not only to produce fine athletes but to produce athletes who will represent their country with pride and with central values intact.

THE ORIENTAL AND EAST ASIAN POSITION

Because of the brevity of this survey, disparate nations will be combined within the same cultural tradition in order to illustrate contrasting cultural values and how they may be reflected in sport performance. In the present discussion the focus is upon China and Japan, even though these nations have never been particularly compatible. However, they do have some values in common in spite of one nation being communist in orientation and one capitalist. The distinguishing feature which is common to both cultures is the sense of loyalty, training in tradition, and allegiance to the past. The upholding of family traditions and pride in the corporate body is emphasized. The individual is deemphasized in family life and is socialized to become part of the group and to function as part of the whole. Japanese society does not emphasize the individuality and self-assertion that one finds in Western societies. When a Japanese does show these traits they will usually be in the service of the group.

Extrapolating from these characteristics, the Japanese athlete is usually an excellent team member, and when self-assertion is manifested, it is again usually in the service of the group effort. Individual athletes such as mountain climbers and daredevils will often execute their feats as a form of self-discipline. Sumo wrestlers are steeped in the values and traditions of their sport. The Japanese rarely expresses emotions against the group or against tradition. Although the child is particularly indulged in terms of impulse gratification, an indulgence which continues into adult life for some male behaviors (for example, sexual), such liberties are not seen to damage the Japanese man's loyalty to the group traditions. In sport training, the Japanese are characterized by a great amount of collective activity. Whole schools can be seen going through exercise motions of unity, a style replayed when the Japanese worker stands beside his desk for group relaxation exercises. Sport activities take place under the corporate banner and Sundays are often spent engaged in company recreation programs which highlight group activities. There is great attention to aesthetics and form in Japan, and although a team may be matched in competition against another, there will usually be considerable emphasis on manners, politeness, and deference in non-game interactions. This was illustrated in the international field hockey study (Butt, 1980) cited previously. The Japanese women's team showed the most ideal profile out of 15 international teams competing in a world championship. The team leaders, that is, those most identified with by the players, showed very high scores on competence and cooperation as sport motivations. Such value dynamics within a team will lead to a continuation of the group, little disruption, and high morale.

Sport usually has a low profile or is absent in countries that are undergoing fast social change through revolution or civil war. Cuba and socialist China did not participate in international sport during their revolutions. However, as previously noted for Cuba, both are now emerging with what appear to be some excellent sports programs and equally excellent sports results. Socialist China, which initially captured the attention of the West with its diplomatic breakthrough via table tennis, has since developed world class athletes in several sports. Putnam (1974) reported the philosophy expressed by Chinese officials during the Asian games, held in Teheran in 1974. Friendship was placed above winning in importance, and good health was more important than monetary reward. At the present time we find China undergoing economic change and establishing new policies and links with the Western world. It has also recently emerged from several years' absence from the international sporting scene with some very highly developed athletes. The Chinese have continued to use sport for national development, for training purposes, for the development of health in the population, and for the encouragement of international goodwill. China provides major financial support for the development of sport in third world nations (Clumpner and Pendleton, 1981). With the broadening of business and cultural partnerships between China and North America one can expect to see many more sport exchanges between the regions.

Mao Tse-tung popularized the idea of physical fitness by promoting swimming. Pictures of Mao swimming the Yangtze River were publicized in both China and the Western world. Mao wrote papers promoting physical culture and strongly believed in the benefits of fitness. Direct attempts were made in China to integrate physical culture training into the schools and to keep it noncompetitive. China has a long history of interest in sports and games and although it had been a relatively unknown entity to the Western world until the Los Angeles Olympics, in fact, its athletes have always competed formidably when travelling abroad. They have been particularly well known for their performances in archery, pistol shooting, and table tennis, and promise much more in the future.

As China takes its place on the world stage in trade, politics, and cultural exchange, the Western world can expect to see unprecedented performances and participation from Chinese athletes. Socialization into sport will emphasize a strong commitment to the corporate body and to the past. The athletes will be ready to sacrifice and to be inspired by culturally set goals and values. They will be strongly supported by the system and they will be selected from a population of one billion people At the end of their careers there will be a vast population to absorb their knowledge and skills. China is still seen as a developing nation. Sport facilities are in short supply, and although sport may not yet touch the masses of people living in rural villages, the Western world should expect strong influence from China in sport of the future.

THE THIRD AND THE FOURTH WORLDS

It has been noted that since historic times, humans have engaged in sport and games. If we look closely at the cultures in even the least developed nations, we find forms of fun such as competition and demonstrations which resemble, to varying degrees, sport and games. Thus we turn from the First and the Second Worlds (the capitalistic and communistic nations) to those parts of the world which are not as developed economically. The Third World is made up of nations in which most of the population lives in relative poverty with little economic development (e.g., Brazil, the Philippines, Mexico). The Fourth World represents the indigenous peoples or natives of various regions such as the native Indians of North America and Scandanavia, the Aboriginals of Australia, and the tribal communities of Africa. These peoples themselves are in various stages of development, integration, or disarray and they present new dimensions of sport and games to the Western student.

Some cultures have originated sports that the Western world has adopted. The game of lacrosse was the invention of North American Indians. Kayaking comes directly from the Eskimo. Humans in all cultures have engaged in running and swimming. Children's games are of great interest in the Third and Fourth Worlds because they are so often cooperative in nature and message. Adult activities also often have social or cooperative significance. In villages in India (Beiser et al., 1981) Carstairs has noted that leisure time is often associated with the playful riddance of annoyances in everyday life. Babies, mothers-in-law, or husbands may be scapegoated in the singing of playful songs. In other words the activities have social significance and meaning, just as the highly organized commercial games have significance and meaning to the Western world. The same sport or activity can be enacted in different cultures, but the values and motivations of the participants may be quite different. Thus some nations might highlight the aesthetics of figure skating while another will stress the pursuit of medals and financial reward. We have already discussed the finding that rural children playing experimental games play more cooperatively than urban children. They are also more cooperative the less they identify with urban capitalistic values and the more they identify with a specific ethnicity such as Chicano or native Indian. Sport is increasingly being questioned as it is portrayed to the Western world. Recent meetings of the Psychoanalytic Society condemned much sport as bad for spectators and bad for society. Many athletes are on record as questioning the great amounts of money they make in professional sport.

It is not only the prosperous urban world that needs to question its values in the presentation of and the participation in sport. Third World countries which are plagued with the destructive use of leisure like gambling and drug taking are a serious concern (de Maderios in Beiser, Butt and Carstairs, 1981). How, for example do the unemployed and impoverished youth in a country such as Brazil use their free time? Do they waste and squander it on destructive activities because others are not available or do they have the opportunity to explore and be creative and thus increase enjoyment and future horizons? The mental and physical health of peoples throughout the world continues to be a primary theme in mental health circles. First, physical needs must be met. Second, emotional needs must be met. Third, programs and people must be free to explore various avenues of leisure and cultural development. There are many lessons to be learned by the Occidental world from the pastimes and peaceful leisure activities in less developed countries. To assume that the competitive Western model is the major and only vehicle for the expression of leisure activity is to miss the possibility of future world cooperation and the necessity for a world perspective on human values.

THE SOUTH AFRICAN ISSUE

In South Africa, sport is accorded a special status and a close relationship to government. In a society where a small white elite class economically and socially dominates the other four-fifths of the population, there has been much time and energy for sport involvement by the white elite. They enjoy a land of sunshine and plenty, large homes with tennis courts and swimming pools, excellent club facilities, and the leisure time to enjoy the pleasures of sport. These conditions are accompanied by an intense South African nationalism and concern for world opinion. South Africa has been ostracized by the world of sport time and again in cricket, swimming, tennis, and other events. The South African Government and sports federations are a wealthy group and they continually court the world of athletics with hospitality, money, and a share in the charmed way of life during visiting tours. They are willing, in addition, to make concessions to allay world opinion by allowing token black participation in sport. The hope is that by conforming to a few rules on a superficial level, they can placate world opinion. For some seeking change, there is the hope that blacks may feel some pride even in their token performance and that they too will realize they can achieve through sport and begin to perceive themselves differently. That faint hope has done little beyond enabling South Africa to continue propagating the world folk model of sport that merely reinforces the values of Apartheid: white supremacy, position maintained through privilege and power, and the exclusive right to dominate nonparticipants.

South Africa occupies an ambiguous position in world politics. Although it is ostracized by many nations, its wine and gold are often transhipped through other countries to disguise their origin and can be readily sold abroad. There is little doubt that the blacks in South Africa are subject to some of the most oppressive laws devised by modern regimes. A minority elite enslaves black labor in mines, in industry, in agriculture, and in domestic duty. The participation of South African teams abroad is often accompanied by riots and disruptions. Sport has offered a suitable vehicle for protest which politicians cannot ignore. International sports representatives signed the so-called "Gleneagles agreement" in 1977 in which governments agreed they would not financially support any athlete who competes against a South African. Some teams have been trained and sent abroad only to be removed from competition when drawn against a South African representative. South African athletes sometimes bear the brunt of the problem. The saga of Zola Budd and her bid for a berth on Britain's 1984 Olympic team is an outstanding example. So is the development of the black runner Sydney Maree, now living in the United States. In spite of the struggles of these athletes, those in the more established sports which are fully professional have an easier time. The legendary golfer Gary Player lives in luxury in Johannesburg. Tennis players have typically competed on the world circuit without problem. This is because in professional sport they are considered to be independent businessmen and not representatives of their country.

With the education and advancement of blacks throughout the world and with blacks taking on new political significance in the United States, it is inevitable that South Africa must change. Barring outright revolution, the reins of power will not be easily wrenched from the current generation of white leaders. But as more blacks from South Africa excel in sport and other endeavors and act as models for those who follow, new possibilities will be opened for the coming generation. As more blacks from South Africa get their education from communist universities and from capitalist colleges, they will take on new influence at home. If problems can be solved increasingly by peaceful negotiation, South African policies will also evolve and adjust. It remains to be seen whether the process of adjustment will continue to be violent as events in 1986 have shown them to be.

24
The Emerging World System

THE EMERGENCE OF A GLOBAL PERSPECTIVE

This final chapter will examine the significance of sport within world society and the role sport might play in the future. Throughout this book we have argued that the competitive values of the athletic field are obsolete and should be changed. The arguments for this position are expanded now to include the international situation. We will examine the sources that sanction and sponsor competitive sport, as well as the sources of possible change. A discussion of essential changes in social values and of the powers that resist those changes is a good starting point.

The problems faced by the human race as a whole have come to the forefront of international attention. Worldwide conferences convene to permit representatives of world nations to work toward developing common policies on such problems as population, diminishing resources, the use of the natural environment, the attainment of peace, and the distribution of wealth and industry. While countries still compete for the rights to waterways, space, and other environmental resources, they also now search for compromise and common approaches. The problems faced by humankind are the concern of average citizens around the world, student groups, representatives of local governments and churches who have become increasingly involved in human rights, environmental issues, and future planning. Literate people need no longer be ignorant of the tides in world affairs, provided they have access to education and communication, and are not politically oppressed. On the international front, negotiation and compromise are replacing confrontation and conflict for the same reasons that on the local front people are becoming involved with the problems of their neighbors. It is clear that conflict will not lead to victory for some and losses for others, but that all will suffer setbacks as a result of it. If nations use their full military power, if environmental resources are used indiscriminately, the losses affect all. This realization by a significant proportion of the world's population may be strong enough to influence even the competitive elements in world society to take a more cooperative stance. Common survival may be a superordinate goal that can unite people who had previously thought they had little in common.

The emphasis upon cooperation and interdependence is not a new way of thinking. Altruism is required for childrearing, neighborhood living, and caring for the less fortunate in any society. The individual is nurtured, raised, protected, and educated and in all societies, these are functions of interdependence and cooperation. In native communities there is usually sufficient trust, interdependence, and interrelatedness that those of superior status are kept in check and act in the interests of all. It is when these qualities are lost, when leaders exploit and corrupt their offices, when competition and Machiavellianism triumph, that competence in social living can be dominated by incompetence. Social competence is sacrificed, for example, when interrelatedness and mutual obligations to others are ignored. This unfortunately reflects the conduct of many multinational corporations in the Third World today. Hazardous products have been identified and exposed in the First World (drugs, tobacco, chemicals) and regulated, at least in part. As a consequence, the corporations have expanded into the Third World to push and peddle the same products with little consideration for the welfare of the new consumers.

World perspectives must replace insular thinking and the welfare of all must take precedence over self-aggrandizement and the aggrandizement of one's own group. This theme, as recently summed up by Roy Megarry, publisher of the *Globe and Mail* and member of the Club of Rome (*Globe and Mail,* Feb. 2, 1984), is as follows:

> Unless a new sense of morality emerges quickly in the developed world, a set of circumstances already in motion will indeed make it "just a question of how long it will be before a revolution arrives."

He notes the major problems as: pollution of land, water, and atmosphere; starvation and malnutrition; strain on limited agricultural lands due to urban sprawl; the overuse of fertilizers and pesticides; deforestation of the world's rainforests; salt erosion and salination; and the explosive growth of population in Third World cities. He states:

> Soon, we will not have the choice of token assistance or outright neglect. The dimensions of the problems are global and affluent nations of the world are being directly affected. Global solutions will be needed.

On the corrective side he notes action groups working toward reducing pollution, life styles changing to produce less waste, environmental groups which are becoming potent political forces, and the emergence of the peace movement. He sees political and moral will as the ingredients necessary to solve these problems.

The Club of Rome provides one major impetus for movement toward world cooperation. Founded in 1969 by Aurelio Peccei, the Italian industrialist, the club comprises about 100 influential industrialists and scientists of various nationalities who are interested in drawing attention to global problems. Alexander King, 75, a Scottish chemist, became president of the club upon Peccei's death in 1984. Other important leadership has come from the World Council of Churches, which strives for a world view. Made up of Christian churches throughout the world, the Council meets every four years and is observed but not sanctioned by the Roman Catholic Church. It is controversial in the West for its political involvement in Latin America and trade unions and for its liaisons with Moscow. It is on the other hand remarkably world wide in its representation. Since its formation after the Second World War, the Council has been calling for global unity, a heightened sense of morality, and global action to deal with global problems. A hard-won consensus was reached in the Nairobi Assembly of 1975, when basic human rights were agreed upon: life, self-determination, cultural identity, rights for minorities, participation in the decision-making of one's community, right to dissent, right to personal dignity, and the right to religious freedom. The execution of these rights by the Council of Churches has suffered as a result of the East-West split between the delegations. It seems that the passage of the Helsinki human rights accord was seen by some Eastern leaders as vindicating a strategy of cooperation with other political regimes, whereas some Western leaders saw the Helsinki agreement as a tool for pressuring Eastern governments into change. And, among the Third World countries there was a deep suspicion that the agreements could be used by both the East and the West to continue their subjugation of the poorer nations. Thus even this World Council of global thinking is bothered by internal strife. A very wealthy organization, the Council receives 98 percent of its funds from member churches and agencies in 13 countries. West Germany and the United States contribute over 60 percent. Thus it is little surprise that Western critics of the Council say that it cares more for the success of revolutionary movements in the Third World than for tackling religious persecution where it is found most blatantly – in the Soviet Union. In spite of this internal strife, the World Council of Churches is one cooperative body which can act as a barometer of the abilities of human groups to achieve cooperative goals.

There are many views, books, and scientific models which have debated the current global problems. Stavrianos (1981) has argued that the ever-increasing gap between the rich and poor nations may lead to nuclear war unless the poor nations are helped to achieve parity. Sampson (1981) believes money not to be the answer. He thinks that many international banks are so irretrievably dependent upon the fate of the Third World nations to whom they have lent vast sums of money that we are truly in a "global village." After the defaults of Iran, Poland and Mexico, the promise of more monetary exchange will do little to rescue the situation. Sampson quotes Celso Ming, the Brazilian economist, as saying: "If I owe a million dollars, then I am lost. But if I owe fifty billion, the bankers are lost." When speaking of world debt today, we are speaking of hundreds of billions of U.S. dollars. For many of these there is no hope of retrieval. It is as though the wealthy nations have an option on Third World development. But do Third World nations intend to develop according to Western plans?

If the answer to world stability cannot be found in economic development, are there other possible solutions? Quadeer (1981) thinks that there are and calls for a change in attitude. The answer is in partnership and not in domination. He writes (1981, p. 16): "with the exception of newly independent small states in Southern and Central Africa and Oceania, most of the Third World now produces enough administrators, agronomists, engineers, scientists and even doctors to take care of normal developmental tasks." He calls for more cross-cultural enlightenment and the ability to experience other cultures with a value-explicit and comparative perspective.

The possibility of annihilation by nuclear armaments has been a horrifying but a unifying theme to peoples throughout the world. Since the dropping of the Atom Bomb on Hiroshima in 1945, the peace movement has been gaining momentum. In the 1950s and 60s Bertrand Russell and others demonstrated in Trafalgar Square in London. Since those early demonstrations the consciousness of people throughout the world has been raised and it is not unusual now to see peace marches 50,000 strong.

Another powerful reminder of thinking the unthinkable comes from the publication of Schell's 1982 *The Fate of the Earth*. Schell describes the possible annihilation of life on earth from nuclear war. This would be the most brutal and wicked act ever committed, its results so irrevocable that they are difficult to imagine. The author sets out to make this ultimate crime conceivable and force people to face the horror of it. He also notes the responsibility which the present generation has not only to itself and its children but to all the children who might follow in generations to come. Similar arguments can be made with regard to the widespread environmental pollution perpetrated by technological and industrial development. The Bhopal and Chernobyl disasters which killed and maimed thousands of people stand as grim beacons of current corruptions of the environment.

It is now more important than ever that individuals, families, groups, and political parties work against the evils of arms and environmental destruction in increasing numbers. With vast numbers of citizens earning their livelihood from the arms race and from technological development and with leaders who do not understand the evils they perpetrate (Jung, 1957), the question is whether people of good will can influence their leaders toward global peace and stability. In order for world problems to be dealt with effectively it seems increasingly evident that they must be dealt with from a position of competence and not of competition, from a position of interdependence and not exploitation, and from a position of wanting survival and not profit.

THE LIMITS TO GROWTH AND
COMPETITIVE EXPANSION

In spite of the many criticisms of The Club of Rome's *Limits to Growth,* (Meadows et al., 1972) it was one of the first and most significant attempts to present the common problems faced by mankind. The authors used a systems program approach developed by Jay Forrester to combine the curves resulting from the predicted growth or decline of the following variables: population, industrial output per capita, food per capita, pollution, nonrenewable resources, birthrate, deathrate and services per capita. The resulting prediction was that present rates of growth would lead to catastrophe for large numbers of humans before the year 2100. As Meadows et al. (1972) summarize their argument: the exact date of the end to growth is not significant. What is significant is that even in this figure, in which every allowance is made for the most optimistic prediction, the reversal sets in within the next century. The point to be drawn is that the encouragement of cooperation, knowledge, and insight is required if the peoples of the world and their representatives are to work together in a common effort to solve the problems resulting from increasing population and decreasing resources. Indeed, some of the problems seem upon us now.

In order to cope with the necessary decision-making and planning for the future, cooperative social and psychological approaches are needed. The aggression, low self-insight, and egocentricity of the competitor, which are encouraged by the competitive situation, will, one hopes, become obsolete or at least move far to the background in human affairs. Common or superordinate goals will provide most encouragement for cooperation, and *The Limits to Growth* offers a strong argument in providing such goals. Yet as long as the competitively oriented think they can come out on top, the possibility of world disaster may not affect their behavior, and many may choose to ignore our common goals. The violent incidents in world affairs that involve innocent people have also led to the realization that the political repression and hate that exist between some peoples of the world cannot be ignored by other world citizens. Highjackings, bombings, and massacres can involve neutral citizens and countries. The desperation and dedication of the terrorists who carry out such acts cannot continually be written off as lawlessness and dealt with by lengthy and costly legal procedures. The message of these disasters should be that the world cannot afford to ignore the intolerable suffering, the injustice, and the problems that people face in many parts of the world. Their problems are world problems and the people of the world should, therefore, work toward finding solutions. The acts in many of these incidents are so bizarre that they can only call attention to the failure of men to deal with some of the grave and critical problems involving the qualities of life and justice that our ideologies so often proclaim. The incidents are often blundered by those who perpetrate them, are seldom managed successfully by the authorities who deal with them, while the citizens of the world read the stories in newspapers and are appalled, crying out for revenge and the locking up of the "madmen." Stark cries of help and desperation are met with withdrawal, indignation, and indifference. Yet at the same time these indignant people will gather in the sports stadiums of the world, 100,000 and more strong, to spend their emotions and enthusiasms on an athletic contest that pits contestants against each other so that there will be a winner and a loser, thus endorsing in principle the desperate acts and tactics of the terrorists. The competitive athletic model is as archaic as the terrorists' attacks, but both are still endorsed by the values we subscribe to. Although competition never maximizes welfare to the point that it could be called personally functional for all, it was once probably socially functional when the Protestant Ethic prevailed in North America, when there were frontiers to be conquered, when territories were to be settled and empires were to be built. This is no longer the case. The human population itself is now often described as the world cancer, and the problems of humankind is not that it cannot master nature, but that it is destroying nature and does not know itself.

Cooperation, peace, and rationality are essential processes that must be developed in the world today so that men and women can begin to solve the pressing problems before them. Cities face problems of crime, of supplies, and of the inequalities of rights of their citizens. Some peoples of the world, as in parts of India and Africa, starve, while others, as in some Western and European countries, overeat and overdrink to the point of ill health. People struggle over property, power, and position, while the very structure over which they struggle to become part of is changing. One of the most constructive personality traits for the future is the willingness to change. For social structure and values seem destined to change and the people who live with such changes will be called upon to adjust, and perhaps to give up what they once had in order to make room for others in a more humane way than is now the case. Egocentricity and fighting only for onself and one's close identities will no longer be useful traits. For this reason the personaltiy attributes fostered in competitive athletes and sustained by the high reward system of athletics today will become dysfunctional. The sooner the emphasis on winning is discontinued the more easily adjustment to the demands of the future will become for masses of people.

In a crowded world where people must live peacefully together, humans find themselves with increasing numbers of dysfunctional responses. They must learn to develop other responses and other reactions; for example, they must learn to act more out of empathy and insight and less out of greed and self-righteousness. These traits will grow as human identification with the world and the people of the world grow. Although many of the major problems in the world used to develop between nations, the present division of the world into nation states belies the way most current problems in the world are developing. Increasing numbers are not international problems, but intranational problems, where the people and governments of different countries deal with similar conflicts within their boundaries, such as between the rich and the poor, between people of different ideological orientations, between those who would lead and those who would follow, and between those who would develop and use natural resources and those who would preserve them. Because more nations now share problems than are divided by them, the emergence of cooperative worldwide organizations was inevitable. The existence of the United Nations, founded in the interest of world peace, is perhaps the most visible organization dedicated to cooperative goals between nations; yet its policies and goals are still undermined by the competitive behaviors of its members.

Nationalism is still much alive and is fanned by international sports competitions. The ill will and bitterness caused by many international competitions have been obvious since sporting contests have been recorded. McIntosh (1971) has observed that the strong desire of people to win, when backed by political identifications and pressures, often causes outright conflict during international sporting competitions.

George Orwell (1968) wrote: "...that sport is an unfailing cause of ill-will, and if such a visit as this has had any effect at all on Anglo-Soviet relations, it could only be to make them slightly worse than before.... Serious sport has nothing to do with fair play. It is bound up with hatred, jealousy, boastfulness, disregard of all rules, and sadistic pleasure in witnessing violence: in other words, it is war minus the shooting." Orwell was commenting on a series of soccer games between the Moscow Dynamos and several British soccer clubs in 1945: The follies of nationalism have been the concern of many writers, philosophers and historians. Natan (1958) concludes that nationalism is destructive to sport, causing it to become a vehicle of conflict and competitive strength instead of enjoyment. He also notes the jargon of international sporting events is more comprehensible to the military chief of staff than to a "genuine sportsman." Bertrand Russell (1932) called for a lessening of nationalistic feelings, as has Otto Klineburg (1966). Perhaps poetry offers the most vivid plea, as in the conclusion of Wilfred Owen's "Dulce et Decorum Est":

> If in some smothering dreams, you too could pace
> Behind the wagon that we flung him in,
> And watch the white eyes wilting in his face,
> His hanging face, like a devil's sick of sin,
> If you could hear, at every jolt, the blood
> Come gargling from the froth-corrupted lungs
> Bitten as the cud
> Of vile, incurable sores on innocent tongues,—
> My friend, you would not tell with such high zest
> To children ardent for some desperate glory,

The old lie: *Dulce et decorum est*
Pro patria mori. *

The problem is that if men are led to believe that either dying or playing for their country is good, they are not encouraged to assess the significance of what they are doing or the rights and privileges of others. They are not made aware of the effects, consequences, and broader implications of their behaviors, but are caught up in the emotional climate of the contest often to the disadvantage of themselves and others. Why is such insular identification encouraged in sport? It is encouraged on two levels. First, national associations, Olympic committees, and international sports organizations are often chartered to foster and to encourage sports on the national and international levels. These associations are usually also supposed to encourage sports at the "grass roots" level, and they assume that national and international events will encourage the participation of many in sport. They tend to assess their success by how well their teams do in international competition and how many top players they develop. These organizations are not set up for monetary gain and they have the potential for change. They could encourage competence values in sport if they reorganized, and they also could arrange the close relationship between competent athletes and developing youth which is essential for sport to be constructive. The second major alignment with international sporting events comes from the commercial spheres in which the television networks, the multinational corporations, business enterprise, and wealthy owners are prominent. Through their strong influence and control over the staging of sport events, the publicizing of sports events through television and newspapers, and the presentation of the events to the public, these enterprises are able to keep a model of conflict and competition alive in front of millions. The impoverishment of these enterprises in terms of human values and social benefit has been a theme of this book. Players are cast as representing countries when they have not lived there for years; players are supposed to represent cities when they are bought and sold like produce; players are cast as being identified with their team when their major concern is money. These kinds of sports enterprises lead to the manipulation, the exploitation, and the deception of the crowd; to the continuation of values that should be questioned and probably altered; and the accumulation of wealth by promoters and a few athletes quite out of proportion the extent of their social contribution.

Because of the positions of centrality and power that corporations such as ITT occupy in the world, much of the hope for value changes and world leadership

---

*Wilfred Owen, COLLECTED POEMS. Copyright Chatto & Windus, Ltd., 1946 © 1963. Reprinted by permission of New Directions Publishing Corporation, New York. The Latin sentence translates: "It is sweet and glorious to die for one's country."

must also rest upon them. Thus, Barnet and Muller (1974), in *Global Reach*, call for changes in the multinationals. If the leaders of corporations, as well as nations and world organizations, were to become familiar with the relationship between the future and human values, and were to act upon them, a stable, cooperative, and competence-oriented world situation might be achieved. That such hopes are possible to realize is perhaps foreshadowed in the sponsorship of effort that produced *The Limits to Growth*. Aurelio Peccei, founder of The Club of Rome (the sponsoring group), was an industrialist and economist associated with Fiat and Olivetti. The Volkswagon Foundation was one of the original sponsors (at the instigation of one of its directors, Eduard Pestel), as was the Xerox Corporation. With additional backing by the U. S. Department of Health, Education and Welfare and by its secretary, Elliot Richardson, the project represented an experimental effort directed toward clarifying the predicament of humankind within the world without respect to the current value systems operating. *The Limits to Growth* project was a cooperative project with the backing of large corporations and concerned citizens. There is a need for many more similar projects, both on larger and smaller scales, and for a center to coordinate and report results.

THE PROMISES OF CHANGE FROM WITHIN CORPORATIONS

The late Barbara Ward Jackson (as quoted by Rowland, 1972) is one economist who has argued that people and not profit should be the major concern of economics:

> To act without rapacity, to use knowledge with wisdom, to respect interdependence, to operate without hubris and greed are not simply, moral imperatives. They are an accurate scientific description of the means of survival.

Francois Partant, an ex-banker who has taken on anti-establishment values, was once head of the foreign department of the Banque de Paris et des Pays-Bas. He resigned and went to Malagasy with the Central Fund for Economic Cooperation, eventually managing a development bank in the Upper Volta. Frustrated as a mediator between financiers and local communities, he and a handful of colleagues are now working on a reanalysis of the modern economic system, and its restructuring, in order to overcome "economaniac fantasies." He has written several books including *La Guerilla economique, Que la crise s'aggrave*, and *Le Pedalo ivre*. He is quoted in 1981 (Delaunay, 1981) as saying:

> Crisis isn't the right word. It would be more accurate to talk of the system decaying, the apotheosis of competition, and the apogee of arms proliferation, if not nuclear war.

He believes progress in the West is being achieved at the expense of the rest of humankind. Although economically interdependent, Partant suggests that capitalism has resulted in laws that allow some societies to develop at the expense of others. He thinks competition as a "source of progress" has "long outlived its usefulness."

Corporations may change as the result of both outside demands and inside pressures. An example of each follows. The giant monopoly of Nestlé's was forced, by a long process, to change its marketing techniques in the Third World. Its aggressive campaign of marketing baby formula led to the deaths of thousands of Third World infants who were denied the immunity to disease that would have resulted from breast feeding. A worldwide boycott was conducted, mostly by churchwomen, before the Swiss-based company's executive vice-president, Carl Angst, agreed to end the promotional campaigns. He agreed that the proceedings were "very sophisticated, lengthy and painful – for Nestlé," and that, "If I look back today at what the marketing practices were in some developing countries 10, 20 years ago in the infant formula industry, I would say yes, the industry has gone too far in many cases in the promotion of these products." Sister Regina Murphy, chairman of the International Nestlé's Boycott Committee, is quoted as saying, "Let not one more mother weep, or one more child weaken, or one more health worker either – because we failed to act." The committee planned to boycott Nestlé's activities for six months, relying on the network of Third World workers developed during the seven-year struggle. Another worker states: "The one big lesson for companies is that they have to be accountable to consumers." Nestlé's commanded 50 percent of the Third World market for infant formula.

Other struggles to make corporations more responsible have not yet been won, but are being played out. The story of Stanley Adams (1984), is an alarming account of what happened to one man who argued that corporations should be responsible to consumers. World product manager of the huge multinational drug company Hoffman-La Roche, Adams revealed its illicit trading practices to the European Economic Community. Price-fixing, market-sharing with competitors, and oppressive control of the worldwide vitamin market were Adams's major concerns. He stated that Librium was overpriced by 6,478 percent, that Colombian subsidiaries were overcharged 155 percent for ingredients, and "When news came of an influenza epidemic, for instance in India, instead of putting vitamin C out in greater quantities, we (Roche) would control the quantities going out and usually increase the price." After Roche was fined approximately $430,000 by the EEC, Adams, who now lives in England, was arrested for his efforts, put in solitary confinement in a Swiss jail on charges of industrial espionage and treason, and taunted by his powerful antagonist. Adams's wife committed suicide while he was jailed, and he was not allowed to attend her funeral. Given a three-year suspended sentence, Adams faced bankruptcy and could not borrow money for his new business of farming in Italy, as he had talked to the press and connected Italian politicians and Roche over the dioxin chemical scandal in Seveso. Adams has documented the illicit practices and exploitation by this major corporation in the Third World. Yet Hoffman-La Roche do little to curb their exploitation of world markets, particularly in their overtures to Third World countries, where they sponsor conferences, appear, advertise, and promote, not facts, but images.

An educated public is essential if the multinational corporations are to be kept in line and if those rising to power within them are going to have the leverage to impose a new morality. One positive sign is the efforts within the United Nations to adopt a code of ethics for multinational corporations with regard to responsibility and world marketing. When such codes do come into practice, the multinational corporations and those within them who want to adopt a new morality will be vastly supported. They will have high potential for achieving constructive aims through competent and responsible practices and cooperative concern for others, including their consumers. This will allow more enlightened management and participation from multinational corporations to emerge.

THE REFORMATION IN SPORT

Change is essential in the values of the sports world, just as change is essential in the world values of international politics. Countries, groups, and individuals cannot be permitted to struggle for position and supremacy as in the past. On an international level, the use of weapons and the development of destructive power previously unthought of have made the motives for power and supremacy a threat to all. The biological struggle for position and the use of conflict to establish power are now obsolete. Humankind has reached a level of evolution where rational considerations must surpass the motives of egocentrism and greed. Many of humankind's cultivated needs and old habits must be curbed; for example, we can no longer be the unmitigated consumers we have been in the past. Competitive sport and competitive play are no longer functional folk models for society. If we are correct in asserting that play is a forerunner of later life activity and significant in the development of the individual and society, just as it is significant in the development of animals, then surely it is worthwhile attempting to change and to reform sport on several levels.

1. Changes from Sport Sponsorship. The greatest potential for change in sport lies with the corporate sponsorship. Corporate sponsors gain in image, promotion, and hence profit through their relationship to sport. From time to time that relationship will become fickle and sport sponsors will retreat from sport to other areas. For example, Rothmans has changed on occasion from sport sponsorship to the sponsorship of art and culture. However, values are changing on the world scene. Public tastes increasingly favor grass roots sport movements, and corporate sponsors are being forced to re-examine their policies and privileges by both internal and external criticism. These factors may well lead to important reform and a new dignity being restored to sport. Two examples of such changes follow. First, sponsors of the U. S. Davis Cup team objected to the boorish and rude behavior of the U. S. team in 1984 in Sweden, and plans were made to have all future players sign a code of conduct. Second, a full page ad in a national Canadian magazine proclaimed Esso's sponsorship of minor hockey throughout Canada and emphasized the values of fun, skill, and team cooperation among the players. Girls and boys are depicted in the promotion, along with Tony, chosen his team's most valuable player.

> Not because he's the top scorer. In fact, his record is 0 goals, 1 assist. He was chosen because he demonstrated his importance to his team. Which just goes to show how valuable this kind of team training is to all our kids.

Even if image making is at the heart of such a promotion campaign, the message shows a major change and innovation over the last decade in sport.

Such innovations signal alterations and adjustments in the values and investments of corporations and businesses that have previously supported the competitive folk model of sport without question. Corporations are in a strategic position to initiate changes in sport and also in other areas of life, as noted in the previous section. For example, a significant proportion of prize money and gate receipts from sport could be assigned to the education and assistance of the world's underprivileged, to social reform, and to achieving global equilibrium. The transformation of the goals and values of the executives of multinational corporations would only come through the realization that their present paths and strategies are self-defeating. The reformation of economic man cannot be relied upon even in the face of disaster, since he will still strive to attain maximum profit. It is possible, however, that broadly educated, thinking businessmen and women, and specifically the leaders of corporations, will provide the major leadership that is necessary for crucial value changes within the world of sport.

Corporations are in an excellent position for world leadership, and as they cease being concerned with image at the expense of substance and as increasing amounts of information are available on them, giving them less secrecy and less ability to hide from the public, one would predict this leadership role to grow. Corporations are much courted in times of economic setback throughout the world due to their capacity to generate jobs, tax revenue, and better tax balances. They show a faster rate of growth than most national economies. Their ethics are being addressed and needed corrections are being attempted. As noted, there are signs that the people within corporations who are being promoted may show changes in perspective from those promoted in the past. International experience, global perspectives on decision-making, and the ability to mediate value disputes and to consider value orientations in local communities are all being emphasized as corporations seek new personnel. The domestic and multinational corporations referred to are not necessarily U.S. based. The poor records of several corporations based in Switzerland and the United States have been noted. Perhaps the emerging corporations from Japan and elsewhere will conduct themselves with more world perspective. On the other hand, American democracy and power may combine to give American corporations most potential for change and world leadership. Yet, many writers (for example, Anderson, 1984; Hayes and Abernathy, 1980) have focused upon the decline in U.S. world influence. Not only do the internal policies and practices in the United States seem to undermine the success of U.S. corporations, but external evaluations of U.S. policies are also unfavorable. Immense problems with U.S. businesses and politics in Latin America and elsewhere have led to Jean Fitzpatrick's (1984) comment at the United Nations: "The United Nations is against us. Who is with us?" It is interesting that even as the United States declines in world power (Barraclough, 1980), U.S. capital is being channeled into the building of a 3,700 mile natural gas pipeline from Siberia in the Soviet Union to Western Europe. In spite of overwhelming scientific and engineering odds against it, the pipeline is going ahead with world monies to support it. It is also going ahead inspite of the U.S. administration's vehement objections.

Both the business world and the sports world seem to benefit from communication and exchange which is worldwide. That is, there are benefits from learning from alternative programs and values, and costs associated with insularity. In sport, Canada has been quite successful in adopting Eastern models of sport development as opposed to Western ones from Great Britain and the United States. The point is that more will be achieved through working with and learning from alternative programs than from preserving the extreme emphasis upon competition enshrined in many Western minds. As corporations change, sport will change. Thus we rate corporations as in the key position to encourage global concern and a shift from egocentric to cooperative values.

2. The Athletes. The author cited athletes as the major source of potential change in sport in 1976. In fact leadership behavior from athletes emerged much less than expected, the reason being that immense amounts of money were poured into sport. Because athletes, particularly the prominent ones, benefited so greatly from this flow of funds, they had little incentive to initiate change. Athletes were bought off and became part of the establishment. Today the best athletes are in the process of acquiring quick fortunes, hence there is a low probability of them exerting pressures for change in sport. Second, many athletes suffer from both stress and distress in their personal lives and are attempting to shore up their own stability. Thus they are hardly in a position to lead others.

In spite of these facts, there are some initiatives for change from the participants in sport. Athletes are becoming increasingly aware of the inner athlete and the importance of competence in sustaining their own motivations and careers. Others have turned their backs on the unrestrained materialism within sport and have elected other life styles than the pursuit of sport. Athletes have stood up against corporate sponsorship, which they have considered to be unethical; the case of the Canadian skiers who refused trophies from a tobacco company has been described earlier (pp. 260). Still other athletes have made ongoing statements through their life styles or their own forms of sponsorship. A good example is golfer Patty Sheehan's sponsorship of a home for girls with behavioral problems. A whole new era of sport involvement may have begun in British Columbia with Terry Fox's run across Canada to raise money for cancer research. Although the one-legged runner died himself from cancer at the halfway point in his run, he raised over $20 million for cancer research. Steve Fonyo, another one-legged cancer victim, later completed the entire cross Canada run and raised $9 million. In the meantime Rick Hansen, a third British Columbia athlete, has executed an around the world expedition in his wheel chair to raise funds for spinal cord research. Such leadership from the disabled and their ability to reach the populace during their athletic feats as well as their ability to command the media has been a major innovation in the fitness and sport movement.

As more athletes abandon the old notion that organized sports will bring them personal glory and happiness, there will be increasing potential for change. The more the athlete adopts a pure competence model for sports involvement, the more he or she will pursue sport for its intrinsic merits and will question the old system in which it is staged. When only a few athletes think this way, they may be called radical but when such athletes are in the majority they will become a major impetus for change.

3. Educators and Education. A third source of change may come through educators and education. Many people fully recognize the destructiveness of competition. Parents, school teachers, and other educators can change the reward system in the school structure so that young children are not conditioned to follow the follies of organized sport. The adult world can be directed to place its encouragement elsewhere so that children with cooperative social perspectives and behaviors become group leaders. Children do not need reinforcement and praise for the development of competence and skill. They are quite capable of feeling their own internal pleasures and rewards. With a change in the school system from emphasis on competitive masterful domination to the genuine enjoyment of doing and experiencing from day to day, a significant step would be taken forward by humankind, much larger than that of Neil Armstrong when his foot touched the surface of the moon; this step would bring humans closer to themselves.

4. Women. A fourth source of change in sport may come from women. At prior writing the author thought that women in public office and positions of power would retain their old values of communal concern and care. This is often not the case, since the influence process functions in two directions. Women in office are influenced as well as influencers, making the process of change slower and perhaps less disruptive. Although women are still not as immediately involved in the present power hierarchy or economic structure as are men, women are making increasing inroads and at the same time are increasing their own autonomy and freedom of choice in affecting decisions. Although some may be very conforming, influential women in politics and positions of leadership are markers for others to follow. Ghandi, Thatcher, Fitzpatrick, and Ferraro are all important figures in the evolution of women's roles and influence. At the same time, older women are in possession of vast amounts of economic wealth which they could, and sometimes do, allocate according to their own judgments and desires for reform. Women in sport, politics, and economics are capable of innovative reform. An example is provided by the political behavior of Mrs. Rene Egan, a Republican, who once campaigned against Vincent Massari, a Democrat, for the state senate in Colorado. She withdrew from the competition because, in her view, the only reason one runs is to contribute to and improve the community, a job that, she was confident, could be ably done by Massari. In sport, as well, women may be the purveyors of reform providing they look for guidance within their own minds and from their own visions.

5. Study in the Social Sciences. The fifth source for change in the world of sport may come from the application of study in the social sciences. If play in young children and animals foreshadows their future activities and development, so does sport in adult society. It is a reflection of where society is and where it may be headed. Youth is influenced by major social pastimes, therefore sport and its significance are worth extended study and should be the subject of social prediction and planning regarding what forms of sports activity are most beneficial to a society. Since sport is a leisure activity, the opportunity for experimental programs would be excellent if athletes, audiences, and social scientists were to cooperate. Many significant questions could be asked and answered in a way that would be meaningful to reasonable men and women. For example, one might ask which organized sport programs are most beneficial to children, if competence motivations can be encouraged and if such motivations result in the psychological benefits described in this book. Long-term studies of the development of male and female athletes within different sporting environments could be undertaken, as could studies of the psychological significance of different sports. Studies of Olympic events could tell us the extent to which international good will and communication and trust are, in fact, encouraged and under what conditions.

It is unfortunate that the thrust of most work has not been value-oriented nor invested itself in the necessary longitudinal work to answer value-oriented questions. Too often money and support go toward efforts and research study in order to improve the performances of athletes. Frequently this effort has to do with the development of new techniques and machinery in which the social significance of the findings is minimal. These efforts mean that the promise of sport psychology is in the future, not in the present. There is at present too much unimaginative work which follows the experimental model with the same rigidity that the competitive model is followed in sport. Research should not advance the researcher but the future of society, and for this reason it should always be creative and innovative. It should also advance the interests and well-being of the participants in the research, or of the public whom the participants represent, and not technology.

Most important, sports programs should be evaluated so that proper planning is possible in educational curricula. The idea of experimental studies providing data for social policy planning is not new. Campbell (1971) called for the use of true experimental societies where all social planning would depend upon the moral and ethical use of scientific study. There are methods by which many social questions could be answered if people would take the time and become aware of the methods, studies, and conclusions to be drawn. Objective data should be used considerably more by governments and their organizations where decisions are being made and acted on. However, part of the blame for social science being so slow to take its place by demonstrating its skills in the service of all must be attributed to the social scientists themselves who have rarely bothered with the application or readability of their studies, and whose students have been trained in the use of group jargon rather than encouraged to use expressive communication. Surely much more evaluation should be carried out on experimental living programs, new types of communities, new forms of government administration and leadership, as well as on sporting programs. For example, it has become fashionable to sponsor junior teams to all varieties of championships in North America (often called world championships even though they are confined to North America). Children are trained, frequently taken out of school, and sometimes pampered and feted, just as adult sports teams are. The long-term effects of these experiences have never been tested, but certainly from the results reported in Ralbovsky's (1974) article, it seems not all benefit. Similarly, on an adult level, large amounts of money are put into college and national team development and sponsorship. These programs rarely assessed in terms of their social significance. All that is known is that they provide a continual source of players for commercial leagues. What good do these programs do the countries and the colleges who sponsor them so freely? In football, there is financial gain for the institution, but for governments, national team sponsorships sometimes result in little feedback to the country as a whole. The sport may not be played by most of the public at large, and the teams may merely be climbing onto an Olympic bandwagon. The sport may be controlled by an elitist association in which only a certain stratum of the population is involved, or it might be that the public does not have access to facilities for the sport. Members of national teams generally do little to help the public. Our present crop of professionals do a little more only because they are paid to appear before youth groups, at dinners, and at developmental as well as community programs. However, the impact of these national teams, even though large sums of money are sunk into them, is rarely assessed.

There would be great benefit from knowing more about, for another example, the reactions of audiences to sports spectacles. How much do people enjoy the aggression of hockey and football and how much are they attracted by the skills displayed? Would they rather be doing something else than attending these sport spectacles? Why are they there? If the media did not emphasize sport would the audience show up at all? Surely governments should have answers to such questions and many others in formulating policies about sport, just as they should have parallel data before making decisions in other areas. The relationship between socialization and sports experiences should be studied. There are numerous studies on socialization, but few have focused on the interaction between personality, predisposition, and sports experiences. The reports of people viewing the results of competitive experiences in schools are not favorable. Few observers of our school systems conclude that competence is developed as a result of school sports. Actually there are more often complaints about the stress on competition. A frequent comment heard from school children is: "If you don't make the team, you are nothing." The most competitive individuals are then attracted to sport and stay in sport, while those oriented toward competence frequently drop out.

The riddle with which we are left is, how can cooperative tendencies and potentials be developed in the face of socially sanctioned competition? The answer may well hold the key to our future and the study of sport may allow us to find it. The playing of sport has not and the spectatorship of sport has not.

THE REPETITION AND SECURITY OF THE GAME

Why do so many engage so repetitively in sports and sports spectatorship if it does disservice to the human condition? The answer lies in the security sport, as a folk model, provides for the public and for athletes. Life is full of pastimes that reinforce the value systems within which individuals operate and which they are trained to accept as permanent and valid. Moore and Anderson (1962) have studied the folk model concept and the social function it serves. Their study, "Some Puzzling Aspects of Social Interaction," emphasized the significance of daily activities that seemingly appear to have no payoff and little importance.

These activities are described as "fun," "leisure pastimes," "hobbies," and "escapes." In fact, our games, entertainments, and small pleasures are all "inexpensive" ways of rehearsing in the abstract the values and the problems with which we must deal in everyday life. They allow the members of a society to experiment and to practice inexpensively the kind of situations met in society at large. Watching sports, reading magazines, listening to music, as well as participation in sports and the like may be analyzed in terms of social significance. The type of activity featured in a culture carries a message. As Roberts, Arth, and Bush (1959) point out in their article "Games and Culture," the games favored by a society, carry within them the expressions of mastery that are of concern in the culture. On the basis of data from 52 tribes, the authors concluded that games of strategy tend to be related to complexity in social systems, usually hierarchical complexities; games of chance tend to be related to the investment of the society in the supernatural or religious beliefs; and games of statistical skill tend to be related to stress upon interaction with conditions in the physical environment. There is tremendous security in being able to repeat or watch an event over and over again with only slight variations that confirm the content, structure, and course of life events. The sports contest is an abstraction of life. It can have validity and value in representing life's struggle for survival and in offering an arena for the exercise of competence and psychological and physical excellence.

The exercise of sport has taken on a different significance, however, because of the conflict and competition it has come to represent for so many. It has become a confirmation for a value system based upon a hierarchical structure that, in turn, is based upon economic position. It represents a struggle to preserve or to improve position. This value system should be questioned. The public has become locked in and accepting because so much money, time, and propaganda have been devoted to one particular form of folk model at the expense of other forms and other folk models. The message of sport, in much of its present context, is a message of devastation and self-assertion, of complying with rules when forced to and of little concern for others. The message, the structure, and the social significance of the sporting contest is becoming more and more representative of the struggle for status, position, and self-survival in society at the expense of others. Through sports people are mistakenly led to believe they are secure because they are better than somebody else. Sometimes the justification is even more removed. They are secure and supported and feel better because their team is better than another team. The quality of the sport has little meaning and, with the expansion of leagues, the quality of the model will decrease so that competence will give away even more to a message of, and a sanction of, competition. When commercial contests proliferate, whether tennis, hockey, or football, there is room for some mediocre athletes to try to make a living. When the best perform too often, their level of performance becomes weaker. With commercial expansion in sport, excellence and competence are decreasing at the expense of the entrenchment in society of a model signifying a struggle for mastery, power, and position over others. But the problems humankind faces in the future will not be problems resolved by a model related to personal position and superiority. The future will be based upon the human animal's ability to share, cooperate, and work out solutions for the good of all. Thus, security may be found temporarily in competitive sport as a folk model, but safety cannot be.

Social Science References

Acosta, R.V., and Carpenter, L.J. (1985). *Women in Sports: A Status Report.* N.Y.: Brooklyn College.

Adler, A. (1917). *The Neurotic Constitution: Outlines of a Comparative Individualistic Psychology and Psychotherapy* (B. Glueck and J.E. Lind, Trans.). New York: Moffat Yard (original work published 1912).

Ager, L.P. (1974). Play among Alaskan Eskimos. *Theory into Practice,* 13(4), 252–256.

Ahlgren, A. and Johnson, D.W. (1979). Sex differences in cooperation and competitive attitudes from the 2nd through the 12th grades. *Developmental Psychology,* 15(2), 45–49.

Alderman, R.B. and Wood, N.L. (1976). An analysis of incentive motivation in young Canadian athletes. *Canadian Journal of Applied Sports Sciences,* 1(2), 169–175.

Altman, I. (1977). Privacy as an interpersonal boundary process. In: M. von Cranach, K. Foppa, W. Lepenies and D. Ploog (Eds.). *Human Ethology: Claims and Limits of a New Discipline.* New York: Cambridge.

Alvarez, C.M. and Pader, O.F. (1979). Cooperative and competitive behavior of Cuban-American children. *Journal of Psychology,* 101(2), 265–271.

Anastasi, A. (1982). *Psychological Testing* (5th ed.). New York: MacMillan.

Arms, R.L., Russell, G.W., and Sandilands, M.L. (1979). Effects on the hostility of spectators of viewing aggressive sports. *Social Psychology Quarterly,* 42, 275–279.

Axelrod, R.M. (1984). *The Evolution of cooperation.* New York: Basic Books.

Balazs, E.K. (1975). Psycho-social study of outstanding female athletes. *The Research Quarterly,* 46(3), 267–273.

Ball, D.W. (1976). Failure in sport. *American Sociological Review,* 41, 726–739.

Ball, J.R., and Carron, A.V. (1976). The influence of team cohesion and participation motivation upon performance success in intercollegiate ice hockey. *Canadian Journal of Applied Sport Sciences,* 1, 271–275.

Bandura, A. (1969a). *Principles of Behavior Modification.* New York: Holt, Rinehart, & Winston.

Bandura, A. (1969b). Social-learning theory of identificatory processes. In D.A. Goslin (Ed.). *Handbook of Socialization Theory and Research* (pp. 213–262). Chicago: Rand McNally.

Bandura, A. (1973). *Aggression: A Social Learning Analysis.* Toronto: Prentice-Hall.

Bandura, A. (1977a). Psychological mechanisms of aggression. In: M. von Cranach, K. Foppa, W. Lepenies and D. Ploog (Eds.). *Human Ethology: Claims and Limits of a New Discipline* pp. 316–356. Cambridge: Cambridge Univ.

Bandura, A. (1977b). Self-efficacy: Toward a unifying theory of behavioral change. *Psychological Review,* 84, 191–215.

Bandura, A. (1982). Self-efficacy mechanism in human agency. *American Psychologist,* 37(2), 122–147.

Bandura, A. and Cervone, D. (1983). Self-evaluative and self-efficacy mechanisms governing the motivational effects of goal systems. *American Psychologist,* 45(5), 1017–1028.

Banerjee, D. and Pareek, U. (1974). Development of co-operative and competitive behavior in children of some sub-cultures. *Indian Journal of Psychology*, 49(3), 237–256.

Barber, T.X. (1970). *Suggested ('Hypnotic') Behavior: The Trance Paradigm Versus an Alternative Paradigm*. Harding, Mass.: Medfield Foundation.

Barber, T.X. (1974). Toward a convergence in hypnosis research. *American Psychologist*, 29, 500–511.

Barber, T.X. (1980). *Advances in Altered States of Consciousness and Human Potentialities*. Vol. 1. Psychological Dimensions.

Bardwick, J.M. (1971). *Psychology of Women: A Study of Bio-Cultural Conflicts*. New York: Harper and Row.

Barnet, R.J. and Müller, R.E. (1974). *Global Reach*. New York: Simon and Schuster.

Barnett, L. (1976). Play and intrinsic rewards: A reply to Csikszentmihalyi. *Journal of Humanistic Psychology*, 16(3), 83–87.

Barnett, M.A., Matthews, K.A. and Corbin, C.B. (1979). The effect of competitive and cooperative instructional sets on children's generosity. *Personality and Social Psychology Bulletin*, 5(1), 91–94.

Barnett, S.A. (1981). *Modern Ethology: The Science of Animal Behavior*. Oxford: Oxford Univ.

Barnouw, E. (1978). *The Sponsor: Notes on a Modern Potentate*. Oxford: Oxford Univ.

Barraclough, G. (1980). Retrospect for the 20th Century and prospect for the 21st Century. Paper presented at the 1980 International Conference on Human Values, Tskuba, Japan.

Beck, A.T. (1967). *Depression*. Philadelphia: Univ. of Pennsylvania.

Beeman, E.A. (1947). The effect of male hormone on aggressive behavior in male mice. *Physiological Zoology*, 20, 373–405.

Beiser, R.L., Butt, D.S., and Carstairs, G.M. (1981). Creative leisure for children and families. In: S.H. Fine, R. Krell & T. Lin (Eds.). *Today's Priorities in Mental Health* (pp. 215–218). Dordrecht, Holland: Reidel Publishing.

Beisser, A.R. (1977). *The Madness in Sports*. (2nd edition). Bowie, Maryland: Charles.

Bell, A.P., Weinberg, M.S. and Hammersmith, S.K. (1981). *Sexual Preference: Its Development in Men and Women*. Bloomington: Indiana Univ.

Bell, K.F. (1983). *Championship Thinking*. Englewood Cliffs, N.J.: Prentice-Hall.

Bem, S.L. (1974). The measurement of psychological androgyny. *Journal of Consulting and Clinical Psychology*, 42, 155–162.

Bem, S.L. (1975). Sex role adaptability: One consequence of psychological androgyny. *Journal of Personality and Social Psychology*, 31, 634–643.

Bem, S.L. (1977). On the utility of alternative procedures for assessing psychological androgyny. *Journal of Consulting and Clinical Psychology*, 45, 196–205.

Bender, L. (1938–77). *Bender-Gestalt Test*. Albany, N.Y.: American Orthopsychiatric Association, Inc.

Benson, H. and Klipper, M. (1976). *The Relaxation Response*. New York: Avon Books.

Berlyne, D.E. (1960). *Conflict, Arousal and Curiosity*. New York: McGraw Hill.

Bird, A.M. (1977). Team structure and success as related to cohesiveness and leadership. *The Journal of Social Psychology*, 103, 217–223.

Blau, T.H. (1984). *The Psychologist as Expert Witness*. New York: Wiley.

Black, J.D. (1956). MMPI results for fifteen groups of female college students. In: G.S. Welsh and W.G. Dahlstrom (Eds.). *Basic Readings on the MMPI in Psychology and Medicine* pp. 562–573. Minneapolis: Univ. of Minnesota.

Block, J.H. (1973). Conceptions of sex role: Some cross-cultural and longitudinal perspectives. *American Psychologist*, 28, 512–526.

Bond, C.F., and Titus, L.J. (1983). Social facilitation: A meta-analysis of 241 studies. *Psychological Bulletin*, 94, 265–292.

Bonen, A., and Keizer, H.A. (1984). Athletic menstrual cycle irregularity: Endocrine response to exercise and training. *The Physician and Sports Medicine.* 12(8), 78–91.

Booth, E.G. (1958). Personality traits of athletes as measured by the MMPI. *Research Quarterly,* 29, 127–138.

Bowles, J.W., Hanley, J.L., Hodgins, B.W., and Rawlyk, G.A. (1972). *Protest Violence and Social Change.* Scarborough, Ont.: Prentice Hall.

Bradburn, N.M. (1969). *The structure of Psychological Well-Being.* Chicago: Aldine.

Bradburn, N.M. and Caplovitz, D. (1965). *Reports on Happiness.* Chicago: Aldine.

Bramel, D., and Friend, R. (1981). Hawthorne, the myth of the docile worker, and class bias in psychology. *American Psychologist,* 36(8), 867–878.

Bredemeier, B.J. (1984). Sport, gender, and moral growth. In: J.M. Sliva and R.S. Weinberg (Eds.) *Psychological Foundations of Sport.* Champaign: Human Kinetics, 400–414.

Bretherton, I. (Ed.) (1984). *Symbolic play: The Development of Social Understanding.* New York: Academic.

British Medical Association Report on Boxing (1984). BMA, Tavistock Square, London, WC1H.

Bronfenbrenner, U. (1970). *Two Worlds of childhood: U.S. and U.S.S.R.* New York: Russell Sage Foundation.

Brown, R. (1986). Sources of erotic orientation. In: *Social Psychology: The Second Edition.* pp. 344–377. New York: Free Press.

Browne, M.A., and Mahoney, M.J. (1984). Sport psychology. In: *Annual Review of Psychology,* 35, 605–625.

Bryan, J.H. (1975). Children's cooperation and helping behaviors. In: E.M. Hetherington (Ed.). *Review of Child Development Research* pp. 127–181. Chicago: Univ. of Chicago.

Burisch, M. (1984). Approaches to personality inventory construction: A comparison of merits. *American Psychologist,* 39, 214–227.

Buros, O.K. (Ed.) (1978). *The Eighth Mental Measurements Yearbook.* Highland Park, N.J.: Gryphon Press.

Buss, A.H., and Durkee, A. (1957). An inventory for assessing different kinds of hostility. *Journal of Consulting Psychology,* 21(4), 343–349.

Butler, R.A. and H.F. Harlow (1957). Discrimination learning and learning sets to visual exploration incentives. *Journal of General Psychology,* 57, 257–264.

Butt, D.S. (1973a). Aggression, neuroticism and competence: Theoretical models for the study of sports motivation. *International Journal of Sports Psychology,* 4, 3–15.

Butt, D.S. (1973b). A factorial facet analysis of Gough's socialization scale. *Social Behavior and Personality,* 1(1), 50–57.

Butt, D.S. (1976). *Psychology of Sport: The Behavior, Motivation, Personality and Performance of Athletes* (1st ed.). New York: Van Nostrand Reinhold.

Butt, D.S. (1979a). Children and sport: Competition or free play? Paper presented at World Congress on Mental Health, Saltzburg.

Butt, D.S. (1979b, March). Psychological measurement in sport and leisure: The use of the Sport Protocol Form B in student participants from Tsukuba University, Japan. Working paper.

Butt, D.S. (1979c). Psychological motivation in figure skating: Some considerations for coaches. Paper presented at meetings of Figure Skating Coaches of Canada, Victoria, B.C.

Butt, D.S. (1979d). Short scales for the measurement of sport motivation. *International Journal of Sport Psychology,* 10, 203–216.

Butt, D.S. (1979e). Sport psychology in Canada. *International Journal of Sport Psychology,* 10, 280–281.

Butt, D.S. (1979f). Who is doing what: A viewpoint on psychological treatments for athletes. In: P. Klavora and J.V. Daniel (Eds.), *Coach, Athlete and the Sport Psychologist.* Toronto: School of Physical and Health Education, Univ. of Toronto.

Butt, D.S. (1980a). The motivational profiles of field hockey teams. *Canadian Field Hockey Research Reports,* Ottawa.

Butt, D.S. (1980b). Psychological studies of athletes: Some technique and applications. In: A. Popma (Ed.). *The Female Athlete: Proceedings of a National Conference about Women in Sports and Recreation* pp. 99–104. Burnaby, B.C.: Institute for Human Performance, Simon Fraser Univ.

Butt, D.S. (1980c). Perspectives from women on sport and leisure. In C.S. Adamec (Ed.). *Sex Roles: Origins, Influences and Implications for Women* pp. 70–88. Montreal: Eden.

Butt, D.S. (1985). Psychological motivation and sports performance in world class women field hockey players. *International Journal of Women's Studies.* 8(4), 328–337.

Butt, D.S., and Schroeder, M.C. (1980). Sex role adaptation, socialization and sport participation in women. *International Journal of Sport Psychology,* 11, 91–99.

Campbell, D.T. (1971). Methods for the experimenting society. Paper presented at the annual meeting of the American Psychological Association, Washington, D.C.

Cantelon, H., and Gruneau, R. (Eds.) (1982). *Sport, Culture and the Modern State.* Toronto: Univ. of Toronto.

Carron, A.V. (1980). *Social Psychology of Sport.* Ithaca, N.Y.: Mouvement.

Carron, A.V. (1984). Cohesion in sport teams. In: Silva, J.M., and Weinberg, R.S. (Eds.). *Psychological Foundation of Sport.* Champaign: Human Kinetics.

Cattell, R.B., Eber, H.W., and Tatsuoka, M.M. (1976). *Sixteen Personality Factor Questionnaire.* Institute for Personality and Ability Testing.

Cautela, J.R., and Wisocki, P.A. (1977). Thought stopping procedure: Description, application, and learning theory interpretations. *Psychological Record,* 27, 255–264.

Childs, D. (1981). The German Democratic Republic. In: J. Riordan (Eds.). *Sport under Communism,* pp. 68–101. London: Hurst.

Clumpner, R.A., and Pendleton, B.B. (1981). The People's Republic of China. In: J. Riordan (Ed.). *Sport under Communism,* 104–140. London: Hurst.

Cochrane, C.T., Strodtbeck, F.L., and Parkman, M.A. (1965). A Masculinity-Femininity Measure to Predict Defensive Behavior, Social Psychology Laboratory, Univ. of Chicago (mimeographed).

Cockburn, A. (1974). *Idle Passion: Chess and the Dance of Death.* New York: New American Library.

Colker, R., and Widom, C.S. (1980). Correlates of female athletic participation: Masculinity, femininity, self-esteem, and attitudes towards women. *Sex Roles,* 6(1), 47–58.

Cook, H., and Stingle, S. (1974). Cooperative behavior in children. *Psychological Bulletin,* 81(2), 918–933.

Corsini, R.J., and Marsella, A.J. and contributors (1983). *Personality Theories, Research, and Assessment.* Itasca, Ill.: F.E. Peacock.

Craighead, W., Kazdin, A.E., and Mahoney, M.J. (1981). *Behavior Modification: Principles, Issues and Applications.* Boston: Houghton–Mifflin.

Cratty, B.J. (1981). *Social Psychology in Athletics.* Englewood Cliffs, N.J.: Prentice-Hall.

Cratty, B.J., and Davis, P.A. (1984). The content of athletes' mental lives: Process decisions when considering modifications. In: W.F. Straub and J.M. Williams (Eds.). *Cognitive Sports Psychology* pp. 317–330. Lansing, New York: Sport Science Associates.

Crockenberg, S.B. and Bryant, B.K. (1978). Socialization: The implicit curriculum of learning environments. *Journal of Research and Development in Education,* 12(1), 69–78.

Crockenberg, S.B., Bryant, B.K., and Wilce, L.S. (1976). The effects of cooperatively and competitively structured learning environments of inter- and intrapersonal behavior. *Child Development*, 47(2), 386–396.

Cronbach, L.J. (1984). *Essentials of Psychological Testing* (4th ed.). New York: Harper & Row.

Csikszentmihalyi, M. (1975). Play and intrinsic rewards. *Journal of Humanistic Psychology*, 15(3), 41–63.

Csikszentmihalyi, M. (1976). Replay to Barnett. *Journal of Humanistic Psychology*, 16(3), 89–91.

Danish, S.J., and Hale, B.D. (1981). Toward an understanding of the practice of sport psychology. *Journal of Sport Psychology*, 3, 90–99.

Danish, S.J., and Hale, B.D. (1982). Let the discussion continue: Further considerations on the practice of sport psychology. *Journal of Sport Psychology*, 4, 10–12.

Dawes, R.M. (1980) Social dilemmas. *Annual Review of Psychology.*, 31, 169–93.

de Charms, R., and Muir, M.S. (1978). Motivation: Social approaches. *Annual Review of Psychology*, 29, 91–113.

Deci, E.L. (1975). *Intrinsic Motivation.* New York: Plenum.

Denzin, N.K. (1975). Play, games and interaction: The contexts of childhood socialization. *The Sociological Quarterly*, 16, 458–478.

Derlega, V.J. and Grzelak, J. (1982). *Cooperation and Helping Behavior.* New York: Academic.

Deutsch, M. (1960). A theory of cooperation and competition. In: D. Cartwright and A. Zander (Eds.). *Group Dynamics: Research and Theory.* New York: Harper & Row. (Original work published 1949 in *Human Relations.*)

Deutsch, M. (1965). The effects of cooperation and competition upon group processes. In: D. Cartwright and A. Zander (Eds.). *Group Dynamics: Research and Theory* (2nd ed.) pp. 414–448. New York: Harper & Row.

Deutsch, M. (1969). Socially relevant science: Reflections on some studies of interpersonal conflict. *American Psychologist*, 24, 1076–1092.

Deutsch, M. (1973). *The Resolution of Conflict: Constructive and Destructive Processes.* New Haven: Yale Univ.

Deutsch, M. (1982). Interdependence and psychological orientation. In: V.J. Derlega and J. Grzelak (Eds.). *Cooperation and Helping Behavior.* New York: Academic.

Douglas, N. (1931). *London Street Games.* London: Chatto and Windus.

Dyer, K.F. (1976a). Social factors influencing female swimming performance. *Journal of Biosocial Science*, 8, 131–136.

Dyer, K.F. (1976b). Social influences on female athletic performance. *Journal of Biosocial Science*, 8, 123–129.

Dyer, K.F. (1982). *Challenging the Men: Women in Sport.* St. Lucia: Queensland: Univ. of Queensland.

Eberhart, J.A., Keverne, E.B., and Meller, R.E. (1980). Social influences on plasma testosterone levels in male Talapoin monkeys. *Hormones and Behavior*, 14, 247–66.

Edwards, A.L. (1963). *Edwards Personal Preference Schedule.* New York: Psychological Corp.

Edwards, H. (1969). *The Revolt of the Black Athlete.* New York: Free Press.

Edwards, H. (1973). *The Sociology of Sport.* Homewood, Ill.: Dorsey.

Edwards, H. (1983). Educating Black Athletes. *The Atlantic Monthly*, August, 31–38.

Ehrhardt, A.A., Evers, K., and Money, J. (1968). Influence of androgen and some aspects of sexually dimorphic behavior in women with late-treated adronogenital syndrome. *Johns Hopkins Medical Journal*, 123, 115–22.

Ellis, A. (1973). Rational-emotive therapy. In: R. Corsini (Ed.). *Current Psychotherapies.* pp. 167–206. Itasca, Ill.: Peacock.

Ellis, H. (1936). Sexual inversion, In: *Studies in the Psychology of Sex.* Vol. II, Part II. New York: Random House.

Erikson, E. (1950). *Childhood and Society.* New York: W.W. Norton.

Eysenck, H.J. (1952). The effects of psychotherapy: An evaluation. *Journal of Consulting Psychology,* 16, 319–324.

Eysenck, H.J. (1976). *Sexualität und Persönlichkeit.* Berlin: Ullstein.

Eysenck, H.J., and Eysenck, S.B.G. (1969). *Personality Structure and Measurement.* London: Routledge & Kegan Paul.

Eysenck, H.J., and Eysenck, S.B.G. (1963–69). *Eysenck Personality Questionnaire.* United States: Educational and Industrial Testing Service; England: Hodder & Stoughton Educational.

Eysenck, H.J. and Eysenck, S.B.G. (1976). *Psychoticism as a Dimension of Personality.* London: Hodder & Stoughton.

Eysenck, H.J, Nias, D.K.B., and Cox, D.N. (1982). Sport and personality. *Advances in Behavior Research and Therapy,* 4(1), 1–56.

Fabian, L., and Ross, M. (1984). The development of the Sports Competition Trait Inventory. *Journal of Sport Behavior,* 7, 13–27.

Farley, F.H. (1985). Psychology and cognition. In: J. Strelau, F.H. Farley and A. Gale, (Eds.). *The Biological Basis of Personality and Behavior. Vol. 1: Theories, Measurement Techniques and Development.* New York: Hemisphere.

Feder, H.H. (1984). Hormones and sexual behavior. *Annual Review of Psychology,* 35, 165–200.

Feltz, D.L., and Landers, D.M. (1983). The effects of mental practice on motor skill learning and performance: A meta analysis. *Journal of Sport Psychology,* 5, 25–57.

Fine, R. (1967). *The Psychology of the Chess Player.* New York: Dover.

Fiske, D.W. (1971). *Measuring the Concepts of Personality.* Chicago: Aldine.

Fiske, D.W. (1978). *Strategies for Personality Research* pp. 76–97. San Francisco: Josey-Bass.

Fiske, D.W. (1983). The meta-analytic revolution in outcome research. *Journal of Consulting and Clinical Psychology,* 51, 65–70.

Fiske, D.W., and Maddi, S.R. (Eds.) (1961). *Functions of Varied Experience.* Homewood, Ill.: Dorsey.

Folkins, C.H., and Sime, W.E. (1981). Physical fitness training and mental health. *American Psychologist,* 4, 373–389.

French, J.A. (1981). Individual differences in play in *Macaca fuscata:* The role of maternal status and proximity. *International Journal of Primatology,* 2, 237–46.

Freud, S. *Group Psychology and the Analysis fo the Ego.* In: J. Strachey (Ed.). *The Standard Edition of the Complete Works of Sigmund Freud.* Vol. 18. London: Hogarth. (Original work published 1922.)

Freud, S. (1961). *Three Essays on Sexuality.* In: J. Strachey (Ed.). *The Standard Edition of the Complete Works of Sigmund Freud.* Vol. 7. London: Hogarth. (Original work published 1905.)

Freud, S. (1961). *Instincts and Their Vicissitudes.* In: J. Strachey (Ed.). *The Standard Edition of the Complete Works of Sigmund Freud.* Vol. 14. London: Hogarth. (Original work published 1913.)

Freud, S. (1961). *Civilization and Its Discontents.* In: J. Strachey (Ed.). *The Standard Edition of the Complete Works of Sigmund Freud.* Vol. 21. London: Hogarth. (Original work published 1930.)

Freud, S. (1961). *The Ego and the Id.* In: J. Strachey (Ed.). *The Standard Edition of the Complete Works of Sigmund Freud.* Vol. 19. London: Hogarth. (Original work published 1923.)

Friedan, B. (1963). *The Feminine Mystique.* New York: Norton.

Gallwey, T. (1974). *The Inner Game of Tennis.* New York: Random House.

Gallwey, T., and Kriegal, B. (1979). *Inner Skiing.* New York: Bantam.

Garfield, S.L. (1981). Psychotherapy: a 40-year appraisal. *American Psychologist,* 36(2) 174–183.

Giese, H., and Schmidt, A. (1968). *Studenten Sexualitäte.* Hamburg: Rohwalt.

Gladue, B.A., Green, R., and Hellman, R.E. (1984). Neuroendocrine response to estrogen and sexual orientation. *Science,* 225 (4669), 1496–1500.

Glass, G.V., McGaw, B., and Smith, M.L. (1981). *Meta-Analysis in Social Research.* Beverly Hills, Calif.: Russel Sage.

Goldstein, J.H. (1983). *Sports Violence.* New York: Springer-Verlag.

Goldstein, K. (1939). *The Organism: A Holistic Approach to Biology Derived from Pathological Data in Man.* New York: American Book Publishing Company.

Goodhart, P., and Chataway, C. (1968). *War Without Weapons.* London: W.H. Allen.

Gough, H.G. (1952). Identifying psychological femininity. *Educational and Psychological Measurement,* 12, 427–439.

Gough, H.G. (1956–75). *California Psychological Inventory.* Consulting Psychologist Press, Inc.

Gough, H.G., and Pederson, D. (1952). The identification and measurement of predispositional factors in crime and delinquency. *Journal of Consulting Psychology,* 16, 207–212.

Graham, F.K. and Kendall, B.S. (1946–1960). *Bender-Gestalt Memory for Designs Test.* Psychological Test Specialists.

Green, R. (1974). *Sexual Identity Conflict in Children and Adults.* New York: Basic Books.

Greenwald, A.G. (1980). The totalitarian ego: Fabrication and revision of personal history. *American Psychologist.* 35, 603–618.

Greer, G. (1984). *Sex and Destiny: The Politics of Human Fertility.* London: Martin Secker & Warburg Ltd.

Gruneau, R. (1983). *Class, Sport, and Social Development.* Amherst: Univ. Massachusetts.

Guthrie, E.R. (1935). *The Psychology of Learning.* New York: Harper & Row.

Hall, E.T. (1969). *The Hidden Dimension.* New York: Anchor.

Hall, M.A. (1973). Women and physical education: A causal analysis. Paper presented at Woman and Sport Symposium, The Univ. Birmingham, Birmingham, England.

Hall, M.A. (1978). *Sport and Gender: A Feminist Perspective on the Sociology of Sport.* Calgary: Univ. Calgary.

Hall, M.A., and Richardson, D.A. (1982). *Fair Ball.* Ottawa: Canadian Advisory Council on the Status of Women.

Hampson, J.L., and Hampson, J.G. (1961). The ontogenesis of sexual behavior in man. In: W.C. Young (Ed.). *Sex and Internal Secretions.* Baltimore: Williams and Wilkins Co., pp. 1401–1432.

Hardman, K. (1973). A dual approach to the study of personality and performance in sport. In: H.T.A. Whiting, K. Hardman, L.B. Hendry and M.G. Jones (Eds.). *Personality and Performance in Physical Education and Sport.* London: Henry Kimpton.

Harris, D.S., and Eitzen, D.S. (1978). The consequences of failure in sport. *Urban Life,* 7(2), 177–188.

Harris, J.C. (1980). Play: A definition and implied interrelationships with culture and sport. *Journal of Sport Psychology,* 2, 46–61.

Harrison, R.P., and Feltz, D.L. (1979). The professionalization of sport psychology: Legal considerations. *Journal of Sport Psychology*, 1, 182–190.

Harvey, O.J. (1953). An experimental approach to the study of status relations in informal groups. *American Sociological Review*, 18, 357–367.

Hathaway, S.R., and McKinley, J.C. (1943–67). *The Minnesota Multiphasic Personality Inventory*. Psychological Corporation.

Hayes, R.H., and Abernathy, W.J. (1980). Managing our one way economic decline. *Harvard Business Review*, July–August.

Heider, F. (1944). Social perception and phenomenal causality. *Psychological Review*, 51, 358–374.

Heider, F. (1958). *The psychology of Interpersonal Relations*. New York: Wiley.

Helmreich, R.L., Spence, J.T., and Holahan, C.K. (1979). Psychological androgyny and sex role flexibility: A test of two hypotheses. *Journal of Personality and Social Psychology*, 37(10), 1631–1643.

Hennig, M., and Jardim, A. (1977). *The Managerial Woman*. Garden City, N.Y.: Anchor Doubleday.

Hertz-Lazarowitz, R., Sharan, S., and Steinberg, R. (1980). Classroom learning style and cooperative behaviour of elementary school children. *Journal of Educational Psychology*, 72(1), 99–106.

Hilgard, E.R. (1981). *Theories of Learning* (5th ed). Englewood Cliffs, N.J.: Prentice-Hall.

Hilgard, E.R., and Hilgard, J.R. (1983). *Hypnosis in the Relief of Pain*. Los Altos, Calif.: Kaufmann.

Hoch, P. (1972). *Rip Off the Big Game: The Exploitation of Sports by the Power Elite*. New York: Anchor.

Horner, M.S. (1972). Toward an understanding of achievement-related conflicts in women. *Journal of Social Issues*, 28(2), 157–176.

Horney, K. (1966). *Our Inner Conflicts*. New York: Norton. (Original work published 1945.)

Howard, D.R. (1976). Multivariate relationships between leisure and personality. *Research Quarterly*. 47, 226–237.

Hull, C.F. (1943). *Principles of Behavior*. New York: Appleton-Century-Crofts.

Hutt, C. (1972). *Males and Females*. Harmondsworth, Middlesex: Penguin.

Jackson, D.N. (1974). *Personality Research Form Manual*. London, Ontario: Research Psychologists Press.

Jackson, D.N., and Paunonen, S.V., (1980). Personality structure and assessment. *Annual Review of Psychology*. 31, 503–551.

Jacobson, E. (1976). *You Must Relax* (5th ed.). New York: McGraw-Hill.

Jain, U. (1978). Competition tolerance in high- and low-density urban rural areas. *Journal of Social Psychology*, 105(2), 297–298.

Janis, I.L. (Ed.) (1982). *Counseling and Personal Decisions: Theory and Research on Short-term Helping Relationships*. New Haven, Conn.: Yale Univ.

Janis, I.L. (1983). The role of social support in adherence to stressful decisions. *American Psychologist*, February, 143–160.

Johnson, D.W., and Ahlgren, A. (1976). Relationship between student attitudes about cooperative, competition and attitudes toward schooling. *Journal of Educational Psychology*, 68(1), 92–102.

Johnson, D.W., and Johnson, R.T. (1978). Cooperative, competitive, and individualistic learning. *Journal of Research and Development in Education*, 12(1), 3–15.

Johnson, D.W., Johnson, R.T., and Anderson, D. (1978). Student cooperative, competitive, and individualistic attitudes toward schooling. *Journal of Psychology,* 100(2), 183–199.

Johnson, D.W., Johnson, R.T., and Scott, L. (1978). The effects of cooperative and individualized instruction on student attitudes and achievement. *Journal of Social Psychology,* 104(2), 207–216.

Johnson, D.W., Johnson, R.T., and Skon, L. (1979). Student achievement on different types of tasks under cooperative, competitive and individualistic conditions. *Contemporary Educational Psychology,* 4(2), 99–106.

Johnson, P.A. (1972). A comparison of personality traits of superior skilled women athletes in basketball, bowling, field hockey, and golf. *Research Quarterly,* 43, 409–415.

Johnson, R.T., and Johnson, D.W. (1979). Type of task and student achievement and attitudes in interpersonal cooperation, competition and individualization. *Journal of Social Psychology,* 108(1), 37–48.

Johnson, W.R., Hutton, D.C., and Johnson, G.B. (1954). Personality traits of some champion athletes as measured by two projective tests: The Rorschach and H-T-P. *Research Quarterly,* 25, 484–485.

Jung, C.G. (1933). *Psychological Types.* New York: Harcourt, Brace & World.

Jung, C.G. (1957). God, the devil, and the human soul. *Atlantic Monthly,* November.

Kagan, J. (1984). *The Nature of the Child.* New York: Basic Books Inc.

Kane, J.E. (Ed.) (1972). *Psychological aspects of physical education and sport.* London: Routledge Kegan Paul.

Kelly, H.H. and Stahelski, A.J. (1970). Social interaction basis of cooperators' and competitors' beliefs about others. *Journal of Personality and Social Psychology,* 16, 66–91.

Kihlstrom, J.F. (1985). Hypnosis. *Annual Review of Psychology,* 36, 385–418.

Kirk, R. (1960). *The Conservative Mind.* Chicago: Henry Regnery.

Klavora, P., and Daniel, J.V. (Eds.) (1979). *Coach, Athlete and the Sport Psychologist.* Champaign, Ill.: Human Kinetics.

Klavora, P., and Flowers, J. (Eds.). (1980). *Motor Learning and Biomechanical Factors in Sport.* Toronto: School of Physical and Health Education, Univ. Toronto.

Klavora, P., and Wipper, K.A.W. (Eds.) (1980). *Psychological and Sociological Factors in Sport.* Toronto: School of Physical and Health Education, Univ. Toronto.

Klineburg, O. (1966). *The Human Dimension in International Relations.* New York: Holt, Rinehart & Winston.

Knight, G.P., and Kagan, S. (1977). Acculturation of prosocial and competitive behaviors among second- and third-generation Mexican-American children. *Journal of Cross-Cultural Psychology,* 8(3), 273–284.

Kohn, A. (1986). *No Contest: The Case Against Competition.* Boston: Houghton–Mifflin.

Kroll, W. (1970). Current strategies and problems in personality assessment of athletes. In: L.E. Smith (Ed.). *Psychology of Motor Learning.* Chicago: Athletic Institution.

Kruglanski, A.W. (1975). The endogenous-exogenous partition in attribution theory. *Psychology Review,* 82, 387–406.

Kuhlman, D.M., Wimberley, D.L. (1976). Expectations of choice behavior held by cooperations, competitors, and individualists across four classes of experimental games. *Journal of Personality and Social Psychology,* 34, 69–81.

Langer, E.J., and Rodin, J. (1976). The effects of choice and enhanced personal responsibility for the aged: A field experiemnt in an institutional setting. *Journal of Social Psychology,* 34, 191–198.

Langer, E.J. (1975). The illusion of control. *The Journal of Social Psychology,* 32, 311–328.

Langer, E. (1983). *The Psychology of Control.* Beverly Hills, Calif.: Sage.

Lasch, C. (1979). *The Culture of Narcissism.* New York, Warner.

Lau, R.R. and Russell, D. (1980). Attributions in the sports pages. *Journal of Personality and Social Psychology*, **39**, 29–38.

Leet, P.M. (1979). The psychological impact of competition. *Devereux Forum*, **14**(1), 16–25.

Lefcourt, J.M. (1976). *Locus of Control*. Hillsdale, N.J.: Erlbaum.

Ledwidge, R. (1980). Run for your mind: Aerobic exercise as a means of alleviating anxiety and depression. *Canadian Journal of Behavioral Science*, **12**, 126–140.

Lefebvre, L.M. and Cunningham, J.D. (1977). The successful football team: Effects of coaching and team cohesiveness. *International Journal of Sports Psychology*, **8**, 29–41.

Lenk, H. (1979). *Social Philosophy of Athletics*. Champaign, Ill.: Stipes.

Lerch, H.A. (1976). Four female collegiate track athletes: An analysis of personal constructs. *The Research Quarterly*, **47**(4), 687–691.

Lerner, M.J. (1982). The justice motive in human relations and the economic model of man: A radical analysis of facts and fictions. In: V.J. Derlega and J. Grzelak (Eds.). *Cooperation and Helping Behavior*, pp. 250–278. New York: Academic.

Lever, J. (1983). *Soccer Madness*. Chicago: Univ. of Chicago.

Lewin, J. (1935). *A Dynamic Theory of Personality*. New York: McGraw-Hill.

Lewin, K. (1936). *Principles of Topological Psychology*. New York: McGraw-Hill.

Locksley, A., and Colten, M.E. (1979). Psychological androgyny: A case of mistaken identity? *Journal of Personality and Social Psychology*, **37**(6), 1017–1031.

London, P., and Fuhrer, M. (1961). Hypnosis, motivation and performance. *Journal of Personality*, **29**, 321–333.

Lorenz, K. (1966). *On Aggression*. New York: Harcourt, Brace & World (Original work published 1963.)

Lorenz, K. (1970). *Studies in Animal and Human Behavior*, Volume 1 (R. Martin, Trans.) Cambridge: Harvard Univ.

Lott, B.E. (1973). Who wants the children? Some relationships among attitudes toward children, parents, and the liberation of women. *American Psychologist*, July, 573–582.

Loy, J.W., Kenyon, G.S., and McPherson, B.D. (1981). *Sport, Culture and Society: A Reader on the Sociology of Sport* (2nd ed.), Philadelphia: Lea & Febiger.

Loy, J.W., McPherson, B.D., and Kenyon, G.S. (1978). *The Sociology of Sport as an Academic Speciality: An Episodic Essay on the Development and Emergence of an Hybrid Subfield in North America*. Ottawa: Canadian Association for Health, Physical Education and Recreation.

MacLean, P.D. (1962). New findings relevant to the evaluation of the psychosexual functioning of the brain. *Journal of Nervous and Mental Disease*, **135**, 289–301.

MacLean, P.D. (1967). The brain in relation to empathy and medical education. *The Journal of Nervous and Mental Disease*, **144**, 374–382.

McBryde, C.M. (Ed.) (1964). *Signs and Symptoms: Applied Pathologic Physiology and Clinical Interpretation*. Toronto: J.B. Lippincott.

McClelland, D.C. (1961). *The Achieving Society*. New York: Van Nostrand.

McClelland, D.C. (1973). Testing for competence rather than for intelligence. *American Psychologist*, **28**, 1–14.

McClelland, D.C. (1985). How motives, skills, and values determine what people do. *American Psychologist*, **40**, 812–825.

McClintock, C.G., Moskowitz, J.M., and McClintock, E. (1977). Variations in preferences for individualistic, competitive, and cooperative outcomes as a function of age, game class, and task in nursery school children. *Child Development*, **48**(3), 1080–1085.

McClintock, C.G., and Moskowitz, J.M. (1976). Chiildren's preferences for individualistic, cooperative, and competitive outcomes. *Journal of Personality and Social Psychology*, **34**(4), 543–555.

McGuire, J.M., and Thomas, M.H. (1975). Effects of sex, competence, and competition on sharing behavior in children. *Journal of Personality and Social Psychology*, 32(3), 490–494.

McIntosh, P.C. (1971). *Sport in Society*. London: C.A. Watts and Co.

Maccoby, E. (Ed.) (1966). *Sex Differences in Intellectual Functioning. The Development of Sex Differences*. Stanford: Standford Univ.

Maccoby, E., and Jacklin, C. (1974). *The Psychology of Sex Differences*. Stanford: Stanford Univ.

Maddi, S.R. (1967). The existential neurosis. *Journal of Abnormal Psychology*, 72, 311–325.

Maddi, S.R. (1976). *Personality Theories: A Comparitive Analysis* (3rd ed.). Homewood, Ill.: Dorsey.

Madsen, M.C. (1971). Development and cross-cultural differences in the cooperation and competitive behavior of young children. *Journal of Cross-Cultural Psychology*, 4, 365–371.

Madsen, M.C., and Shapira, A. (1970). Cooperative and competitive behavior of urban Afro-American, Anglo-American, Mexican-American and Mexican Village children. *Developmental Psychology*, 3, 16–20.

Madsen, M.C., and Shapira, A. (1977, August). Corporation and challenge in four cultures. *Journal of Social Psychology*, 102(2), 189–195.

Madsen, M., and Lancy, D. (1981). Cooperative and competitive behavior: Experiments related to ethnic identity and urbanization in Papua New Guinea. *Journal of Cross Cultural Psychology*, 12, 389–408.

Maehr, M.L. (1974). Culture and achievement motivation. *American Psychologist*, 29, 887–896.

Maehr, M.L., and Nicholls, J.G. (1980). Culture and achievement motivation: A second look. In: N. Warren (Ed.). *Studies in Cross-Cultural Psychology* Vol. 3. New York: Academic.

Maehr, M.L., and Kleiber, D.A. (1981). The graying of achievement motivation. *American Psychologist*, 36(7), 787–793.

Mahoney, M.J. (1974). *Cognitive and Behavior Modification*. Cambridge, Mass.: Balinger.

Mahoney, M.J., and Avener, M. (1977). Psychology of the elite athlete: An exploratory study. *Cognitive Therapy and Research*, 1(2), 135–141.

Mahoney, M.J., and Avener, M. (1980). Mahoney-Avener gymnast questionnaire. In: R.M. Suinn (Ed.), *Psychology in Sports: Methods and Applications*, pp. 351–355. Minneapolis: Burgess.

Malmo, R.R. (1959). Activation: A neuopsychological dimension. *Psychological Review*, 66, 367–386.

Maltz, M. (1966). *Psycho-Cybernetics*. New York: Pocket Books, Simon & Schuster.

Mandell, A.J. (1974). A psychiatric study of professional football. *Saturday Review*, October, 5, 12–16.

Mandell, A. (1976). *The Nightmare Season*. New York: Random House.

Marko, J. (1978). The attitude of pupils toward competing. *Psycholögia a Patopsychölogia Dietata*, 13(3), 219–227.

Martens, R. (1971). Anxiety and motor behavior: A review. *Journal of Motor Behavior*, 3(2), 151–180.

Martens, R. (1975). The paradigmatic crisis in American sport personology. *Sportwissenshaft*, 5, 9–24.

Martens, R. (1976). Kid sports: A den of iniquity or land of promise? Proceedings of the National College of Physical Education Association for Men, Univ. of Illinois at Chicago Circle.

Martens, R. (1977). *Sport Competition Anxiety Test*. Champaign, Ill.: Human Kinetics.

Martens, R., Singer, R.N., and Harris, D.V. (1977). Psychology Testing within Sport: Committee report. *North American Society for the Psychology of Sport and Physical Activity Newsletter*, 2(3), 2–4.

Martin, G.L., and Hrycaiko, D. (1984). *Behavior Modification and Coaching: Principles, Procedures and Research*. Springfield, Ill.: Charles C. Thomas.

Maslow, A. (1970). *Motivation and Personality*. New York: Harper & Row. (Original work published 1954.)

Masters, R.D. (1977). Beyond reductionism: Five basic concepts in human ethology. In: M. von Cranach, K. Foppa, W. Lepenies, and D. Ploog (Eds.). *Human Ethology: Claims and Limits of a New Discipline*. New York: Cambridge Univ.

Mead, M. (1937). *Cooperation and Competition Among Primitive Peoples*. New York: McGraw-Hill.

Meadows, D.H., Meadows, D.L., Randers, J., and Behrens, W.W. III (1972). *The Limits to Growth: A Report for the Club of Rome's Project on the Predicament of Mankind*. New York: Universe Books.

Mechikoff, R.A., and Kozar, B. (1983). *Sport Psychology: The Coach's Perspective*. Springfield, Ill., Charles C. Thomas.

Medeiros, E.B. (1980). Should leisure be a matter for social concern in developing countries? Paper presented at meetings of World Federation of Mental Health. Saltzburg.

Meichenbaum, D. (1977). *Cognitive-Behavior Modification*. New York: Plenum.

Meuris, G., and Bougard, J. (1982). Le gardien de but de football considéré sous l'angle des motivations profondes. *Revue de l'éducation physique*, 22(4), 29–31.

Michaels, J.W., Blommel, J.M., Brokato, R.M., Linkous, R.A., and Rowe, J.S. (1982). Social facilitation and inhibition in a natural setting. *Replications in Social Psychology*, 2, 21–24.

Miller, A.G. (1973). Integration and acculturation of cooperative behavior among Blackfoot Indian and non-Indian Canadian children. *Journal of Cross-Cultural Psychology*, 4, 374–380.

Miller, L.K. and Hamblin, R.L. (1963). Interdependence, differential rewarding, and productivity. *American Sociological Review*, 28, 768–778.

Mintz, A. (1951). Non-adaptive group behavior. *Journal of Abnormal and Social Psychology*, 46, 150–159.

Mitchell, J.V. (Ed.). (1985). *The Ninth Mental Measurements Yearbook*. Lincoln, Nebraska: Univ. Nebraska.

Mohr, D. (1971). Mental Practice. I. *Encyclopedia of Sports Sciences and Medicine*. New York: MacMillan, 52–55.

Money, J. (1973). Prenatal hormones and postnatal socialization in gender identity differentiation. In: J.K. Cole and R. Dienstbier (Eds.). *Nebraska Symposium on Motivation 1973*, pp. 221–296. Lincoln: Univ. of Nebraska.

Money, J. (1980). *Love and Love Sickness: The Science of Sex, Gender Differences, and Peer-Bonding*. Baltimore: Johns Hopkins Press.

Money, J., and Ehrhardt, A.A. (1972). *Man and Woman, Boy and Girl: The Differentiation and Dimorphism of Gender Identity from Conception to Maturity*. Baltimore: Johns Hopkins Press.

Moore, O.K., and Anderson, A.R. (1962). Some puzzling aspects of social interaction. *Review of Metaphysics*, 15, 409–433.

Moore, N.V., Evertson, C.M., and Brophy, J.E. (1974). Solitary play: Some functional reconsiderations. *Developmental Psychology*, 10(6), 830–834.

Morgan, W.P. (Ed.) (1972a). *Ergogenic Aids and Muscular Performance*. New York: Academic.

Morgan, W.P. (1972b). Sport psychology. In: R.N. Singer (Ed.). *The Psychomotor Domain: Movement Behavior* pp. 199–228. Philadelphia: Lea & Febiger.

Morgan, W.P. (1978). Sport personology: The credulous, skeptical argument in perspective. In: W.F. Straub (Ed.). *Sport psychology: An analysis of athlete behavior* (pp. 330–339). Ithaca, N.Y.: Mouvement.

Morgan, W.P. (1979). Prediction of performance in athletes. In: P. Klavora and J.V. Daniel (Eds.), *Coach, Athlete and the Sport Psychologist*, pp. 173–186. Toronto: Univ. of Toronto.

Morgan, W.P. (1980). The trait psychology controversy. *Research Quarterly*, 51, 50–76.

Morgan, W.P. Psychophysiology of self-awareness during vigorous physical activity. *Research Quarterly*, 1981. 52, 385–427.

Morgan, W.P., and Costill, D.L. (1972). Psychological characteristics of the marathon runner. *Journal of Sports Medicine and Physical Fitness*, 12, 42–46.

Morgan, W.P. and Johnson, R.W. (1977). Psychologic characterization of the elite wrestler: A mental health model. Paper presented at the Annual Meeting of the American College of Sports Medicine. Chicago.

Morgan, W.P. and Johnson, R.W. (1978). Personality characteristics of successful and unsuccessful oarsmen. *International Journal of Sport Psychology*, 9, 119–133.

Morgan, W.P. and Pollock, M.L. (1977). Psychologic characterization of the elite distance runner. *Annals of the New York Academy of Sciences*, 301, 382–403.

Moss, C.S. (1965). *Hypnosis in perspective*. New York: MacMillan.

Munroe, R.L., and Munroe, R.H. (1977). Cooperation and competition among East African and American children. *Journal of Social Psychology*, 101(1), 145–146.

Murray, H.A., et al. (1938). *Explorations in Personality*. New York: Oxford Univ.

Murray, H.A. (1943). *Thematic Apperception Test*. Cambridge, Mass.: Harvard Univ.

Myers, A.M., and Gonda, G. (1982). Empirical validation of the Bem Sex-Role Inventory. *Journal of Personality and Social Psychology*, 43, 304–318.

Myers, A.M., and Lips, H.M. (1978). Participation in competitive amateur sports as a function of psychological androgyny. *Sex Roles*, 4, 571–588.

Naditch, M.P., and DeMaio, T. (1975). Locus of control and competence. *Journal of Personality*, 43(4), 542–559.

Nagle, F.J., Morgan, W.P., Hellickson, R.O., Serfass, R.C., and Alexander, J.F. (1975). Spotting success traits in Olympic contenders. *Physician and Sports Medicine*, 3, 31–34.

Nann, R.C., Butt, D.S., and Ladrido-Ignacio, L. (Eds.) (1984). *Mental Health, Culture Values and Social Development: A Look into the Eighties*. Dordrecht, Holland: Reidel.

Natan, A. (1958). *Sport and Society*. London: Bowes & Bowes.

Nelson, L.L. and Kagan, S. (1972). Competition: The star-spangled scramble. *Psychology Today*, September, pp. 53 ff.

Nideffer, R.M. (1976a). *The Inner Athlete: Mind Plus Muscle for Winning*. New York: Thomas Y. Crowell.

Nideffer, R.M. (1976b). *The Test of Attentional and Interpersonal Style and Interpreter's Manual*. Rochester, N.Y.: Brag.

Nideffer, R.M. (1976c). The test of attentional and interpersonal style. *Journal of Personality and Social Psychology*, 34(3), 394–404.

Nideffer, R.M., and Sharpe, R. (1978). *A.C.T.: Attention Control Training*. New York: Wyder.

Nideffer, R.M. (1981). *The Ethics and Practice of Applied Sport Psychology*. Ithaca, New York: Mouvement.

Nieciunski, S. (1978). Cooperation of 6 and 7 year-old children in task groups and the general regularities of their social development. *Polish Psychological Bulletin*, 9(1), 27–36.

Nixon, H.L. Jr. (1974). Team orientations, interpersonal relations and team success. *Research Quarterly,* 47(3), 429–435.

Novak, M. (1976). *The Joy of Sports: End Zones, Bases, Baskets, Balls and the Conservation of the American Spirit.* New York: Basil Books.

Ogilvie, B.C. (1974). Personality traits of competitors and coaches. In: G.H. McGlynn (Ed.). *Issues in Physical Education and Sports.* Palo Alto, Calif.: National.

Ogilvie, B.C. (1978). Walking the perilous path of the team psychologist. In: W.F. Straub (Ed.). *Sport Psychology: An Analysis of Athlete Behavior,* pp. 321–329, Ithaca, N.Y.: Mouvement.

Ogilvie, B.C., Johnsgard, K. and Tutko, T.A. (1971). Personality. *Encyclopedia of Sports Sciences and Medicine,* pp. 229–237. New York: MacMillan.

Ogilvie, B.C., and Tutko, T.A. (1966). *Problem Athletes and How to Handle Them.* London: Pelham.

Oglesby, C.A. (1984). Interactions between gender identity and sport. In: J.M. Sliva and R.S. Weinberg (Eds.). *Psychological Foundations of Sport.* pp. 387–399. Champaign. Human Kinetics.

Orlick, T. (1978). *Winning Through Cooperation.* Washington, D.C.: Acropolis.

Orlick, T. (1979). Children's games: Following the path that has heart. *Elementary School Guidance and Counseling,* 14(2), 156–161.

Orlick, T. (1980). *In Pursuit of Excellence.* Ottawa, Coaching Association of Canada.

Orlick, T.D. (1974). Sport Participation: A process of shaping behavior. *Human Factors,* 16(5), 558–561.

Pareek, U., and Banerjee, D. (1976). Achievement motive and competitive behavior. *Manas,* 23(1), 9–15.

Pareek, U., and Banerjee, D. (1974). Developmental trends in the dimensions of cooperative and competitive game behavior in some subcultures. *Indian Educational Review,* 9(1), 11–37.

Partington, J.T., Orlick, T., and Salmela, J. (1982). *Sport in Perspective:* Proceedings of Fifth World Sport Psychology Conference. Ottawa: Coaching Assocation of Canada.

Pattison, E.M. (1984). Towards a psychosocial cultural analysis of religion and mental health. In: R.L. Nann, D.S. Butt, L.L. Ignacio (Eds.). *Mental Health, Cultural Values and Social Development.* Dordrecht, Holland: Reidel.

Pavlov, I.P. (1902). *The Work of the Digestive Glands.* London: Griffin

Pedhazur, E.J., and Tetenbaum, T.J. (1979). Bem sex role inventory: A theoretical and methodological critique. *Journal of Personality and Social Psychology,* 37, 996–1016.

Percival, L. (Ed.). (1974). Proceedings of the first international symposium in the art and science of coaching, Vol. 2. Willowdale, Ontario: F.I. Productions.

Peterson, S.L., Weber, J.C., and Trousdale, W.W. (1967). Personality traits of women in team sports, versus women in individual sports. *Research Quarterly,* 38, 686–690.

Phares, E.J. (1957). Expectancy changes in skill and chance situations. *Journal of Abnormal and Social Psychology,* 54, 339–342.

Phares, E.J. (1976). *Locus of Control in Personality.* Morristown, N.J.: General Learning.

Piaget, J. (1952). *The Origins of Intelligence in Children.* New York: International Univ. (Original work published 1936.)

Piaget, J. (1966). Response to Brian Sutton-Smith. *Psychological Review,* 73(1), 111–112.

Piaget, J. (1962). *Play, Dreams, and Imitation in Childhood.* (C. Gatteano and F.M. Hodgson, Trans.). New York: Norton.

Piaget, J. (1965). *The Moral Judgment of the Child.* (M.W. Gabain, Trans.). New York: Free. (Original work published 1932.)

Plattner, S., and Minturn, L. (1975). A comparative and longitudinal study of the behavior of communally raised children. *Ethos*, 3(4), 469–480.

Popma, A. (Ed.) (1980). The female athlete: Proceedings of a national conference about women in sports and recreation. Vancouver: Institute for Human Performance, Simon Fraser Univ.

Pruitt, D.G., and Kimmel, M.J. (1977). Twenty years of experimental gaming: critique, synthesis, and suggestions for the future. *Annual Review of Psychology*, 28, 363–392.

Pulos, L. (1979). Athletes and self-hypnosis. In: P. Klavora and J.V. Daniel (Eds.). *Coach, Athlete and the Sport Psychologist*, pp. 144–154. Champaign, Ill.: Human Kinetics.

Quadeer, M.A. (1982). Third World studies: Paternalism or enlightenment. *Canadian Association of University Teachers Bulletin*, April, pp. 15–16.

Rabbie, J.M. (1982). The effects of intergroup competition and cooperation in intragroup and intergroup relationships. In: V.J. Derlega and J. Grzelak (Eds.). *Cooperation and Helping Behavior*, pp. 128–151. New York: Academic.

Rachman, S. (1984). Fear and courage. *Behaviour Therapy*, 15(16), 109–120.

Rae, D. (1981). *Equalities*. Cambridge: Harvard Univ.

Reber, A.S. (1985). *The Penguin Dictionary of Psychology*. Hammondsworth, England: Penguin.

Rhodewalt, F., Saltzman, A.T., and Wittmer, J. (1982). Self-Handicapping among competitive athletes: The role of practice in self-esteem protection. Unpublished manuscript, Univ. of Utah.

Richmond, B.O., and Vance J.J. (1974–1975). Cooperative competitive game strategy and personality characteristics of black and white children. *Interpersonal Development*, 5(2), 78–85.

Riecke, L. (1969). Five ways to increase athletic performance through using hypnosis. *Hypnosis Quarterly*, 14(3) p. 7, ff.

Riegal, K. (1975). Adult life crisis: a dialectic interpretation of development. In: N. Datan and L. Ginsberg (Eds.). *Life-Span Developmental Psychology: Normative Life Crisis*. New York: Academic.

Reitan, R.M. (1981). *Halstead-Reitan Neuropsychological Test Battery*. Tucson: Reitan Neuropsychological Lab.

Riordan, J. (1977). *Sport in Soviet Society*. Cambridge: Cambridge Univ.

Riordan, J. (1980). *Soviet Sport: Background to the Olympics*. Oxford: Blackwells.

Riordan, J. (Ed.) (1981). *Sport Under Communism* (2nd ed.). London: Hurst.

Riordan, J. (1982). Sport and the Soviet State: Response to Morton and Cantelon. In: H. Cantelon and R. Gruneau (Eds.). *Sport, Culture and the Modern State*, pp. 265–280. Toronto: Univ. of Toronto.

Roberts, J.M., Arth, M.J., and Bush, R.R. (1959). Games in culture. *American Anthropologist*. 61, 597–605.

Robinson, A. (1977). Play the arena for acquisition of rules for competent behavior. *American Journal of Occupational Therapy*, 31(4), 248–253.

Rodin, J., and Langer, E.J. (1977). Long-term effects of a control-relevant intervention with the institutionalized aged. *Journal of Personality and Social Psychology*, 35, 897–902.

Roethlisberger, F.J., and Dickson, W.J. (1966). *Counselling in an Organization: A sequel to the Hawthorne researches*. Cambridge, Mass.: Harvard Univ.

Rogers, C.R. (1951). *Client-Centered Therapy*. Boston: Houghton Mifflin.

Rogers, C.R. (1961). *On Becoming a Person*. Boston: Houghton Mifflin.

Rogers, C.R. (1970). *Carl Rogers on Encounter Groups*. New York: Harper & Row.

Rohrbaugh, J.B. (1979). Femininity on the line. *Psychology Today*. August, 30–42.

Rorschach, H. (1921–51). *Rorschach test.* Switzerland: Hans Huber.

Rosenberg, B.G., and Sutton-Smith, B. (1973). Family structure and sex-role variations. In: J.K. Cole and R. Dienstbier (Eds.), *Nebraska Symposium on Motivation.* pp. 195–220. Lincoln: Univ. of Nebraska.

Ross, H.S., Goldman, B.D., and Hay, D.F. (1976). *Features and Functions of Infant Games.* Toronto: Univ. of Waterloo.

Rotter, J.B. (1966). Generalized expectancies for internal vs. external control of reinforcement. *Psychological Monographs,* 80 (whole number 609).

Rowell, T.E. (1974). Social dominance. *Journal of Behavioral Biology,* 11, 131–154.

Rowland, W. (1973). *The Plot to Save the World.* Toronto: Clarke, Irwin.

Rushall, B.S. (1972). The status of personality research and application in sport and physical education. Paper presented at Physical Education Forum. Dalhousie Univ., Halifax, N.S.

Rushall, B.S. (1978). Environment specific behavior inventories: developmental procedures. *International Journal of Sport Psychology,* 9.

Rushall, B., and Siedentop, D. (1972). *The Development and Control of Behavior in Sport and Physical Education.* Philadelphia: Lea and Febiger.

Russell, B. (1930). *The Conquest of Happiness.* New York: Liveright.

Russell, B. (1932a). *Education and the Modern World.* New York: Norton.

Russell, B. (1932b). *Education and the Social Order.* London: Allen & Unwin.

Russell, B. (1961). *Education of Character.* New York: Philosophical Library.

Russell, G.W. (1979). Hero selection by Canadian ice hockey players: Skill or aggression? *Canadian Journal of Applied Sports Sciences,* 4(4), 309–313.

Russell, G.W. (1981a). Aggression in sport. In: P.F. Brain and D. Benton (Eds.). *Multidisciplinary Approaches to Aggression Research.* Elsevier: North Holland Biomedical.

Russell, G.W. (1981b). Spectator moods at an aggressive sports event. *Journal of Sport Psychology,* 3, 217–227.

Russell, G.W. (1983a). Crowd size and density in relation to athletic aggression and performance. *Social Behavior and Personality,* 11(1), 9–15.

Russell, G.W. (1983b). Psychological issues in sports aggression. In: J.H. Goldstein (Ed.). *Sports Violence.* New York: Springer-Verlag.

Russell, G.W., and Russell, A.M. (1984). Sports penalties: An alternative means of measuring aggression. *Social Behavior & Personality.* 12(1), 69–74.

Ryan, R.M., Vallerand, R.J. and Deci, E.L. (1984). Intrinsic motivation in sport: A cognitive evaluation theory interpretation. In: W.F. Staub and J.M. Williams (Eds.). *Cognitive Sport Psychology.* Lansing, New York: Sports Sciences Associates, 231–242.

Ryde, D. (1971). Hypnosis. *Encyclopedia of Sports Sciences and Medicine.* New York: Macmillan, pp. 42–46.

Salmela, J.H. (1984). Comparative sport psychology. In: J.M. Sliva and R.S. Weinberg (Eds.) *Psychological Foundations of Sport.* Champaign: Human Kinetics, 23–34.

Sampson, E.E. (1981). Cognitive psychology as ideology. *American Psychologist,* 36, 730-743.

Sarason, S.B. (1981). *Psychology Misdirected.* New York: Free.

Sartre, J.P. (1962). *Existential Psychoanalysis.* Chicago: Henry Regnery. (Original work published 1953.)

Scott, J. (1971). *The Athletic Revolution.* New York: Free.

Schendel, J. (1965). Psychological differences between athletes and non-participants in athletics at three educational levels. *Research Quarterly,* 36, 52–67.

Schilling, G. (1980). Psycho-regulative procedure in Swiss sport: More as an alibi or fire-brigade? *International Journal of Sports Psychology,* 11(3), 189–201.

Schorr, K.T., Ashley, M.A., and Joy, K.L. (1977). A multivariate analysis of male athlete characteristics: Sport type and success. *Multivariate Experimental Clinical Research.* 3, 53–68.

Schultz, J., and Luthe, W. (1959). *Autogenic Training: A Physiological Approach in Psychotherapy.* New York: Grune and Stratten.

Schwartz, G.E., Davidson, R.J., and Goleman, D.J. (1978). Patterning of cognitive and somatic processes in the self-regulation of anxiety: effects of meditation versus exercise. *Psychosomatic Medicine,* **40,** 321–328.

Sears, R.R., Rau, L., and Alpert, R. (1965). *Identification and child Training.* Stanford, Calif.: Stanford Univ.

Secretariate of the 1978 Tskuba Conference, (1980). Enter the new society: The quest for reconciliation between economic and cultural values. Tokyo: Leisure Development Center.

Seligman, M.E.P. (1975). *Helplessness: On Depression, Development and Death.* San Francisco: Freeman.

Selye, H. (1936). Syndrome produced by diverse nocuous agents. *Nature.* **138,** 32.

Selye, H. (1976). *The Stress of Life.* (rev. ed.). New York: McGraw-Hill.

Selye, H. (1981). Dealing with stress in a depressed economy. *Spectrum,* **2**(2), 1–11.

Selye, H.H. (1983). *Stress Research: Issues for the Eighties.*

Senior, K., and Brophy, J. (1973). Praise and group competition as motivating incentives for children. *Psychological Reports,* **32**(3, pt. 1), 951–958.

Shaffer, T.E. (1972). Physiological considerations of the female participant. In: D.V. Harris (Ed.). *Woman and Sport: A National Research Conference,* pp. 321–332. Penn State HPER series, No. 2. Pennsylvania State Univ.

Shapira, A. (1976). Developmental differences in competitive behavior of Kibbutz and city children in Isreal. *Journal of Social Psychology,* **98**(1), 19–26.

Sherif, M., and Sherif, C.W. (1969). *Social Psychology.* pp. 221–266. New York: Harper & Row.

Sherif, M., White, B.J., and Harvey, O.J. (1955). Status in experimentally produced groups. *American Journal of Sociology.* **60,** 370–379.

Silverman, L.H. (1976). Psychoanalytic theory: The reports of my death are greatly exaggerated. *American Psychologist,* **31,** 621–637.

Silverman, L.H., and Weinberger, J. (1985). Mommy and I are one: Implications for psychotherapy. *American Psychologist,* **40,** 1296–1308.

Simon, N.G. (1981). Hormones and human aggression: A comparative perspective. *International Journal of Mental Health,* **10,** 60–74.

Singer, R.N. (1972). *Coaching, Athletics, and Psychology.* New York: McGraw-Hill.

Sipes, R.G. (1973). War, sports and aggression: an empirical test of two rival theories. *American Anthropologist,* **75**(1), 64–86.

Skinner, B.F. (1953a). *Science and Human Behavior.* New York: Free.

Skinner, B.F. (1953b). Punishment. *Science and Human Behavior,* Chapter 12, pp. 182–193. New York: Free.

Skinner, B.F. (1971). *Beyond Freedom and Dignity.* New York: Knopf.

Slavin, R.E., and Tanner, A.M. (1979). Effects of cooperative reward structures and individual accountability on productivity and learning. *Journal of Educational Research,* **72**(5), 294–298.

Sliva, J.M., and Weinberg, R.S. (Eds.) (1984). *Psychological Foundations of Sport.* Champaign: Human Kinetics.

Smith, A. (1975). *Powers of Mind.* New York: Ballantine.

Smith, M.D. (1974). Significant others' influence on the assaultive behaviour of young hockey players. *International Review of Sport Sociology,* **3–4,** 45–56.

Smith, M.D. (1976). Precipitants of crowd violence. *Sociological Inquiry,* **48,** 121–131.

Smith, M.D. (1979). Towards an explanation of hockey violence: A reference other approach. *Canadian Journal of Sociology,* **4,** 105–124.

Smith, M.D. (1983). *Violence in Sport.* Toronto: Butterworths.

Smith, M.L., Glass, G.V., and Miller, T.I. (1980). *The Benefits of Psychotherapy*. Baltimore: Johns Hopkins Univ.

Smith, M.L., and Glass, G.V. (1977). Meta-analysis of psychotherapy outcome studies. *American Psychologist, 32,* 752–60.

Snyder, E.E., and Kivlin, J.E. (1975). Women athletes and aspects of psychological well-being and body image. *The Research Quarterly,* 46(2), 191–199.

Snyder, E.E., and Kivlin, J.E. (1977). Perceptions of the sex role among female athletes and nonathletes. *Adolescence,* 12(45), 23–29.

Snyder, E.E., and Spreitzer, E. (1976). Correlates of sport participation among adolescent girls. *The Research Quarterly,* 47(4), 804–809.

Snyder, E.E., and Spreitzer, E. (1977). Participation in sport as related to educational expectations among high school girls. *Sociology of Education,* 50, 47–55.

Snyder, E.E., and Spreitzer, E. (1983). *Social Aspects of Sport* (2nd ed.). Englewood Cliffs, N.J.: Prentice-Hall.

Spence, J.T. (1985). Achievement American style: The rewards and costs of individualism. *American Psychologist,* 40(12), 1285–1295.

Spence, J.T., Helmreich, R., and Stapp, J. (1975). Ratings of self and peers on sex role attitudes and their relation to self-esteem and conceptions of masculinity and femininity. *Journal of Personality and Social Psychology,* 32(1), 29–39.

Spence, J.T., Helmreich, R.L., and Holahan, C.K. (1979). Negative and positive components of psychological masculinity and femininity and their relationship to self-reports of neurotic and acting out behaviors. *Journal of Personality and Social Psychology,* 37(10), 1673–1682.

Spence, J.T., and Helmreich, R.L. (1980). Masculine instrumentality and feminine expressiveness: Their relationships with sex role attitudes and behaviors. *Psychology of Women Quarterly.* 5(2), 147–163.

Spielberger, C.C., Gorsuch, R.L., and Lushene, R. (1968–1970). *State-trait Anxiety Inventory*. Palo Alto, Calif.: Consulting Psychologists.

Stanford-Binet Intelligence Scale, Third Revision. (1916–73). Chicago: Riverside.

Stavrianos, L.S. (1981). *Global Rift, The Third World Comes of Age.* New York: Morrow.

Stein, P.J., and Hoffman, S. (1978). Sports and male role strain. *Journal of Social Issues,* 34(1), 136–150.

Stevens, R.S. (1981). Psycho-physiological variables and hockey playing ability. Unpublished master's thesis, Simon Fraser Univ., Burnaby, B.C.

Straub, W.F. (1975). Team cohesiveness in athletics. *International Journal of Sports Psychology,* 6(3), 125–133.

Straub, W.F. (1978). *Sport Psychology: An Analysis of Athlete Behavior.* Ithaca, N.Y.: Mouvement.

Straub, W.F., and Williams, J.M. (1984). *Cognitive Sport Psychology.* Lansing, New York. Sport Science Associates.

Strauss, A. (1973). Regularized status - passage. In: W. Bennis et al. (Eds.). *Interpersonal Dynamics,* pp. 267–273. Homewood, Ill.: Dorsey. (Original work published 1959.)

Suinn, R.M. (Ed.) (1980a). *Psychology in Sports: Methods and Application's.* Minneapolis. Burgess.

Suinn, R.M. (1980b). Body thinking: Psychology for olympic champs. *Psychology in sports: Methods and Applications.* pp. 306–315. Minneapolis: Burgess.

Sutton-Smith, B. (1966, January). Piaget on play: a critique. *Psychological Review,* 173 (1), 104–110.

Sutton-Smith, B. (Eds.) (1979). *Play and Learning.* New York: Garnder.

Sutton-Smith, B. (1984). *The Masks of Play.* New York: Leisure.

Sutton-Smith, B. (1985). The child at play. *Psychology Today*, 19(10), 64–65.

Taylor, J.A. (1953). A personality scale of manifest anxiety. *Journal of Abnormal and Social Psychology*, 48, 285–290.

Terman, L.M., and Merrill, M.A. (1916–73). *Stanford-Binet Intelligence Scale*, Third revision. Boston: Houghton Mifflin.

Thomas, D.R. (1975). Effects of social class on cooperation and competition among children. *New Zealand Journal of Educational Studies*, 10(2), 135–139.

Thomas, D.R. (1978). Cooperation and competition among children in the Pacific Islands and New Zealand: The school as an agent of social change. *Journal of Research and Development in Education*, 12(1), 88–96.

Thorpe, J.A. (1958). Personality patterns of successful women physical educators. *Research Quarterly*. 29, 83–92.

Thorndike. E.L. (1898). *Animal Intelligence*. New York: Macmillan.

Tinbergen, N. (1951). *The Study of Instinct*. Oxford: Clarendon.

Tinbergen, N. (1973). *The Animal in its World*, Vols. 1 and 2. London: Allen and Unwin.

Toda, M., Shinotsuka, H., McClintock, C.G., and Stech, F.J. (1978). Development of competitive behavior as a function of culture, age and social comparison. *Journal of Personality and Social Psychology*, 36(8), 825–839.

Tolman, E.C. (1932). *Purposive Behavior in Animals and Men*. New York: Appleton-Century-Crofts.

Triplett, N. (1898). The dynamogenic factors in pacemaking and competition. *American Journal of Psychology*, 9, 507–533.

Tutko, T., and Bruns, W. (1976). *Winning is Everything and Other American Myths*. New York: Macmillan.

Tutko, T.A., Lyon, L.P., and Ogilvie, B.C. (1969–77). *Athletic Motivation Inventory*. Chicago: Science Research Associates.

Underwood, J. (1979). *The Death of an American Game*. Boston: Little, Brown.

Veblen, T. (1953). *The Theory of the Leisure Class*. New York: Mentor. (Original work published 1899.)

Vinacke, W.E. (1969). Variables in experimental games: Toward a field theory. *Psychological Bulletin*, 71, 293–318.

Vincent, M.F. (1977). Comparison of self-concepts of college women: Athletes and physical education majors. *The Research Quarterly*, 47(2), 218–225.

von Cranach, M., Foppa, K., Lepenies, W., and Ploog, D. (Eds.) (1977). *Human Ethology: Claims and Limits of a New Discipline*. New York: Cambridge Univ.

von Neumann, J., and Morgenstern, O. (1953). *Theory of Games and Economic Behavior*, 3rd ed. Princeton, N.J., Princeton Univ.

Watson, J.B. (1913). Psychology as the behaviorist views it. *Psychological Review*, 20, 158–177.

Watson, J.B. (1919). *Psychology from the Standpoint of a Behaviorist*. Philadelphia: Lippincott.

Weber, M. (1930). *The Protestant Ethic and the Spirit of Capitalism*. (T. Parsons, Trans.) New York: Scribner.

Wechsler, D. (1949–74). *Wechsler Intelligence Scale for Children*. Cleveland, Ohio: Psychological corporation.

Wechsler, D. (1939–55). *Wechsler adult intelligence scale*. Cleveland, Ohio: Psychological Corporation.

Weinberg, S.K., and Arond, H. (1952). The occupational culture of the boxer. *The American Journal of Sociology*, 5, 460–469.

Weisler, A., and McCall, R.B. (1976). Exploration and play, resume and redirection. *American Psychologist,* July, 492–508.

Werner, A.C., and Gottheil, E. (1966). Personality development and participation in college athletics. *Research Quarterly,* 37, 126–131.

Whalen, R.E., and Simon, N.G. (1984). Biological motivation, *Annual Review of Psychology,* 35, 257–276.

Whannel, G. (1983). *Blowing the Whistle: The Politics of Sport.* London: Pluto.

White, R.W. (1959). Motivation reconsidered: The concept of competence. *Psychological Review,* 66, 297–333.

White, R.W. (1961). Competence and the psychosexual stages of development. In: D.W. Fiske and S.R. Maddi (Eds.). *Functions of Varied Experience.* Homewood, Ill.: Dorsey.

White, R.W. (1960). Competence and the psychosexual stages of development. In: M.R. Jones (Ed.). *Nebraska Symposium on Motivation.* Lincoln, Neb.: Univ. Nebraska.

White, R.W. (1963). Ego and reality in psychoanalytic theory: a proposal regarding independent ego energies. *Psychological Issues,* 3(3), Monograph 11. New York: International Univ.

Whyte, W.F. (1943). *Street Corner Society: The Social Structure of an Italian Slum.* Chicago: Univ. Chicago.

Widmeyer, W.N., and Martens, R. (1978). When cohesion predicts performance outcome in sport. *The Research Quarterly,* 49(3), 372–380.

Wilson, E.O. (1978). *On Human Nature.* Cambridge: Harvard Univ.

Wilson, E.O. (1975–1980). *Sociobiology: The New Synthesis.* Cambridge: Harvard Univ.

Wilson, E.O. (1985). Altruism and ants. *Discover,* 6(8), 46–51.

Williams, J.M. (1978). Personality characteristics of the successful female athlete. In: W.F. Straub (Ed.). *Sport Psychology: An Analysis of Athlete Behavior.* Ithaca, New York: Mouvement.

Wolk, S. and Kurtz, J. (1975). Positive adjustment and involvement during aging and expectancy for internal control. *Journal of Consulting and Clinical Psychology,* 43, 173–178.

Wolpe, J. and Lazarus, A.A. (1966). *Behavior Therapy Techniques: A Guide to the Treatment of Neurosis.* New York: Pergamon.

Wolpe, J. (1982). *The Practice of Behavior Therapy.* New York: Pergamon.

Worringham, C.J., and Messick, D.M. (1983). Social facilitation of running: An unobtrusive study. *Journal of Social Psychology,* 121, 23–29.

Wrightsman, L.S., O'Connor, J.O. and Baker, N.J. (1972). *Cooperation and Competition: Reading and Mixed-Motive Games.* Belmont, Calif.: Brooks/Cole.

Wrisberg, C.A., Donovan, T.J., Britton, S.E., and Ewing, S.J. (1984). Assessing the motivations of athletes: Further tests of Butt's theory. In: D.M. Landers (Ed.). *Sport and Elite Performers.* Champaign: Human Kinetics.

Wrong, D.H. (1962). The over-socialized concept of man in modern sociology. *Psychoanalysis and the Psychoanalytic Review,* 49, 53–69.

Yaffe, M. (1975). Some variables affecting team success in soccer. In: H.T.A. Whiting (Ed.), *Readings in Sports Psychology,* pp. 63–71. London: Lepus.

Zaharieva, E. (1971). Sex. *Encyclopedia of Sports Sciences and Medicine,* pp. 81–82. New York: Macmillan.

Zajonc, R.B. (1965). Social facilitation. *Science,* 149, 269–274.

Zander, A.F. (1974). Team spirit vs. the individual achiever. *Psychology Today,* November, pp. 64–68.

Zander, A.R. (1981). *Motives and Goals in Groups.* New York: Academic.

Ziferstein, I. (1983). Soviet personality theory. In: R.J. Corsini and A.J. Marsella (Eds.). *Personality, Research and Assessment,* pp. 489–535. Itasca, Illinois: F.E. Peacock Pub.

Zuckerman, M. (1979). *Sensation Sacking: Beyond the Optimal Level of Arousal.* New Jersey: Lawrence Earlbaum.

Zuckerman, M., Bone, R., Neary, R., Mangelsdorff, P., and Brustman, B. (1972). What is the sensation seeker? Personality trait and experience correlates of the sensation-seeking scales. *Journal of Consulting and Clinical Psychology,* 39, 308–321.

Illustrative References

Adams, S. (1984). *Roche Versus Adams.* London: Cape.

Alfano, P. (1982). Kush with the Colts: Controversial architect of change. *The New York Times,* July 26. p. C6.

Anderson, R. (1984). World class trading status seen linked to multi-nationals. *The Globe and Mail,* week of March 7. p. B2.

Ashe, A. with Amdur, N. (1981). *Off the Court.* New York: New American Library.

Atyeo, D. (1979). *Blood and Guts: Violence in Sports.* New York: Paddington.

Bannister, R. (1955). *First Four Minutes.* London: Putnam.

Barnes, L. (1973). *The Plastic Orgasm.* Richmond Hill, Ontario: Simon & Schuster.

Berkow, I. (1982). The twin temples of boxing. *The New York Times,* November 20, p. 15.

Blackaller, T. (1984). Why we lost the America's cup. *Sport Illustrated,* 60(11), pp. 66–80.

Bock, H. (1982). Rumors drove homosexual from baseball. *The Vancouver Sun,* September 16, p. B1.

Bouton, J. (1970). *Ball Four: My Life and Hard Times Throwing the Knuckleball in the Big Leagues.* New York: World.

Bouton, J. (L. Shecter, Ed.). (1971). *I'm Glad you Didn't Take it Personally.* New York: Dell.

Bradley, B. You can't buy heart. *Sports Illustrated,* 47(18), 103–114.

Brady, F. (1965). *Profile of a Prodigy: The Life and Games of Bobby Fischer.* New York: David McKay.

Briner, B. (1973). Making sport of us all. *Sports Illustrated,* 39, December 10, pp. 36–42.

Brosnan, J. (1964). The fantasy world of baseball. *Atlantic Monthly,* 213, 69–72.

Brown, R.M. (1983). *Sudden Death.* New York: Bantam.

Bruce, H. (1984). And may the best cheater win. *Quest,* 13(7), 68–69.

Burke, Glenn (1976). Formerly an L.A. Dodger/Oakland Athletic. *Inside Sports.* September, 1982.

Callahan, Tom (1983). How's the weather up there? *Time,* January 17, p. 60.

Cleary, W. (1967). *Surfing: All the Young Wave Hunters.* New York: New American Library.

Cocking, C. (1976). Goon hockey: Entertainment for a sick society. *The Vancouver Sun Magazine,* 26(4), p. 4.

Cooper, H. (1972). *An Autobiography,* London: Hodder Paperbacks.

Coover, R. (1968). *The Universal Baseball Association, Inc.* New York: Random House.

Creamer, R.W. (1974). *Babe.* New York: Simon and Schuster.

Deford, F. (1984). A head to head. *Sports Illustrated,* 61(2), 72–86.

Deford, F. (1975a). Hero with a tragic flaw. (Part 1). *Sports Illustrated,* 42(2), 50–58.

Deford, F. (1975b). Out of the sun, into the shadows. (Part 2). *Sports Illustrated,* 42(3), 30–37.

Delaunay, J. (1981). The system is beginning to strangle itself. *The Guardian*, December 20, p. 14.

Devaney, J. (1974). *Tom Seaver*. Toronto: Popular Library.

Dolson, F. (1975). *Always Young: A Biography*. Mountain View, Calif.: Anderson World.

Dowling, T. (1970). *Coach: A Season with Lombardi*. New York: W.W. Norton.

Dryden, K. (1983). *The Game*. Toronto: Macmillan.

Durso, J. (1971). *The All-American Dollar: The Big Business of Sports*. Boston: Houghton Mifflin.

Fischler, S. (1969). *Gordie Howe*. New York: Grosset and Dunlap Tempo Books. (Original work published 1967.)

Fox, C. (1975). Lella Lombardi shifts for herself. *WomenSports*, January, pp. 42ff.

Franks, L. (1973). See Jane run. *Ms. Magazine*, January, pp. 98ff.

Gasher, M. (1984). Baumann's mentor went a little deeper. *The Province*, August 1, p. 46.

Gibson, A. (1958). *I Always Wanted to be Somebody*. New York: Perennial.

Ginzburg, R. (1962). Portrait of a genuis as a young chess master. *Harper's*, January, pp. 49–55.

Grimble, A. (1952). *A Pattern of Islands*. London: John Murray.

Grimsley, W. (1982). "Lack of respect" biggest problem facing pro tennis. *The Vancouver Sun*, June 28, p. C3.

Guttmann, A. (1983). *The Games Must Go On: Avery Brundage and the Olympic Movement*. New York: Columbia Univ.

Halberstam, D. (1981). The stakes of the game. *Playboy*, November, pp. 124–126, 150, 196–201.

Hart, M. (1971). Sport: women sit in the back of the bus. *Psychology Today*, October.

Hentoff, N. (1967). The murderous pleasures of tennis. *Atlantic Monthly*, April, pp. 98–100.

Hopcraft, A. (1971). *The Football Man: People and Passions in Soccer*. Harmondsworth, Middlesex: Penguin. (Original work published 1968.)

Housman, A.E. (1950). To an athlete dying young. In: L. Untermeyer's *Modern British Poetry*. New York: Harcourt, Brace.

Johnson, W.O. (1984a). They saved the best for last. *Sports Illustrated*, 60(9), 14–22.

Johnson, W.O. (1984b). A rich harvest from a sea of trouble. *Sports Illustrated*, 61(28), pp. 60–85.

Johnson, W.O. (1985a). Steroids: A problem of huge dimensions. *Sports Illustrated*, 62(19), 38–61.

Johnson, W.O. (1985b). Rub-a-dub-dub. *Sports Illustrated*, 62(4), pp. 34–45.

Jordan, P. (1974). *The Suitors of Spring*. New York: Warner Paperbacks.

Kahn, L. (1979). *Tony Jacklin: The Price of Success*. London: Hamlyn.

Kennedy, R. (1974). 427: a case in point (part 1). *Sports Illustrated*, 40(23), 87ff.

Kennedy, R. (1974b). 427: The payoff (part 2). *Sports Illustrated*. 40(24), 24ff.

King, B.J., with Deford, F. (1982). *Billie Jean*. New York: Viking.

Kopay, D., and Young, P.D. (1977). *The David Kopay Story: An Extraordinary Self-Revelation*. New York: Random House.

Kramer, G. (1969). *Instant Replay*. Toronto: Signet. (Original work published 1968.)

Lamblin, B. (1975). *My Skin Barely Covers Me*. Perris, Ca.: Uncle John's Art Publication.

Large, P. (1978). X marks the computer revolution at Vernons. *Financial Guardian*, London, August 22, p. 17.

Lever, J. (1969). Soccer: Opium of the Brazilian people. *Trans-Action*, January.

Levine, D. (1983). On target for the games. *Sports Illustrated*, 59(16), 37.

Levitt, M., and Lloyd, B. (1983). *Upset: Australia Wins the America's Cup*. New York: Workman.

Lieber, J., and Kirschenbaum, J. (1982). Stormy weather at South Carolina. *Sports Illustrated,* 56(5), 30–37.

Look who's on Tony's team: Esso. (1984). *Maclean's,* 97(6).

Looney, D.S. (1983). He has seen the light. *Sports Illustrated,* 58(16), 48–54.

Luciano, R., and Fisher, D. (1983). *The Umpire Strikes Back.* New York: Bantam.

Lunn, A. (1957). *A Century of Mountaineering (1857–1957).* Switzerland: Allen and Unwin.

McCabe, N. (1977). Glennie loses a tooth and feels like a champ. *The Globe and Mail,* December 24, p. 37.

McDermott, B. (1982). More than a pretty face. *Sports Illustrated,* 56(2), pp. 29–35.

McDermott, B. (1983). Wrong image but the right touch. *Sports Illustrated,* 59(4) p. 39, 44.

McMurtry, J. (1971). Philosophy of a corner linebacker. *The Nation,* January 18, 83–84.

McRae, E. (1974). Athlete's anonymous: Keeping old jocks off skid row. *The Canadian Magazine in The Vancouver Province,* November 9.

Magnussen, K. with J. Cross. (1973). *Karen: The Karen Magnussen story.* Don Mills, Ontario: Collier-MacMillan.

Magnusson, S. (1981). *The Flying Scotsman,* London: Quartet.

Megarry, A.R. (1984). A population explosion the planet can't duck. *The Globe and Mail,* February 2, p. 7.

Meggyesy, D. (1970). *Out of Their League.* New York: Simon and Schuster.

Menaker, E. (1982). Casualty of a failed system. *The New York Times,* October 3, pp. 25, 27.

Mendelssohn, K. (1971). A scientist looks at the pyramids. *American Scientist,* 59, 210–220.

Mewshaw, M. (1983). *Short Circuit.* New York: Atheneum.

Michener, J.A. (1983). *Sports in America.* New York: Ballantine. (Original work published 1976.)

Moore, K. (1984). He's a perfect 10. *Sports Illustrated,* 61(4), 194–218.

Moore, K. (1983). She runs and we are lifted. *Sports Illustrated.* 57(27), 32–44.

Murphy, J.A. (1985). The Arcel Medical Center is a start toward the care of retired boxers. *Sports Illustrated,* 62(6), 44–46.

Navratilova, M., with Vecsey, G. (1985). *Martina.* New York: Knopf.

Neff, C. (1983). Caracas: a scandal and a warning. *Sports Illustrated,* 59(11), 18–23.

Oh, S., and Falkner, D. (1984). *A Zen Way of Baseball.* Fitzhenry & Whiteside.

O'Hara, J.E. (S. Fell) (1983). Gentleman of the old school. *Racquets,* pp. 12–26, May.

Orwell, G., and Angus, I., (Eds.) (1968). *The Collected Essays, Journalism and Letters of George Orwell, Vol. 4: In Front of Your Nose.* London: Secker and Warburg.

Ottum, B. (1984). Only you, Mary Lou. *Sports Illustrated,* 61(4), 462–476.

Ottum, B. (1983). A fight to the Finnish. *Sports Illustrated,* 59(24), pp. 44–50.

Owen, W. (1963). *Collected Poems.* New York: New Directions Publishing Corporation.

Palango, P. (1982). Sport doctors more concerned over civil suits. *The Globe and Mail,* October 7, p. 15.

Parrish, B. (1972). *They Call It a Game.* New York: New American Library.

Paul, L. (1974). A three-letter word for sport. *Univ. of Chicago Magazine,* March/April, pp. 19ff.

Piersall, J., and Hirshberg, A. (1955). *Fear Strikes Out.* Boston: Little, Brown.

Papanek, J., and Brubaker, B. (1984). The man who rules hockey. *Sports Illustrated,* 61(1), 60–74.

Pileggi, S. (1982). The lady in the white silk dress. *Sports Illustrated,* 57(12), pp. 63–79.

Ralbovsky, M. (1974). Destiny's forgotten darlings. *Atlantic Monthly,* 233, 106–118.

Rentzel, L. (1973). *When All the Laughter Died in Sorrow.* New York: Bantam. (Original work published 1972.)

Richards, R. (1984). *Second Serve.* Briarcliff Manor, N.Y.: Stein and Day.

Schell, J. (1982). *The Fate of the Earth.* New York: Knopf.

Schneider, C. (1983). Talk about racquets. *Los Angeles,* 28(11), 182–190.

Scott, A.C. (1974). Closing the muscle gap. *Ms. Magazine,* September, pp. 49ff.

Seligson, T. (1984). The challenge of her life. *Parade magazine,* January 8, pp. 4–7.

Shaw, G. (1973). *Meat on the Hoof: The Hidden World of Texas Football.* New York: Dell. (Original work published 1972.)

Shecter, L. (1970). *The Jocks.* New York: Warner Paperbacks. (Original work published 1969.)

Sheehan, G. (1980). *This Running Life.* New York: Simon & Schuster.

Sobol, K. (1974). *Babe Ruth and the American Dream.* New York: Ballantine Books.

Sports Illustrated, 61(2) (Scorecard Section), p. 12.

Surface, B. (1977). Get the rook! *New York Times Magazine,* January 9, pp. 52–53.

Taafe, W. (1986). TV to Sports: The bucks stop here. *Sports Illustrated,* 64(8), 20–27.

Tarasov, A. (1972). *Road to Olympus: Russian hockey secrets.* Richmond Hill, Ontario: Pocket Books. Originally published, 1969.

Tatum, J., with B. Koshner (1979). *They Call me Assassin.* New York: Everest House.

Tekeyan, C. (1976). Why does he play so hard? *The New York Times,* December 9, Section 5, p. 20.

Todd, T. (1983). The steroid predicament. *Sports Illustrated,* 55(9), 62–78.

Todd, T. (1984). The use of human growth hormone poses a grave dilemma for sport. *Sports Illustrated,* 61(18), 6–15.

Vipond, J. (1971). *Gordie Howe Number 9.* Toronto: McGraw-Hill. (Original work published 1958.)

Wilkinson, J. (1982). A great leap forward has left the rest far behind. *MacLeans,* May 31, pp. 38–39.

Wilmore, J.H. (1974). They told you you couldn't compete with men and you, like a fool, believed them. Here's hope. *Women-Sports,* June, pp. 40ff.

Wilson, B. (1964). *My Side of the Net.* London: Stanley Paul.

Wolf, D. (1972). *Foul! Connie Hawkins.* New York: Warner.

Wooden, J. (1973). *They Call me Coach.* New York: Bantam.

Woodley, R. (1974). How to win the soap box derby. *Harper's,* 249, 62–69.

Wulf, S. (1981). Tricks of the trade. *Sports Illustrated,* 54, (16), 92–108.

Young, D. (1969). *Sonny Liston: the champ nobody wanted.* Chicago: Johnson.

Zimmerman, P. (1983). An overdose of problems. *Sports Illustrated,* 59(10), 16–22.

Name Index

Subject Index